Writing Arguments

A Rhetoric with Readings

CONCISE EDITION

Seventh Edition

John D. Ramage
Arizona State University

John C. Bean
Seattle University

June Johnson
Seattle University

New! 2016 MLA Updates

Boston   Columbus   Hoboken   Indianapolis   New York   San Francisco
Amsterdam   Cape Town   Dubai   London   Madrid   Milan   Munich   Paris   Montréal   Toronto
Delhi   Mexico City   São Paulo   Sydney   Hong Kong   Seoul   Singapore   Taipei   Tokyo

Senior Acquisitions Editor: Brad Potthoff
Program Manager: Anne Shure
Development Editor: Kassi Radomski
Product Marketing Manager: Ali Arnold
Field Marketing Manager: Mark Robinson
Executive Digital Producer: Stefanie A. Snajder
Content Specialist: Erin Jenkins
Project Manager: Savoula Amanatidis
Project Coordination, Text Design, and Page Makeup: Integra
Program Design Lead and Cover Designer: Barbara Atkinson
Cover Images: *Clockwise from top left:* Drill rig set up for winter drilling in Wyoming (Tom Grundy/Shutterstock); Urban teenagers using multimedia devices (Csondy, Getty); American Female Soldier in combat uniform saluting a flag at sunset (Steve Cukrov/Shutterstock); Working bees on honey cells (Kotomiti Okuma/Shutterstock).
Photo Research: QBS Learning
Senior Manufacturing Buyer: Roy L. Pickering, Jr.
Printer and Binder: LSC Communications, Inc. North Chemsford, Massachusetts
Cover Printer: LSC Communications, Inc. North Chelmsford, Massachusetts
Text Font: 10.5/12 Minion Pro

Acknowledgments of third-party content appear on pages 296–297, which constitute an extension of this copyright page.

PEARSON, ALWAYS LEARNING, and MyWritingLab are exclusive trademarks in the United States and/or other countries, of Pearson Education, Inc., or its affiliates.

Unless otherwise indicated herein, any third-party trademarks that may appear in this work are the property of their respective owners and any references to third-party trademarks, logos, or other trade dress are for demonstrative or descriptive purposes only. Such references are not intended to imply any sponsorship, endorsement, authorization, or promotion of Pearson's products by the owners of such marks, or any relationship between the owner and Pearson Education, Inc., or its affiliates, authors, licensees, or distributors.

Library of Congress Cataloging-in-Publication Data
Ramage, John D., author.
  Writing arguments: a rhetoric with readings/John D. Ramage, John C. Bean, June Johnson.—Concise edition; 7th edition.
    p. cm
  ISBN 978-0-321-96428-1
  1. English language—Rhetoric.   2. Persuasion (Rhetoric)   3. College readers.   4. Report writing.
  I. Bean, John C., author.   II. Johnson, June, author.   III. Title.
  PE1431.R33 2016
  808'.0427—dc23
                                                                    2014033973

4   18

Complete Edition
ISBN-10:   0-13-458651-4
ISBN-13: 978-0-13-458651-9

Brief Edition
ISBN-10:   0-13-458650-6
ISBN-13: 978-0-13-458650-2

Concise Edition
ISBN-10:   0-13-458649-2
ISBN-13: 978-0-13-458649-6

www.pearsonhighered.com

Brief Contents

Detailed Contents

Preface

Through many editions, *Writing Arguments* has established itself as a leading college textbook in argumentation. By focusing on argument as dialogue in search of solutions to problems instead of as pro-con debate with winners and losers, *Writing Arguments* treats argument as a process of inquiry as well as a means of persuasion. Users and reviewers have consistently praised the book for teaching the critical thinking skills needed for *writing* arguments: how to analyze the occasion for an argument; how to ground an argument in the values and beliefs of the targeted audience; how to develop and elaborate an argument; and how to respond sensitively to objections and alternative views. We are pleased that in this seventh concise edition, we have made many improvements while retaining the text's signature strengths.

What's New in the Seventh Edition?

- **An updated, revised, and streamlined Chapter 2 on "Argument as Inquiry," exploring the "living wage" controversy.** Chapter 2 now has all new student examples, visual arguments, and professional readings on the timely issue of raising the minimum wage for fast-food workers or retail store clerks. A new annotated student exploratory essay models the process of rhetorical reading and dialogic thinking.
- **Six new student model essays, many of which are annotated.** New student model arguments, including newly annotated models, help demonstrate argument strategies in practice. Showing how other students have developed various types of arguments makes argument concepts and strategies easier for students to grasp and use themselves. New student essays address timely and relevant issues such as raising the minimum wage, analyzing the ethics of downloading films from person-to-person torrent sites on the Web, critiquing a school culture that makes minorities "invisible," opposing women in combat roles, and evaluating the effect of social media on today's college students.
- **Expanded treatment of evidence.** A revised and expanded Chapter 5 explains with greater clarity the kinds of evidence that can be used in argument and shows students how to analyze evidence rhetorically. A new section shows students how to evaluate evidence encountered in secondary sources by tracing it back to its primary sources.
- **Expanded treatment of Rogerian communication and other means of engaging alternative views.** In Chapter 7, we expand our treatment of Rogerian argument by reframing it as Rogerian communication, which focuses more on mutual listening, negotiation, and growth than on persuasion. In addition, a new annotated student essay illustrates how a classical argument appealing to a neutral, undecided, or mildly resistant audience addresses alternative views.
- **Four new professional readings.** New readings about issues such as a living wage, the use of dietary supplements among athletes, and therapeutic cloning have been chosen for their illustrative power and student interest.
- **New visual examples throughout the text.** New images, editorial cartoons, and graphics throughout the text highlight current issues such as living wage, climate

change, bullying, sexual trafficking, date rape, rainwater conservation, fracking, and gender or racial stereotypes.

- **Streamlined organization of each chapter now keyed to learning outcomes.** Each chapter now begins with learning outcomes. Each main heading in a chapter is linked to an outcome, enhancing the explanatory power of the outcomes and helping students learn the high-level take-away points and concepts in each chapter.

What Hasn't Changed? The Distinguishing Features of *Writing Arguments*

Building on earlier success, we have preserved the signature features of earlier editions praised by students, instructors, and reviewers:

- **Integration of four different approaches to argument.** This text uses:
  - **The enthymeme as a rhetorical and logical structure.** This concept, especially useful for beginning writers, helps students "nutshell" an argument as a claim with one or more supporting *because* clauses. It also helps them see how real-world arguments are rooted in assumptions granted by the audience rather than in universal and unchanging principles.
  - **The three classical types of appeal—*logos, ethos,* and *pathos*.** These concepts help students place their arguments in a rhetorical context focusing on audience-based appeals; they also help students create an effective voice and style.
  - **Toulmin's system of analyzing arguments.** Toulmin's system helps students see the complete, implicit structure that underlies an enthymeme and develop appropriate grounds and backing to support an argument's reasons and warrants. It also highlights the rhetorical, social, and dialectical nature of argument.
  - **Stasis theory concerning types of claims.** This approach stresses the heuristic value of learning different patterns of support for different types of claims and often leads students to make surprisingly rich and full arguments.
- **Focus throughout on writing arguments.** Grounded in composition theory, this text combines explanations of argument with exploratory writing activities, sequenced writing assignments, and class-tested discussion tasks with the aim of helping students produce their own strong arguments. The text emphasizes the critical thinking that underlies effective arguments, particularly the skills of critical reading, of active questioning and listening, of believing and doubting, of negotiating ambiguity and seeking synthesis, and of developing effective reasons and evidence to support claims.
- **Emphasis on argument as a rhetorical act.** Analyzing the audience, understanding the real-world occasions for argument, appreciating the context and genre of arguments, and tying arguments to the audience's beliefs and values are all treated as equally important rhetorical considerations.
- **Generous treatment of the research process.** Appendix 2 covers a variety of research skills, including reading and evaluating sources rhetorically, taking notes, integrating source material, avoiding plagiarism and patch writing, and citing sources using two academic citation systems: MLA (8th edition) and APA.
- **Well-sequenced writing assignments.** The text provides a variety of sequenced writing assignments that include an argument summary, a researched exploratory

essay, a "supporting-reasons" argument, a classical argument, a delayed-thesis argument or Rogerian letter, a rhetorical analysis of a written argument, a rhetorical analysis of a visual argument (an advocacy ad or poster), a definition argument, a causal argument, an evaluation or ethical argument, a proposal argument, and a speech with PowerPoint slides.

■ **"For Class Discussion" exercises and "Examining Visual Arguments" exercises.** These class-tested informal activities, which teach critical thinking and build argumentative skills, are designed to produce active class discussion and debate. All "For Class Discussion" exercises can be used either for whole-class discussions or for collaborative group tasks.

Resources for Instructors and Students

Now Available for Composition   MyWritingLab™

Integrated Solutions for Writing. *MyWritingLab* is an online homework, tutorial, and assessment program that provides engaging experiences for today's instructors and students. New features designed specifically for composition instructors and their course needs include a new writing space for students, customizable rubrics for assessing and grading student writing, multimedia instruction on all aspects of composition, and advanced reporting to improve the ability to analyze class performance.

Adaptive learning. *MyWritingLab* offers pre-assessments and personalized remediation so students see improved results and instructors spend less time in class reviewing the basics.

Visit www.mywritinglab.com for more information.

eTextbooks

Pearson eText gives students access to *Writing Arguments*, Seventh Edition, whenever and wherever they can access the Internet. The eText pages look exactly like the printed text, and include powerful interactive and customization functions. Users can create notes, highlight text in different colors, create bookmarks, zoom, click hyperlinked words and phrases to view definitions, and view as a single page or as two pages. Pearson eText also links students to associated media files, enabling them to view videos as they read the text, and offers a full-text search and the ability to save and export notes. The Pearson eText also includes embedded URLs in the chapter text with active links to the Internet.

The Pearson eText app is a great companion to Pearson's eText browser-based book reader. It allows existing subscribers who view their Pearson eText titles on a Mac or PC to additionally access their titles in a bookshelf on the iPad or an Android tablet either online or via download.

Instructor's Manual, Tenth Edition

The Instructor's Manual, tenth edition, includes suggestions for designing an argument course, sequencing writing assignments, and teaching each chapter, as well as sample syllabi and an introduction to Toulmin.

Acknowledgments

We are happy for this opportunity to give public thanks to the scholars, teachers, and students who have influenced our approach to composition and argument.

We are particularly grateful to our talented students—Trudie Makens, Lauren Shinozuka, Alex Mullen, Lorena Mendoza-Flores, and Ivan Snook—who contributed to this edition their timely arguments built from their intellectual curiosity, ideas, personal experiences, and research. We also thank Janie Bube for her environmental advocacy poster and Trey Tice for his film criticism. Additionally, we are grateful to all our students whom we have been privileged to teach in our writing classes. Their insights and growth as writers have inspired our ongoing study of rhetoric and argumentation.

We thank, too, the many users of our texts who have given us encouragement about our successes and offered helpful suggestions for improvements. Particularly we thank the following scholars and teachers who reviewed this revision of *Writing Arguments* in its various stages: Alicia Alexander, Cape Fear Community College; Elijah Coleman, Washington State University; Shannon Collins, Owensboro Community and Technical College; Veronda Hutchinson, Johnston Community College; A. Abby Knoblauch, Kansas State University; Beth Lewis, Moberly Area Community College; Layne Neeper, Morehead State University; Jessie Nixon, University of Alaska Anchorage; Thomas Riddle, Guilford Technical Community College; Dixie A. Shaw-Tillmon, The University of Texas San Antonio; Janice R. Showler, Holy Family University; Coreen Wees, Iowa Western Community College; and Stephen H. Wells, Community College of Allegheny County.

We thank our editor, Brad Potthoff, for his publishing knowledge and cordial leadership, and our two development editors, Kassi Radomski and Marion Castellucci, who shepherded this project through every stage, giving us timely insight, collaborative feedback, and their professional support. We also thank Martha Beyerlein, our production editor, who has worked with us for years and patiently ushered us into the paperless stages of text preparation.

As always we thank our families, who ultimately make this work possible. John Bean thanks his wife, Kit, also a professional composition teacher, and his children, Matthew, Andrew, Stephen, and Sarah, all of whom have grown to adulthood since he first began writing textbooks. Our lively conversations at family dinners, which now include spouses, partners, and grandchildren, have kept him engaged in arguments that matter about how to create a just, humane, and sustainable world. June Johnson thanks her husband, Kenneth Bube, a mathematics professor and researcher, and her daughter, Janie Bube, now a student contributor to this text. Ken and Janie have played major roles in the ongoing family analysis of argumentation in the public sphere on wide-ranging subjects. Janie's knowledge of environmental issues and Kenneth's knowledge of mathematical thinking, online education, energy resources, and technology have broadened June's understanding of argument hotspots. They have also enabled her to meet the demands and challenges of continuing to infuse new ideas and material into this text in each revision.

John C. Bean
June Johnson

PART ONE
Overview of Argument

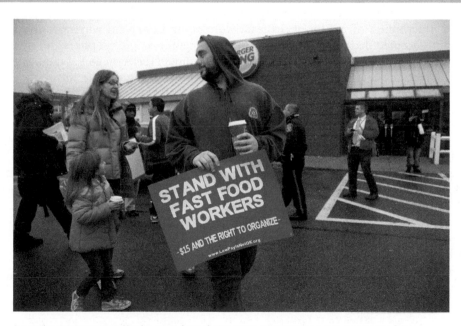

Across the country, protests like this one in front of a Burger King in Boston are raising awareness of the poverty-level wages of fast-food workers, who are not represented by unions and who often depend on public assistance such as food stamps to get by every month. While protestors argue for a minimum wage of $15 per hour, opponents argue that raising the minimum wage would increase food prices and reduce the number of jobs. If you were making a brochure or poster in favor of an increased minimum wage for fast-food workers, how effective would this realistic, low-keyed photo be in raising sympathy for the cause? Chapters 2 and 7 explore the issue of a living wage for unskilled workers.

Argument: An Introduction

1

What you will learn in this chapter:

1.1 To explain common misconceptions about the meaning of argument
1.2 To describe defining features of argument
1.3 To understand the relationship of argument to the problem of truth

At the outset of a book on argument, you might expect us to provide a simple definition of argument. Instead, we're going to explain why no universally accepted definition is possible. Over the centuries, philosophers and rhetoricians have disagreed about both the meaning of the term and about the goals that arguers should set for themselves. This opening chapter introduces you to some of these controversies.

We begin by showing some common misconceptions about argument while also explaining how arguments can be either implicit or explicit. We then discuss three defining features of argument: It requires writers or speakers to justify their claims, it is both a product and a process, and it combines elements of truth seeking and persuasion. Finally, we explore more deeply the relationship between truth seeking and persuasion by asking questions about the nature of "truth" that arguments seek.

What Do We Mean by Argument?

1.1 To explain common misconceptions about the meaning of argument

Let's begin by examining the inadequacies of two popular images of argument—fight and debate.

Argument Is Not a Fight or a Quarrel

The word *argument* often connotes anger, as when we say, "I just got in a huge argument with my roommate!" We may picture heated disagreements, rising pulse rates, and slamming doors. We may conjure up images of shouting talk-show guests or flaming bloggers.

But to our way of thinking, argument doesn't necessarily imply anger. In fact, arguing is often pleasurable. It is a creative and productive activity that engages us at high levels of inquiry and critical thinking, often in conversation with people we like and respect. For your primary image of argument, we invite you to think not of a shouting match on cable news but of a small group of reasonable people seeking the best solution to a problem. We will return to this image throughout the chapter.

Argument Is Not Pro-Con Debate

Another popular conception of argument is debate—a presidential debate, perhaps, or a high school or college debate tournament. According to one popular dictionary, *debate* is "a formal contest of argumentation in which two opposing teams defend and attack a given proposition." Although formal debates can develop our critical thinking powers, they stress winning and losing, often to the detriment of cooperative inquiry.

To illustrate the limitations of debate, consider one of our former students, a champion high school debater who spent his senior year debating prison reform. Throughout the year he argued for and against such propositions as "The United States should build more prisons" and "We must find innovative alternatives to prison." One day we asked him, "What do you personally think is the best way to reform prisons?" He replied, "I don't know. I've never thought about what I would actually choose."

Here was a bright, articulate student who had studied prisons extensively for a year. Yet nothing in the atmosphere of pro-con debate had engaged him in truth-seeking inquiry. He could argue for and against a proposition, but he hadn't experienced the wrenching process of clarifying his own values and taking a personal stand. As we explain throughout this text, argument entails a desire for truth; it aims to find the best solutions to complex problems. We don't mean that arguers don't passionately support their own points of view or expose weaknesses in views they find faulty. Instead, we mean that their goal isn't to win a game but to find and promote the best belief or course of action.

Arguments Can Be Explicit or Implicit

Before proceeding to some defining features of argument, we should also note that arguments can be either explicit or implicit. An explicit argument directly states its controversial claim and supports it with reasons and evidence. An implicit argument, in contrast, may not look like an argument at all. It may be a bumper sticker, a billboard, a poster, a photograph, a cartoon, a vanity license plate, a slogan on a T-shirt, an advertisement, a poem, or a song lyric. But like an explicit argument, it persuades its audience toward a certain point of view.

Consider the striking photograph in Figure 1.1—a baby wearing a bib labeled "POISON." This photograph enters a conversation about the safety of toys and other baby products sold in the United States, prompted in part by the discovery that a substance used to make plastics pliable and soft—*phthalates* (pronounced "thalates")—may be harmful. Phthalates have been shown to interfere with hormone production in rat fetuses and, based on other rodent studies, may produce cancers and other ailments.

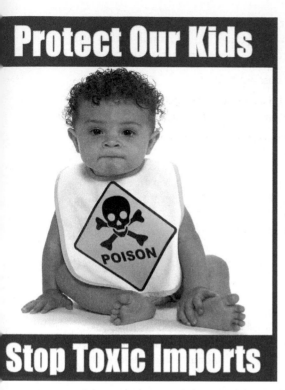

FIGURE 1.1 Baby and bib

Because many baby products contain phthalates—bibs, edges of cribs, rubber duckies, and other soft rubbery toys—parents worry that babies can ingest phthalates by chewing on these items.

The photograph of the baby and bib makes the argumentative claim that baby products are poisonous; the photograph implicitly urges viewers to take action against phthalates. But a skilled arguer would recognize that this photograph is just one voice in a surprisingly complex conversation. Is the bib in fact poisonous? An examination of explicit arguments about phthalates—that is, verbal arguments with stated reasons and evidence—reveals a number of disputed questions about the risk posed by phthalates. To what extent do studies on rats apply to humans? How much exposure to phthalates should be considered dangerous? (Experiments on rats used large amounts of phthalates—amounts that, according to many scientists, far exceed anything a baby could absorb by chewing on a toy.) Also at issue is the level of health risks a free market society should be willing to tolerate. A U.S. agency generally doesn't ban a substance unless it has been *proven* harmful to humans, not merely suspected of being harmful. In defense of free markets, the toy and chemical industries accused opponents of phthalates of using "junk science" to produce scary—but inaccurate—data.

Our point in summarizing the toxic toy controversy is to demonstrate the persuasive roles of both implicit and explicit arguments in resolving civic disputes.

The Defining Features of Argument

1.2 To describe defining features of argument

We turn now to examine arguments in more detail. (Unless we say otherwise, by *argument* we mean explicit arguments that attempt to supply reasons and evidence to support their claims.) This section examines three defining features of such arguments.

Argument Requires Justification of Its Claims

To begin defining argument, let's turn to a humble but universal site of disagreement: the conflict between a parent and a teenager over rules. In what way and in what circumstances do such conflicts constitute arguments?

Consider the following dialogue:

YOUNG PERSON (*racing for the front door while putting coat on*):   Bye. See you later.

PARENT: Whoa! What time are you planning on coming home?

YOUNG PERSON (*coolly, hand still on doorknob*):   I'm sure we discussed this earlier. I'll be home around 2 A.M. (*The second sentence, spoken very rapidly, is barely audible.*)

PARENT (*mouth tightening*):   We did *not* discuss this earlier, and you're *not* staying out till two in the morning. You'll be home at twelve.

At this point in the exchange, we have a quarrel, not an argument. Quarrelers exchange antagonistic assertions without any attempt to support them rationally. If the dialogue never gets past the "Yes-you-will/No-I-won't" stage, it either remains a quarrel or degenerates into a fight.

Let us say, however, that the dialogue takes the following turn:

YOUNG PERSON (*tragically*):   But I'm *sixteen years old!*

Now we're moving toward argument. Not, to be sure, a particularly well-developed or cogent one, but an argument all the same. It's now an argument because one of the quarrelers has offered a reason for her assertion. Her choice of curfew is satisfactory, she says, *because* she is sixteen years old.

The parent can now respond in one of several ways that will either advance the argument or turn it back into a quarrel. The parent can simply invoke parental authority ("I don't care—you're still coming home at twelve"), in which case the argument ceases. Or the parent can provide a reason for his or her view ("You will be home at twelve because your dad and I pay the bills around here!"), in which case the argument takes a new turn.

So far we've established two necessary conditions that must be met before we're willing to call something an argument: (1) a set of two or more conflicting assertions and (2) the attempt to resolve the conflict through an appeal to reason.

But good argument demands more than meeting these two formal requirements. For an argument to be effective, the arguer must clarify and support the reasons presented. For example, "But I'm sixteen years old!" is not yet a clear support for the assertion "I should be allowed to set my own curfew." On the surface, Young Person's argument seems absurd. Her parent, of all people, knows precisely how old she is. What makes it an argument is that behind her claim lies an unstated assumption—all sixteen-year-olds are old enough to set their own curfews. What Young Person needs to do now is to support that assumption.* In doing so, she must anticipate the sorts of questions the assumption will raise in the minds of her parent: What is the legal status of sixteen-year-olds? How psychologically mature, as opposed to chronologically

---

*In Chapter 4 we will call the assumption underlying a line of reasoning its *warrant*.

mature, is Young Person? What is the actual track record of Young Person in being responsible? Each of these questions will force Young Person to reexamine and clarify her assumptions about the proper degree of autonomy for sixteen-year-olds. And her response to those questions should in turn force the parents to reexamine their assumptions about the dependence of sixteen-year-olds on parental guidance and wisdom. (Likewise, the parents will need to show why "paying the bills around here" automatically gives them the right to set Young Person's curfew.)

As the argument continues, Young Person and Parent may shift to a different line of reasoning. For example, Young Person might say, "I should be allowed to stay out until 2 A.M. because all my friends get to stay out that late." (Here the unstated assumption is that the rules in this family ought to be based on the rules in other families.) The parent might in turn respond, "But I certainly never stayed out that late when I was your age"—an argument assuming that the rules in this family should follow the rules of an earlier generation.

As Young Person and Parent listen to each other's points of view (and begin realizing why their initial arguments have not persuaded their intended audience), both parties find themselves in the uncomfortable position of having to examine their own beliefs and to justify assumptions that they have taken for granted. Here we encounter one of the earliest senses of the term *to argue,* which is "to clarify." As an arguer begins to clarify her own position on an issue, she also begins to clarify her audience's position. Such clarification helps the arguer see how she might accommodate her audience's views, perhaps by adjusting her own position or by developing reasons that appeal to her audience's values. Thus Young Person might suggest an argument like this:

> I should be allowed to stay out until 2 A.M. on a trial basis because I need enough space to demonstrate my maturity and show you I won't get into trouble.

The assumption underlying this argument is that it is good to give teenagers freedom to demonstrate their maturity. Because this reason is likely to appeal to her parent's values (the parent wants the daughter to mature) and because it is tempered by the qualifier "on a trial basis" (which reduces some of the threat of Young Person's initial demands), it may prompt productive discussion.

Whether or not Young Person and Parent can work out the best solution, the preceding scenario illustrates how argument leads people to clarify their reasons and provide justifications that can be examined rationally. The scenario also illustrates two specific aspects of argument that we will explore in detail in the next sections: (1) Argument is both a process and a product. (2) Argument combines truth seeking and persuasion.

Argument Is Both a Process and a Product

In the preceding scenario, argument functioned as a *process* whereby two or more parties sought the best solution to a question or problem. Argument can also be viewed as a *product,* each product being any person's contribution to the conversation at a given moment. In an informal discussion, these products are usually short, whatever time a person uses during his or her turns in the conversation. Under more formal settings, an orally delivered product might be a short, impromptu speech (say, during an open-mike discussion of a campus issue) or a longer, carefully prepared formal speech (as in a PowerPoint presentation at a business meeting or an argument at a public hearing on a city project).

Similar conversations occur in writing. Roughly analogous to a small-group discussion is an exchange of the kind that occurs regularly online through informal chat groups or more formal blog sites. In an online discussion, participants have more thinking time to shape their messages than they do in a real-time oral discussion. Nevertheless, messages are usually short and informal, making it possible over the course of several days to see participants' ideas shift and evolve as conversants modify their initial views in response to others' views.

Roughly equivalent to a formal speech would be a formal written argument, which may take the form of an academic argument for a college course; an online blog posting; a guest column for the op-ed* section of a newspaper; a legal brief; or an article for an organizational newsletter, popular magazine, or professional journal. In each of these instances, the written argument (a product) enters a conversation (a process)—in this case, a conversation of readers, many of whom will carry on the conversation by writing their own responses or by discussing the writer's views with others. The goal of the community of writers and readers is to find the best solution to the problem or issue under discussion.

Argument Combines Truth Seeking and Persuasion

In thinking about argument as a product, the writer will find herself continually moving back and forth between truth seeking and persuasion—that is, between questions about the subject matter (What is the best solution to this problem?) and about audience (What reasons and evidence will most persuade them?). Back and forth she'll weave, alternately absorbed in the subject of her argument and in the audience for that argument.

Rarely is either focus ever completely ignored, but their relative importance shifts during different phases of the argument's development. We could thus place arguments on a kind of continuum that measures the degree of attention a writer gives to subject matter versus audience (see Figure 1.2). At the far truth-seeking end might be an exploratory piece that lays out several alternative approaches to a problem and weighs the strengths and weaknesses of each. At the other end of the continuum would be outright propaganda, such as a political campaign advertisement that reduces a complex issue to sound bites. (At its most blatant, propaganda obliterates truth seeking; it will do anything, including distorting or inventing

---

*Op-ed stands for "opposite-editorial." It is the generic name in journalism for signed arguments that voice the writer's opinion on an issue, as opposed to news stories, which are supposed to report events objectively.

FIGURE 1.2 Continuum of arguments from truth seeking to persuasion

evidence, to win over an audience.) In the middle ranges of the continuum, writers shift their focuses back and forth between truth seeking and persuasion, but with varying degrees of emphasis.

As an example of a writer focusing primarily on truth seeking, consider the case of Kathleen who, in her college argument course, addressed the definitional question "Should American Sign Language meet the university's foreign language requirement?" Kathleen had taken two years of ASL at a community college. When she transferred to a four-year college, her ASL proficiency was dismissed by the foreign language department chair. "ASL isn't a 'language,'" he said summarily. "It's not equivalent to learning French, German, or Japanese."

Kathleen disagreed, so she immersed herself in developing her argument. In her initial research she focused almost entirely on subject matter, searching for what linguists, neurologists, cognitive psychologists, and sociologists had said about ASL. She was only tacitly concerned with her audience, whom she mostly envisioned as her classmates and those sympathetic to her view. She wrote a well-documented paper, citing several scholarly articles that made a good case to her classmates (and her professor) that ASL is indeed a distinct language.

Proud of the big red A the professor had placed on her paper, Kathleen decided for a subsequent assignment to write a second paper on ASL—but this time aimed it directly at the chair of foreign languages, petitioning him to accept her ASL proficiency for the foreign language requirement. Now her writing task falls closer to the persuasive end of our continuum. Kathleen once again immersed herself in research, but this time focused not on subject matter—whether or not ASL is a distinct language—but on audience. She researched the history of the foreign language requirement at her college and discovered some of the politics behind it. She also interviewed foreign language teachers to find out what they knew and didn't know about ASL. She discovered that many teachers thought ASL was "easy to learn" and would allow students to avoid the rigors of a "real" foreign language class. Additionally, she learned that foreign language teachers valued immersing students in a foreign culture; in fact, the foreign language requirement was part of her college's effort to create a multicultural curriculum.

This new understanding of her target audience helped Kathleen reconceptualize her argument. Her claim that ASL was a real language (the subject of her first paper) became only one section of her second paper, much condensed and abridged. She added sections showing (1) that learning ASL is difficult (to counter her audience's belief that learning ASL was easy), (2) that the deaf community formed a distinct culture with its own customs and literature (to show how ASL met the goals of multiculturalism), and (3) that the number of transfer students with ASL credits would be negligible (to allay fears that accepting ASL would threaten enrollments in language classes). She ended her argument with an appeal to her college's emphasis—declared in its mission statement—on eradicating social injustice and reaching out to the oppressed. She described the isolation of deaf people in a world where almost no hearing people learn ASL, and she argued that the deaf community on her campus could be integrated more fully into campus life if more students could "talk" with them. Thus the ideas included in her new argument—the reasons selected, the evidence used, the arrangement and tone—all were determined by her primary focus on persuasion.

Our point, then, is that all along the continuum writers are concerned with truth seeking and persuasion, but not necessarily with equal balance. Kathleen could not have written her second paper, aimed specifically at persuading the chair of the foreign language department, if she hadn't first immersed herself in truth-seeking research that convinced her that ASL is indeed a distinct language. Nor are we saying that her second argument was better than her first. Both involved truth seeking and persuasion, but the first focused primarily on subject matter and the second primarily on audience.

Argument and the Problem of Truth

1.3 To understand the relationship of argument to the problem of truth

The tension that we have just examined between truth seeking and persuasion raises an ancient issue in the field of argument: Is the arguer's first obligation to truth or to winning the argument? And just what is the nature of the truth to which arguers are supposed to be obligated?

In Plato's famous dialogues from ancient Greek philosophy, these questions were at the heart of Socrates' disagreement with the Sophists. The Sophists were professional rhetoricians who specialized in training orators to win arguments. Socrates, who valued truth seeking over persuasion and believed that truth could be discovered through philosophic inquiry, opposed the Sophists. For Socrates, Truth resided in the ideal world of forms, and through philosophic rigor humans could transcend the changing, shadowlike world of everyday reality to perceive the world of universals where Truth, Beauty, and Goodness resided. Through his method of questioning his interlocutors, Socrates would gradually peel away layer after layer of false views until Truth was revealed. The good person's duty, Socrates believed, was not to win an argument but to pursue this higher Truth. Socrates distrusted rhetoricians because they were interested only in the temporal power and wealth that came from persuading audiences to the orator's views.

Let's apply Socrates' disagreement with the Sophists to a modern instance. Suppose your community is divided over the issue of raising environmental standards versus keeping open a job-producing factory that doesn't meet new guidelines for waste discharge. The Sophists would train you to argue any side of this issue on behalf of any lobbying group willing to pay for your services. If, however, you followed the spirit of Socrates, you would be inspired to listen to all sides of the dispute, peel away false arguments, discover the Truth through reasonable inquiry, and commit yourself to a Right Course of Action.

But what is the nature of Truth or Right Action in a dispute between jobs and the environment? The Sophists believed that truth was determined by those in power; thus they could enter an argument unconstrained by any transcendent beliefs or assumptions. When Socrates talked about justice and virtue, they could reply contemptuously that these were fictitious concepts invented by the weak to protect themselves from the strong. Over the years, the Sophists' relativist beliefs were so repugnant to people that the term *sophistry* became synonymous with trickery in argument.

However, in recent years the Sophists' critique of a transcendent Universal Truth has been taken seriously by many philosophers, sociologists, and other thinkers who doubt Socrates' confident belief that arguments, properly conducted, necessarily arrive at a single Truth. For these thinkers, as for the Sophists, there are often different degrees of truth and different kinds of truths for different situations or cultures. From this perspective, when we consider questions of interpretation or value, we can never demonstrate that a belief or assumption is true—not through scientific observation, not through reason, and not through religious revelation. We get our beliefs, according to these contemporary thinkers, from the shared assumptions of our particular cultures. We are condemned (or liberated) to live in a pluralistic, multicultural world with competing visions of truth.

If we accept this pluralistic view of the world, do we then endorse the Sophists' radical relativism, freeing us to argue any side of any issue? Or do we doggedly pursue some modern equivalent of Socrates' truth?

Our own sympathies are with Socrates, but we admit to a view of truth that is more tentative, cautious, and conflicted than his. For us, truth seeking does not mean finding the "Right Answer" to a disputed question, but neither does it mean a valueless relativism in which all answers are equally good. For us, truth seeking means taking responsibility for determining the "best answer" or "best solution" to the question for the good of the whole community when taking into consideration the interests of all stakeholders. It means making hard decisions in the face of uncertainty. This more tentative view of truth means that you cannot use argument to "prove" your claim, but only to make a reasonable case for your claim.

To seek truth, then, means to seek the best or most just solution to a problem while observing all available evidence, listening with an open mind to the views of all stakeholders, clarifying and attempting to justify your own values and assumptions, and taking responsibility for your argument. It follows that truth seeking often means delaying closure on an issue, acknowledging the pressure of alternative views, and being willing to change one's mind. Seen in this way, learning to argue effectively has the deepest sort of social value: It helps communities settle conflicts in a rational and humane way by finding, through the dialectic exchange of ideas, the best solutions to problems without resorting to violence or to other assertions of raw power.

■ ■ ■   **FOR CLASS DISCUSSION** Role-Playing Arguments

On any given day, the media provides evidence of the complexity of living in a pluralistic culture. Issues that could be readily decided in a completely homogeneous culture raise questions in a society that has fewer shared assumptions. Use the following case as the subject of a "simulation game" in which class members present the points of view of the people involved.

Case: Political Asylum for German Family Seeking Right to Homeschool Their Children

In 2010 an Evangelical Christian family from Germany, Uwe and Hannelore Romeike and their five children, moved to the United States seeking asylum from political persecution. At the U.S. immigration hearings, the couple argued that if they remained in Germany their decision to homeschool their children would result in fines, possible arrest, and even forced separation from their children. German law forbids homeschooling on the grounds that failure to attend recognized schools will create "parallel societies" whose members will fail to integrate into Germany's open and pluralistic culture. In early 2011, a U.S. federal immigration judge granted political asylum to the family, denouncing the German government's policy against homeschooling. He called it "utterly repellent to everything we believe as Americans." However, in 2013 the Sixth Circuit Court unanimously overturned the original decision and revoked the family's status as political refugees. Stating that the United States cannot give political asylum to every victim of perceived unfairness in another country's laws, the court declared that Germany's ban on homeschooling did not constitute political persecution. The decision led to international debate about the role of homeschooling in a pluralistic society and about the definition of political persecution. In the United States, the Homeschooling Legal Defense Association urged that the case be heard by the United States Supreme Court and sponsored a petition drive supporting the Romeike family.

Your task: Imagine a public hearing on this issue where all stakeholders are invited to present their points of view. The U.S. Immigration Web site offers the following definition of refugee status:

> Refugee status or asylum may be granted to people who have been persecuted or fear they will be persecuted on account of race, religion, nationality, and/or membership in a particular social group or political opinion.

Your goal isn't to make your own decision about this case but to bring to imaginative life all the points of view in the controversy. Hold a mock public hearing in which classmates play the following roles: (a) An American parent advocating homeschooling; (b) an American teacher's union representative opposing homeschooling; (c) an attorney arguing that the Romeike family meets the criteria for "refugee status"; (d) an attorney arguing that the Romeike family does not meet the criteria for refugee status; (e) a German citizen supporting the German law against homeschooling; (f) a Romeike parent arguing that they would be persecuted if they returned to Germany; (g) other roles that your class thinks are relevant to this case.   ■ ■ ■

Argument as Inquiry
Reading and Exploring

2

What you will learn in this chapter:

2.1 To find issues to explore

2.2 To read sources rhetorically by analyzing a text's genre, purpose, and degree of advocacy

2.3 To read to believe an argument's claims

2.4 To read to doubt an argument's claims

2.5 To delay closure by thinking dialectically

In the previous chapter we explained that argument focuses on both truth seeking and persuasion. In this chapter, we focus on inquiry (truth seeking) as the entry point into argumentative conversations. Unfortunately, in today's wired environment argument is often carried on within isolated echo chambers of like-minded participants who believe they already possess the truth. In contrast, this chapter argues that argument is better approached as an exploratory process in which participants try to suspend judgment and delay closure by engaging thoughtfully with alternative points of view, truly listening to other perspectives, examining their own values and assumptions, and perhaps even changing their views. We value the insight of rhetorician Wayne Booth, who proposes that when we enter an argumentative conversation, we should not ask first "How can I change your mind?" but rather "When should I change my mind?"*

In this chapter, we present some practical strategies for reading and exploring arguments in an open-minded and intellectually responsible way. To illustrate argument as inquiry, we will show you how one student, Trudie Makens, explored the problem of whether fast-food workers and other low-wage laborers should be paid a "living wage" of $15 per hour.

Finding Issues to Explore

2.1 To find issues to explore

Argument as inquiry begins when you find yourself in disagreement with someone else's point of view. Sometimes you will be confused about the issue. At other times, you will have a visceral

---

*Wayne Booth raised these questions in a featured session with Peter Elbow titled "Blind Skepticism vs. the Rhetoric of Assent: Implications for Rhetoric, Argument, and Teaching," presented at the CCCC annual convention, Chicago, Illinois, March 2002.

gut reaction that causes you to take an immediate position, even though you haven't thought through the issue in depth. At the start of the arguing process, being confused is often preferable to having a strong stand. Initial confusion disposes you to uncover your issue's complexity and let your thinking evolve. In this section we show you ways to find issues worth exploring.

Do Some Initial Brainstorming

As a first step, make an inventory of issues that interest you. Many of the ideas you develop may become subject matter for arguments that you will write later in this course. The chart on pages 13–14 will help you generate a productive list.

Once you've made a list, add to it as new ideas strike you and return to it each time you are given a new argumentative assignment.

Be Open to the Issues All around You

We are surrounded by argumentative issues. You will be invited into argumentative conversations by posters, bumper stickers, blog sites, newspaper editorial pages, magazine articles, movie reviews, song lyrics, class discussions, and so forth. When you read or listen, watch for "hot spots"—passages or moments that evoke strong agreement, disagreement, or confusion. As an illustration of how arguments are all around us, try the following exercise on the issue of a living wage for low-wage workers.

Brainstorming Issues to Explore

What You Can Do	How It Works
Make an inventory of the communities to which you belong. Consider classroom communities; clubs and organizations; residence hall, apartment, neighborhood, or family communities; church/synagogue or work communities; communities related to your hobbies or avocations; your city, state, region, nation, and world communities.	Because arguments arise out of disagreements within communities, you can often think of issues for argument by beginning with a list of the communities to which you belong.
Identify controversies within those communities. Think both big and small: ■ Big issue in world community: What is the best way to prevent destruction of rain forests? ■ Small issue in residence hall community: Should quiet hours be enforced?	To stimulate thinking, use prompts such as these: ■ People in this community frequently disagree about _____. ■ Within my work community, Person X believes _____; however, this view troubles me because _____.

(Continued)

What You Can Do	How It Works
Narrow your list to a handful of problematic issues for which you don't have a position; share it with classmates. Identify a few issues that you would like to explore more deeply. When you share with classmates, add their issues to yours.	Sharing your list with classmates stimulates more thinking and encourages conversations. The more you explore your views with others, the more ideas you will develop. Good writing grows out of good talking.
Brainstorm a network of related issues. Any given issue is always embedded in a network of other issues. To see how open-ended and fluid an argumentative conversation can be, try connecting one of your issues to a network of other issues including subissues and side issues.	Brainstorm questions that compel you to look at an issue in a variety of ways. For example, if you explored the controversy over whether toys with phthalates should be banned (see Chapter 1), you might generate questions such as these about related issues:

- How dangerous are phthalates?
- Is the testing that has been done on rats adequate or accurate for determining the effects on humans?
- To what extent are controversies over phthalates similar to controversies over steroids, genetically modified foods, nitrites in cured meat, or mercury in dental fillings?

■ ■ ■   **FOR CLASS DISCUSSION**   Responding to Visual Arguments about a Living Wage

Suppose, in your initial search for a controversial issue, you encounter three visual texts related to raising the minimum wage for fast-food workers: the protest photo (page 1), the cartoon (Figure 2.1), and the graph (Figure 2.2). Working individually or in small groups, generate exploratory responses to these questions:

1. What claim is each of these visual texts making?
2. What network of related issues do these visual texts suggest?
3. What questions or ideas do these visual texts raise for you?   ■ ■ ■

Explore Ideas by Freewriting

Freewriting is useful at any stage of the writing process. When you freewrite, you put fingers to keyboard (or pen to paper) and write rapidly *nonstop,* usually five to ten minutes at a stretch, without worrying about structure, grammar, or correctness. Your goal is to generate as many ideas as possible without stopping to edit your work. If you can't think of anything to say, write "relax" or "I'm stuck" over and over until new ideas emerge. Here is how Trudie Makens did a freewrite in response to the protest photo at the beginning of Part 1 (p. 1).

FIGURE 2.1 Political cartoon on minimum wage

Trudie's Freewrite

Working in the food and service industry as a busser, I relate to the man in the picture holding the sign reading "Stand with Fast Food Workers." It's hard to live off of minimum wage, and if it weren't for my tips, I wouldn't be able to pay some of my bills. And that is with help from my parents since I am a college student. I can't imagine what it would be like for full time workers in the fast food industry where orders are taken via counter. I remember when I worked counter service jobs, as a barista and at a dumpling café, no one ever tipped. They didn't feel like they needed too since it was not formal wait service. My work, and my coworkers' work, was not valued. What some people don't realize is that whether you are working at McDonalds or in an upscale restaurant, you are still working hard to provide good service. If anything, it is harder to work jobs like McDonalds where customers are dismissive and don't value the service they are receiving. Think, relax. Why do people not value the work of fast food and counter service workers? Because it is considered unskilled labor? A lot of the people I have worked with didn't have the time or money to go to college because they were burdened with the financial strains of having children or caring for sick or elderly relatives. I remember my co-worker Maria who was always stressed out because she couldn't pay her rent and had

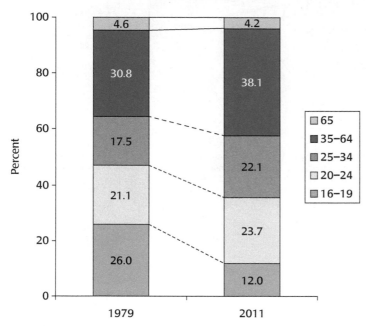

FIGURE 2.2 Graph offering employment statistics relevant to minimum wage controversy

Adapted from Schmitt, John, and Janelle Jones, "Low-Wage Workers Are Older and Better Educated Than Ever." Center for Economic and Policy Research. April 2012.

a child to support. A living wage would help people who haven't been lucky enough to inherit wealth to pull themselves out of poverty. And it wouldn't hurt corporations like McDonalds to live with a little less profit.

Explore Ideas by Idea Mapping

Another good technique for exploring ideas is *idea mapping*. When you make an idea map, draw a circle in the center of a page and write some trigger idea (a broad topic, a question, or working thesis statement) in the center of the circle. Then record your ideas on branches and subbranches extending from the center circle. A major advantage of "picturing" your thoughts is that you can see them as part of an emerging design rather than as strings of unrelated ideas.

Idea maps usually generate more ideas, though less well-developed ones, than freewrites. Figure 2.3 shows an idea map that student Trudie Makens created on the issue of minimum wage after class discussion of the visual texts in Figures 2.1 and 2.2.

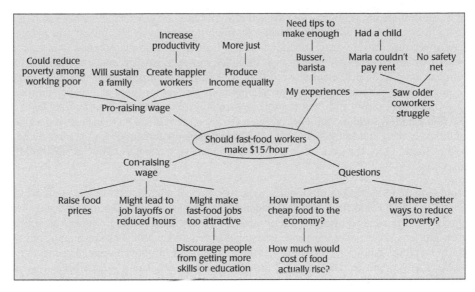

FIGURE 2.3 Trudie's idea map

Explore Ideas by Playing the Believing and Doubting Game

The believing and doubting game, a critical thinking strategy developed by rhetorician Peter Elbow, is an excellent way to stretch your thinking.

- **As a believer, your role is to be wholly sympathetic to an idea.** You must listen carefully to the idea and suspend all disbelief. You must identify all the ways in which the idea may appeal to different audiences and all the reasons for believing the idea. The believing game can be difficult, even frightening, if you are asked to believe an idea that strikes you as false or threatening.
- **As a doubter, your role is to be judgmental and critical, finding fault with an idea.** The doubting game is the opposite of the believing game. You do your best to find counterexamples and inconsistencies that undermine the idea you are examining. Again, it can be threatening to doubt ideas that you instinctively want to believe.

When you play the believing and doubting game with an assertion, simply write two different chunks, one chunk arguing for the assertion (the believing game) and one chunk opposing it (the doubting game). Freewrite both chunks, letting your ideas flow without censoring. Or, alternatively, make an idea map with believing and doubting branches. Here is how student writer Trudie Makens played the believing and doubting game with the assertion "Fast-food workers should be paid $15 per hour."

Trudie 's Believing and Doubting Game

Believing: I doubt anyone strives to become a full-time fast-food worker, but many people become stuck in those jobs and can't advance because they don't have a college education or because there are no better jobs available. Sometimes the workers are college students, so an increase in minimum pay would help them not accrue so much debt and perhaps have more time to study because they wouldn't have to work so many hours. But the real benefit would come to the uneducated, unskilled fast-food worker whose financial situation has led him or her to the fast-food job. The current minimum wage is barely livable. If the fast-food worker were to receive $15 per hour, there is far more of a chance for them to support themselves and their family comfortably without the stress of poverty. Even if the full-time fast-food worker does not go on to get more skills or go to college, it becomes more likely their children will be able to go to college if the fast-food worker is receiving a higher wage. Thus, the cycle of poverty as it is inherited generationally is, at least mildly, disrupted.

Doubting: If a $15 per hour minimum wage were to be implemented, the fast-food corporations would have to find ways to compensate for the profit loss. The most obvious way would be to raise food prices. If prices were to rise, fast food would no longer be affordable. This could have damaging and reversing effects on the working class who may rely on cheap fast food. Another problem is that the $15 per hour minimum wage may encourage workers to stay put in their jobs and not strive for a career. The student worker may no longer see the benefit of going into debt to get a degree and be satisfied with their current fast-food job. The effect of more desirable fast-food jobs may put pressure on other companies to raise the hourly wage of their entry-level positions. The rise in wage may, again, have the ripple effect of higher-priced products, thus reducing sales and forcing these companies to lay off some workers. No matter what scenario is dreamt up, it would seem that raising the minimum wage to $15 per hour, even if just for fast-food workers, might have damaging effects on the economy that diminish any benefits or advantages that theoretically come from receiving a higher wage.

Although Trudie sees the injustice of paying low wages to fast-food workers, she also sees that paying such workers $15 per hour might raise the cost of food, reduce the number of jobs available, or have other negative consequences. Playing the believing and doubting game has helped her articulate her dilemma and see the issue in more complex terms.

■ ■ ■   **FOR CLASS DISCUSSION**   Playing the Believing and Doubting Game

Individual task: Choose one or more of the following controversial claims and play the believing and doubting game with it, through either freewriting or idea mapping.

1. Federal law should forbid the purchase of assault weapons or high-capacity magazines.
2. Athletes should be allowed to take steroids and human growth hormone under a doctor's supervision.
3. Illegal immigrants already living in the United States should be granted amnesty and placed on a fast track to U.S. citizenship.

Group task: Working in pairs, in small groups, or as a whole class, share your results with classmates.   ■ ■ ■

Reading Texts Rhetorically

2.2 To read sources rhetorically by analyzing a text's genre, purpose, and degree of advocacy

Once you become engaged with an issue, you will typically research it to understand the various voices in the conversation, the points of disagreement, the uses of evidence and counterevidence, and the underlying assumptions and beliefs of different stakeholders. In this section, we focus on reading sources rhetorically by analyzing their genre, their author's purpose and intended audience, and the text's degree of advocacy. In later chapters, we discuss rhetorical reading in more depth: Chapter 5 teaches the concept of "angle of vision" based on the way an argumentative text selects and frames evidence; Chapter 8 teaches you how to write a rhetorical analysis of a text; and finally, Appendix 2 teaches the skills of research writing from a rhetorical perspective.

Genres of Argument

To situate an argument rhetorically, you should try to identify its genre. A *genre* is a recurring type or pattern of argument such as a letter to the editor, a scholarly journal article, or the home page of an advocacy Web site. Genres are often categorized by recurring features, formats, and styles. The genre of any given argument helps determine its length, tone, sentence complexity, level of informality or formality, use of visuals, kinds of evidence, and the presence or absence of documentation. When you do your own Internet research, you therefore need to be aware of the original genre of the text you are reading—to know, for example, whether the piece published on the Web was originally a newspaper editorial, a blog, a peer-reviewed scholarly article, or something else.

In the following chart we identify most of the genres of argument through which readers and writers carry on the conversations of a democracy.

Genres of Argument

Genre	Explanation and Examples	Stylistic Features
Personal correspondence	■ Letters or e-mail messages ■ Often sent to specific decision makers (complaint letter, request for an action)	■ Style can range from a formal business letter to an informal note
Letters to the editor	■ Published in newspapers and some magazines ■ Provide a forum for citizens to voice views on public issues	■ Very short (fewer than 300 words) and time sensitive ■ Can be summaries of longer arguments, but often focus in "sound bite" style on one point

(Continued)

Genre	Explanation and Examples	Stylistic Features
Newspaper editorials and op-ed pieces	■ Published on the editorial or op-ed ("opposite-editorial") pages ■ Editorials promote views of the newspaper owners/editors ■ Op-ed pieces, usually written by professional columnists or guest writers, range in bias from ultraconservative to socialist ■ Often written in response to political events or social problems in the news	■ Usually short (500–1,000 words) ■ Vary from explicit thesis-driven arguments to implicit arguments with stylistic flair ■ Have a journalistic style (short paragraphs) without detailed evidence ■ Sources usually not documented
Blogs and postings to chat rooms and electronic bulletin boards	■ Web-published commentaries, usually on specific topics and often intended to influence public opinion ■ Blogs are gaining influence as alternative commentaries to the established media ■ Reflect a wide range of perspectives	■ Often blend styles of journalism, personal narrative, and formal argument ■ Often difficult to determine identity and credentials of blogger ■ Often provide hyperlinks to related sites on the Web
Articles in public affairs or niche magazines	■ Usually written by staff writers or freelancers ■ Appear in public affairs magazines such as *National Review* or *The Progressive* or in niche magazines for special-interest groups such as *Rolling Stone* (popular culture) or *The Advocate* (gay and lesbian issues) ■ Often reflect the political point of view of the magazine	■ Frequently include narrative elements rather than explicit thesis-and-reasons organization ■ Often provide well-researched coverage of various perspectives on a public issue
Articles in scholarly journals	■ Peer-reviewed articles published by nonprofit academic journals subsidized by universities or scholarly societies ■ Characterized by scrupulous attention to completeness and accuracy in treatment of data	■ Usually employ a formal academic style ■ Include academic documentation and bibliographies ■ May reflect the biases, methods, and strategies associated with a specific school of thought or theory within a discipline

Genre	Explanation and Examples	Stylistic Features
Legal briefs and court decisions	■ Written by attorneys or judges ■ "Friend-of-the-court" briefs are often published by stakeholders to influence appeals courts ■ Court decisions explain the reasoning of justices on civic cases (and often include minority opinions)	■ Usually written in legalese, but use a logical reasons-and-evidence structure ■ Friend-of-the-court briefs are sometimes aimed at popular audiences
Organizational white papers	■ In-house documents or PowerPoint presentations aimed at influencing organizational policy or decisions or giving informed advice to clients ■ Sometimes written for external audiences to influence public opinion to be favorable to the organization ■ External white papers are often posted on Web sites or sent to legislators	■ Usually desktop or Web published ■ Often include graphics and other visuals ■ Vary in style from the dully bureaucratic (satirized in *Dilbert* cartoons) to the cogent and persuasive
Public affairs advocacy advertisements	■ Published as posters, fliers, Web pages, or paid advertisements ■ Condensed verbal/visual arguments aimed at influencing public opinion ■ Often have explicit bias and ignore alternative views	■ Use succinct "sound bite" style ■ Employ document design, bulleted lists, and visual elements (graphics, photographs, or drawings) for rhetorical effect
Advocacy Web sites	■ Usually identified by the extension ".org" in the Web site address ■ Often created by well-financed advocacy groups such as the NRA (National Rifle Association) or PETA (People for the Ethical Treatment of Animals) ■ Reflect the bias of the site owner	■ Often contain many layers with hyperlinks to other sites ■ Use visuals and verbal text to create an immediate visceral response favorable to the site owner's views ■ Ethically responsible sites announce their bias and purpose in an "About Us" or "Mission Statement" link on the home page

(Continued)

Genre	Explanation and Examples	Stylistic Features
Visual arguments	<ul><li>Political cartoons, usually drawn by syndicated cartoonists</li><li>Other visual arguments (photographs, drawings, graphics, ads), usually accompanied by verbal text</li></ul>	<ul><li>Make strong emotional appeals, often reducing complex issues to one powerful perspective (see Chapter 9)</li></ul>
Speeches and PowerPoint presentations	<ul><li>Political speeches, keynote speeches at professional meetings, informal speeches at hearings, interviews, business presentations</li><li>Often made available via transcription in newspapers or on Web sites</li><li>In business or government settings, often accompanied by PowerPoint slides</li></ul>	<ul><li>Usually organized clearly with highlighted claim, supporting reasons, and transitions</li><li>Accompanying PowerPoint slides designed to highlight structure, display evidence in graphics, mark key points, and sometimes provide humor</li></ul>
Documentary films	<ul><li>Formerly nonfiction reporting, documentary films now range widely from efforts to document reality objectively to efforts to persuade viewers to adopt the filmmaker's perspective or take action</li><li>Usually cost less to produce than commercial films and lack special effects</li><li>Cover topics such as art, science, and economic, political, environmental, and military crises</li></ul>	<ul><li>Often use extended visual arguments, combined with interviews and voice-overs, to influence as well as inform viewers</li><li>The filmmaker's angle of vision may dominate, or his or her perspective and values may be more subtle</li></ul>

Authorial Purpose and Audience

A democratic society depends on the lively exchange of ideas—people with stakes in issues and different perspectives advocating for their positions. In reconstructing the rhetorical context of an argument, consider how any given writer is spurred to write by a motivating occasion and by the desire to change the views of a particular audience. The following list identifies the wide range of writers, as well as cartoonists, filmmakers, and others, who are apt to produce arguments on public issues.

- **Lobbyists and advocacy groups.** Lobbyists and advocacy groups commit themselves to a cause, often with passion, and produce avidly partisan arguments aimed at persuading voters, legislators, government agencies, and other decision makers. They often maintain advocacy Web sites, buy advertising space in newspapers and magazines, and lobby legislators face-to-face.

■ **Legislators, political candidates, and government officials.** Whenever new laws, regulations, or government policies are proposed, staffers do research and write white papers recommending positions on an issue. Often these are available on the Web.

■ **Business professionals, labor union leaders, and bankers.** Business spokespeople often try to influence public opinion in ways that support corporate or business interests, whereas labor union officials support wage structures favorable to union members. Typically businesspeople produce "corporate image" advertisements, send white papers to legislators, or write op-ed pieces that frame issues from a business perspective, whereas labor unions produce arguments favorable to workers.

■ **Lawyers and judges.** Many controversial issues are entangled in legal matters. Lawyers write briefs supporting their clients' cases. Sometimes lawyers or legal experts not directly connected to a case, particularly law professors, file "friend-of-the-court" briefs aimed at influencing the decision of judges. Finally, judges write court opinions explaining their decisions on a case.

■ **Media commentators.** Many controversial issues are in the news and attract the attention of media commentators (journalists, editorial writers, syndicated columnists, bloggers, political cartoonists) who write articles and blogs or op-ed pieces on the issue or produce editorial cartoons, filtering their arguments through the perspective of their own political views.

■ **Professional freelance or staff writers.** Some of the most thoughtful analyses of public issues are composed by freelance or staff writers for public forum magazines such as *Atlantic Monthly, The Nation, Ms., National Review*, and *The New Yorker*, or for online news sites or blogs such as *The Daily Kos* or *Little Green Footballs*. These can range from in-depth background pieces to arguments with a highly persuasive aim.

■ **Think tanks.** Because today many political, economic, and social issues are very complex, policy makers and commentators often rely on research institutions or think tanks to supply statistical studies and in-depth investigation of problems. These think tanks range across the political spectrum, from conservative (the Hoover Institute, the Heritage Foundation) or libertarian (the Cato Institute) to the centrist or liberal (the Brookings Institution, the Pew Foundation, the Economic Policy Institute). They usually maintain many-layered Web sites that include background on research writers, recent publications, and archives of past publications, including policy statements and white papers.

■ **Scholars and academics.** College professors play a public role through their scholarly research, contributing data, studies, and analyses to public debates. Scholarly research differs substantially from advocacy argument in its systematic attempt to arrive at the best answers to questions based on the full examination of relevant data. Scholarly research is usually published in refereed academic journals rather than in popular magazines.

■ **Independent and commercial filmmakers.** Testifying to the growing popularity of film and its power to involve people in issues, documentary filmmakers often reflect on issues of the day, and commercial filmmakers often embed arguments within their dramatic storytelling. The global film industry is adding international perspectives as well.

■ **Citizens and students.** Engaged citizens influence social policy through letters, contributions to advocacy Web sites, guest editorials for newspapers, blogs, and speeches in public forums. Students also write for university communities, present their work at undergraduate research conferences, and influence public opinion by writing to political leaders and decision makers.

Determining Degree of Advocacy

As you read any given source connected to your issue, try to determine whether it is an advocacy piece that supports a position, a background piece that provides the context for an issue, or an overview article that tries to summarize the various positions in the controversy. If it is an argument, also try to determine its degree of advocacy along the continuum from "truth seeking" to "persuasion" shown in Figure 1.2 (page 8). Particularly pay attention to how an argument selects and frames evidence. When you encounter any argumentative text, use the following guide questions to help you read the text rhetorically.

Questions for Reading Texts Rhetorically

1. What genre of argument is this? How do the conventions of that genre help determine the depth, complexity, and even appearance of the argument?
2. Who is the author? What are the author's credentials and what is his or her investment in the issue?
3. What audience is he or she writing for?
4. What motivating occasion prompted the writing? The motivating occasion could be a current event, a crisis, pending legislation, a recently published alternative view, or another ongoing problem.
5. What is the author's purpose? The purpose could range from strong advocacy to inquiring truth seeker.
6. What information about the publication or source (magazine, newspaper, advocacy Web site) helps explain the writer's perspective or the structure and style of the argument?
7. What is the writer's angle of vision? By angle of vision, we mean the filter, lens, or selective seeing through which the writer is approaching the issue. What is left out from this argument? What does this author not see? (Chapter 5, pages 80–87, discusses how angle of vision operates in the selection and framing of evidence.)

This rhetorical knowledge becomes important in helping you select a diversity of voices and genres of argument when you are exploring an issue. Note how Trudie Makens makes use of her awareness of rhetorical context in her exploratory paper on pages 36–42.

■ ■ ■ **FOR CLASS DISCUSSION** **Placing Readings in Their Rhetorical Context**
Find two recent arguments on the subject of minimum wage* or on another subject specified by your instructor. Your arguments should (1) represent different genres and (2) represent different kinds of arguers (syndicated newspaper columnists, bloggers, freelance magazine writers, scholars, and so forth).

For each argument, answer the "Questions for Reading Texts Rhetorically" on page 24. Then share your findings with classmates.   ■ ■ ■

Reading to Believe an Argument's Claims

2.3 To read to believe an argument's claims

A powerful strategy for reading an argument rhetorically is to follow the spirit of the believing and doubting game, beginning with "believing." When you read to believe an argument, you practice what psychologist Carl Rogers calls *empathic listening*. Empathic listening requires that you see the world through the author's eyes, temporarily adopt the author's beliefs and values, and suspend your scepticism and biases in order to hear what the author is saying.

To illustrate what we mean by reading to believe, we will continue with our example of raising the minimum wage, a highly controversial issue. The following article, "The Pay Is Too Damn Low," is by James Surowiecki, an American journalist who writes the "Financial Page" column in *The New Yorker*, a magazine with a liberal perspective. This article appeared in *The New Yorker* in August 2013. Please read this article carefully in preparation for the exercises and examples that follow.

The Pay Is Too Damn Low

JAMES SUROWIECKI

A few weeks ago, Washington, D.C., passed a living-wage bill designed to make Walmart pay its workers a minimum of $12.50 an hour. Then President Obama called on Congress to raise the federal minimum wage (which is currently $7.25 an hour). McDonald's was widely derided for releasing a budget to help its employees plan financially, since that only underscored how brutally hard it is to live on a McDonald's wage. And last week fast-food workers across the country staged walkouts, calling for an increase in their pay to fifteen dollars an hour. Low-wage earners have long been the hardest workers to organize and the easiest to ignore. Now they're front-page news.

The workers' grievances are simple: low wages, few (if any) benefits, and little full-time work. In inflation-adjusted terms, the minimum wage, though higher than it was a decade ago, is still well below its 1968 peak (when it was worth about $10.70 an hour in today's dollars), and it's still poverty-level pay. To make matters worse, most fast-food and retail work is part time, and the weak

---

*For help on how to find articles through Web or licensed database searches, see Chapter 15.

job market has eroded what little bargaining power low-wage workers had: their earnings actually fell between 2009 and last year, according to the National Employment Law Project.

Still, the reason this has become a big political issue is not that the jobs have changed; it's that the people doing the jobs have. Historically, low-wage work tended to be done either by the young or by women looking for part-time jobs to supplement family income. As the historian Bethany Moreton has shown, Walmart in its early days sought explicitly to hire underemployed married women. Fast-food workforces, meanwhile, were dominated by teenagers. Now, though, plenty of family breadwinners are stuck in these jobs. That's because, over the past three decades, the U.S. economy has done a poor job of creating good middle-class jobs; five of the six fastest-growing job categories today pay less than the median wage. That's why, as a recent study by the economists John Schmitt and Janelle Jones has shown, low-wage workers are older and better educated than ever. More important, more of them are relying on their paychecks not for pin money or to pay for Friday-night dates but, rather, to support families. Forty years ago, there was no expectation that fast-food or discount-retail jobs would provide a living wage, because these were not jobs that, in the main, adult heads of household did. Today, low-wage workers provide 46 percent of their family's income. It is that change which is driving the demand for higher pay.

The situation is the result of a tectonic shift in the American economy. In 1960, the country's biggest employer, General Motors, was also its most profitable company and one of its best-paying. It had high profit margins and real pricing power, even as it was paying its workers union wages. And it was not alone: firms such as Ford, Standard Oil, and Bethlehem Steel employed huge numbers of well-paid workers while earning big profits. Today, the country's biggest employers are retailers and fast-food chains, almost all of which have built

their businesses on low pay—they've striven to keep wages down and unions out—and low prices.

5   This complicates things, in part because of the nature of these businesses. They make plenty of money, but most have slim profit margins: Walmart and Target earn between three and four cents on the dollar; a typical McDonald's franchise restaurant earns around six cents on the dollar before taxes, according to an analysis from Janney Capital Markets. In fact, the combined profits of all the major retailers, restaurant chains, and supermarkets in the Fortune 500 are smaller than the profits of Apple alone. Yet Apple employs just 76,000 people, while the retailers, supermarkets, and restaurant chains employ 5.6 million. The grim truth of those numbers is that low wages are a big part of why these companies are able to stay profitable while offering low prices. Congress is currently considering a bill increasing the minimum wage to $10.10 over the next three years. That's an increase that the companies can easily tolerate, and it would make a significant difference in the lives of low-wage workers. But that's still a long way from turning these jobs into the kind of employment that can support a middle-class family. If you want to accomplish that, you have to change the entire way these companies do business. Above all, you have to get consumers to accept significantly higher, and steadily rising, prices. After decades in which we've grown used to cheap stuff, that won't be easy.

Realistically, then, a higher minimum wage can be only part of the solution. We also need to expand the earned-income tax credit and strengthen the social-insurance system, including child care and health care (the advent of Obamacare will help in this regard). Fast-food jobs in Germany and the Netherlands aren't much better-paid than in the United States, but a stronger safety net makes workers much better off. We also need many more of the "middle-class jobs" we're always hearing about. A recent McKinsey report suggested that the government should invest almost a trillion dollars over the next five years in repairing and upgrading the national infrastructure, which seems like a good place to start. And we really need the economy as a whole to grow faster, because that would both increase the supply of good jobs and improve the bargaining power of low-wage workers. As Jared Bernstein, an economist at the Center for Budget and Policy Priorities told me, "The best friend that low-wage workers have is a strong economy and a tight job market." It isn't enough to make bad jobs better. We need to create better jobs.

Summary Writing as a Way of Reading to Believe

One way to show that you have listened well to an article is to summarize its argument in your own words. A summary (also called an *abstract,* a *précis,* or a *synopsis*) presents only a text's major points and eliminates supporting details. Writers often incorporate summaries of other writers' views into their own arguments, either to support their own views or to represent alternative views that they intend to oppose. Summaries can be any length, depending on the writer's purpose, but usually they range from several sentences to one or two paragraphs.

To help you write an effective summary, we recommend the following steps:

Step 1: *Read the argument for general meaning.* Don't judge it. Put your objections aside; just follow the writer's meaning, trying to see the issue from the writer's perspective. Try to adopt the writer's values and belief system.

Step 2: *Reread the article slowly, writing brief* does *and* says *statements for each paragraph (or group of closely connected paragraphs).* A *does* statement identifies a paragraph's function, such as "summarizes an opposing view," "introduces a supporting reason," "gives an example," or "uses statistics to support the previous point." A *says* statement summarizes a paragraph's content. What follows are *does* and *says* statements for the first three paragraphs of Surowiecki's article:

Does/Says Analysis of Surowiecki's Article

Paragraph 1: *Does:* Gives examples of recent news stories about protests of low-wage workers. *Says:* Hard-to-organize, low wage earners are now in the news demanding an increase in the minimum wage.

Paragraph 2: *Does:* Provides details about the workers' grievances. *Says:* A weakening job market combined with low wages, lack of benefits, and mainly part-time hours keeps low-wage workers at poverty levels.

Paragraph 3: *Does:* Explains the changing demographics of those who hold low-wage jobs. *Says:* In the past, minimum-wage jobs were held primarily by teenagers or by women desiring part-time work to supplement family incomes, but today many primary breadwinners depend on minimum-wage jobs to support a family.

■ ■ ■ **FOR CLASS DISCUSSION** Writing *Does/Says* **Statements**

Working individually or in small groups, write *does* and *says* statements for the remaining paragraphs of Surowiecki's article.   ■ ■ ■

Step 3: *Examine your* does *and* says *statements to determine the major sections of the argument.* Create a list of the major points (and subpoints) that must appear in a summary in order to represent that argument accurately. If you are visually oriented, you may prefer to make a flowchart or scratch outline of the sections of Surowiecki's argument.

Step 4: *Turn your list, outline, or flowchart into a prose summary.* Typically, writers do this in one of two ways. Some start by joining all their *says* statements into a lengthy paragraph-by-paragraph summary and then prune it. Others start with a one-sentence summary of the argument's thesis and major supporting reasons and then flesh it out with more supporting ideas. Your goal is to be as neutral as possible by keeping your own response to the writer's ideas out of your summary. You also need to cover all the writer's main points and give them the same emphasis as in the original article.

Step 5: *Revise your summary until it is the desired length and is sufficiently clear, concise, and complete.* Your goal is to spend your words wisely, making every word count. When you incorporate a summary into your own essay, you must distinguish that author's views from your own by using *attributive tags* (expressions such as "Surowiecki asserts" or "according to Surowiecki"). You must also put any directly borrowed wording in quotation marks. Finally, you must cite the original author using appropriate conventions for documenting sources.

What follows are two summaries of Surowiecki's article—a one-paragraph version and a one-sentence version—by student writer Trudie Makens.

Trudie's One-Paragraph Summary of Surowiecki's Argument

In his *New Yorker* article "The Pay Is Too Damn Low," James Surowiecki analyzes the grievances of workers at fast-food franchises, Walmart, or Target. In the past, it didn't matter that these jobs were low-pay, part-time, and without benefits because they were held mainly by teenagers or married women seeking to supplement a husband's wages. But today, says Surowiecki, a growing number of primary breadwinners rely on these poverty-level wages to support families. The problem stems from a "tectonic shift in the American economy." While in 1960, "firms like Ford, Standard Oil, and Bethlehem Steel employed huge numbers of well-paid workers while earning big profits," nowadays America's biggest employers are fast-food and retail companies with low profit margins. These companies depend on low-wage workers to keep prices cheap for the American consumer. Paying living wages to workers would completely change the business model, resulting in steadily rising prices. According to Surowiecki raising the minimum wage is only one tool for fighting poverty. America also needs to create a social insurance system like that of Germany or the Netherlands. Surowiecki calls for an increase in earned income tax credit, universal health insurance, affordable child care, and investment of almost a trillion dollars in infrastructure to create good middle-class jobs.

Work Cited

Surowiecki, James. "The Pay Is Too Damn Low." *The New Yorker,* 12 Aug. 2013, p. 35, www.newyorker.com/magazine/2013/08/12/the-pay-is-too-damn-low.

Trudie's One-Sentence Summary of Surowiecki's Argument

In his *New Yorker* article, "The Pay Is Too Damn Low," James Surowiecki argues that raising the minimum wage is only a partial solution to the problem of poverty and needs to be supplemented with a European-style social security network including an increase in earned income tax credit, universal health insurance, affordable child care, and investment of almost a trillion dollars in infrastructure to create good middle-class jobs.

Practicing Believing: Willing Your Own Belief in the Writer's Views

Although writing an accurate summary of an argument shows that you have listened to it effectively and understood it, summary writing by itself doesn't mean that you have actively tried to enter the writer's worldview. We want to stress the importance of believing it. Rhetorician Peter Elbow reminds us that before we critique a text, we should try to "dwell with" and "dwell in" the writer's ideas—play the believing game—in order to "earn" our right to criticize.* To help you "believe" a writer, find places in the text that resonate positively for you, look for values and beliefs you hold in common (however few), and search for personal experiences and values that affirm his or her argument.

Reading to Doubt

2.4 To read to doubt an argument's claims

After willing yourself to believe an argument, will yourself to doubt it by questioning the writer's logic, the writer's evidence and assumptions, and the writer's strategies for developing the argument. You also think about what is *not* in the argument by noting what the author has glossed over or left out. You add a new layer of marginal notes, articulating what is bothering you, asking questions, demanding proof, doubting evidence, challenging the author's assumptions and values, and so forth.

■ ■ ■ **FOR CLASS DISCUSSION** **Raising Doubts about Surowiecki's Argument**
Return now to Surowiecki's article and read it skeptically. Raise questions, offer objections, and express doubts. Then, working as a class or in small groups, list all the doubts you have about Surowiecki's argument.

■ ■ ■

Now that you have doubted Surowiecki's article, compare your questions and doubts to some raised by student writer Trudie Makens.

---

*Peter Elbow, "Bringing the Rhetoric of Assent and the Believing Game Together—Into the Classroom," *College English,* 67.4 (March 2005), 389.

Trudie's Doubts about Surowiecki's Article

- In his second paragraph, Surowiecki outlines three workers' grievances: "low wages, few (if any) benefits, and little full-time work." But increasing the minimum wage addresses only one of the grievances. A higher minimum wage might make it less likely for a worker to receive benefits or obtain full-time rather than part-time work. Moreover, with a higher wage, large companies may try to maintain profits by cutting jobs.

- Surowiecki asserts that large retailers and fast-food companies would absorb the cost of a higher minimum wage by raising prices on consumer goods. But if low-wage workers are also consumers, won't higher prices on previously cheap products defeat the benefits of a higher wage?

- Though he ends his article by calling for a multifaceted solution to poverty, he does so without offering a way to accomplish this goal. Where would the money come from in order to expand the earned income tax credit, strengthen the United States' current social insurance system, or invest in infrastructure? Further, how would the United States effectively implement and sustain these nationwide social programs without upsetting the already delicate economy?

- In his article Surowiecki mentions several studies, but there is no way to tell if these are widely respected studies or controversial ones. Would other studies, for example, conclude that low-wage workers today are responsible for 46 percent of their family's income?

These are only some of the objections that might be raised against Surowiecki's argument. The point here is that doubting as well as believing is a key part of the exploratory process and purpose. *Believing* urges you to adapt the views of others so that you can expand your own thinking and try on ideas that might begin to modify your own views or even change them. *Doubting* helps protect you from becoming overpowered by others' arguments and teaches you to stand back, consider, and weigh points carefully. It also leads you to new questions and points you might want to explore further.

Thinking Dialectically

2.5 To delay closure by thinking dialectically

This chapter's final strategy—thinking dialectically to bring texts into conversation with each other—encompasses all the previous strategies and can have a powerful effect on your growth as a thinker and arguer. The term *dialectic* is associated with the German philosopher Georg Wilhelm Friedrich Hegel, who postulated that each thesis prompts an opposing thesis (which he calls an "antithesis") and that the conflict between these views can lead thinkers to a new claim (a "synthesis") that incorporates aspects of both views. Dialectic thinking is the philosophical underpinning of the believing and doubting game, pushing us toward new and better ideas. As Peter Elbow puts it, "Because it's so hard to let go of an idea we are holding (or more to the point, an idea that's holding us), our best hope for leverage in learning to doubt such ideas is *to take on different ideas.*"* Dialectic thinking means playing ideas against each other, creating a tension that forces you to keep expanding your perspective.

---

*Peter Elbow, "Bringing the Rhetoric of Assent and the Believing Game Together—Into the Classroom," *College English* 67.4 (March 2005), 390.

As you listen to differing views, try to identify sources of disagreement among arguers, which often fall into two categories: (1) disagreement about the facts of the case and (2) disagreement about underlying values, beliefs, or assumptions. We saw these disagreements in Chapter 1 in the conversation about phthalates in children's toys. At the level of facts, disputants disagreed about the amount of phthalates a baby might ingest when chewing a rubber toy or about the quantity of ingested phthalates needed to be harmful. At the level of values, disputants disagreed on the amount of risk that must be present in a free market economy before a government agency should ban a substance. As you try to determine your own position on an issue, consider what research you might have to do to resolve questions of fact; also try to articulate your own underlying values, beliefs, and assumptions.

As you consider multiple points of view on an issue, try using the following questions to promote dialectic thinking:

Questions to Promote Dialectic Thinking

1. What would writer A say to writer B?
2. After I read writer A, I thought _____; however, after I read writer B, my thinking on this issue had changed in these ways: _____.
3. To what extent do writer A and writer B disagree about facts and interpretations of facts?
4. To what extent do writer A and writer B disagree about underlying beliefs, assumptions, and values?
5. Can I find any areas of agreement, including shared values and beliefs, between writer A and writer B?
6. What new, significant questions do these texts raise for me?
7. After I have wrestled with the ideas in these two texts, what are my current views on this issue?

Responding to questions like these—either through class discussion or through exploratory writing—can help you work your way into a public controversy. Earlier in this chapter you read James Surowiecki's article expressing liberal support for raising the minimum wage and enacting other government measures to help the poor. Now consider an article expressing a quite different point of view, an op-ed piece written by Michael Saltsman, the research director at the Employment Policies Institute—a pro-business, free market think tank opposed to raising the minimum wage. It appeared in *The Huffington Post* in April 2013. We ask you to read the article and then use the preceding questions to stimulate dialectic thinking about Surowiecki versus Saltsman.

■ ■ ■   **FOR CLASS DISCUSSION** Practicing Dialectic Thinking with
                                    Two Articles

Individual task: Freewrite your responses to the preceding questions, in which Surowiecki is writer A and Saltsman is writer B.

Group task: Working as a whole class or in small groups, share your responses to the two articles, guided by the dialectic questions.   ■ ■ ■

To Help the Poor, Move Beyond "Minimum" Gestures

MICHAEL SALTSMAN

Actor and director Ben Affleck made news this week with the announcement that he'll spend five days living on just $1.50—the U.S.-dollar daily equivalent of extreme poverty, according to the Global Poverty Project.

Affleck's heart is in the right place, but his actions won't provide a measurable benefit for people who actually live in poverty. On that score, Affleck's actions are not unlike a series of recently-introduced proposals to raise the federal minimum wage—well-intentioned but ultimately empty gestures that will do little to raise poor families out of poverty.

For poverty-reducing policies to benefit the poor, the benefits first have to be properly targeted to people living in poverty. On this count, a higher minimum wage fails miserably. Census Bureau data shows that over 60 percent of people living below the poverty line don't work. They don't need a raise—they need a job.

Among those who do earn the minimum wage, a majority actually don't live in poverty. According to a forthcoming Employment Policies Institute analysis of Census Bureau data, over half of those covered by President Obama's $9 proposal live in households with income at least twice the poverty level—and one-third are in households with an income three times or greater than the poverty level.

5   That's because nearly 60 percent of affected employees aren't single earners, according to the EPI report—they're living in households where a parent or a spouse often earns an income far above the minimum. (The average family income of this group is $50,789). By contrast, we found that only nine percent of people covered by President Obama's $9 minimum wage are single parents with children.

It's for reasons like these that the majority of academic research shows little connection between a higher minimum wage and reductions in poverty. For instance, economists from American and Cornell Universities examined data from the 28 states that raised their minimum wages between 2003 and 2007, and found no associated reductions in poverty.

Of course, poor targeting isn't the only problem. The vast majority of economic research—including 85 percent of the most credible studies from the last two decades—finds that job loss for the least-skilled employees follows on the heels of minimum wage hikes.

That's why better-targeted policies like the Earned Income Tax Credit (EITC) deserve the support of politicians and public figures who want to do something about poverty. It's been empirically proven to boost employment and incomes, without the unintended consequences of a wage hike. Accounting for the EITC, the full-time hourly wage for many minimum wage earners is already above the $9 figure that President Obama has proposed.

Boosting the EITC might not have the same media appeal of a higher minimum wage (or of Ben Affleck's pledge, for that matter), but it does what neither wage hikes or the Affleck pledge can—actually make a measurable difference for the poor.

Three Ways to Foster Dialectic Thinking

In this concluding section, we suggest three ways to stimulate and sustain the process of dialectic thinking.

Effective Discussions   Good, rich talk is one of the most powerful ways to stimulate dialectic thinking. The key is to keep these discussions from being shouting matches or bully pulpits for those who like to dominate the airtime. Discussions are most productive if people are willing to express different points of view or to role-play those views for the purpose of advancing the conversation.

Reading Logs   In our classes, we require students to keep reading logs or journals in which they use freewriting and idea mapping to explore their ideas as they encounter multiple perspectives on an issue. One part of a journal or reading log should include summaries of each article you read. Another part should focus on your own dialectic thinking as you interact with your sources while you are reading them. Adapt the questions for promoting dialectic thinking on page 31.

A Formal Exploratory Essay   A formal exploratory essay tells the story of an intellectual journey. It is both a way of promoting dialectical thinking and a way of narrating one's struggle to negotiate multiple views. The keys to writing successful exploratory essays are: (1) choosing an issue to explore on which you don't yet have an answer or position (or on which you are open to changing your mind); (2) wrestling with an issue or problem by resisting quick, simple answers and by exploring diverse perspectives; and (3) letting your thinking evolve and your own stance on the issue grow out of this exploration.

Exploratory essays can be powerful thinking and writing experiences in their own right, but they can also be a valuable precursor to a formal argument. Many instructors assign a formal exploratory paper as the first stage of a course research project—what we might call a "thesis-seeking" stage.

An exploratory essay includes these thinking moves and parts:

- The essay is opened and driven by the writer's issue question or research problem—not a thesis.
- The introduction to the essay presents the question and shows why it interests the writer, why it is significant, and why it is problematic rather than clear-cut or easy to resolve.
- The body of the essay shows the writer's inquiry process. It demonstrates how the writer has kept the question open, sincerely wrestled with different views on the question, accepted uncertainty and ambiguity, and possibly redefined the question in the midst of his or her reading and reflection on multiple perspectives.
- The body of the essay includes summaries of the different views or sources that the writer explored and often includes believing and doubting responses to them.
- In the essay's conclusion, the writer may clarify his or her thinking and discover a thesis to be developed and supported in a subsequent argument. But the conclusion can also remain open because the writer may not have discovered his or her own position on the issue and may acknowledge the need or desire for more exploration.

One of the writing assignment options for this chapter is a formal exploratory paper. Trudie Makens's exploratory essay on pages 36–42 shows how she explored different voices in the controversy over raising the minimum wage to $15 per hour.

WRITING ASSIGNMENT An Argument Summary or A Formal Exploratory Essay

Option 1: An Argument Summary Write a 250-word summary of an argument selected by your instructor. Then write a one-sentence summary of the same argument. Use as models Trudie Makens's summaries of James Surowiecki's argument on raising the minimum wage (pages 28 and 29).

Option 2: A Formal Exploratory Essay Write an exploratory essay in which you narrate in first-person, chronological order the evolution through time of your thinking about an issue or problem. Rather than state a thesis or claim, begin with a question or problem. Then describe your inquiry process as you worked your way through sources or different views. Follow the guidelines for an exploratory paper shown on page 33. When you cite the sources you have considered, be sure to use attributive tags so that the reader can distinguish between your own ideas and those of the sources you have summarized. If you use research sources, use MLA documentation for citing ideas and quotations and for creating a Works Cited at the end. ■

Organization Plan for an Exploratory Essay

Introduction (one to several paragraphs)	• Establish that your question is complex, problematic, and significant. • Show why you are interested in it. • Present relevant background on your issue. Begin with your question or build up to it, using it to end your introductory section.
Body section 1: First view or source	• Introduce your first source and show why you started with it. • Provide rhetorical context and information about it. • Summarize the source's content and argument. • Offer your response to this source, including both believing and doubting points. • Talk about what this source contributes to your understanding of your question: What did you learn? What value does this source have for you? What is missing from this source that you want to consider? Where do you want to go from here?
Body section 2: Second view or source	• Repeat the process with a new source selected to advance the inquiry. • Explain why you selected this source (to find an alternative view, pursue a sub-question, find more data, and so forth). • Summarize the source's argument. • Respond to the source's ideas. Look for points of agreement and disagreement with other sources. • Show how your cumulative reading of sources is shaping your thinking or leading to more questions.
Body sections 3, 4, 5, etc.	• Continue exploring views or sources.
Conclusion	• Wrap up your intellectual journey and explain where you are now in your thinking and how your understanding of your problem has changed. • Present your current answer to your question based on all that you have learned so far, or explain why you still can't answer your question, or explain what research you might pursue further.

Reading

What follows is Trudie Makens's exploratory essay on the subject of raising the minimum wage. Her research begins with the articles by Surowiecki and Saltsman that you have already read and discussed. She then moves off in her own direction.

Title as question indicates an exploratory purpose.

Should Fast-Food Workers Be Paid $15 per Hour?

TRUDIE MAKENS (STUDENT)

Introduction identifies the issue, explains the writer's interest in it, and acknowledges its complexity.

Having worked as a busser in a pizza restaurant, a part-time barista, and a server at a dumpling cafe, I was immediately attracted to our class discussions of minimum wage, sparked by recent protests of fast-food workers demanding pay of $15 per hour. My first job as a barista exposed me to the harsh reality of living on today's existing minimum wage as I witnessed my coworker Maria lose her home because she couldn't pay rent and support her kids at the same time. As a single mother of two, Maria had to bounce from relative to relative putting a strain on her family relations, her image of herself as an able provider, and her children. I am lucky because, as a student, I am blessed to have my family operate as a safety net for me. If I am ever short on a bill or get sick or hurt, my parents will assist me financially. Many of the individuals I have worked with do not have that same safety net. These individuals are often older and have children or are beginning a family. Understanding the hardships of minimum-wage jobs, I entered our class discussions in support of the $15/hour demand because this pay rate would give workers a living wage. However, despite my personal affinities with these workers, I also understood that raising the minimum wage might have negative consequences for our economy. I wanted to explore this issue in more depth so I decided to pose my research question as "Should fast-food workers be paid a living wage of $15 per hour?"

Writer states her research question.

Writer identifies her first source.

My exploration began with an article that our instructor assigned to the whole class: "The Pay Is Too Damn Low" by James Surowiecki from *The New Yorker*. In the past, according to Surowiecki, it didn't matter that jobs at Walmart, Target, or fast-food franchises were low-pay, part-time, and without benefits because they were held mainly by teenagers or married women seeking to supplement a husband's wages.

Writer summarizes the article.

But today, says Surowiecki, a growing number of primary breadwinners rely on these poverty-level wages to support families. The problem stems from a "tectonic shift in the American economy." While in 1960, "firms like Ford, Standard Oil, and Bethlehem Steel employed huge numbers of well-paid workers while earning big profits," nowadays America's biggest employers are fast-food and retail companies with low profit margins. While Surowiecki acknowledges that these retail companies and food franchises depend on low-wage workers to keep prices cheap for the American consumer, he still supports increasing the minimum wage but sees it as only one tool for fighting poverty. He argues that America also needs to create a European-style safety net system and calls for an increase in earned income tax credit, universal health insurance, affordable child care, and investment of almost a trillion dollars in infrastructure to create good middle-class jobs.

Writer shows how this article has advanced her thinking by strengthening her previous mention of "safety nets."

Surowiecki's concluding remarks about a safety net system resonated with me. I understood that what protected me from a financial crisis was my family acting like a safety net. The government, Surowiecki argues, should perform the same function for low-wage earners through such programs as childcare and health care. He points to Germany and the Netherlands, arguing the stronger safety net put in place for workers by these European governments provides a better economic and social situation for low-wage workers, even though they are paid around the same amount as United States low-wage workers. Surowiecki also addressed some of my concerns regarding the economic consequences of implementing a living wage. Even though some low-wage jobs might be eliminated and food costs might go up, government investment in infrastructure might create more high-paying, middle-class jobs, resulting in a net benefit. But I still wasn't convinced or completely satisfied. How exactly would the government raise the money for a redesigned social insurance system? Would the country accept the needed higher taxes? While Surowiecki had convinced me that the government had an important role to play in creating the conditions for a living wage, I still was unclear on how the government could effectively do so without detrimentally upsetting the economy.

Writer includes doubting points by identifying problems not resolved in first source.

Writer shows rhetorical thinking by purposely seeking an argument from a business perspective; she identifies conservative credentials of author and summarizes his argument.

Writer summarizes second source.

I wanted to know more about raising the minimum wage from the business perspective, so I Googled "living wage" and found an anti-minimum wage article from Michael Saltsman, the research director of the Employment Policy Institute. The op-ed piece was published online in *The Huffington Post* and entitled, "To Help the Poor, Move Beyond 'Minimum' Gestures." I also found a full page ad from the same conservative institute depicting a robot doing the work of a fast food employee. Saltsman believes that despite the good intentions of living wage proponents a higher federal minimum wage will do more harm than good. Within his piece, Saltsman equates the symbolic value of Ben Affleck's pledge to live five days on $1.50, "the U.S. dollar equivalent of extreme poverty," to proposals for a higher federal minimum wage. Both, according to Saltsman, are "ultimately empty gestures" that do little to lift families out of poverty. What the poor need, Saltsman asserts, is "not a raise" but a job. Saltsman claims that over "60% of people living below the poverty line don't work" and those who do earn a minimum wage don't live in poverty households. Even if a member of the working poor were to receive a living wage, Saltsman argues, "job loss for the least-skilled employees follows on the heels of a minimum wage hike." What helps to reduce poverty, according to Saltsman, is not a higher minimum wage but the Earned Income Tax Credit, "empirically proven to boost employment and incomes" and thus providing "a measurable difference for the poor."

Writer includes both believing and doubting points.

5   Prior to reading Saltsman, I had not fully considered the potential that workers would be laid off because it would be cheaper for businesses to use robots or other automation than to employ higher-wage workers. Though Saltsman got me thinking about the dangers of job displacement, I wasn't convinced by his argument that an increased minimum wage would primarily benefit people who didn't need it such as teenagers or second earners in an already middle-class family. I could see that an increased minimum wage wouldn't help the 60 percent of the poor who were unemployed, but I also realized that the Earned Income Tax Credit wouldn't help the unemployed either because it is goes only to poor people who report income. (I Googled "earned income tax credit" just to make sure I understood how it works by giving a boost of income to poor but working tax filers.) Though Saltsman persuaded me to consider the negative economic consequences of a living wage, I wasn't convinced the living wage was entirely ineffective. I thought back to Surowiecki who, unlike Saltsman, saw a living wage as one component in a larger solution to reduce poverty. Both recommended an expanded Earned Income Tax Credit, but Surowiecki went further and also encouraged a stronger social-insurance system in addition to a higher minimum wage. Neither article persuaded me the living wage was either fully beneficial or fully injurious. To clarify my position, I needed to do more research.

I wanted another economist's perspective, so I typed in "economic impact and living wage" into ProQuest, an interdisciplinary research database. One of the articles that caught my attention was "Living Wage: Some Gain, Neediest Lose Out." The article was an interview with labor economist Richard Toikka by author Charles Oliver featured in *Investor's Business Daily,* a conservative financial newspaper focused on stock and bond investments. In the interview, Oliver prompts Toikka to discuss the unintended consequences of a higher minimum wage.

Toikka asserts that in order to absorb the cost of a higher wage, companies seek to hire higher-skilled workers who require less training, and thus cost the company less money. With a higher wage offered, Toikka argues, more high-skilled workers, such as college students, seek these jobs, increasing "the competition low skilled workers face." Thus an increased minimum wage reduces the number of low-skilled jobs available. Toikka also makes the same argument as Saltsman, concluding that the benefits of a higher wage don't go towards the families who need it, but instead to second-earners who aren't living below the poverty line. Toikka cites a survey among labor economists asked to rate the efficiency of anti-poverty measures, and "69% said living wages weren't at all efficient in meeting the needs of poor families." The more efficient way to combat poverty, Toikka argues, is not a living wage but an expansion of the Earned Income Tax Credit.

Putting Toikka in conversation with Saltsman, I began to understand and heed the warnings of both economists. Though well-intentioned, increasing the minimum wage by itself is not apt to reduce poverty and would ultimately injure the poor rather than helping. If a living wage does lead to heightened competition and employers slashing jobs, then perhaps a living wage is ineffective and therefore should be abandoned in favor of the Earned Income Tax Credit. So far, all the articles agreed the Earned Income Tax Credit was a good way to reduce poverty, even though it too benefits only those with jobs. Even so, I couldn't help but think that abandoning a living wage was a concession to a flawed economic system that doesn't value the working poor or the impoverished unemployed enough. I thought back to Surowiecki when he praised Germany and the Netherlands for providing a strong social insurance system that served as a safety net for those in low-wage jobs. If Europe can ensure dignity and security to its citizens, then why can't the United States? Although 69 percent of labor economists say that a living wage is an inefficient way to alleviate poverty, we don't know what they would say if the government also invested in infrastructure to create well-paying jobs. Right now, it seems from my readings, that the current market doesn't value low-wage workers. What is valued in our economy is capital, profit, and cheap goods, all of which come at the expense of millions of workers. Is the structure of the economy where wealth is unequally distributed and workers are exploited really inevitable? Or is it an economic trend that can be reversed? I wanted to believe the latter, so I returned to ProQuest to find another article addressing the economic impact of a living wage but from a pro-labor perspective.

In my search, I found an article entitled "The Task Rabbit Economy," authored by Robert Kuttner and published in the progressive magazine *The American Prospect*. Kuttner begins by describing a successful San

Writer shows how the pro-business sources have complicated her initial tentative position.

Writer uses believing and doubting strategies to think dialectically, looking for a synthesis.

Writer purposefully seeks a different perspective.

Writer identifies next source and places it in rhetorical context.

Francisco company whose Web site matches people who have an odd job they need done with people who will do the work for a fee. The company, named the Task Rabbit, is like an online temp agency that operates by having would-be workers bid against each other, driving the price down for their labor. Kuttner argues that Task Rabbit's business model, which produces cheap labor, is analogous to our current economy, where workers have lost "bargaining power" and work has become casual and unstable (46). Kuttner argues that this low-wage economy has produced less economic growth, less prosperity, and more unemployment than earlier eras when there was more job stability and higher wages. According to Kuttner, the claim made by labor economists that a higher minimum wage leaves low-skilled workers without a job ignores how an unregulated labor market has allowed corporations to "weaken labor … and extract abnormal profits" (47). Kuttner draws on the economy of Sweden to provide an example where a living wage, full employment, and a "deliberate effort to narrow wage gaps" has been implemented effectively (48). What's more, Kuttner addresses the concern of rising prices by citing a Demos study that found raising wages so retail workers "earned at least \$25,000 a year" only cost large retailers "1 percent of the \$2.17 trillion annual sales" (52). Kuttner closes out his article by emphasizing that "organized labor" is what will change the labor market, using both collective bargaining and "political force" (55).

Kuttner's article moved me in a way that Toikka and Saltsman's pieces could not. Instead of accepting an economic system where low-wage workers are exploited for stockholder profits and cheap goods, Kuttner criticizes the labor market for its failure to value workers. Kuttner acknowledges that a higher minimum wage will upset the present economy, but he argues that the present economic system isn't inevitable but the result of large employers choosing to value capital over people without strong governmental policies protecting labor and the poor. Moreover, Kuttner's article illuminates the inefficiency of our economy. The studies Kuttner references reveal that the United States was better off in the years after World War II, when jobs were stable, plentiful, and paid a living wage. Most of all, I appreciated Kuttner's concluding call to action, and his assurance that such action will not lead to economic suicide but create the "dynamic, supple, and innovative" economy our nation strives for. According to Kuttner, we can choose to allow the market to continue unregulated, or, through organizing workers, we can push towards policies that value people—their rights, health, and dignity. As I read Kuttner, I wondered what current labor movements are in existence today and the progress they are making in their fight to gain rights and a living wage. I, again, turned to ProQuest.

Writer identifies next source and places it in rhetorical context.

10   My search handed me a long list of results, but I found one article that provided a relevant look into a labor campaign organized by Walmart sales associates. Titled "Job Insecurity," the article was written by Kevin Clarke and published in the Catholic magazine *America*. Clarke begins by introducing William Fletcher, a twenty-three-year-old retail sales associate at Walmart. According to Fletcher, he loves his job and "working with the public" but, he says, he and other employees constantly struggle with "low wages, chaotic scheduling, and insensitive management." Both Fletcher and Clarke wonder why being a retail sales associate for Walmart warrants not receiving enough to "have a home, have health insurance, have all the basic things in life." In order to improve his working conditions, Fletcher joined Organization United for Respect at Walmart, or OUR Walmart. OUR Walmart, Clarke states, is "part of an emerging labor phenomenon of non-union activism against Walmart and other powerful, profitable U.S. corporations that maintain large, low paid work forces." Walmart, according to both Fletcher and Clarke, is a trend-setting company. If labor conditions improve at Walmart, other companies could follow suit. The organization draws from the tactics of "community organizing and the civil rights movement." Unfortunately, Clarke states, Walmart management continues to thwart protests or walkouts. Despite obstacles, OUR Walmart persists, marking a major moment in the contemporary labor movement. The article ends with Clarke's appeal to the Catholic social justice tradition of solidarity with the poor. He notes that Walmart sales associates depend on government support programs such as food stamps and housing assistance. He reminds his readers that our continual search for the cheapest goods makes us partially guilty for the exploitation of workers. He urges us to shop conscientiously and thoughtfully.

Writer pulls together the results of her dialectic thinking, which has resulted in a synthesis.

I reached the end of the article feeling shocked. In lieu of everything I read from Kuttner, I was amazed that Walmart could dismiss the demands of OUR Walmart. Clarke states the owners of Walmart, the Walton family, possess "48% of Walmart stock and [are] the richest family on earth, with over $107 billion in net worth." Hearing numbers like these confirmed my forming conviction that the unregulated labor market dangerously exploits workers in order to gain cheap labor, cheap goods, and bloated profits. What's more, Walmart actively tries to scare workers from organizing—threatening to take away their jobs. Though there is much more to read and learn about the growing labor movement in the United States, Clarke's article, as well as Surowiecki, Saltsman, Toikka, and Kuttner's pieces, allowed me to

Final sentences reveal synthesis that goes beyond original leanings in first paragraph.

round out my position on a higher minimum wage. As I end my exploratory paper, I understand that a living wage is possible and should be provided to service workers as a basic human right. But it also needs to be supplemented with the kinds of social insurance systems stressed by Surowiecki and Kuttner.

Works Cited

Writer compiles an MLA-formatted "Works Cited" page that lists alphabetically all the sources discussed in the paper.

Clarke, Kevin. "Job Insecurity." *America,* 18 Feb. 2013, americamagazine.org/issue/article/job-insecurity.

Kuttner, Robert. "The Task Rabbit Economy." *The American Prospect,* 24 Sept. 2013, pp. 45-55.

Oliver, Charles. "Living Wage: Some Gain, Neediest Lose Out." *Investor's Business Daily,* 5 Sept. 2000. *ProQuest,* 10 Jan. 2014, search.proquest.com/docview/1026806044/fulltext/DA48476F0F254E4CPQ/1?accountid=10226.

Saltsman, Michael. "To Help the Poor, Move Beyond 'Minimum' Gestures." *The Huffington Post,* 26 Apr. 2013, updated 26 June 2013, www.huffingtonpost.com/michael-saltsman/earned-income-tax-credit-minimum-wage_b_3165459.html.

Surowiecki, James. "The Pay Is Too Damn Low." *The New Yorker,* 12 Aug. 2013, p. 35.

PART TWO
Writing an Argument

This still from the *Tomb Raider* video game series features main character Lara Croft engaged in one of her typical combats with humans, beasts, or supernatural creatures. Lara, an adventurer and archaeologist, represents both a sexualized and an empowered woman. Women and violent video games are the focus of student Carmen Tieu's argument developed in Chapters 3–5; however, Carmen explores gender roles from the perspective of a woman playing a "male" video game, *Halo*.

The Core of an Argument

A Claim with Reasons

3

In Part One, we explained that argument combines truth seeking with persuasion. Part One, by highlighting the importance of exploration and inquiry, emphasizes the truth-seeking dimension of argument, offering a variety of writing assignments ranging from freewriting to playing the believing and doubting game to writing a formal exploratory essay. In Part Two, we show you how to convert your exploratory ideas into a thesis-governed classical argument that uses effective reasons and evidence to support its claims. Each chapter in Part Two focuses on a key skill or idea needed for responsible and effective persuasion.

The Classical Structure of Argument

3.1 To describe the key elements of classical argument

Classical argument is patterned after the persuasive speeches of ancient Greek and Roman orators. It typically has the organizational structure shown on page 45, which shows these typical sections:

- **The introduction.** Writers of classical argument typically begin by establishing the timeliness of the issue at stake and connecting the audience to the issue with a current event, memorable scene, illustrative story, or startling statistic—something that grabs the audience's attention. They continue the introduction by focusing the issue—often by stating it directly as a question or by briefly summarizing opposing views—and providing needed background and context. They conclude the introduction by presenting their claim (thesis statement) and forecasting the argument's structure.

- **The presentation of the writer's position.** The presentation of the writer's position is usually the longest part of a classical argument. Here writers present the reasons and evidence supporting their claims, typically choosing reasons that tie into their audience's values, beliefs, and assumptions. Usually each reason is developed in its own paragraph or sequence of paragraphs.

■ **The summary and critique of alternative views.** When summarizing and responding to opposing views, writers have several options. If there are several opposing arguments, writers may summarize all of them together and then compose a single response, or they may summarize and respond to each argument in turn. As we explain in Chapter 7, writers may respond to opposing views either by refuting them or by conceding to their strengths and shifting to a different field of values.

■ **The conclusion.** Finally, in their conclusion, writers sum up their argument, often calling for some kind of action, thereby creating a sense of closure and leaving a strong final impression.

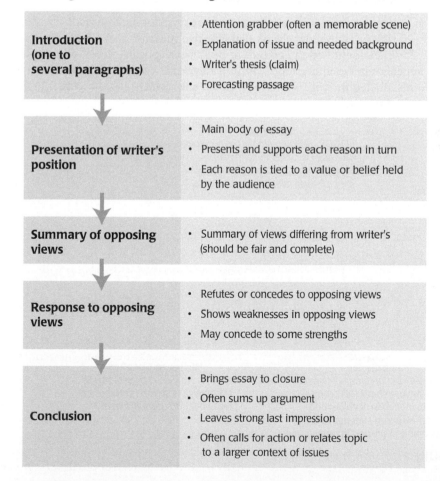

Organization Plan for an Argument with a Classical Structure

Introduction (one to several paragraphs)	• Attention grabber (often a memorable scene) • Explanation of issue and needed background • Writer's thesis (claim) • Forecasting passage
Presentation of writer's position	• Main body of essay • Presents and supports each reason in turn • Each reason is tied to a value or belief held by the audience
Summary of opposing views	• Summary of views differing from writer's (should be fair and complete)
Response to opposing views	• Refutes or concedes to opposing views • Shows weaknesses in opposing views • May concede to some strengths
Conclusion	• Brings essay to closure • Often sums up argument • Leaves strong last impression • Often calls for action or relates topic to a larger context of issues

In this organization, the body of a classical argument has two major sections—the one presenting the writer's position and the other summarizing and critiquing alternative views. Our organization plan has the writer's position coming first, but it is possible to reverse that order. (In Chapter 7 we consider the factors affecting this choice.)

For all its strengths, the classical structure may not always be your most persuasive strategy. In some cases, you may be more effective by delaying your thesis, by ignoring alternative views altogether, or by showing great sympathy for opposing views (see Chapter 7). Even in these cases, however, the classical structure is a useful planning tool. Its call for a thesis statement and a forecasting statement in the introduction helps you see the whole of your argument in miniature. And by requiring you to summarize and consider opposing views, classical argument alerts you to the limits of your position and to the need for further reasons and evidence. As we will show, the classical structure is a particularly persuasive mode of argument when you address a neutral or undecided audience.

Classical Appeals and the Rhetorical Triangle

3.2 To explain the rhetorical appeals

Besides developing a template or structure for an argument, classical rhetoricians analyzed the ways that effective speeches persuaded their audiences. They identified three kinds of persuasive appeals—*logos, ethos,* and *pathos.* These appeals can be understood within a rhetorical context illustrated by a triangle with points labeled *message, writer or speaker,* and *audience* (see Figure 3.1). Effective

Message
LOGOS: *How can I make the argument internally consistent and logical? How can I find the best reasons and support them with the best evidence?*

Audience
PATHOS: *How can I make the reader open to my message? How can I best appeal to my reader's values and interests? How can I engage my reader emotionally and imaginatively?*

Writer or Speaker
ETHOS: *How can I present myself effectively? How can I enhance my credibility and trustworthiness?*

FIGURE 3.1 The rhetorical triangle

arguments pay attention to all three points on this *rhetorical triangle*. As Figure ↲.↥ shows, each point on the triangle corresponds to one of the three persuasive appeals:

■ ***Logos*** (Greek for "word") focuses attention on the quality of the message—that is, on the internal consistency and clarity of the argument itself and on the logic of its reasons and support. The impact of *logos* on an audience is referred to as its logical appeal.

■ ***Ethos*** (Greek for "character") focuses attention on the writer's (or speaker's) character, or credibility, as it is projected in the message. *Ethos* is conveyed through the writer's investment in his or her claim, through the fairness with which the writer considers alternative views, through the tone and style of the message, and even through the message's professional appearance on paper or screen, including correct grammar, flawless proofreading, and appropriate formats for citations and bibliography. In some cases, *ethos* is also a function of the writer's reputation for honesty and expertise independent of the message. The impact of *ethos* on an audience is referred to as its *ethical appeal* or *appeal from credibility*.

■ ***Pathos*** (Greek for "suffering" or "experience") focuses attention on the values and beliefs of the intended audience. It is often associated with emotional appeal, but *pathos* appeals more specifically to an audience's imaginative sympathies—their capacity to feel and see what the writer feels and sees. Thus, when we turn the abstractions of logical discourse into a tangible and immediate story, we are making a pathetic appeal. Whereas appeals to *logos* and *ethos* can further an audience's intellectual assent to our claim, appeals to *pathos* engage the imagination and feelings, moving the audience to a deeper appreciation of the argument's significance.

A related rhetorical concept, connected to the appeals of *logos*, *ethos*, and *pathos*, is that of *kairos*, from the Greek word for "right time," "season," or "opportunity." This concept suggests that for an argument to be persuasive its timing must be effectively chosen and its tone and structure in right proportion or measure. You may have had the experience of composing an argumentative e-mail and then hesitating before clicking the "send" button. Is this the right moment to send this message? Is my audience ready to hear what I'm saying? Would my argument be more effective if I waited for a couple of days? If I send this message now, should I change its tone and content? This attentiveness to the unfolding of time is what is meant by *kairos*. We will return to this concept in Chapter 6, when we consider *ethos* and *pathos* in more depth.

Given this background on the classical appeals, let's turn now to *logos*— the logic and structure of arguments.

Issue Questions as the Origins of Argument

3.3 To distinguish between issue and information questions and between genuine and pseudo-arguments

At the heart of any argument is an issue, which we can define as a controversial topic area, such as "the labeling of genetically engineered foods" or "racial profiling," that gives rise to differing points of view and conflicting claims. A writer can usually focus an issue by asking an issue question that invites at least two alternative answers. Thus the topic area "abortion" gives rise to issue questions such as "Should abortion be legal?" "Should the federal government underwrite the cost of abortion?""When does a fetus become a human being?" Each of these issue questions opens up one strand of the complex debate on abortion.

Difference between an Issue Question and an Information Question

Of course, not all questions are issue questions that can be answered reasonably in two or more differing ways; thus not all questions can lead to effective arguments. Some may simply call for more information, not argument. Keeping this distinction in mind, consider the following two questions:

> How does the teenage pregnancy rate in the United States compare with the rate in Sweden? If the rates are different, why?

Although both questions seem to call for information rather than for argument, we believe that the second one would be an issue question if reasonable people disagreed on the answer. Thus, different writers might agree that the teenage pregnancy rate in the United States is seven times higher than the rate in Sweden. But they might disagree about why. One writer might emphasize Sweden's practical, secularized sex education courses in the schools, leading to more consistent use of contraceptives among Swedish teenagers. Another writer might point to the higher use of oral contraceptives among teenage girls in Sweden (partly a result of Sweden's generous national health program) and to less reliance on condoms for preventing pregnancy. Another might argue that moral decay in the United States is at fault. Thus, underneath the surface of what looks like a simple explication of the "truth" is really a controversy.

How to Identify an Issue Question

You can generally tell whether a given question is an issue question or an information question by examining your purpose in relationship to your audience. If your relationship to your audience is that of teacher to learner, so that your audience hopes to gain new information, knowledge, or understanding that you possess, then your question is probably an information question. But if your relationship to your audience is that of advocate to decision maker or jury, so that your audience needs to make up its mind on something or is weighing different points of view, then the question you address is an issue question. Often the same question can be an information question in one context and an issue question in another. Consider the following examples:

- **How does a diesel engine work?** (Probably an information question, posed by an audience of learners who regard you as a teacher.)
- **What is the most cost-effective way to produce diesel fuel from crude oil?** (This could be an information question if experts agree and you are addressing new

learners. But if you are addressing engineers and one engineer says process X is the most cost-effective and another argues for process Y, then the question is an issue question.)

■ **Should the present highway tax on diesel fuel be increased?** (This is certainly an issue question. One person says yes; another says no; another offers a compromise.)

■ ■ ■ **FOR CLASS DISCUSSION** **Information Questions versus Issue Questions**

Working as a class or in small groups, decide whether the following questions are information questions or issue questions. Some questions could be either, depending on the context. For such questions, create hypothetical contexts that justify your choice.

1. What percentage of public schools in the United States are failing?
2. What is the effect on children of playing first-person-shooter games?
3. Is genetically modified corn safe for human consumption?
4. Should people get rid of their land lines and have only cell phones?   ■ ■ ■

Difference between a Genuine Argument and a Pseudo-Argument

Although every argument features an issue question with alternative answers, not every dispute over answers is a rational argument. Rational arguments require two additional factors: (1) reasonable participants who operate within the conventions of reasonable behavior and (2) potentially sharable assumptions that can serve as a starting place or foundation for the argument. Lacking one or both of these conditions, disagreements remain stalled at the level of pseudo-arguments.

Pseudo-Arguments: Committed Believers and Fanatical Skeptics

A reasonable argument assumes the possibility of growth and change; disputants may modify their views as they acknowledge strengths in an alternative view or weaknesses in their own. Such growth becomes impossible—and argument degenerates to pseudo-argument—when disputants are so firmly committed to their own positions that they can't "hear" each other. Consider the case of the committed believer or the fanatical skeptic.

From one perspective, committed believers are admirable. They are persons of conviction, unwilling to compromise their principles or bend to the prevailing winds. But from another perspective, committed believers can seem rigidly fixed, incapable of growth or change. When committed believers from two clashing belief systems try to engage in dialog with each other, a truth-seeking exchange of views becomes difficult. They talk past each other; dialogue is replaced by monologue from within isolated silos. Once committed believers push each other's buttons on climate change, guns, health care, taxes, religion, or some other issue, each disputant resorts to an endless replaying of the same prepackaged arguments. Disagreeing with a committed believer is like ordering the surf to quiet down. The only response is another crashing wave.

In contrast to the committed believer, the fanatical skeptic dismisses the possibility of ever believing anything. Skeptics often demand proof where no proof is possible. So what if the sun has risen every day of recorded history? That's no proof that it will rise tomorrow. Short of absolute proof, which never exists, fanatical skeptics accept nothing. In a world where the most we can hope for is increased audience adherence to our ideas, the skeptic demands an ironclad, logical demonstration of our claim's rightness.

A Closer Look at Pseudo-Arguments: The Lack of Shared Assumptions

As we have seen, rational argument degenerates to pseudo-argument when there is no possibility for listening, learning, growth, or change. In this section, we look more closely at a frequent cause of pseudo-arguments: lack of shared assumptions.

Shared Assumptions and the Problem of Ideology   As our discussion of committed believers suggests, reasonable argument is difficult when the disputants have differing "ideologies," which is an academic word for belief systems or worldviews. We all have beliefs and values that are shaped by our family backgrounds, friends, culture, particular time in history, race or ethnicity, gender or sexual orientation, social class, religion, education, and so forth. Because we tend to think that our particular lens for looking at the world is natural and universal rather than peculiar to ourselves, we must be aware that persons who disagree with us may not share our deepest assumptions and beliefs. To participate in rational argument, we and our audience must seek *shared assumptions*—certain principles or values or beliefs that can serve as common ground.

The failure to find shared assumptions often leads to pseudo-arguments, particularly if one disputant evokes assumptions that another disputant cannot accept. For example, consider differences within the Christian community over how to interpret the Bible. Some Christians choose a straightforward, literal interpretation of the Bible as God's word while others read some passages metaphorically or mythically; still others read it as an ethical blueprint for social justice. These Christians may not be able to argue rationally about, say, evolution or gay marriage because they have very different ways of reading Biblical passages and invoking the authority of the Bible. Similar disagreements about assumptions occur in the political arena as well. Our point is that certain religious or political beliefs or texts cannot be evoked for evidence or authority when an audience does not assume the belief's truth or does not agree on the way that a given text should be read or interpreted.

Shared Assumptions and the Problem of Personal Opinions   Lack of shared assumptions also dooms arguments about purely personal opinions—for example, someone's claim that opera is boring or that pizza is better than nachos. Of course, a pizza-versus-nachos argument might be possible if the disputants assume a shared criterion about nutrition. For example, a nutritionist could argue that pizza is better than nachos because it provides more balanced nutrients per calorie. But if one of the disputants responds, "Nah, nachos are better than pizza because nachos taste better," then he makes a different assumption—"My sense of taste is better than your sense of taste." This is a wholly personal standard, an assumption that others are unable to share.

■ ■ ■   **FOR CLASS DISCUSSION**   **Reasonable Arguments versus Pseudo-Arguments**

The following questions can all be answered in alternative ways. However, not all of them will lead to reasonable arguments. Try to decide which questions will lead to reasonable arguments and which will lead only to pseudo-arguments.

1. Are the *Star Wars* films good science fiction?
2. Is it ethically justifiable to capture dolphins and train them for human entertainment?
3. Is an abstract oil painting by a monkey a true work of art?
4. Are nose rings and tongue studs attractive?

■ ■ ■

Frame of an Argument: A Claim Supported by Reasons

3.4 To describe the basic frame of an argument

We said earlier that an argument originates in an *issue question*, which by definition is any question that promotes disagreement about the best answer. When you write an argument, your task is to take a position on an issue and to support it with reasons and evidence. The *claim* of your essay is the position you want your audience to accept. To put it another way, your claim is your essay's *thesis statement*, a one-sentence summary answer to your issue question. Your task, then, is to make a claim and support it with reasons.

What Is a Reason?

A *reason* (also called a *premise*) is a claim used to support another claim. A reason is usually linked to a claim with words such as *because, since, for, so, thus, consequently,* and *therefore*, indicating that the claim follows logically from the reason.

Let us take an example. In one of our recent classes, students heatedly debated the ethics of capturing wild dolphins and orcas (killer whales) and training them to perform in marine parks. This issue—made public by news stories and films such as *The Cove* (2009) and *Blackfish* (2012)—has many dimensions, including safety concerns for both the animals and their human trainers, as well as moral, scientific, legal, and economic considerations. Here are the frameworks the class developed for two alternative positions on this issue:

One View

CLAIM: The public should not support marine parks.

REASON 1:   Marine parks stressfully separate dolphins and orcas from their natural habitat.

REASON 2: The education these parks claim to offer about marine mammals is just a series of artificial, exploitive tricks taught through behavior modification.

REASON 3: The motive behind these parks is big business profit.

REASON 4: Marine parks encourage artificial breeding programs and inhumane hunts and captures.

REASON 5: Marine parks promote an attitude of human dominance over animals.

Alternative View

CLAIM: The public should continue to enjoy marine parks.

REASON 1: These parks observe accreditation standards for animal welfare, health, and nutrition.

REASON 2: These marine parks enable scientists and veterinarians to study animal behavior in ways not possible with field studies in the wild.

REASON 3: These marine parks provide environmental education and memorable entertainment.

REASON 4: Marine parks use some of their profits to support research, conservation, and rescue and rehabilitation programs.

REASON 5: In their training of dolphins and orcas, these marine parks reinforce natural behaviors, exercise the animals' intelligence, and promote beneficial bonding with humans.

Formulating a list of reasons in this way breaks your argumentative task into a series of subtasks. It gives you a frame for building your argument in parts. In the previous example, the frame for the argument opposing commercial use of sea mammals suggests five different lines of reasoning a writer might pursue. A writer might use all five reasons or select only two or three, depending on which reasons would most persuade the intended audience. Each line of reasoning would be developed in its own separate section of the argument, where the reason would be supported with evidence and details.

Expressing Reasons in *Because* Clauses

Chances are that when you were a child, the word *because* contained magical explanatory powers. Later, as you got older, you discovered that *because* only introduced your arguments and that it was the reasons following *because* that made the difference. Still, *because* introduced you to the powers potentially residing in the adult world of logic.

Of course, there are many other ways besides "because" to express the logical connection between a reason and a claim:

- The public should not support marine parks because these parks stressfully separate dolphins and orcas from their natural habitat.
- Marine parks stressfully separate dolphins and orcas from their natural habitat. Therefore the public should not support them.
- One reason that the public should not support marine animal parks is that they stressfully separate dolphins and orcas from their natural habitat.

Even though logical relationships can be stated in various ways, writing out one or more *because* clauses seems to be the most succinct and manageable way to clarify an argument for oneself. We therefore suggest that sometime in the writing process, you create a *working thesis statement* that summarizes your main reasons as *because* clauses attached to your claim.* Just when you compose your own working thesis statement depends largely on your writing process—whether you like to create a whole outline at the beginning or discover your ideas as you write. Composing *because* clauses can be a powerful discovery tool, causing you to think of many different kinds of arguments to support your claim. But it is often difficult to wrestle your ideas into the *because* clause shape, which sometimes seems to be overly tidy for the complex network of ideas you are trying to work with. Nevertheless, trying to summarize your argument as a single claim with reasons should help you see more clearly what you have to do.

■■■   **FOR CLASS DISCUSSION** Developing Claims and Reasons

Try this exercise to help you see how writing *because* clauses can be a discovery procedure.

Divide into small groups. Each group member should contribute an issue that he or she might like to explore. Discussing one person's issue at a time, help each member develop a claim supported by several reasons. Express each reason as a *because* clause. Then write out the working thesis statement for each person's argument by attaching the *because* clauses to the claim. Finally, try to create *because* clauses in support of an alternative claim for each issue. Recorders should select two or three working thesis statements from the group to present to the class as a whole.

■ ■ ■

WRITING ASSIGNMENT An Issue Question and Working Thesis Statements

Decide on an issue and a claim for a classical argument that you would like to write. Create a one-sentence question that summarizes the controversial issue that your claim addresses. Then draft a working thesis statement for your proposed argument. Organize the thesis as a claim using bulleted *because* clauses for reasons. You should have at least two reasons, but it is okay to have three or four. Also include an "opposing thesis statement"—a claim with *because* clauses for an alternative position on your issue.

Recall that in Part One we emphasized exploratory writing as a way of resisting closure and helping you wrestle with multiple perspectives. Now we ask you to begin a process of closure by developing a thesis statement that condenses your argument into

---

*A working thesis statement opposing the commercial use of captured dolphins and orcas might look like this: The public should not support marine parks because marine parks stressfully separate dolphins and orcas from their natural habitat; because they are mainly big businesses driven by profit; because they create inaccurate and incomplete educational information about dolphins and orcas; because they encourage inhumane breeding programs and hunts and captures; and because they promote an attitude of human dominance over animals. You might not put a bulky thesis statement like this into your essay; rather, a working thesis statement is a behind-the-scenes way of summarizing your argument so that you can see it whole and clear.

a claim with supporting reasons. However, as we emphasize throughout this text, drafting itself is an exploratory process. Writers almost always discover new ideas when they write a first draft; as they take their writing project through multiple drafts, their views may change substantially. Often, in fact, honest writers can switch positions on an issue by discovering that a counterargument is stronger than their own. So the working thesis statement that you submit for this assignment may evolve substantially once you begin to draft.

In this chapter, as well as in Chapters 4 and 5, we will follow the process of student writer Carmen Tieu as she constructed an argument on violent video games. During earlier exploratory writing, she wrote about a classroom incident in which her professor had described video game playing as gendered behavior (overwhelmingly male). The professor indicated his dislike for such games, pointing to their antisocial, dehumanizing values. In her freewrite, Carmen described her own enjoyment of violent video games—particularly first-person shooter games—and explored the pleasure that she derived from beating boys at Halo. She knew that she wanted to write an argument on this issue. What follows is Carmen's submission for this assignment.

Carmen's Issue Question and Working Thesis Statements

Issue Question: Should girls be encouraged to play first-person shooter video games?

My claim: First-person shooter (FPS) video games are great activities for girls

- because beating guys at their own game is empowering for girls
- because being skilled at FPS games frees girls from feminine stereotypes
- because they give girls a different way of bonding with males
- because they give girls new insights into a male subculture

Opposing claim: First-person shooter games are a bad activity for anyone, especially girls

- because they promote antisocial values like indiscriminate killing
- because they amplify the bad macho side of male stereotypes
- because they waste valuable time that could have been spent on something constructive
- because FPS games could encourage women to see themselves as objects ∎

The Logical Structure of Arguments

In Chapter 3 you learned that the core of an argument is a claim supported by reasons and that these reasons can often be stated as *because* clauses attached to a claim. In the present chapter we examine the logical structure of arguments in more depth.

An Overview of *Logos:* What Do We Mean by the "Logical Structure" of an Argument?

4.1 To explain the logical structure of argument in terms of claim, reason, and assumption granted by the audience

As you will recall from our discussion of the rhetorical triangle, *logos* refers to the strength of an argument's support and its internal consistency. *Logos* is the argument's logical structure. But what do we mean by "logical structure"?

Formal Logic versus Real-World Logic

First of all, what we *don't* mean by logical structure is the kind of precise certainty you get in a philosophy class in formal logic. Logic classes deal with symbolic assertions that are universal and unchanging, such as "If all ps are qs and if r is a p, then r is a q." This statement is logically certain so long as p, q, and r are pure abstractions. But in the real world, p, q, and r turn into actual things, and the relationships among them suddenly become fuzzy. For example, p might be a class of actions called "Sexual Harassment," while q could be the class called "Actions That Justify Getting Fired from One's Job." If r is the class "Telling Off-Color Stories," then the logic of our p–q–r statement suggests that telling off-color stories (r) is an instance of sexual harassment (p), which in turn is an action justifying getting fired from one's job (q).

Now, most of us would agree that sexual harassment is a serious offense that might well justify getting fired. In turn, we might agree that telling off-color stories, if the jokes are sufficiently raunchy and are inflicted on an unwilling audience, constitutes sexual harassment. But few of us would want to say categorically that all people who tell off-color stories are harassing their listeners and ought to be fired. Most of us would want to know the particulars of the case before making a final judgment.

In the real world, then, it is difficult to say that rs are always ps or that every instance of a p results in q. That is why we discourage students from using the word *prove* in claims they write for arguments (as in "This paper will prove that euthanasia is wrong"). Real-world arguments seldom *prove* anything. They can only make a good case for something, a case that is more or less strong, more or less probable. Often the best you can hope for is to strengthen the resolve of those who agree with you or weaken the resistance of those who oppose you.

The Role of Assumptions

A key difference, then, between formal logic and real-world argument is that real-world arguments are not grounded in abstract, universal statements. Rather, as we shall see, they must be grounded in beliefs, assumptions, or values granted by the audience. A second important difference is that in real-world arguments, these beliefs, assumptions, or values are often unstated. So long as writer and audience share the same assumptions, it's fine to leave them unstated. But if these underlying assumptions aren't shared, the writer has a problem.

To illustrate the nature of this problem, consider one of the arguments we introduced in the last chapter.

> The public should not support marine parks because they stressfully separate dolphins and orcas from their natural habitat.

On the face of it, this is a plausible argument. But the argument is persuasive only if the audience agrees with the writer's assumption that it is wrong to separate wild animals from their natural habitats. What if you believed that confinement of wild animals is not always harmful or stressful to the animals, that the knowledge derived from the capture of wild animals enables humans to preserve the natural environment for these animals, and that the benefits to be gained from the captivity of a small number of wild animals outweigh the animals' loss of freedom? If this were the case, you might believe that marine parks have positive consequences so long as they strive to provide humane conditions for the animals, with minimal stress. If these were your beliefs, the argument wouldn't work for you because you would reject the underlying assumption. To persuade you with this line of reasoning, the writer would have to defend this assumption, showing why it is unwise or unethical to remove animals from their free and wild conditions.

The Core of an Argument: The Enthymeme

The previous core argument ("The public should not support marine parks because they stressfully separate dolphins and orcas from their natural habitat") is an incomplete logical structure called an *enthymeme*. Its persuasiveness depends on an underlying assumption or belief that the audience must accept. To complete the enthymeme and make it effective, the audience must willingly supply a missing premise—in this case, that it is wrong to separate wild animals from their natural environments. The Greek philosopher Aristotle showed how successful enthymemes root the speaker's argument in assumptions, beliefs, or values held by the audience. The word *enthymeme* comes from the Greek *en* (meaning "in") and *thumos* (meaning "mind"). Listeners or readers must have in mind an assumption, belief, or value that lets them willingly supply the missing premise. If the audience is unwilling to supply the missing premise, then the argument fails. Our point is that successful arguments depend both on what the arguer says and on what the audience already has "in mind."

To clarify the concept of "enthymeme," let's go over this same territory again, this time more slowly, examining what we mean by "incomplete logical structure." The sentence "The public should not support marine parks because they stressfully separate dolphins and orcas from their natural habitat " is an enthymeme. It combines a claim (the public should not support marine parks) with a reason expressed as a *because* clause (because they stressfully separate dolphins from their natural habitat). To render this enthymeme logically complete, the audience must willingly supply a missing assumption—that it is wrong to separate wild animals from their natural habitat. If your audience accepts this assumption, then you have a starting place on which to build an effective argument. If your audience doesn't accept this assumption, then you must supply another argument to support it, and so on until you find common ground with your audience.

To sum up:

1. Claims are supported with reasons. You can usually state a reason as a because clause attached to a claim (see Chapter 3).
2. A because clause attached to a claim is an incomplete logical structure called an enthymeme. To create a complete logical structure from an enthymeme, the underlying assumption (or assumptions) must be articulated.
3. To serve as an effective starting point for the argument, this underlying assumption should be a belief, value, or principle that the audience grants.

Let's illustrate this structure by putting the previous example into schematic form.

ENTHYMEME

CLAIM The public should not support marine parks

REASON because they stressfully separate dolphins and orcas from their natural habitat.

Audience must supply this assumption ⟶

UNDERLYING ASSUMPTION
It is wrong to separate wild animals from their natural habitats.

The Power of Audience-Based Reasons

Aristotle's concept of the enthymeme focuses on the writer's need to create what we can now call "audience-based reasons" as opposed to "writer-based reasons." A reason that is persuasive to you might not be persuasive to your audience. Finding audience-based reasons means finding arguments effectively anchored within your audience's beliefs and values. To illustrate the difference between an audience-based reason and a writer-based reason, suppose that you are a vegetarian persuaded mainly by ethical arguments against causing needless suffering to animals. Suppose further that you wanted to persuade others to become vegetarians or at least to reduce their consumption of meat. Your "writer-based reason" for vegetarianism could be stated as follows:

> You should become a vegetarian because doing so will help reduce the needless suffering of animals.

The underlying assumption here is that it is wrong to cause the suffering of animals. This writer-based reason might also be an audience-based reason for persons who are wrestling with the moral dimension of animal suffering. But this assumption might not resonate with people who have made their own peace with eating meat. How might you use audience-based reasons to appeal to these meat-eaters? Here are two more possible enthymemes:

> You should become a vegetarian because doing so may help you lower your cholesterol.

> You should become a vegetarian because doing so will significantly lower your carbon footprint.

These arguments hook into the assumption that it is good to lower one's cholesterol (health values) or that it is good to lower one's carbon footprint (environmental values). All three of the arguments—whether based on ethics, health, or the environment—might further the practice of vegetarianism or at least reduce the amount of meat consumed, but they won't appeal equally to all audiences. From the perspective of logic alone, all three arguments are equally sound. But they will affect different audiences differently.

■ ■ ■   **FOR CLASS DISCUSSION** Identifying Underlying Assumptions and Choosing Audience-Based Reasons

Working individually or in small groups, identify the unstated assumption that the audience must supply in order to make the following enthymemes persuasive.

Example

Enthymeme: Rabbits make good pets because they are gentle.

Underlying assumption: Gentle animals make good pets.

1. We shouldn't elect Joe as committee chair because he is too bossy.
2. Airport screeners should use racial profiling because doing so will increase the odds of stopping terrorists.

3. Racial profiling should not be used by airport screeners because it violates a person's civil rights.
4. We should strengthen the Endangered Species Act because doing so will preserve genetic diversity on the planet.
5. The Endangered Species Act is too stringent because it severely damages the economy.

Adopting a Language for Describing Arguments: The Toulmin System

4.2 To use the Toulmin system to describe an argument's logical structure

Understanding a new field usually requires us to learn a new vocabulary. For example, if you were taking biology for the first time, you'd have to learn dozens and dozens of new terms. Luckily, the field of argument requires us to learn a mere handful of new terms. A particularly useful set of argument terms, one we'll be using occasionally throughout the rest of this text, comes from philosopher Stephen Toulmin. In the 1950s, Toulmin rejected the prevailing models of argument based on formal logic in favor of a very audience-based courtroom model.

Toulmin's courtroom model differs from formal logic in that it assumes that (1) all assertions and assumptions are contestable by "opposing counsel" and that (2) all final "verdicts" about the persuasiveness of the opposing arguments will be rendered by a neutral third party, a judge or jury. As writers, keeping in mind the "opposing counsel" forces us to anticipate counterarguments and to question our assumptions. Keeping in mind the judge and jury reminds us to answer opposing arguments fully, without rancor, and to present positive reasons for supporting our case as well as negative reasons for disbelieving the opposing case. Above all else, Toulmin's model reminds us not to construct an argument that appeals only to those who already agree with us. In short, it helps arguers tailor arguments to their audiences.

The system we use for analyzing arguments combines Toulmin's language with Aristotle's concept of the enthymeme. It builds on the system you have already been practicing. We simply need to add a few key terms from Toulmin. The first term is Toulmin's *warrant*, the name we will now use for the underlying assumption that turns an enthymeme into a complete, logical structure as shown at the top of the next page.

Toulmin derives his term *warrant* from the concept of "warranty" or "guarantee." The warrant is the value, belief, or principle that the audience has to hold if the soundness of the argument is to be guaranteed or warranted. We sometimes make similar use of this word in ordinary language when we say, "That is an unwarranted conclusion," meaning one has leaped from information about a situation to a conclusion about that situation without any sort of general principle to justify or "warrant" that move. Thus the warrant—once accepted by the audience—"guarantees" the soundness of the argument.

ENTHYMEME

CLAIM The public should not support marine parks

REASON because they stressfully separate dolphins and orcas from their natural habitat.

Audience must supply this warrant ──────────┐
                                              ↓

WARRANT

It is wrong to separate wild animals from their natural habitats.

But arguments need more than claims, reasons, and warrants. These are simply one-sentence statements—the frame of an argument, not a developed argument. To give body and weight to our arguments and make them convincing, we need what Toulmin calls *grounds* and *backing*. Let's start with grounds. Grounds are the supporting evidence that causes an audience to accept your reason. Grounds are facts, data, statistics, causal links, testimony, examples, anecdotes—the blood and muscle that flesh out the skeletal frame of your enthymeme. Toulmin suggests that grounds are "what you have to go on" in an argument—the stuff you can point to and present before a jury. Here is how grounds fit into our emerging argument schema:

ENTHYMEME

CLAIM The public should not support marine parks

REASON because they stressfully separate dolphins and orcas from their natural habitat.

Grounds support ──→ **GROUNDS**
the reason

Evidence and arguments showing stressful difference between dolphin and orca behavior in the wild and in captivity:

- In the wild, dolphins and orcas swim in pods, dolphins around forty miles a day, and orcas around sixty miles a day, in the open ocean whereas marine park tanks provide only a tiny fraction of that space.

- Evidence that separation from their family members and pods in their natural habitats creates emotional distress that can't be remedied by the presence of randomly selected other dolphins and orcas in these marine parks.

- Statistics that the stress caused by confinement and the echoes and noise of concrete pools, audiences, and music often results in the animals needing medication.

- Statistics that show that dolphins and orcas don't live as long in captivity as in their natural habitat.

In many cases, successful arguments require just these three components: a claim, a reason, and grounds. If the audience already accepts the unstated assumption behind the reason (the warrant), then the warrant can safely remain in the background, unstated and unexamined. But if there is a chance that the audience will question or doubt the warrant, then the writer needs to back it up by providing an argument in its support. *Backing* is the argument that supports the warrant. It may require no more than one or two sentences or as much as a major section in your argument. Its goal is to persuade the audience to accept the warrant. Here is how *backing* is added to our schema:

Backing supports the warrant

WARRANT
It is wrong to separate wild animals from their natural habitats.

BACKING
Arguments showing why it is unwise, unethical, or otherwise wrong to separate wild animals from their natural environments:

• Examples of wild animals (those in aquariums and zoos) that do not thrive in artificially constructed environments, that don't live long, or that suffer psychological stress from confinement

• An ecological argument about the beauty of animals in the wild and of the complexity of the natural webs of which animals are a part

• A philosophical argument that humans shouldn't treat animals as instruments for their own enjoyment or profit

Toulmin's system next asks us to imagine how a resistant audience would try to refute our argument. Specifically, the adversarial audience might challenge our reason and grounds by arguing that dolphins in captivity are not as stressed as we claim (evidence provided by veterinarians, caretakers, or animal trainers verifying that most dolphins in captivity are in good health). Or the adversary might attack our warrant and backing by showing how the captivity of some wild animal might save the species from extinction or how animals are often saved from illness and predators by caring humans. An adversary might attack our philosophical or spiritual arguments by saying that the same reasoning, taken to its logical conclusion, would eliminate zoos and require all humans to become vegetarians or vegans. An adversary might even argue that dolphins enjoy being with humans and have the same capacity to be animal companions as dogs or cats.

In the case of the argument opposing dolphins in captivity, an adversary might offer one or more of the following rebuttals.

Writer must anticipate these attacks from skeptics

ENTHYMEME

CLAIM The public should not support marine parks

REASON because they stressfully separate dolphins and orcas from their natural habitat.

GROUNDS

Evidence and arguments showing stressful difference between dolphin behavior in the wild and in captivity:

- In the wild, dolphins and orcas swim in pods, dolphins about forty miles a day in the open ocean and orcas about sixty, whereas marine park tanks provide only a tiny fraction of that space.

- Evidence that the echoes from concrete pools, music of dolphin shows, and the applause and noise of audiences are stressful and harmful

- Statistics about the excessive number of performances or about the levels of stress hormones produced in dolphins

"POSSIBLE CONDITIONS OF REBUTTAL
A skeptic can attack the reason and grounds":

- Argument that these programs must observe strict accreditation standards for animal welfare, health, and education

- Marine parks exercise dolphins' and orcas' intelligence and abilities and build on their natural behaviors.

- Many dolphins and orcas have been bred in captivity, so they aren't "wild."

- The education and entertainment provided by marine parks promote public concern for dolphins and orcas.

WARRANT

It is wrong to separate wild animals from their natural habitats.

BACKING

Arguments showing why it is unwise, unethical, or otherwise wrong to separate wild animals from their natural environments:

- Examples of wild animals (those in aquariums and zoos) that do not thrive in artificially constructed environments, that don't live long, or that suffer psychological stress from confinement

- An ecological argument about the beauty of animals in the wild and of the complexity of the natural webs of which animals are a part

- A philosophical argument that humans shouldn't treat animals as instruments for their own enjoyment or profit

"POSSIBLE CONDITIONS OF REBUTTAL
A skeptic can attack the warrant and backing."

- The natural habitat is not always the best environment for wild animals.

- Captivity may actually preserve some species.

- Scientists have been able to conduct valuable studies of dolphins and learn more about orcas in captivity, which would have been impossible in the wild.

As this example shows, adversarial readers can question an argument's reasons and grounds or its warrant and backing or sometimes both. Conditions of rebuttal remind writers to look at their arguments from the perspective of skeptics.

Toulmin's final term, used to limit the force of a claim and indicate the degree of its probable truth, is *qualifier*. The qualifier reminds us that real-world arguments almost never prove a claim. We may say things such as *very likely, probably,* or *maybe* to indicate the strength of the claim we are willing to draw from our grounds and warrant. Thus if there are exceptions to your warrant or if your grounds are not very

strong, you will have to qualify your claim. For example, you might say, "Exce
limited cases of scientific research, dolphins and orcas should not be held in capti
ity." In our future displays of the Toulmin scheme we will omit the qualifiers, but you
should always remember that no argument is 100 percent conclusive.

■ ■ ■   **FOR CLASS DISCUSSION** Developing Enthymemes with the Toulmin Schema

Working individually or in small groups, imagine that you have to write arguments
developing the five enthymemes listed in the For Class Discussion exercise on pages 58–59.
Use the Toulmin schema to help you determine what you need to consider when
developing each enthymeme. We suggest that you try a four-box diagram structure
as a way of visualizing the schema. We have applied the Toulmin schema to the first
enthymeme: "We shouldn't elect Joe as committee chair because he is too bossy."

ENTHYMEME

CLAIM We shouldn't elect Joe as committee chair
REASON because he is too bossy.

GROUNDS

Evidence of Joe's bossiness:

• Examples of the way he dominates meetings—doesn't
  call on people, talks too much
• Testimony about his bossiness from people who have
  served with him on committees
• Anecdotes about his abrasive style

CONDITIONS OF REBUTTAL
Attacking the reason and grounds

Evidence that Joe is not bossy or is only
occasionally bossy:

• Counterevidence showing his collaborative style
• Testimony from people who have liked Joe as a
  leader and claim he isn't bossy; testimony about his
  cooperativeness and kindness
• Testimony that anecdotes about Joe's bossiness
  aren't typical

WARRANT
Bossy people make bad committee chairs.

BACKING
Problems caused by bossy committee chairs:

• Bossy people don't inspire cooperation and enthusiam.
• Bossy people make others angry.
• Bossy people tend to make bad decisions because
  they don't incorporate advice from others.

CONDITIONS OF REBUTTAL
Attacking the warrant and backing

• Arguments that bossiness can be a good trait
  • Sometimes bossy people make good chairpersons.
  • This committee needs a bossy person who can
    make decisions and get things done.
• Argument that Joe has other traits of good
  leadership that outweigh his bossiness

■ ■ ■

Using Toulmin's Schema to Plan and Test Your Argument

4.3 To use the Toulmin
system to generate ideas for
your argument and test it
for completeness

So far we have seen that a claim, a reason, and a warrant form
the frame for a line of reasoning in an argument. Most of the
words in an argument, however, are devoted to grounds and
backing.

Hypothetical Example: Cheerleaders as Athletes

For an illustration of how a writer can use the Toulmin schema to generate ideas for an argument, consider the following case. In April 2005, the Texas house of representatives passed a bill banning "sexually suggestive" cheerleading. Across the nation, evening television show comics poked fun at the bill, while newspaper editorialists debated its wisdom and constitutionality. In one of our classes, however, several students, including one who had earned a high school varsity letter in competitive cheerleading, defended the bill by contending that provocative dance moves hurt the athletic image of cheerleading. In the following example, which draws on ideas developed in class discussion, we create a hypothetical student writer (we'll call her Chandale) who argues in defense of the Texas bill. Chandale's argument is based on the following enthymeme:

> The bill banning suggestive dancing for high school cheerleaders is a good law because it promotes a view of female cheerleaders as athletes rather than exotic dancers.

Chandale used the Toulmin schema to brainstorm ideas for developing her argument. Here are her notes:

Chandale's Planning Notes Using the Toulmin Schema

Enthymeme: The bill banning suggestive dancing is a good law because it promotes a view of female cheerleaders as athletes.

Grounds: First, I've got to use evidence to show that cheerleaders are athletes.

- Cheerleaders at my high school are carefully chosen for their stamina and skill after exhausting two-week tryouts.
- We begin all practices with a mile run and an hour of warm-up exercises. We are also expected to work out on our own for at least an hour on weekends and on days without practice.
- We learned competitive routines and stunts consisting of lifts, tosses, flips, catches, and gymnastic moves. This requires athletic ability! We'd practice these stunts for hours each week.
- Throughout the year cheerleaders have to attend practices, camps, and workshops to learn new routines and stunts.
- Our squad competed in competitions around the state.
- Competitive cheerleading is a growing movement across the country—University of Maryland has made it a varsity sport for women.
- Skimpy uniforms and suggestive dance moves destroy this image by making women eye candy like the Dallas Cowboys cheerleaders.

Warrant: It is a good thing to view female cheerleaders as athletes.

Backing: Now I need to make the case that it is good to see cheerleaders as athletes rather than as eye candy.

- Athletic competition builds self-esteem, independence, a powerful sense of achievement—it contributes to health, strength, conditioning.

- Competitive cheerleading is one of the few sports where teams are made up of both men and women. (Why is this good? Should I use this?)
- The suggestive dance moves turn women into sex objects whose function is to be gazed at by men, which suggests that women's value is based on their beauty and sex appeal.
- We are talking about HIGH SCHOOL cheerleading—it is a very bad early influence on girls to model themselves on Dallas Cowboys cheerleaders or sexy MTV videos of rock stars.
- Junior high girls want to do what senior high girls do—suggestive dance moves promote sexuality way too early.

Conditions of Rebuttal: Would anybody try to rebut my reasons and grounds that cheerleading is an athletic activity?

- No. I think it is obvious that cheerleading is an athletic activity once they see my evidence.
- However, they might not think of cheerleading as a sport. They might say that the University of Maryland just declared it a sport as a cheap way to meet Title IX federal rules to have more women's sports. I'll have to make sure that I show this is really a sport.
- They also might say that competitive cheerleading shouldn't be encouraged because it is too dangerous—lots of serious injuries including paralysis have been caused by mistakes in doing flips, lifts, and tosses. If I include this, maybe I could say that other sports are dangerous also—and it is in fact danger that makes this sport so exciting.

Would anyone doubt my warrant and backing that it is good to see female cheerleaders as athletes?

- Yes, all those people who laughed at the Texas legislature think that people are being too prudish and that banning suggestive dance moves violates free expression. I'll need to make my case that it is bad for young girls to see themselves as sex objects too early.

The information that Chandale lists under "grounds" is what she sees as the facts of the case—the hard data she will use as evidence to support her contention that cheerleading is an athletic activity. The paragraph that follows shows how this argument might look when placed in written form.

First Part of Chandale's Argument

Summarizes opposing view

States her claim

Although evening television show comedians have made fun of the Texas legislature's desire to ban "suggestive" dance moves from cheerleading routines, I applaud this bill because it promotes a healthy view of female cheerleaders as athletes rather than showgirls. I was lucky enough to attend a high school where cheerleading is a sport, and I earned a varsity letter as a cheerleader.

For grounds, uses personal experience details to show that cheerleading is an athletic activity

To get on my high school's cheerleading squad, students have to go through an exhausting two-week tryout of workouts and instruction in the basic routines; then they are chosen based on their stamina and skill. Once on the squad, cheerleaders begin all practices with a mile run and an hour of grueling warm-up exercises and are expected to exercise on their own on weekends. As a result of this regimen, cheerleaders achieve and maintain a top level of physical fitness. In addition, to get on the squad, students must be able to do handstands, cartwheels, handsprings, high jumps, and the splits. Each year the squad builds up to its complex routines and stunts consisting of lifts, tosses, flips, catches, and gymnastic moves that only trained athletes can do. In tough competitions at the regional and state levels, the cheerleading squad demonstrates its athletic talent. This view of cheerleading as a competitive sport is also spreading to colleges. As reported recently in a number of newspapers, the University of Maryland has made cheerleading a varsity sport, and many other universities are following suit. Athletic performance of this caliber is a far cry from the sexy dancing that many high school girls often associate with cheerleading. By banning suggestive dancing in cheerleading routines, the Texas legislature creates an opportunity for schools to emphasize the athleticism of cheerleading.

Provides more grounds by showing emerging views of cheerleading as a competitive sport

As you can see, Chandale has plenty of evidence for arguing that competitive cheerleading is an athletic activity quite different from sexy dancing. But how effective is this argument as it stands? Is this all she needs? The Toulmin schema encourages writers to include—if needed for the intended audience—explicit support for their warrants as well as attention to conditions for rebuttal. Because the overwhelming national response to the Texas law was ridicule at the perceived prudishness of the legislators, Chandale decides to expand her argument as follows:

Continuation of Chandale's Argument

Supplies warrant: It is good to see cheerleaders as athletic and bad to see them as sex objects

This emphasis on cheerleaders as athletes rather than sexy dancers is good for girls. The erotic dance moves that many high school cheerleaders now incorporate into their routines show that they are emulating the Dallas Cowboys cheerleaders or pop stars on MTV. Our already sexually saturated culture (think of the suggestive clothing marketed to little girls) pushes girls and women to measure their value by their beauty and sex appeal. It would be far healthier, both physically and psychologically, if high school cheerleaders were identified as athletes. For women and men both, competitive cheerleading can build self-esteem, pride in teamwork, and a powerful sense of achievement, as well as promote health, strength, and fitness.

Supplies backing: Shows benefits that come from seeing cheerleaders as athletes

Anticipates an objection

Responds to objection by supplying more evidence that cheerleading is a sport; in fact it is a dangerous sport

Some people might object to competitive cheerleading by saying that cheerleading isn't really a sport. Some have accused the University of Maryland of making cheerleading a varsity sport only as a cheap way of meeting Title IX requirements. But anyone who has watched competitive cheerleading, and imagined what it would be like to be thrown high into the air, knows instinctively that this is a sport indeed. In fact, other persons might object to competitive cheerleading because it is too dangerous, with potential for very severe injuries, including paralysis. Obviously the sport is dangerous—but so are many sports, including football, gymnastics, diving, and trampoline. The danger and difficulty of the sport is part of its appeal. Part of what can make cheerleaders as athletes better role models for girls than cheerleaders as erotic dancers is the courage and training needed for success. Of course, the Texas legislators might not have had athleticism in mind when they banned suggestive dancing. They might only have been promoting their vision of morality. But at stake are the role models we set for young girls. I'll pick an athlete over a Dallas Cowboys cheerleader every time.

Sums up by returning to claim

Our example suggests how a writer can use the Toulmin schema to generate ideas for an argument. For evidence, Chandale draws primarily on her personal experiences as a cheerleader/athlete and on her knowledge of popular culture. She also draws on her reading of several newspaper articles about the University of Maryland's making cheerleading a varsity sport. A more detailed discussion of evidence in arguments occurs in Chapter 5.

Extended Student Example: Girls and Violent Video Games

Let's look at one more example of how the Toulmin system can help you generate ideas for your argument. In this case we will look at a complete essay from student writer Carmen Tieu, whose evolving argument about girls and violent video games was introduced in the last chapter. Carmen's assignment was to write a "supporting reasons" argument, which is a shortened form of the classical argument described on pages 44–46. It has all the features of a classical argument except for the requirement to summarize and rebut opposing views. In planning her argument, Carmen decided to use four lines of reasoning, as shown in her because clauses listed on page 54. She then created basic Toulmin frames for each reason and used those frames to plan out the needed examples and evidence. Based on her planning notes, Carmen's composed argument went through several drafts. Here is her final version.

Title makes persuasive claim

Why Violent Video Games Are Good for Girls

CARMEN TIEU (STUDENT)

Attention-grabbing scene

It is ten o'clock P.M., game time. My entire family knows by now that when I am home on Saturday nights, ten P.M. is my gaming night when I play my favorite first-person-shooter games, usually *Halo 3,* on Xbox Live. Seated in my mobile chair in front of my family's 42-inch flat screen HDTV, I log onto Xbox Live. A small message in the bottom of the screen appears with the words "Kr1pL3r is online," alerting me that one of my male friends is online and already playing. As the game loads, I send Kr1pL3r a game invite, and he joins me in the pre-game room lobby.

Continues scene and provides more background

In the game room lobby, all the players who will be participating in the match are chatting aggressively with each other: "Oh man, we're gonna own you guys so bad." When a member of the opposing team notices my gamer tag, "embracingapathy," he begins to insult me by calling me various degrading, gay-associated names: "Embracing apa-what? Man, it sounds so emo. Are you some fag? I bet you want me so bad. You're gonna get owned!" Players always assume from my gamer tag that I am a gay male, never a female. The possibility that I am a girl is the last thing on their minds. Of course, they are right that girls seldom play first-person-shooter games. Girls are socialized into activities that promote togetherness and talk, not high intensity competition involving fantasized shooting and killing. The violent nature of the games tends to repulse girls. Opponents of violent video

Sums up an opposing view

games typically hold that these games are so graphically violent that they will influence players to become amoral and sadistic. Feminists also argue that violent video games often objectify women by portraying them as sexualized toys for men's gratification. Although I understand these objections, I argue that playing first-person-shooter

States claim
States first reason

games can actually be good for girls.

First, playing FPS games gives girls the chance to beat guys at their own game. When I first began playing *Halo 2,* I was horrible. My male friends constantly put me down for my lack of skills, constantly telling

For grounds, uses personal narrative to show how she can beat guys

me that I was awful, "but for a girl, you're good." But it didn't take much practice until I learned to operate the two joy sticks with precision and with quick instinctual reactions. While guys and girls can play many physical games together, such as basketball or touch football, guys will always have the advantage because on average they are taller, faster, and stronger than females. However, when it comes to video games, girls can compete equally because physical strength isn't required, just quick reaction time and manual dexterity—skills that

Briefly backs warrant

women possess in abundance. The adrenaline rush that I receive from

<table>
<tr><td>

by showing the
good feeling of
empowerment

States second
reason

Details focus on
backing for warrant:
It is good for girls to be
freed from feminine
stereotypes

Provides third reason

Uses a narrative
example for grounds;
shows how FPS games
give her a different
way of bonding with
males

Backing for warrant:
This new kind of
bonding is good

Provides final reason

Provides grounds:
gives examples of
what she learned
about male subculture

</td><td>

beating a bunch of testosterone-driven guys at something they suppos-edly excel at is empowering and exciting; I especially savor the look of horror on their faces when I completely destroy them.

Since female video gamers are so rare, playing shooter games allows girls to be freed from feminine stereotypes and increases their confidence. Culture generally portrays females as caring, nonviolent, and motherly beings who are not supposed to enjoy FPS games with their war themes and violent killings. I am in no way rejecting these traditional female values since I myself am a compassionate, tree-hugging vegan. But I also like to break these stereotypes. Playing video games offers a great way for females to break the social mold of only doing "girly" things and introduces them to something that males commonly enjoy. Playing video games with sexist males has also helped me become more outspoken. Psychologically, I can stand up to aggressive males because I know that I can beat them at their own game. The confidence I've gotten from excelling at shooter games may have even carried over into the academic arena because I am majoring in chemical engineering and have no fear whatsoever of intruding into the male-dominated territory of math and science. Knowing that I can beat all the guys in my engineering classes at *Halo* gives me that little extra confidence boost during exams and labs.

5   Another reason for girls to play FPS games is that it gives us a different way of bonding with guys. Once when I was discussing my latest *Halo 3* matches with one of my regular male friends, a guy whom I didn't know turned around and said, "You play *Halo*? Wow, you just earned my respect." Although I was annoyed that this guy apparently didn't respect women in general, it is apparent that guys will talk to me differently now that I can play video games. From a guy's perspective I can also appreciate why males find video games so addicting. You get joy from perfecting your skills so that your high-angle grenade kills become a thing of beauty. While all of these skills may seem trivial to some, the acknowledgment of my skills from other players leaves me with a perverse sense of pride in knowing that I played the game better than everyone else. Since I have started playing, I have also noticed that it is much easier to talk to males about lots of different subjects. Talking video games with guys is a great ice-breaker that leads to different kinds of friendships outside the realm of romance and dating.

Finally, playing violent video games can be valuable for girls because it gives them insights into a disturbing part of male subculture. When the testosterone starts kicking in, guys become blatantly homophobic and misogynistic. Any player, regardless of gender, who cannot play well (as measured by having a high number of kills and a low number of deaths) is made fun of by being called gay, a girl, or worse. Even

</td></tr>
</table>

when some guys finally meet a female player, they will also insult her by calling her a lesbian or an ugly fat chick that has no life. Their insults towards the girl will dramatically increase if she beats them because they feel so humiliated. In their eyes, playing worse than a girl is embarrassing because girls are supposed to be inept at FPS games. Whenever I play *Halo* better than my male friends, they often comment on how "it makes no sense that we're getting owned by Carmen."

Provides backing for warrant: Shows value of learning about male subculture while keeping separate from it

When males act like such sexist jerks it causes one to question if they are always like this. My answer is no because I know, first hand, that when guys like that are having one-on-one conversations with a female, they show a softer side, and the macho side goes away. They don't talk about how girls should stay in the kitchen and make them dinner, but rather how they think it is cool that they share a fun, common interest with a girl. But when they are in a group of males their fake, offensive macho side comes out. I find this phenomenon troubling because it shows a real problem in the way boys are socialized. To be a real "man" around other guys, they have to put down women and gays in activities involving aggressive behavior where men are supposed to excel. But they don't become macho and aggressive in activities like reading and writing, which they think of as feminine. I've always known that guys are more physically aggressive than women, but until playing violent video games I had never realized how this aggression is related to misogyny and homophobia. Perhaps these traits aren't deeply ingrained in men but come out primarily in a competitive male environment. Whatever the cause, it is an ugly phenomenon, and I'm glad that I learned more about it. Beating guys at FPS games has made me a more confident woman while being more aware of gender differences in the way men and women are socialized. I joined the guys in playing *Halo,* but I didn't join their subculture of ridiculing women and gays.

Sums up why her playing FPS games is valuable

The Thesis-Governed "Self-Announcing" Structure of Classical Argument

Like the complete classical argument explained on pages 44–46, Carmen's supporting-reasons argument has a thesis-governed structure in which she states her claim near the end of the introduction, begins body paragraphs with clearly stated reasons, and uses effective transitions throughout to keep her reader on track. This kind of tightly organized structure is sometimes called a *self-announcing* or *closed-form* structure because the writer states his or her claim before beginning the body of the argument and forecasts the structure that is to follow. In contrast, an *unfolding* or *open-form* structure often doesn't give away the writer's position until late in the essay. (We discuss delayed-thesis arguments in Chapter 7.) A general rule of thumb for arguments using more than one line of reasoning is to place your most important or interesting reason last, where it will have the greatest impact on your readers.

In writing a self-announcing argument, students often ask how much of the argument to summarize in the thesis statement. Consider Carmen's options:

- She might announce only her claim:

  Playing first-person-shooter games can be good for girls.

- She might forecast a series of parallel reasons:

  There are several reasons that playing first-person-shooter games can be good for girls.

- She might forecast the actual number of reasons:

  I will present four reasons that playing first-person-shooter games can be good for girls.

- Or she might forecast the whole argument by including her *because* clauses with her claim:

  Playing first-person-shooter games can be good for girls because it lets girls feel empowered by beating guys at their own game, because it frees girls from feminine stereotypes, because it gives girls a different way of bonding with males, and because it gives girls new insights into a male subculture.

This last thesis statement forecasts not only the claim, but also the supporting reasons that will serve as topic sentences for key paragraphs throughout the body of the paper.

No formula can tell you precisely how much of your argument to forecast in the introduction. However, these suggestions can guide you. In writing a self-announcing argument, forecast only what is needed for clarity. In short arguments, readers often need only your claim. In longer arguments, however, or in especially complex ones, readers appreciate your forecasting the complete structure of the argument (claim with reasons). Also, as we explain in later chapters, the directness of classical argument is not always the best way to reach all audiences. On many occasions more open form or delayed thesis approaches are more effective.

■ ■ ■   **FOR CLASS DISCUSSION**   **Reasons, Warrants, and Conditions of Rebuttal**

Individual task:

1. Choose one of the following reasons. Then write a passage that provides grounds to support the reason. Use details from personal experience or imagine plausible, hypothetical details.

   a. For college students, Web surfing or checking social media can be harmful because it causes you to waste so much study time.

   b. Rap has a bad influence on teenagers because it celebrates angry violence.

   c. The university's decision to charge more for parking permits for solo drivers is a good environmental plan because it encourages students to use public transportation.

2. Now create an argument to support the warrant for the reason you chose in task 1. The warrants for each of the arguments are stated below.
    a. Support this warrant: Wasting study time is harmful for college students.
    b. Support this warrant: It is bad to celebrate angry violence.
    c. Support this warrant: It is good for the environment to encourage students to use public transportation.

Group task: Working in pairs, small groups, or as a whole class, share your strategies for supporting your chosen reason and warrant.

WRITING ASSIGNMENT **Plan of an Argument's Details**

This assignment asks you to return to the working thesis statement that you created for the brief writing assignment in Chapter 3. From that thesis statement extract one of your enthymemes (your claim with one of your *because* clauses). Write out the warrant for your enthymeme. Then use the Toulmin schema to brainstorm the details you might use (grounds, backing, conditions of rebuttal) to convert your enthymeme into a fleshed-out argument. Use as your model Chandale's planning notes on pages 64–65. Note that this is a process-oriented brainstorming task aimed at helping you generate ideas for an argument-in-process. You may end up changing your ideas substantially as you compose the actual argument. (An assignment to write a complete "supporting reasons" argument like Carmen's comes at the end of the next chapter on uses of evidence.) ■

Using Evidence Effectively

5

What you will learn in this chapter:

5.1 To explain the different kinds of evidence

5.2 To make your evidence persuasive by using the STAR criteria and other strategies

5.3 To understand evidence rhetorically by explaining how the selection and framing of evidence reveals an angle of vision

In Chapters 3 and 4, we introduced you to the concept of *logos*—the logical structure of reasons and evidence in an argument. In this chapter, we turn to the uses of evidence in argument. By "evidence," we mean all the verifiable data and information a writer might use as support for an argument. In Toulmin's terms, evidence is part of the *grounds* or *backing* of an argument in support of reasons or warrants.

Kinds of Evidence

5.1 To explain the different kinds of evidence

Writers have numerous options for the kinds of evidence they can use in an argument, including personal experience, observations, interviews, questionnaires, field or laboratory research, or findings derived from researching primary or secondary sources found in libraries, in databases, or on the World Wide Web. Carmen Tieu's argument in the last chapter is based on personal experience. More commonly, college arguments require library and Internet research—what professors call "information literacy" (see Appendix 2). This chapter focuses more basically on how evidence functions rhetorically in an argument and how it is selected and framed.

We will begin by categorizing different kinds of evidence, illustrating how each kind might be incorporated into an argument, and suggesting the strengths and limitations of each.

Data from Personal Experience   One powerful kind of evidence comes from personal experience:

Example	Strengths and Limitations
Despite recent criticism that Ritalin is overprescribed for attention deficit and hyperactivity disorder, it can often seem like a miracle drug. My little brother is a perfect example. Before he was given Ritalin he was a terror in school... [Tell the "before" and "after" story of your little brother]	■ Personal-experience examples help readers identify with writer; they show writer's personal connection to issue. ■ Vivid stories capture the imagination and appeal to *pathos*. ■ Skeptics may argue that personal examples are insufficient (writer is guilty of hasty generalization), not typical, or not adequately scientific or verifiable.

Data from Observation or Field Research   You can also develop evidence from personally observing a phenomenon or from doing your own field research:

Example	Strengths and Limitations
The intersection at 5th and Montgomery is particularly dangerous because pedestrians almost never find a comfortable break in the heavy flow of cars. On April 29, I watched fifty-seven pedestrians cross the street. Not once did cars stop in both directions before the pedestrian stepped off the sidewalk onto the street. [Continue with observed data about danger.]	■ Field research gives feeling of scientific credibility. ■ It increases typicality by expanding database beyond one example. ■ It enhances the *ethos* of writer as personally invested and reasonable. ■ Skeptics may point to flaws in how observations were conducted, showing how data are insufficient, inaccurate, or nontypical.

Data from Interviews, Questionnaires, Surveys   You can also gather data by interviewing stakeholders in a controversy, creating questionnaires, or doing surveys.

Example	Strengths and Limitations
Another reason to ban laptops from classrooms is the extent to which laptop users disturb other students. In a questionnaire distributed to 50 students in my residence hall, a surprising 60 percent said that they were annoyed by fellow students' checking Facebook, paying their bills, or surfing the Web while pretending to take notes in class. Additionally, I interviewed five students, who gave me specific examples of how these distractions interfere with learning. [Report the examples.]	■ Interviews, questionnaires, and surveys enhance sufficiency and typicality of evidence by expanding database beyond experiences of one person. ■ Quantitative data from questionnaires and surveys often increase scientific feel of argument. ■ Surveys and questionnaires often uncover local or recent data not available in published research. ■ Interviews can provide engaging personal stories, thus enhancing *pathos*. ■ Skeptics can raise doubts about research methodology, questionnaire design, or typicality of interview subjects.

Data from Library or Internet Research   For many arguments, evidence is derived from reading, particularly from library or Internet research. Appendix 2 helps you conduct effective research and incorporate research sources into your arguments:

Example	Strengths and Limitations
The belief that a high-carbohydrate, low-fat diet is the best way to lose weight has been challenged by research conducted by Walter Willett and his colleagues in the department of nutrition in the Harvard School of Public Health. Willett's research suggests that complex carbohydrates such as pasta and potatoes spike glucose levels, increasing risk of diabetes. Additionally, some fats—especially monounsaturated and polyunsaturated fats found in nuts, fish, and most vegetable oils—help lower "bad" cholesterol levels (45).	■ Researched evidence is often powerful, especially when sources are respected by your audience. ■ Researched data may take the form of facts, examples, summaries of research studies, quotations from experts, and so forth. ■ Skeptics might doubt the accuracy of facts, the credentials of a source, or the research design of a study. They might also cite studies with different results. ■ Skeptics might raise doubts about sufficiency, typicality, or relevance of your research data.

Testimony   Writers frequently use testimony when direct data are either unavailable or highly technical or complex. Testimonial evidence can come from research or from interviews:

Example	Strengths and Limitations
Although the Swedish economist Bjorn Lomborg claims that acid rain is not a significant problem, many environmentalists disagree. According to David Bellamany, president of the Conservation Foundation, "Acid rain does kill forests and people around the world, and it's still doing so in the most polluted places, such as Russia" (qtd. in BBC News).	■ By itself, testimony generally is less persuasive than direct data. ■ Persuasiveness can be increased if source has impressive credentials, which the writer can state through attributive tags introducing the testimony. ■ Skeptics might undermine testimonial evidence by questioning credentials of source, showing source's bias, or quoting a countersource.

Statistical Data   Many contemporary arguments rely heavily on statistical data, often supplemented by visual graphics such as tables, pie charts, and graphs. (See Chapter 9 for a discussion of the use of graphics in argument.)

Example	Strengths and Limitations
Americans are delaying marriage at a surprising rate. In 1970, 85 percent of Americans between the ages of 15 and 29 were married. In 2010, however, only 45 percent were married (U.S. Census Bureau).	■ Statistics can give powerful snapshots of aggregate data from a wide database. ■ They are often used in conjunction with graphics (see pages 159–165). ■ They can be calculated and displayed in different ways to achieve different rhetorical effects, so readers must be wary (see pages 85–86). ■ Skeptics might question statistical methods, research design, and interpretation of data.

Hypothetical Examples, Cases, and Scenarios   Arguments occasionally use hypothetical examples, cases, or scenarios, particularly to illustrate conjectured consequences of an event or to test philosophical hypotheses.

Example	Strengths and Limitations
Consider what might happen if we continue to use biotech soybeans that are resistant to herbicides. The resistant gene, through cross-pollination, might be transferred to an ordinary weed, creating an out-of-control superweed that herbicides couldn't kill. Such a superweed could be an ecological disaster.	■ Scenarios have strong imaginative appeal. ■ They are persuasive only if they seem plausible. ■ A scenario narrative often conveys a sense of inevitability, even if the actual scenario is unlikely; hence, rhetorical effect may be illogical. ■ Skeptics might show implausibility of the scenario or offer an alternative scenario.

Reasoned Sequence of Ideas   Sometimes arguments are supported with a reasoned sequence of ideas rather than with concrete facts or other forms of empirical evidence. The writer's concern is to support a point through a logical progression of ideas. Such arguments are conceptual, supported by linked ideas, rather than evidential. This kind of support occurs frequently in arguments and often is intermingled with evidentiary support.

Example	Strengths and Limitations
Embryonic stem cell research, despite its promise in fighting diseases, may have negative social consequences. This research encourages us to place embryos in the category of mere cellular matter that can be manipulated at will. Currently we reduce animals to this category when we genetically alter them for human purposes, such as engineering pigs to grow more human-like heart valves for use in transplants. Using human embryos in the same way—as material that can be altered and destroyed at will—may benefit society materially, but this quest for greater knowledge and control involves a reclassifying of embryos that could potentially lead to a devaluing of human life.	■ These sequences often are used in causal arguments to show how causes are linked to effects or in definitional or values arguments to show links among ideas. ■ They have great power to clarify values and show the belief structure upon which a claim is founded. ■ They can sketch out ideas and connections that would otherwise remain latent. ■ Their effectiveness depends on the audience's acceptance of each link in the sequence of ideas. ■ Skeptics might raise objections at any link in the sequence, often by pointing to different values or outlining different consequences.

The Persuasive Use of Evidence

5.2 To make your evidence persuasive by using the STAR criteria and other strategies

We turn now from kinds of evidence to strategies for making evidence as convincing and persuasive as possible. Consider a target audience of educated, reasonable, and careful readers who approach an issue with healthy skepticism; open-minded but cautious. What demands would such readers make on a writer's use of evidence? To begin to answer that question, let's look at some general principles for using evidence persuasively.

Apply the STAR Criteria to Evidence

Our open-minded but skeptical audience would first of all expect your evidence to meet what rhetorician Richard Fulkerson calls the STAR criteria:*

Sufficiency: Is there enough evidence?

Typicality: Is the chosen evidence representative and typical?

Accuracy: Is the evidence accurate and up-to date?

Relevance: Is the evidence relevant to the claim?

Let's examine each in turn.

Sufficiency of Evidence   How much evidence you need is a function of your rhetorical context. In a court trial, opposing attorneys often agree to waive evidence for points that aren't in doubt in order to concentrate on contested points. The more a

---

*Richard Fulkerson, *Teaching the Argument in Writing* (Urbana: National Council of Teachers of English, 1996), 44–53. In this section, we are indebted to Fulkerson's discussion.

claim is contested or the more your audience is skeptical, the more evidence you may need to present. If you provide too little evidence, you may be accused of *hasty generalization* (see Appendix 1, page 273), a reasoning fallacy in which a person makes a sweeping conclusion based on only one or two instances. On the other hand, if you provide too much evidence, your argument may become overly long and tedious. You can guard against having too little or too much evidence by appropriately qualifying the claim your evidence supports.

> **Strong claim:** Working full time seriously harms a student's grade point average. [much data needed—probably a combination of examples and statistical studies]
>
> **Qualified claim:** Working full time often harms a student's grade point average.

Typicality of Evidence   Whenever you select data, readers need to believe the data are typical and representative rather than extreme instances. Suppose that you want to argue that students can combine full-time work with full-time college and cite the case of your friend Pam who pulled a straight-A grade average while working forty hours per week as a night receptionist in a small hotel. Your audience might doubt the typicality of Pam's case since a night receptionist often can use work hours for studying. What about more typical jobs, they'll ask, where you can't study while you work?

Accuracy of Evidence   Evidence can't be used ethically unless it is accurate and up-to-date, and it can't be persuasive unless the audience believes in the credibility of the writer's sources. We'll develop this point more fully later in this section.

Relevance of Evidence   Finally, evidence will be persuasive only if the reader considers it relevant to what is at stake in the dispute. Consider the following student argument: "I deserve an A in this course because I worked exceptionally hard." The student then cites substantial evidence of how hard he worked—a log of study hours, copies of multiple drafts of papers, testimony from friends, and so forth. Such evidence is ample support for the claim "I worked very hard" but is irrelevant to the claim that "I deserve an A."

Establish a Trustworthy Ethos

Besides supplying evidence that meets the STAR criteria, you can make your evidence more persuasive by establishing your own credibility and fairness (see the discussion of *ethos* in Chapter 6, page 90). To be credible you must identify the sources of your evidence through attributive tags (phrases like "according to T. Alvarez" or "as stated by a recent EPA report") along with, in academic papers, in-text citations and a concluding bibliography (see Appendix 2). Also, you need to be fair in the way you select evidence. For example, it is unethical to take quotations out of context or to write an unfair summary that oversimplifies or distorts a source author's intended meaning (see straw man fallacy in Appendix 1, page 273).

Be Mindful of a Source's Distance from the Original Data

When you support an argument through library/Internet research, you often encounter sources that report evidence from a second- or third-hand perspective. You need to imagine where your source author found the information that you now want to use in your own argument. Let's take as an example a passage from James Surowiecki's article on the minimum wage reprinted in Chapter 2. Because this is a magazine article rather than an academic paper, it contains no footnotes or bibliography, but Surowiecki never-theless uses attributive tags to identify his main sources. Here is a passage from page 26:

Passage from "The Pay Is Too Damn Low"
by James Surowieki

Attributive tag (cites this study as his source)

purported factual statement that we are examining

[O]ver the past three decades, the U.S. economy has done a poor job of creating good middle-class jobs; five of the six fastest-growing job categories today pay less than the median wage. That's why, as a recent study by the economists John Schmitt and Janelle Jones has shown, low-wage workers are older and better educated than ever. More important, more of them are relying on their paychecks not for pin money or to pay for Friday-night dates but, rather, to support families.

Much of Surowiecki's argument for increasing the minimum wage depends on evidence that low-wage workers are "older and better educated than ever." But we might ask, How does Surowiecki know about the age and education of low-wage workers? Why should we trust him? Using an attributive tag, he identifies his source as a recent study by economists John Schmitt and Janelle Jones. We plugged these names into a Google search and quickly located the source: A white paper titled "Low-wage Workers Are Older and Better Educated Than Ever," dated April 2012, from the Center for Economic and Policy Research, which, according to its website, is a nonprofit, nonpartisan re-search center aimed at providing factual economic data for public policy makers. So where did Schmitt and Jones get their data? They cite statistical tables compiled by the "Current Population Survey," which is a joint effort of the Census Bureau and Bureau of Labor Statistics. Based on these original data, Schmitt and Jones constructed two graphs showing shifts in distribution of low-wage workers by age and then by education from 1971 to 2011. One of these graphs, for example, shows that in 1979 teenagers held 26 percent of low-wage jobs, but by 2011 that number was only 12 percent. (You can see this graph in Chapter 2, Figure 2.2, page 16). Conversely, the second graph shows that in 1979, only 25 percent of low-wage job holders had completed at least some college, but by 2011, 43 percent had completed some college.

Let's summarize the process we have just traced: The original data came from gov-ernment statistics collected by the Census Bureau and the Bureau of Labor Statistics. Schmitt and Jones then converted these data into detailed graphs. Surowiecki then summarized the message of the graphs into his single sentence. If you were then to cite Surowiecki as your source for this same information, you would be depending on a chain of trust stretching from the original data through Schmitt and Jones and Surowiecki to you. Of course, you can't be expected to trace all your research-gathered evidence back to the original data, but you need to imagine that it is possible to do so.

Rhetorical Understanding of Evidence

5.3 To understand evidence rhetorically by explaining how the selection and framing of evidence reveals an angle of vision

In the previous section, we presented some general principles for the effective use of evidence. We now ask you to look more closely at the rhetorical context in which evidence operates. We'll look first at the kinds of evidence used in arguments, and then show you how writers select and frame evidence for persuasive effect.

Angle of Vision and the Selection and Framing of Evidence

When we enter the argumentative arena, we come as complex, whole persons, not as disembodied computers that reach claims through a value-free calculus. We enter with our own ideologies, beliefs, values, and guiding assumptions as formed by our particular lived lives. These differences help explain why one person's terrorist might be another person's freedom fighter, or why a hand gun in a drawer might be one person's defense against intruders and another person's child accident waiting to happen. In writing about guns, a believer in second amendment rights is apt to cite evidence that having a gun can stop a violent intruder or prevent a rape. Conversely, proponents of gun control are apt to cite evidence about accidental deaths or suicides. In an argument, evidence is always selected to further the arguer's claim and is never simply an inert, neutral "fact."

These guiding beliefs and values work together to create a writer's "angle of vision." By this term we mean a perspective, bias, lens, filter, frame, or screen that helps determine what a writer sees or doesn't see. This angle of vision makes certain items stand out in a field of data and other items become invisible. It both determines and reveals the writer's view of which data are important and which are trivial, which are significant and which can be ignored.

To illustrate how angle of vision creates this kind of selective seeing, consider how two hypothetical speakers might select different data about homeless people when presenting speeches to their city council. The first speaker argues that the city should increase its services to the homeless. The second asks the city to promote tourism more aggressively. Their differing angles of vision will cause the two speakers to select different data about homeless people and to frame these data in different ways. Because the first speaker wants to increase the council's sympathy for the homeless, she frames homeless people positively by telling the story of one homeless man's struggle to find shelter and nutritious food. Her speech focuses primarily on the low number of tax dollars devoted to helping the homeless. In contrast, the second speaker, using data about lost tourist income, might frame the homeless as "panhandlers" by telling the story of obnoxious, urine-soaked winos who pester shoppers for handouts. As arguers, both speakers want their audience to see the homeless from their own angles of vision.

Consequently, lost tourist dollars don't show up at all in the first speaker's argument, whereas the story of a homeless man's night in the cold doesn't show up in the second speaker's argument. As this example shows, one goal writers have in selecting and framing evidence is to bring the reader's view of the subject into alignment with the writer's angle of vision. The writer selects and frames evidence to limit and control what the reader sees.

To help you better understand the concept of selection and framing, we offer the following exercise based on different angles of vision regarding "festival seating" at rock concerts. Because of nationally reported injuries and near-death experiences resulting from stage diving and crowd surfing at rock concerts, many cities have tried to ban festival seating that allows for the spontaneous creation of mosh pits. Critics of mosh pits have pointed to the injuries caused by crowd surfing and to the ensuing lawsuits against concert venues. Meanwhile, supporters cite the almost ecstatic enjoyment of crowd-surfing rock fans who seek out concerts with "festival seating."

Suppose your city has scheduled a public hearing on a proposed city ordinance to ban mosh pits at rock concerts. Among the possible data available to various speakers for evidence are the following:

- Some bands, like Nine Inch Nails, specify festival seating that allows a mosh pit area.
- A female mosher writing on the Internet says: "I experience a shared energy that is like no other when I am in the pit with the crowd. It is like we are all a bunch of atoms bouncing off of each other. It's great. Hey, some people get that feeling from basketball games. I get mine from the mosh pit."
- A student conducted a survey of fifty students on her campus who had attended rock concerts in the last six months. Of the respondents, 80 percent thought that mosh pits should be allowed at concerts.
- Narrative comments on these questionnaires included the following:
  - Mosh pits are a passion for me. I get an amazing rush when crowd surfing.
  - I don't like to be in a mosh pit or do crowd surfing. But I love festival seating and like to watch the mosh pits. For me, mosh pits are part of the ambience of a concert.
  - I know a girl who was groped in a mosh pit, and she'll never do one again. But I have never had any problems.
  - Mosh pits are dangerous and stupid. I think they should be outlawed.
  - If you are afraid of mosh pits, just stay away. It is ridiculous to ban them because they are totally voluntary. They should just post big signs saying, "City assumes no responsibility for accidents occurring in mosh pit area."
  - On September 14, 2013, six people were taken to hospitals with injuries after a mosh pit fight broke out at the Riot Fest music festival in Chicago.
- According to a 2008 ABC news special, a company specializing in crowd management at rock festivals estimated "that 10,000 people have been injured in and around mosh pits in the last decade." The company said further that "most injuries incurred from mosh pits aren't actually by the moshers but by innocent bystanders."

- In 2005, a blogger reported breaking his nose on an elbow while another described having his lip ring pulled out. Another blogger on the same site described having his lip nearly sliced off by the neck of a bass guitar. The injury required seventy-eight stitches. In May 2008, fifty people were treated at emergency rooms for mosh pit injuries acquired at a Bamboozle concert in New Jersey.
- Twenty-four concert deaths were recorded in 2001, most of them in the area closest to the stage, where people are packed in.
- A teenage girl suffered brain damage at a 1998 Pearl Jam concert in Rapid City, South Dakota. According to her attorney, she hadn't intended to bodysurf or enter the mosh pit but "got sucked in while she was standing at its fringe."
- The website Wikihow offers tips on staying safe in a mosh pit. According to the site, "While it may seem otherwise, moshing is by no means a way to hurt someone. Moshing is about releasing aggression, and having fun while enjoying some awesome music."

■ ■ ■ FOR CLASS DISCUSSION Creating Contrasting Angles of Vision

Tasks: Working individually or in small groups, complete the following tasks:

1. Compose two short speeches, one supporting the proposed city ordinance to ban mosh pits and one opposing it. How you use these data is up to you, but be able to explain your reasoning in the way you select and frame your evidence.
2. After you have shared examples of different speeches, explain the approaches that different classmates employed. What principle of selection was used? If arguers included evidence contrary to their positions, how did they handle it, respond to it, minimize its importance, or otherwise channel its rhetorical effect? ■ ■ ■

Rhetorical Strategies for Framing Evidence

What we hope you learned from the preceding exercise is that an arguer's angle of vision causes the arguer to select evidence from a wide field of data and then frame these data through rhetorical strategies that emphasize some data, minimize others, and guide the reader's response. Now that you have a basic idea of what we mean by framing evidence, here are some strategies writers can use to guide what the reader sees and feels.

Strategies for Framing Evidence

- **Controlling the space given to supporting versus contrary evidence:** Depending on their audience and purpose, writers can devote most of their space to supporting evidence and minimal space to contrary evidence (or omit it entirely). Thus, those arguing in favor of mosh pits may have used lots of evidence supporting mosh pits, including enthusiastic quotations from concertgoers, while omitting (or summarizing very rapidly) the data about the dangers of mosh pits.

EXAMINING VISUAL ARGUMENTS

Crowd surfing in a mosh pit

Angle of Vision

Angle of vision can be conveyed visually as well as verbally. These photos display different angles of vision toward mosh pits. Suppose you were writing a blog in support of festival seating and mosh pits. Which image would you include in your posting? Why? Suppose, alternatively, that you were blogging against mosh pits, perhaps urging local officials to outlaw them. Which image would you choose? Why?

Analyze the visual features of these photographs in order to explain how they are constructed to create alternative angles of vision on mosh pits.

An alternative view of a mosh pit

■ **Emphasizing a detailed story versus presenting lots of facts and statistics:** Often, writers can choose to support a point with a memorable individual case or with aggregate data such as statistics or lists of facts. A memorable story can have a strongly persuasive effect. For example, to create a negative view of mosh pits, a writer might tell the heartrending story of a teenager suffering permanent brain damage from being dropped on a mosh pit floor. In contrast, a supporter of mosh pits might tell the story of a happy music lover turned on to the concert scene by the rush of crowd surfing. A different strategy is to use facts and statistics rather than case narratives—for example, data about the frequency of mosh pit accidents, financial consequences of lawsuits, and so forth. The single narrative case often has a more powerful rhetorical effect, but it is always open to the charge that it is an insufficient or nonrepresentative example. Vivid anecdotes make for interesting reading, but by themselves they may not be compelling logically. In contrast, aggregate data, often used in scholarly studies, can provide more compelling logical evidence but sometimes make the prose wonkish and dense.

■ **Providing contextual and interpretive comments when presenting data:** When citing data, writers can add brief contextual or interpretive comments that act like lenses over the readers' eyes to help them see the data from the writer's perspective. Suppose you want to support mosh pits, but want to admit that mosh pits are dangerous. You could make that danger seem irrelevant or inconsequential by saying: "It is true that occasional mosh pit accidents happen, just as accidents happen in any kind of recreational activity from swimming to weekend softball games." The concluding phrase frames the danger of mosh pits by comparing them to other recreational accidents that don't require special laws or regulations. The implied argument is this: banning mosh pits because of an occasional accident would be as silly as banning recreational swimming because of occasional accidents.

■ **Putting contrary evidence in subordinate positions:** Just as a photographer can place a flower at the center of a photograph or in the background, a writer can place a piece of data in a subordinate clause or main clause of a sentence. Note how the structure of the following sentence minimizes the fact that mosh pit accidents are rare: "Although mosh pit accidents are rare, the danger to the city of multimillion-dollar liability lawsuits means that the city should nevertheless ban them for reasons of fiscal prudence." The factual datum that mosh pit accidents are rare is summarized briefly and tucked away in a subordinate "*although* clause," while the writer's own position is elaborated in the main clause where it receives grammatical emphasis. A writer with a different angle of vision might say, "Although some cities may occasionally be threatened with a lawsuit, serious accidents resulting from mosh pits are so rare that cities shouldn't interfere with the desires of music fans to conduct concerts as they please."

■ **Choosing labels and names that guide the reader's response to data:** One of the most subtle ways to control your reader's response to data is to choose labels and names that prompt them to see the issue as you do. If you like mosh pits, you might refer to the seating arrangements in a concert venue as "festival seating, where concertgoers have the opportunity to create a free-flowing mosh pit." If you don't like mosh pits, you might refer to the seating arrangements as "an accident-inviting use of empty space where rowdies can crowd together, slam into each other, and occasionally punch and kick." The labels you choose, along with the connotations of the words you select, urge your reader to share your angle of vision.

■ **Using images (photographs, drawings) to guide the reader's response to data:** Another strategy for moving your audience toward your angle of vision is to include a photograph or drawing that portrays a contested issue from your perspective.

Consider how the photographs on page 83 make arguments about mosh pits. Most people agree that the first photo supports a positive view of mosh pits. The crowd looks happy and relaxed (rather than rowdy or out of control), and the young woman lifted above the crowd smiles broadly, her body relaxed, her arms extended. In contrast, the second photo emphasizes muscular men and threatens danger rather than harmony. The crowd seems on the verge of turning ugly. (See Chapter 9 for a complete discussion of the use of visuals in argument.)

■ **Revealing the value system that determines the writer's selection and framing of data:** Ultimately, how a writer selects and frames evidence is linked to the system of values that organize his or her argument. If you favor mosh pits, you probably favor maximizing the pleasure of concertgoers, promoting individual choice, and letting moshers assume the risk of their own behavior. If you want to forbid mosh pits, you probably favor minimizing risks, protecting the city from lawsuits, and protecting individuals from the danger of their own out-of-control actions. Sometimes you can foster connections with your audience by openly addressing your underlying values that you hope your audience shares with you. You can often frame your selected data by stating explicitly the values that guide your argument.

Special Strategies for Framing Statistical Evidence

Numbers and statistical data can be framed in so many ways that this category of evidence deserves its own separate treatment. By recognizing how writers frame numbers to support the story they want to tell, you will always be aware that other stories are also possible. Ethical use of numbers means that you use reputable sources for your basic data, that you don't invent or intentionally distort numbers for your own purposes, and that you don't ignore alternative points of view. Here are some of the choices writers make when framing statistical data:

■ **Raw numbers versus percentages**. You can alter the rhetorical effect of a statistic by choosing between raw numbers and percentages. In summer 2002, many American parents panicked over what seemed like an epidemic of child abductions. If you cited the raw number of these abductions reported in the national news, this number, although small, could seem scary. But if you computed the actual percentage of American children who were abducted, that percentage was so infinitesimally small as to seem insignificant. You can apply this framing option directly to the mosh pit case. To emphasize the danger of mosh pits, you can say that twenty deaths occurred at rock concerts in a given year. To minimize this statistic, you could compute the percentage of deaths by dividing this number by the total number of persons who attended rock concerts during the year, certainly a number in the several millions. From the perspective of percentages, the death rate at concerts is extremely low.

■ **Median versus mean.** Another way to alter the rhetorical effect of numbers is to choose between the median and the mean. The mean is the average of all numbers on a list. The median is the middle number when all the numbers are arranged sequentially from high to low. In 2006, the mean annual income for retired families in the United States was $41,928—not a wealthy amount but enough to live on comfortably if you owned your own home. However, the median income was only $27,798, a figure that gives you a much more striking picture of income distribution among older Americans. This median figure means that half of all retired families in the United States had annual incomes of $27,798 or less. The much higher mean income indicates that many retired Americans are quite wealthy. This wealth raises the average of all incomes (the mean) but doesn't affect the median.

■ **Unadjusted versus adjusted numbers**. Suppose your boss told you that you were getting a 5 percent raise. You might be happy—unless inflation rates were running at 6 percent. Economic data can be hard to interpret across time unless the dollar amounts are adjusted for inflation. This same problem occurs in other areas. For example, comparing grade point averages of college graduates in 1970 versus 2012 means little unless one can somehow compensate for grade inflation.

■ **Base point for statistical comparisons**. Suppose you create a graph of global average temperatures from 1998 to the present. This graph, with 1998 as a base starting point, will suggest that the earth may be cooling slightly, not heating up. However, if you begin the graph in 1980, the line, though fluctuating, rises steadily. (See graph on page 202). One's choice of the base point for a comparison often makes a significant rhetorical difference.

■ ■ ■   **FOR CLASS DISCUSSION**   Using Strategies to Frame Statistical Evidence

A proposal to build a new publicly-funded sports stadium in a major American city yielded a wide range of statistical arguments. All of the following statements are reasonably faithful to the same facts:

■ The stadium would be paid for by raising the sales tax from 8.2 percent to 8.3 percent over a twenty-year period.

■ The sales tax increase is one-tenth of 1 percent.

■ This increase represents an average of $7.50 per person per year—about the price of a large special coffee drink and a pastry.

■ This increase represents $750 per five-person family over the twenty-year period of the tax.

■ For a family building a new home in this city, this tax will increase building costs by $200.

■ This is a $250 million tax increase for city residents.

How would you describe the costs of the proposed ballpark if you opposed the proposal? How would you describe the costs if you supported the proposal?   ■ ■ ■

Creating a Plan for Gathering Evidence

We conclude this chapter with a list of brainstorming questions that may help you think of possible sources for evidence in your own argument. As you begin contemplating an argument, you can use the following checklist to help you think of possible sources for evidence.

A Checklist for Brainstorming Sources of Evidence

- What personal experiences have you had with this issue? What details from your life or the lives of your friends, acquaintances, or relatives might serve as examples or other kinds of evidence?
- What observational studies would be relevant to this issue?
- What people could you interview to provide insights or expert knowledge on this issue?
- What questions about your issue could be addressed in a survey or questionnaire?
- What useful information on this issue might encyclopedias or specialized references in your university library provide?
- What evidence might you seek on this issue using licensed databases to search for relevant articles from magazines, newspapers, and scholarly journals?
- How might an Internet search engine help you research this issue?
- What evidence might you find on this issue from reliable statistical resources such as U.S. Census Bureau data, the Centers for Disease Control, or *Statistical Abstract of the United States?*

WRITING ASSIGNMENT   **A Supporting-Reasons Argument**

Write an argument that uses at least two reasons to support your claim. Your argument should include all the features of a classical argument, except that you can omit the section on summarizing and responding to opposing views, which we will cover in Chapter 7. This assignment builds on the brief writing assignments in Chapter 3 (create a thesis statement for an argument) and Chapter 4 (brainstorm support for one of your enthymemes using the Toulmin schema). Like a complete classical argument, a supporting-reasons argument has a thesis-governed structure in which you state your claim at the end of the introduction, begin body paragraphs with clearly stated reasons, and use effective transitions throughout to keep your reader on track. In developing your own argument, place your most important, persuasive, or interesting reason last, where it will have the greatest impact on your readers. A model for a supporting reasons argument is Carmen Tieu's "Why Violent Video Games are Good for Girls" on pages 68–70. ■

Moving Your Audience

Ethos, Pathos, and *Kairos*

6

What you will learn in this chapter:

6.1 To explain how the classical appeals of *logos, ethos,* and *pathos* work together to move your audience

6.2 To create effective appeals to *ethos*

6.3 To create effective appeals to *pathos*

6.4 To be mindful of *kairos* or the "timeliness" of your argument

6.5 To explain how images make visual appeals to *logos, ethos, pathos,* and *kairos*

6.6 To explain how audience-based reasons appeal to *logos, ethos, pathos,* and *kairos*

In Chapters 4 and 5 we focused on *logos*—the logical structure of reasons and evidence in argument. In this chapter we turn to *ethos* and *pathos,* which comprise the other two points of the rhetorical triangle introduced in Chapter 3, page 46. We also consider the *kairos,* or timeliness of the argument, and conclude by showing how audience-based reasons appeal simultaneously to *logos, ethos, pathos,* and *kairos.*

Ethos and *Pathos* as Persuasive Appeals: An Overview

6.1 To explain how the classical appeals of *logos, ethos,* and *pathos* work together to move your audience

To see how *logos, ethos,* and *pathos* work together to create an impact on the reader, consider the different impacts of the following arguments, each of which has roughly the same logical appeal.

1. People should adopt a vegetarian diet because doing so will help prevent the cruelty to animals caused by factory farming.

2. If you are planning to eat chicken tonight, please consider how much that chicken suffered so that you can have a tender and juicy meal. Commercial growers cram the chickens so tightly together into cages that they never walk on their own legs, see sunshine, or flap their wings. In fact, their beaks must be cut off to keep them from pecking each other's eyes out. One way to prevent such suffering is for more people to become vegetarians.

3. People who eat meat are no better than sadists who torture other sentient creatures to enhance their own pleasure. Unless you enjoy sadistic tyranny over others, you have only one choice: Become a vegetarian.

4. People committed to justice might consider the extent to which our love of eating meat requires the agony of animals. A visit to a modern chicken factory—where chickens live their entire lives in tiny darkened coops without room to spread their wings—might raise doubts about our right to inflict such suffering on sentient creatures. Indeed, such a visit might persuade us that vegetarianism is a more just alternative.

Each argument has roughly the same logical core:

ENTHYMEME

CLAIM People should adopt a vegetarian diet

REASON because doing so will help prevent the cruelty to animals caused by factory farming.

GROUNDS

• Evidence of suffering in commercial chicken farms, where chickens are crammed together and lash out at one another

• Evidence that only widespread adoption of vegetarianism will end factory farming

WARRANT

If we have an alternative to making animals suffer, we should use it.

But the impact of each argument varies. The difference between arguments 1 and 2, most of our students report, is the greater emotional power of 2. Whereas argument 1 refers only to the abstraction "cruelty to animals," argument 2 paints a vivid picture of chickens with their beaks cut off to prevent their pecking each other blind. Argument 2 makes a stronger appeal to *pathos* (not necessarily a stronger argument), stirring feelings by appealing simultaneously to the heart and to the head.

The difference between arguments 1 and 3 concerns both *ethos* and *pathos*. Argument 3 appeals to the emotions through highly charged words such as *torture, sadists,* and *tyranny.* But argument 3 also draws attention to its writer, and most of our students report not liking that writer very much. His stance is self-righteous and insulting. In contrast, argument 4's author establishes a more positive *ethos.* He establishes rapport with members of his audience by assuming they are committed to justice and by qualifying his argument with conditional terms such as *might* and *perhaps*. He also invites sympathy for his problem—an appeal to *pathos*—by offering a specific description of chickens crammed into tiny coops.

Which of these arguments is best? The answer depends on the intended audience. Arguments 1 and 4 seem aimed at receptive audiences reasonably open to exploration of the issue. Arguments 2 and 3 seem designed to shock complacent audiences or to rally a group of true believers. Even argument 3, which is too abusive to be effective in most instances, might work as a rallying speech at a convention of animal liberation activists.

Our point thus far is that *logos, ethos,* and *pathos* are different aspects of the same whole, different lenses for intensifying or softening the light beam you project onto the screen. Every choice you make as a writer affects in some way each of the three appeals. The rest of this chapter examines these choices in more detail.

How to Create an Effective *Ethos:* The Appeal to Credibility

6.2 To create effective appeals to *ethos*

The ancient Greek and Roman rhetoricians recognized that an argument will be more persuasive if the audience trusts the speaker. Aristotle argued that such trust resides within the speech itself, not in the prior reputation of the speaker. In the speaker's manner and delivery; in tone, word choice, and arrangement of reasons; and in the sympathy with which the speaker treats alternative views, he or she creates a trustworthy persona. Aristotle called the impact of the speaker's credibility the appeal from *ethos*. How does a writer create credibility? We suggest four ways:

- **Be knowledgeable about your issue.** The first way to gain credibility is to *be* credible—that is, to argue from a strong base of knowledge, to have at hand the examples, personal experiences, statistics, and other empirical data needed to make a sound case. If you have done your homework, you will command the attention of most audiences.
- **Be fair.** Demonstrate fairness and courtesy to alternative views. Because true argument can occur only where persons may reasonably disagree with one another, your *ethos* will be strengthened if you demonstrate that you understand and empathize with other points of view.
- **Build a bridge to your audience.** A third means of establishing credibility—building a bridge to your audience—has been treated in our earlier discussions of audience-based reasons. By grounding your argument in shared values and assumptions, you demonstrate your goodwill and enhance your image as a trustworthy person respectful of your audience's views.
- **Demonstrate professionalism.** Finally, you can enhance your *ethos* by the professionalism revealed in your own writing: If your manuscript is sloppy, marred by spelling or grammatical errors, poorly documented, or inattentive to the tone and style of the expected genre, your own credibility will be damaged.

How to Create *Pathos:* The Appeal to Beliefs and Emotions

6.3 To create effective appeals to *pathos*

Although commonly defined as an "appeal to the emotions," *pathos* evokes effects that are subtler and more complex than the word *emotions* suggests. Because our understanding of something is a matter of feeling as well as perceiving, *pathos* can evoke nonlogical, but not necessarily nonrational, ways of knowing. When used effectively, pathetic appeals reveal the fullest human meaning of an issue, touching the heart and mind simultaneously. Although it is difficult to classify all the ways that writers can create appeals from *pathos,* we will focus on four strategies: concrete language; specific examples and illustrations; narratives; and word connotations, metaphors, and analogies.

Use Concrete Language

Concrete language can increase the liveliness, interest level, and personality of one's prose and typically heightens *pathos* in an argument. Consider the differences between the first and second drafts of the following student argument:

First Draft

People who prefer driving a car to taking a bus think that taking the bus will increase the stress of the daily commute. Just the opposite is true. Not being able to find a parking spot when in a hurry to work or school can cause a person stress. Taking the bus gives a person time to read or sleep, etc. It could be used as a mental break.

Second Draft (with Concrete Language)

Taking the bus can be more relaxing than driving a car. Having someone else behind the wheel gives people time to chat with friends or cram for a test. They can balance their checkbooks, do homework, doze off, read the daily newspaper, or get lost in a novel rather than foaming at the mouth looking for a parking space.

In this revision, specific details enliven the prose by creating images that trigger positive feelings. Who wouldn't want some free time to doze off or to get lost in a novel?

Use Specific Examples and Illustrations

Specific examples and illustrations serve two purposes in an argument: they provide evidence that supports your reasons, and they give your argument presence and emotional resonance. Note the flatness of the following draft, arguing for the value of multicultural studies in a university core curriculum:

First Draft

Another advantage of a multicultural education is that it will help us see our own culture in a broader perspective. If all we know is our own heritage, we might not be inclined to see anything bad about this heritage because we won't know anything else. But if we study other heritages, we can see the costs and benefits of our own heritage.

Now note the increase in "presence" when the writer adds a specific example.

Second Draft (Example Added)

Another advantage of multicultural education is that it raises questions about traditional Western values. For example, owning private property (such as buying your own home) is part of the American dream and is a basic right guaranteed in our Constitution. However, in studying the beliefs of American Indians, students are confronted with a very different view of private property. When the U.S. government sought to buy land in the Pacific Northwest from Chief Sealth, he is alleged to have replied:

> The president in Washington sends words that he wishes to buy our land. But how can you buy or sell the sky? The land? The idea is strange to us. If we do not own the freshness of the air and the sparkle of the water, how can you buy them?[…]We are part of the earth and it is part of us[.…]This we know: The earth does not belong to man, man belongs to the earth.

Our class was shocked by the contrast between traditional Western views of property and Chief Sealth's views. One of our best class discussions was initiated by this quotation from Chief Sealth. Had we not been exposed to a view from another culture, we would have never been led to question the "rightness" of Western values.

The writer begins his revision by evoking a traditional Western view of private property, which he then questions by shifting to Chief Sealth's vision of land as open, endless, and as unobtainable as the sky. Through the use of a specific example, the writer brings to life his previously abstract point about the benefit of multicultural education.

Use Narratives

A particularly powerful way to evoke *pathos* is to tell a story that either leads into your claim or embodies it implicitly and that appeals to your readers' feelings and imagination. Brief narratives—whether real or hypothetical—are particularly effective as opening attention grabbers for an argument. To illustrate how an introductory narrative (either a story or a brief scene) can create pathetic appeals, consider the following first paragraph to an argument opposing jet skis:

> I dove off the dock into the lake, and as I approached the surface I could see the sun shining through the water. As my head popped out, I located my cousin a few feet away in a rowboat waiting to escort me as I, a twelve-year-old girl, attempted to swim across the mile-wide, pristine lake and back to our dock. I made it, and that glorious summer day is one of my most precious memories. Today, however, no one would dare attempt that swim. Jet skis have taken over this small lake where I spent many summers with my grandparents. Dozens of whining jet skis crisscross the lake, ruining it for swimming, fishing, canoeing, rowboating, and even waterskiing. More stringent state laws are needed to control jet skiing because it interferes with other uses of lakes and is currently very dangerous.

This narrative makes a case for a particular point of view toward jet skis by winning our identification with the writer's experience. She invites us to relive that experience with her while she also taps into our own treasured memories of summer experiences that have been destroyed by change.

Opening narratives to evoke *pathos* can be powerfully effective, but they are also risky. If they are too private, too self-indulgent, too sentimental, or even too dramatic and forceful, they can backfire on you. If you have doubts about an opening narrative, read it to a sample audience before using it in your final draft.

Use Words, Metaphors, and Analogies with Appropriate Connotations

Another way of appealing to *pathos* is to select words, metaphors, or analogies with connotations that match your aim. We have already described this strategy in Chapter 5 in our discussion of the "framing" of evidence (pages 80–85). By using words with particular connotations, a writer guides readers to see the issue through the writer's angle of vision. Thus if you want to create positive feelings about a recent city council decision, you can call it "bold and decisive"; if you want to create negative feelings, you can call it "haughty and autocratic." Similarly, writers can use favorable or unfavorable metaphors and analogies to evoke different imaginative or emotional responses. A tax bill might be viewed as a "potentially fatal poison pill" or as "unpleasant but necessary economic medicine." In each of these cases, the words create an emotional as well as intellectual response.

■ ■ ■ **FOR CLASS DISCUSSION** Incorporating Appeals to *Pathos*

Outside class, rewrite the introduction to one of your previous papers (or a current draft) to include more appeals to *pathos*. Use any of the strategies for giving your argument presence: concrete language, specific examples, narratives, metaphors, analogies, and connotative words. Bring both your original and your rewritten introductions to class. In pairs or in groups, discuss the comparative effectiveness of these introductions in trying to reach your intended audience.

Kairos: The Timeliness and Fitness of Arguments

6.4 To be mindful of *kairos* or the "timeliness" of your argument

To increase your argument's effectiveness, you need to consider not only its appeals to *logos, ethos,* and *pathos,* but also its *kairos*—that is, its timing, its appropriateness for the occasion. In Greek, *kairos* means "right time," "season," or "opportunity." It differs from the ordinary Greek word for time, *chronos,* the root of our words "chronology" and "chronometer." You can measure *chronos* by looking at your watch, but you measure *kairos* by sensing the opportune time through psychological attentiveness to situation and meaning. To think *kairotically* is to be attuned to the total context of a situation in order to act in the right way at the right moment. If you have ever written an angry e-mail but then debated whether to hit "send," you have been thinking *kairotically*. Here are some examples that illustrate the range of insights contained by the term *kairos*:

■ If you write a letter to the editor of a newspaper or post a response to a blog, you usually have a one- or two-day window before a current event becomes "old news" and is no longer interesting. An out-of-date response may go unread, not because it is poorly written or argued but because it misses its *kairotic* moment.

■ Similar instances of lost timeliness occur in class discussions: You have an important point that you want to contribute, but the professor doesn't acknowledge your raised hand. When you finally are called on, the *kairotic* moment has passed.

■ A sociology major is writing a senior capstone paper for graduation. The due date for the paper is fixed, so the timing of the paper isn't at issue. But *kairos* is still relevant. It urges the student to ask about the "right way" to produce a sociology paper at this moment in the discipline's history. Currently what are leading-edge versus trailing-edge questions in sociology? What theorists or research methods are now in vogue? How would a good capstone paper written in 2015 differ from one written a decade earlier?

As you can see from these examples, *kairos* concerns a whole range of questions connected to the timing, fitness, appropriateness, and proportions of a message within an evolving rhetorical context. There are no rules to help you determine the *kairotic* moment for your argument, but being attuned to *kairos* will help you "read" your audience and rhetorical situation in a dynamic way.

■ ■ ■ **FOR CLASS DISCUSSION** Analyzing an Argument's Appeals

Your instructor will select an argument for analysis. Working in small groups or as a whole class, analyze the assigned argument first from the perspective of *kairos* and then from the perspective of *logos, ethos,* and *pathos.*   ■ ■ ■

Using Images to Appeal to *Logos, Ethos, Pathos,* and *Kairos*

6.5 To explain how images make visual appeals to *logos, ethos, pathos,* and *kairos*

One of the most powerful ways to move your audience is to use photos or other images that can appeal to *logos, ethos, pathos,* and *kairos* in one glance. (Chapter 9 focuses exclusively on visual rhetoric—the persuasive power of images.) Although many written arguments do not lend themselves to visual illustrations, we suggest that when you construct arguments you consider the potential of visual support. When images work well, they are analogous to the verbal strategies of concrete language, specific illustrations, narratives, and connotative words. As an example, suppose you are writing an argument supporting fundraising efforts to help a third-world country that has recently experienced a natural catastrophe. To add a powerful appeal to *pathos,* you might consider incorporating into your argument the photograph shown in Figure 6.1 of the devastation and personal loss caused by typhoon Haiyan in the Philippines in 2013. A photograph such as this one can evoke a strong emotional and imaginative response as well as make viewers think.

■ ■ ■ **FOR CLASS DISCUSSION** Analyzing Images as Appeals to *Pathos*

Working in small groups or as a whole class, share your responses to the following questions:

1. How would you describe the emotional/imaginative impact of Figure 6.1? What details of the photo specifically create its appeal to *pathos*?

FIGURE 6.1 Photo after Typhoon Haiyan in the Philippines

2. Many disaster-relief photos seek to convey the magnitude of the destruc-
    tion and suffering, sometimes shockingly, by depicting destroyed buildings,
    mangled bodies, and images of human misery. How is your response to Figure
    6.1 similar to or different from your response to commonly encountered close-
    up photographs of grief-stricken victims or to distance shots of wide-spread
    destruction? To what extent is Figure 6.1's story—told from the perspective of
    a child—different from the more typical photographs of destroyed buildings or
    anguished faces?

How Audience-Based Reasons Enhance *Logos, Ethos,* and *Pathos*

6.6 To explain how
audience-based reasons
appeal to *logos, ethos, pathos,*
and *kairos*

We conclude this chapter by returning to the concept of audience-
based reasons that we introduced in Chapter 4. Audience-based
reasons enhance *logos* because they are built on underlying assumptions (warrants) that the audience is likely to accept. But they
also enhance *ethos* and *pathos* by helping the writer identify with

EXAMINING VISUAL ARGUMENTS

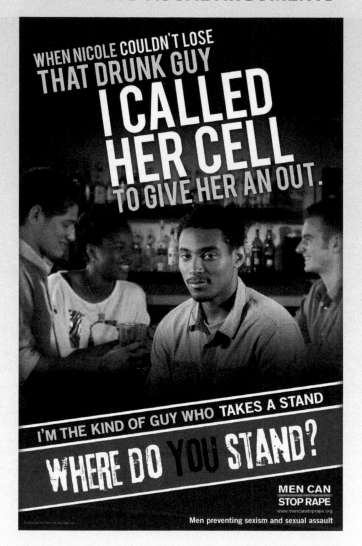

Logos, Ethos, Pathos, and *Kairos*

Efforts to combat sexual assault and the culture of date rape on campuses have figured prominently in public conversation recently, with discussions booming on the Web sites of newly formed organizations and stories of rallies on university campuses appearing on news sites. As this advocacy poster shows, the need to bolster bystander intervention is a critical piece in addressing this problem.

How does this advocacy poster attempt to move its audience? Analyze the poster's visual and verbal appeals to *logos, ethos, pathos* and *kairos.*

the audience, entering into their beliefs and values. To consider the needs of you ence, you can ask yourself the following questions:

Questions for Analyzing Your Audience

What to Ask	Why to Ask It
1. *Who is your audience?*	Your answer will help you think about audience-based reasons.
2. *How much does your audience know or care about your issue?*	Your answer can especially affect your introduction and conclusion. The less the audience knows, the more background you will have to provide.
3. *What is your audience's current attitude toward your issue?*	Your answer will help you decide the structure and tone of your argument.
4. *What will be your audience's likely objections to your argument?*	Your answers will help determine the content of your argument and will alert you to extra research you may need.
5. *What values, beliefs, or assumptions about the world do you and your audience share?*	Your answer will help you find common ground with your audience.

To see how a concern for audience-based reasons can enhance *ethos* and *pathos*, suppose that you support racial profiling (rather than random selection) for determining who receives intensive screening at airports. Suppose further that you are writing a guest op-ed column for a liberal campus newspaper and imagine readers repulsed by the notion of racial profiling (as indeed you are repulsed too in most cases). It's important from the start that you understand and acknowledge the interests of those opposed to your position. Middle Eastern males as well as black males with African passports, the most likely candidates for racial profiling, will object to your racial stereotyping, which lumps all people of Arabic, Semitic, or African appearance into the category "potential terrorists." African Americans and Hispanics, frequent victims of racial profiling by police in U.S. cities, may object to further extension of this hated practice. Also, most political liberals, as well as many moderates and conservatives, may object to the racism inherent in selecting people for airport screening on the basis of ethnicity.

What shared values might you use to build bridges to those opposed to racial profiling at airports? You need to develop a strategy to reduce your audience's fears and to link your reasons to their values. Your thinking might go something like this:

Problem: How can I create an argument rooted in shared values? How can I reduce fear that racial profiling in this situation endorses racism or will lead to further erosion of civil liberties?

Bridge-building goals: I must try to show that my argument's goal is to increase airline safety by preventing terrorism like that of 9/11/01. My argument must show my respect for Islam and for Arabic and Semitic people. I must also show my rejection of racial profiling as normal police practice.

Possible strategies:

- Stress the shared value of protecting innocent people from terrorism.
- Show how racial profiling significantly increases the efficiency of secondary searches. (If searches are performed at random, then we waste time and resources searching those statistically unlikely to be terrorists.)
- Argue that airport screeners must also use indicators other than race to select individuals for searches (for example, traits that might indicate a domestic terrorist).
- Show my respect for Islam.
- Show sympathy for people selected for searching via racial profiling and acknowledge that this practice would normally be despicable except for the extreme importance of airline security, which overrides personal liberties in this case.
- Show my rejection of racial profiling in situations other than airport screening—for example, stopping African Americans for traffic violations more often than whites and then searching their cars for drugs or stolen goods.

These thinking notes about your audience allow you to develop a plan for your argument. Perhaps you might formulate a claim with reasons as follows:

- Airport screeners should use racial profiling rather than random selection to determine which people undergo intensive screening
  - because doing so will be more efficient use of airport screeners' time, increase the odds of finding terrorists, and thus lead to greater airline safety. (*WARRANT: Increased airline safety is good; or, at a deeper level, The positive consequences of increasing airline safety through racial profiling outweigh the negative consequences.*)
  - because racial profiling in this specific case does not mean allowing it in everyday police activities, nor does it imply disrespect for Islam or for Middle Eastern or African males. (*WARRANT: Racial profiling is unacceptable in everyday police practices. It is wrong to show disrespect for Islam or Middle Eastern or African males.*)

■ ■ ■   **FOR CLASS DISCUSSION**   Planning an Audience-Based
Argumentative Strategy

Working individually or in small groups, plan an audience-based argumentative strategy for one or more of the following cases. Follow the thinking process used by the writer of the racial profiling argument: (1) state several problems that the writer must solve to reach the audience, and (2) develop possible solutions to those problems.

1. An argument for the right of software companies to continue making and selling violent video games: aim the argument at parents who oppose their children playing these games.
2. An argument to reverse grade inflation by limiting the number of As and Bs a professor can give in a course: aim the argument at students who fear getting lower grades.
3. An argument supporting the legalization of cocaine: aim your argument at readers of *Reader's Digest,* a conservative magazine that supports the current war on drugs.   ■ ■ ■

WRITING ASSIGNMENT   **Revising a Draft for *Ethos, Pathos,*** **and Audience-Based Reasons**

Part 1: Choose an argument that you have previously written or are currently drafting. Revise the argument with explicit focus on increasing its appeals to *ethos, pathos,* and *logos* via audience-based reasons. Consider especially how you might improve *ethos* by building bridges to the audience or improve *pathos* through concrete language, specific examples, metaphors, or connotations of words. Finally, consider the extent to which your reasons are audience-based.

Or

Multimodal option: Imagine an argument that you have previously written or are currently drafting that could be enhanced with effective photographs or images. Revise your argument to include these images, perhaps creating a desktop published document that wraps text around visuals chosen to enhance *pathos*. Other multimodal possibilities include transforming your argument into a speech supported by Power-Point images (see Chapter 14, pages 269–270), into a poster argument (see Chapter 9, page 152, and Chapter 14, page 257), or even into a podcast that includes music.

Part 2: Attach to your revision or transformed project a reflective letter explaining the choices you made in revising your original argument or in transforming it using a multimodal approach. Describe for your instructor the changes or transformations you made and explain how or why your new version enhances your argument's effectiveness at moving its audience. ▪

Responding to Objections and Alternative Views

7

What you will learn in this chapter:

7.1 To explain the differences between one-sided, multisided, and dialogic argument

7.2 To determine the degree of your audience's resistance to your views in order to shape the content, structure, and tone of your argument

7.3 To use one-sided argument to appeal to supportive audiences

7.4 To use classical argument to appeal to neutral or undecided audiences, using refutation and concession

7.5 To use dialogic, delayed-thesis argument to appeal to resistant audiences

7.6 To use Rogerian communication to open up new channels of understanding between you and an opposing audience

In the previous chapter, we discussed strategies for moving your audience through appeals to *ethos*, *pathos*, and *kairos*. In this chapter, we examine strategies for addressing opposing or alternative views—whether to omit them, refute them, concede to them, or incorporate them through compromise and conciliation.

One-Sided, Multisided, and Dialogic Arguments

7.1 To explain the differences between one-sided, multisided, and dialogic argument

Arguments are said to be one-sided, multisided, or dialogic:

- *A one-sided argument* presents only the writer's position on the issue without summarizing and responding to alternative viewpoints.
- *A multisided argument* presents the writer's position, but also summarizes and responds to possible objections and alternative views.
- *A dialogic argument* has a much stronger component of inquiry, where the writer presents herself as uncertain or searching, where the audience is considered a partner in the dialogue, and where the writer's purpose is to seek common ground, perhaps leading to a consensual solution to a problem.

How can you determine the kind of argument that would be most effective in a given case? As a general rule, one-sided arguments are appropriate when an issue is not highly contested. When an issue is highly contested, then one-sided arguments tend to strengthen the convictions of those who are already in the writer's camp, but alienate those who aren't. In contrast, for those initially opposed to a writer's claim, a multisided argument shows that the writer has considered other views and thus reduces some initial hostility. An especially interesting effect can occur with neutral or undecided audiences. In the short run, one-sided arguments often are persuasive to a neutral audience, but in the long run multisided arguments have more staying power. Neutral audiences who've heard only one side of an issue tend to change their minds when they hear alternative arguments. By anticipating and rebutting opposing views, a multisided argument diminishes the surprise and force of subsequent counterarguments. If we move from neutral to highly resistant audiences, adversarial approaches—even multisided ones—are seldom effective because they increase hostility and harden the differences between writer and reader. In such cases, more dialogic approaches have the best chance of establishing common ground for inquiry and consensus.

In the rest of this chapter, we will show you how your choice of writing one-sided, multisided, or dialogic arguments is a function of how you perceive your audience's resistance to your views as well as your level of confidence in your own views.

Determining Your Audience's Resistance to Your Views

7.2 To determine the degree of your audience's resistance to your views in order to shape the content, structure, and tone of your argument

When you write an argument, you must always consider your audience's point of view. One way to imagine your relationship to members of your audience is to place them on a scale of resistance ranging from strong support of your position to strong opposition (see Figure 7.1). At the "Accord" end of this scale are like-minded people who basically agree with your position on the issue. At the "Resistance" end are those who strongly disagree with you, perhaps unconditionally, because their values, beliefs, or assumptions sharply differ from your own. Between "Accord" and "Resistance" lies a range of opinions. Close to your position will be those leaning in your direction but with less conviction than you. Close to the resistance position will be those basically opposed to your view but willing to listen to your argument and perhaps willing to acknowledge some of its strengths. In the middle are those undecided people who are still sorting out their feelings, seeking additional information, and weighing the strengths and weaknesses of alternative views.

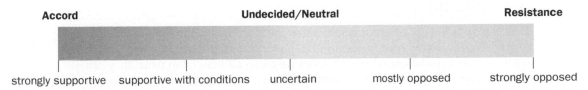

FIGURE 7.1 Scale of resistance

Seldom, however, will you encounter an issue in which all your intended readers fall into one position on the scale of resistance. Often readers will have different degrees of resistance or be resistant for different reasons. Sometimes as a writer you will simply need to "invent" your audience—that is, to assume that a certain category of readers will be your primary audience. Making this decision gives you a stable base from which to create audience-based reasons and to craft an appropriate tone and structure. The next sections show how you can adjust your arguing strategy depending on whether you imagine your audience as supportive, neutral, or hostile.

Appealing to a Supportive Audience: One-sided Argument

7.3 To use one-sided argument to appeal to supportive audiences

One-sided arguments commonly occur when an issue isn't highly contested and the writer's aim is merely to put forth a new or different point of view. When an issue is contested, however, one-sided arguments are used mainly to stir the passions of supporters—to convert belief into action by inspiring a party member to contribute to a senator's campaign or a bored office worker to sign up for a change-your-life weekend seminar.

Typically, appeals to a supportive audience are structured as one-sided arguments that either ignore opposing views or reduce them to "enemy" stereotypes. Filled with motivational language, these arguments list the benefits that will ensue from your donations to the cause and the horrors just around the corner if the other side wins. One of the authors of this text received a fund-raising letter from an environmental lobbying group declaring, "It's crunch time for the polluters and their pals on Capitol Hill." The "corporate polluters" and "anti-environment politicians," the letter continues, have "stepped up efforts to roll back our environmental protections—relying on large campaign contributions, slick PR firms and well-heeled lobbyists to get the job done before November's election." This letter makes the reader feel part of an in-group of good guys fighting big business "polluters." Nothing in the letter examines environmental issues from a business perspective or attempts to examine alternative views fairly. Because the intended audience already believes in the cause, nothing in the letter invites readers to consider the issues more complexly. Rather, the goal is to solidify support, increase the fervor of belief, and inspire action. Most appeal arguments make it easy to act, ending with a toll-free phone number to call, a Web site to visit, a tear-out postcard to send in, or a congressperson's address to write to.

Appealing to a Neutral or Undecided Audience: Classical Argument

7.4 To use classical argument to appeal to neutral or undecided audiences, using refutation and concession

The in-group appeals that motivate an already supportive audience can repel a neutral or undecided audience. Because undecided audiences are like jurors weighing all sides of an issue, they distrust one-sided arguments that caricature other views. Generally the best strategy for appealing to undecided audiences is the classical argument described in Chapter 3 (pages 44–46).

What characterizes the classical argument is the writer's willingness to summarize opposing views fairly and to respond to them openly—either by trying to refute them or by conceding to their strengths and then shifting to a different field of values. Let's look at these strategies in more depth.

Summarizing Opposing Views

The first step toward responding to opposing views in a classical argument is to summarize them fairly. Follow the *principle of charity,* which obliges you to avoid loaded, biased, or "straw man" summaries that oversimplify or distort opposing arguments, making them easy to knock over.

Consider the difference between an unfair and a fair summary of an argument. In the following example, a supporter of genetically engineered foods intends to refute the argument of organic food advocate Lisa Turner, who opposes all forms of biotechnology.

Unfair Summary of Turner's Argument

In a biased article lacking scientific understanding of biotechnology, natural foods huckster Lisa Turner parrots the health food industry's party line that genetically altered crops are Frankenstein's monsters run amok. She ignorantly claims that consumption of biotech foods will lead to worldwide destruction, disease, and death—ignoring the wealth of scientific literature showing that genetically modified foods are safe. Her misinformed attacks are scare tactics aimed at selling consumers on overpriced "health food" products to be purchased at boutique organic food stores.

Fair Summary of Turner's Argument

In an article appearing in a nutrition magazine, health food advocate Lisa Turner warns readers that much of our food today is genetically modified using gene-level techniques that differ completely from ordinary crossbreeding. She argues that the potential, unforeseen, harmful consequences of genetic engineering offset the possible benefits of increasing the food supply, reducing the use of pesticides, and boosting the nutritional value of foods. Turner asserts that genetic engineering is imprecise, untested, unpredictable, irreversible, and also uncontrollable because of animals, insects, and winds.

In the unfair summary, the writer distorts and oversimplifies Turner's argument, creating a straw man argument that is easy to knock over because it doesn't make the opponent's best case. In contrast, a fair summary follows the "principle of charity," allowing the strength of the opposing view to come through clearly.

Refuting Opposing Views

Once you have summarized an opposing view, you can either refute it or concede to its strengths. In refuting an opposing view, you attempt to convince readers that its argument is logically flawed, inadequately supported, or based on erroneous assumptions or wrong values. In refuting an argument, you can rebut (1) the writer's stated reason and grounds, (2) the writer's warrant and backing, or (3) both. Put in less specialized language, you can rebut a writer's reasons and evidence or the writer's underlying assumptions. Suppose, for example, that you wanted to refute this argument:

> Students should limit the number of internships they take because internships are time-consuming.

We can clarify the structure of this argument by showing it in Toulmin terms:

> One way to refute this argument is to rebut the stated reason that internships are time-consuming. Your rebuttal might go something like this:

> I disagree that internships are time-consuming. In fact, organizations and businesses are usually very upfront, realistic, and flexible in the weekly hours that they ask of students. The examples that you cite of overly demanding internships are exceptions. Furthermore, these internships have since been retailored to students' schedules. [The writer could then provide examples of realistic, limited-time internships.]

Or you could concede that internships are time-consuming but rebut the argument's warrant that using time in these apprentice situations is bad for students:

> I agree that internships take sizable chunks of students' time, but investment in real-world work environments is a worthwhile use of students' time. Through this investment, students clarify their professional goals, log work experience, and gain references. Without interning in these work environments, students would miss important career preparation.

Let's now illustrate these strategies in a more complex situation. Consider the controversy inspired by a *New York Times Magazine* article entitled "Recycling Is Garbage." Its author, John Tierney, argued that recycling is not environmentally sound and that it is cheaper to bury garbage in a landfill than to recycle it. In criticizing recycling, Tierney argued that recycling wastes money; he provided evidence that "every time a sanitation department crew picks up a load of bottles and cans from the curb, New York City loses money."

A number of environmentalists responded angrily to Tierney's argument, challenging either his reason, his warrant, or both. Those refuting the reason offered counterevidence showing that recycling isn't as expensive as Tierney claimed. Those refuting the warrant said that even if the costs of recycling are higher than burying wastes in a landfill, recycling still benefits the environment by reducing the amount of virgin materials taken from nature. These critics, in effect, offered a new warrant: Conserving the world's resources is an important goal of garbage disposal.

Strategies for Rebutting Evidence

Whether you are rebutting an argument's reasons or its warrant, you will frequently need to question a writer's use of evidence. Here are some strategies you can use:

- *Deny the truth of the data.* Arguers can disagree about the facts of a case. If you have reasons to doubt a writer's facts, call them into question.

- *Cite counterexamples and countertestimony.* You often can rebut an argument based on examples or testimony by citing counterexamples or countertestimony, which deny the conclusiveness of the original data.
- *Cast doubt on the representativeness or <u>sufficiency of examples.</u>* Examples are powerful only if the audience feels that they are representative and sufficient. Many environmentalists complained that John Tierney's attack on recycling was based too largely on data from New York City and that it didn't accurately take into account the more positive experiences of other cities and states. When data from outside New York City were examined, the cost-effectiveness and positive environmental impact of recycling seemed more apparent.
- *Cast doubt on the relevance or recency of examples, statistics, or testimony.* The best evidence is up-to-date. In a rapidly changing universe, data even a few years out-of-date are often ineffective. For example, as the demand for recycled goods increases, the cost of recycling will be reduced. Out-of-date statistics will skew any argument about the cost of recycling.
- *Question the credibility of an authority.* If an opposing argument is based on testimony, you can undermine its persuasiveness if you show that the person cited lacks up-to-date or relevant expertise in the field.
- *Question the accuracy or context of quotations.* Evidence based on testimony is frequently distorted by being either misquoted or taken out of context. Often scientists will qualify their findings heavily, but these qualifications will be omitted by the popular media. You can thus attack the use of a quotation by putting it in its original context or by restoring the qualifications in its original source.
- *Question the way statistical data were produced or interpreted.* Chapter 5 provides fuller treatment of how to question statistics. In general, you can rebut statistical evidence by calling into account how the data were gathered, treated mathematically, or interpreted. It can make a big difference, for example, whether you cite raw numbers or percentages, or whether you choose large or small increments for the axes of graphs.

Conceding to Opposing Views

In writing a classical argument, a writer must sometimes concede to an opposing argument rather than refute it. Sometimes you encounter portions of an argument that you simply can't refute. For example, suppose that you are a libertarian who supports the legalization of hard drugs such as cocaine and heroin. Adversaries argue that legalizing hard drugs will increase the number of drug users and addicts. You might dispute the size of their numbers, but you reluctantly agree that they are right. Your strategy in this case is not to refute the opposing argument but to concede to it by admitting that legalization of hard drugs will promote heroin and cocaine addiction. Having made that concession, your task is then to show that the benefits of drug legalization still outweigh the costs you've just conceded.

As this example shows, the strategy of a concession argument is to switch from the field of values employed by the writer you disagree with to a different field of values more favorable to your position. You don't try to refute the writer's stated reason and grounds (by arguing that legalization will *not* lead to increased drug usage and addiction) or his warrant (by arguing that increased drug use and addiction is not a problem). Rather, you shift the argument to a new field of values by introducing a new warrant, one that you think your audience can share (that the benefits of legalization—eliminating the black market and ending the crime and violence associated with procurement of drugs—outweigh the costs of increased addiction). To the extent that opponents of legalization share your desire to stop drug-related crime, shifting to this new field of values is a good strategy. Although it may seem that you weaken your own position by conceding to an opposing argument, you may actually strengthen it by increasing your credibility and gaining your audience's goodwill. Moreover, conceding to one part of an opposing argument doesn't mean that you won't refute other parts of that argument.

Example of a Student Essay Using Refutation Strategy

The following student essay illustrates how a classical argument appealing to a neutral, undecided, or even mildly resistant audience engages with alternative views. Note the use of both concession and rebuttal strategies.

Bringing Dignity to Workers: Make the Minimum Wage a Living Wage

TRUDIE MAKENS (STUDENT)

Having worked as a busser in a pizza restaurant, a part time barista, and a server at a dumpling cafe I have had a number of minimum wage jobs. My coworkers have ranged from students like myself to single parents and primary providers for their families. As a student, I have always had my parents as a safety net protecting me from financial hardship. However, my coworkers whose only income is their minimum wage endured financial hardships daily. I witnessed one of my coworkers, Maria, lose her home trying to balance supporting her two children and paying her rent. At work, Maria would describe her anxiety as she bounced from relative to relative, straining her family relations and image of herself as an able provider. Without a living wage or the government's providing social insurance programs to ensure financial security for all citizens, families like Maria's are locked into poverty. Raising the federal minimum wage to a livable standard is an important and necessary step to eradicate poverty and ensure dignified living for individuals and families.

Yet some argue that a higher federal minimum wage will do more harm than good. Michael Saltsman, the research director of the employment policy institute, elaborates the pro-business objections to a minimum wage in several op-ed pieces published in national print or online newspapers. Saltsman primarily makes three arguments against raising the minimum wage. Each of them, I contend, is weak or flawed.

First, Saltsman warns that raising the minimum wage will force businesses to cut jobs. In order to maintain profit and to keep prices low, Saltsman argues, businesses will pay for a higher wage by slashing the number of workers. Worse, businesses may cut entire departments in favor of automation such as having fast-food customers order their meals from computer touch screens. Saltsman's argument, however, depends on older studies that, according to university of California economist Michael Reich, are "fundamentally flawed" (Maclay). In a study published in 2010, Reich and his coauthors find that these earlier studies fail to account for all the critical variables besides wages that influence employment levels. By comparing employment levels between states with higher versus lower minimum-wage levels, Reich and his colleagues provide empirical evidence that raising the minimum wage produces no "adverse employment effects" (954).

Saltsman's second objection to a higher minimum wage is that it targets the wrong people and thus won't reduce overall poverty levels. According to Saltsman, a majority of people living in poverty are unemployed while a majority of minimum-wage workers are from households above the poverty line. Although Saltsman may be correct that a higher minimum wage won't help a jobless person, he ignores the benefits of a living wage to the working poor who would be lifted out of poverty. Moreover, a higher minimum wage might itself stimulate jobs because minimum-wage workers with more money in their pockets are apt to spend it, increasing demand for goods.

5   Finally Saltsman argues that the minimum wage is less effective at reducing poverty than the earned income tax credit, which boosts the income of low-wage workers while not giving any income boost to workers who are already above the poverty level. However, the earned income tax credit, like the minimum wage, does nothing for the jobless poor. Moreover, the earned income tax credit puts the burden of poverty relief on taxpayers rather than employers and corporate shareholders, doing little to shift the economy in an equitable direction. We need both an increased minimum wage and the Earned Income Tax Credit.

It seems clear that to combat poverty, the United States needs a many-pronged effort with a hike in the minimum wage being only one of the prongs. Although a higher minimum wage will not by itself eliminate poverty, it will certainly help. It needs to be combined with investments in infrastructure to create jobs, with affordable higher education, with better job training, and with other safety-net systems such as those in place in Europe to give dignity to all citizens. Rather than our government and market system prioritizing corporations and profit, the rights and dignity of workers should be held foremost important. Raising the minimum wage to a living wage will help change the structure of a market system that often exploits workers.

Works Cited

Maclay, Kathleen. "Minimum Wage Hikes Don't Eliminate Jobs, Study Finds." *UC Berkeley News Center,* 1 Dec. 2010, news.berkeley.edu/2010/12/01/minimumwagejobs.

Reich, Michael, et al. "Minimum Wage Effects across State Borders: Estimates Using Contiguous Counties." *Review of Economics and Statistics,* vol. 92, no. 4, 2010, pp. 945-64.

Saltsman, Michael. "The Wrong Way to Reduce Poverty." *USA Today,* 20 Sept. 2013, www.usatoday.com/story/opinion/2013/09/20/minimum-wages-poverty-column/2839003.

---. "To Help the Poor, Move Beyond 'Minimum' Gestures." *The Huffington Post,* 26 Apr. 2013, updated 26 June 2013, www.huffingtonpost.com/michael-saltsman/earned-income-tax-credit-minimum-wage_b_3165459.html.

■ ■ ■   **FOR WRITING AND CLASS DISCUSSION** **Refutation Strategies**

Individually or in groups, examine Trudi Makens' classical argument "Bringing Dignity to Workers: Making the Minimum Wage a Living Wage." Annotate the parts of this argument (the thesis claim, the reasons, the use of evidence). Particularly note the rebuttal strategies that Trudi employs—where she summarizes and rebuts opposing views. Work out an answer to this question: How persuasive is this argument in its acknowledgment of and response to different perspectives on the higher wage issue?   ■ ■ ■

Appealing to a Resistant Audience: Dialogic Argument

7.5 To use dialogic, delayed-thesis argument to appeal to resistant audiences

Whereas classical argument is effective for neutral or undecided audiences, it is often less effective for strongly resistant audiences who hold values, assumptions, or beliefs widely different from the writer's. They are often unswayed by classical argument, which attacks their worldview too directly. Writers, too, may recognize that progress toward communication on some values-laden issues may require them to take a more open, problem-solving approach. On issues such as abortion, gun control, gay rights, or the role of religion in the public sphere, the distance between a writer and a resistant audience can be so great that persuasion seems impossible. In these cases the writer's goal may be simply to open dialogue by seeking common ground—that is, by finding places where the writer and audience agree. For example, pro-choice and pro-life advocates may never agree on a woman's right to an abortion, but they may share common ground in wanting to reduce teenage pregnancy. There is room, in other words, for conversation, if not for agreement.

Because of these differences in basic beliefs and values, the goal of dialogic argument is seldom to convert resistant readers to the writer's position. The best a writer can hope for is to reduce somewhat the level of resistance, perhaps by increasing the reader's willingness to listen as preparation for future dialogue. In this section and the next, we introduce you to two strategies for reducing the resistance of hostile audiences—delayed-thesis argument and Rogerian communication.

Creating a Dialogic Argument with a Delayed Thesis

Unlike a classical argument, a delayed-thesis argument assumes an exploratory approach to a subject. Instead of declaring a claim and reasons early in the argument, you may work your way slowly to your claim, devoting a large part of the argument to examining different views and re-creating your own inquiry into the subject.

Let's look at a delayed-thesis argument, examining its form and emotional impact. (For another delayed-thesis argument, see Ellen Goodman's commentary piece "Womb for Rent" on pages 137–138.) The following op-ed piece by syndicated columnist Ross Douthat appeared in the *New York Times* during the public debates about the building of a Muslim community center near Ground Zero in lower Manhattan. Note how Douthat takes a nonthreatening tone and pulls readers into his exploration of the issue.

Islam in Two Americas

ROSS DOUTHAT

Writer frames the controversy as a conflict of American identities, two divergent ways that the country thinks of itself.

There's an America where it doesn't matter what language you speak, what god you worship or how deep your New World roots run. An America where allegiance to the Constitution trumps ethnic differences, language barriers and religious divides. An America where the newest arrival to our shores is no less American than the ever-so-great granddaughter of the Pilgrims.

But there's another America as well, one that understands itself as a distinctive culture, rather than just a set of political propositions. This America speaks English, not Spanish or Chinese or Arabic. It looks back to a particular religious heritage: Protestantism originally, and then a Judeo-Christian consensus that accommodated Jews and Catholics as well.

Writer establishes problem and its timeliness but doesn't indicate stand.

Writer explores both perspectives: inclusive constitutional America, which defends the right of all religious groups to worship as they please, and the melting pot America, which emphasizes its Judeo-Christian heritage.

These two understandings of America, one constitutional and one cultural, have been in tension throughout our history. They're in tension in the controversy over the Islamic mosque and cultural center scheduled to go up two blocks from ground zero.

The first America views the project as the consummate expression of our nation's high ideals. "This is America," President Barack Obama intoned last week, "and our commitment to religious freedom must be unshakeable." The construction of the mosque, Mayor Michael Bloomberg told New Yorkers, is as important a test of the principle of religious freedom "as we may see in our lifetimes."

5   The second America begs to differ. It sees the project as an affront to the memory of 9/11, and a sign of disrespect for the values of a country where Islam has only recently become part of the public consciousness. And beneath these concerns lurks the darker suspicion that Islam in any form may be incompatible with the American way of life.

Both understandings of this country have wisdom to offer, and both have been necessary to the American experiment's success. During the great waves of 19th-century immigration, the insistence that new arrivals adapt to Anglo-Saxon culture was crucial to their swift assimilation.

Writer keeps the problem open as he examines how these two identities functioned in American history.

The same was true in religion. The steady pressure to conform to American norms eventually persuaded the Mormons to abandon polygamy, smoothing their assimilation into the American mainstream. Nativist concerns about Catholicism's illiberal tendencies inspired American Catholics to prod their church toward a recognition of the virtues of democracy, making it possible for generations of immigrants to feel unambiguously Catholic and American.

So it is today with Islam. The first America is correct to insist on Muslims' absolute right to build and worship where they wish. But the second America is right to press for something more from Muslim Americans—particularly from figures like Feisal Abdul Rauf, the imam behind the mosque—than simple protestations of good faith.

Writer applies this analysis to Islam and begins foreshadowing his thesis.

Too often, American Muslim institutions have turned out to be entangled with ideas and groups that most Americans rightly consider beyond the pale. Too often, American Muslim leaders strike ambiguous notes when asked to disassociate themselves completely from illiberal causes.

Writer reveals his thesis: American Muslims would best signal their dissociation from Islamic terrorist groups and their respect for melting pot America by not building the mosque close to Ground Zero.

10   For Muslim Americans to integrate fully into our national life, they'll need leaders who don't describe America as "an accessory to the crime" of 9/11 (as Rauf did shortly after the 2001 attacks), or duck questions about whether groups like Hamas count as terrorist organizations (as Rauf did in June). They'll need leaders whose antennas are sensitive enough to recognize that the quest for inter-religious dialogue is ill served by throwing up a high-profile mosque two blocks from the site of a mass murder committed in the name of Islam.

They'll need leaders, in other words, who understand that while the ideals of the first America protect the *e pluribus*, it's the demands the second America makes of new arrivals that help create the *unum*.

In this delayed-thesis argument, conservative Ross Douthat writes to liberal *New York Times* readers who are apt to support the Muslim project. His strategy is to acknowledge the complexity of the issue, admit the legitimacy of different opposing views, and only toward the end of the argument state his own position. If Douthat had chosen to write a classical argument, he would have declared his position in the first paragraph, perhaps with a thesis statement like this:

Muslim Americans should not build their community center near Ground Zero because doing so represents disrespect for America's core cultural identity and insensitivity to Americans' national pain caused by Islamic terrorists.

With this thesis, readers would have no initial doubt where Douthat stands. His in-your-face thesis would activate the emotional objections of readers who support the Islamic community center and might prevent them from even reading the piece. In contrast, both liberal and conservative readers can get drawn into the building momentum of Douthat's delayed-thesis version and appreciate its subtlety and surprise.

Writing a Delayed-Thesis Argument

Clearly, where you place your claim can affect your argument's impact on its audience. We should note, however, that a delayed-thesis argument is not simply a classical argument turned upside down. Instead it promotes dialogue with the audience rather than compelling readers to accept the writer's views. It strives to enrich and complicate the discussion as much as present a stand on the issue. It entails some risk to the writer because it leaves space only at the end of the argument for developing the writer's claim. However, it may lead the writer and readers to a deeper understanding of an issue, provide clarification, and promote further discussion. Although there is no set form, the organization plan below shows characteristic elements often found in delayed-thesis arguments.

Organization Plan for a Delayed-Thesis Argument

Introduction
- Establish the problem under discussion and often the occasion that makes the issue timely (*kairos*).
- Engage the audience in the problem.

Dialogic Discussion
- Explore the problem from multiple perspectives, showing the validity of different views.
- Invite the audience to join with you in considering different perspectives.
- Show how you are wrestling with the problem.
- For a good portion of the argument, keep the problem open, building some suspense.

Delayed Thesis and Support
- Present your thesis-claim toward the end of the argument.
- Support the thesis with several reasons and a brief discussion that may build on points presented earlier.

Conclusion
- Leave the audience thinking about the problem and your position.

A More Open-Ended Approach:
Rogerian Communication

7.6 To use Rogerian communication to open up new channels of under-standing between you and an opposing audience

We now turn to a more complex kind of dialogic method: *Rogerian communication*. We use the term "communication" rather than "argument" because, as we will explain in more detail shortly, this strategy focuses on mutual listening and growth more than on persuasion. All dialogic arguments emphasize problem solving, collaborative thinking, and negotiation with a resistant audience. But Rogerian communication, besides delaying its thesis, works to change the writer as well as the reader. Rogerian communication is named after psychotherapist Carl Rogers, who developed a communication strategy for helping people resolve differences.* The Rogerian strategy emphasizes "empathic listening," which Rogers defined as the ability to see an issue sympathetically from another person's perspective or "frame of reference." He trained people to withhold judgment of another person's ideas until they had walked in that person's shoes. What Carl Rogers understood is that traditional methods of argumentation are threatening. Because Rogerian communication stresses the psychological as well as the logical dimensions of argument, it is particularly effective when dealing with emotion-laden issues.

With Rogerian communication, the writer tries to reduce the sense of difference between writer and reader by releasing her tight hold on her own views. Particularly, she tries to show that *both writer and resistant audience share many basic values.* This search for common ground often has the psychological effect of enlarging, complicating, or deepening the writer's own worldview. By acknowledging that she has empathy for the audience's views, the writer makes it easier for the audience to listen to her views. Ideally, this mutual listening leads to a compromise or synthesis or, at the least, better understanding and more open channels of communication.

The art of listening leads to another essential feature of Rogerian communication—the ability to point out areas of agreement between the writer's and reader's positions. Suppose, for example, that you support rapid development of alternative energy and oppose offshore or wilderness oil exploration. If you are writing to readers who want to maximize oil exploration, you can reduce tension and establish conditions for problem solving if you point out areas of agreement and shared value with your audience. You might begin by sympathetically summarizing your readers' pro-oil argument and then point out areas of agreement. You might say, for example, that you also value U.S. energy independence from foreign oil, that you appreciate recent advances in safe drilling technology, and that you agree that we can't dispense with our oil needs overnight. Your effort to understand your audience's views helps build a bridge that will encourage dialogue and make it more likely that your audience will listen when you offer your perspective.

---

*See Carl Rogers's essay "Communication: Its Blocking and Its Facilitation" in *On Becoming a Person* (Boston: Houghton Mifflin, 1961), 329–37. For a fuller discussion of Rogerian argument, see Richard Young, Alton Becker, and Kenneth Pike, *Rhetoric: Discovery and Change* (New York: Harcourt Brace, 1972).

Rogers's communication strategies have been the subject of intense debate among scholars. On the one hand, some rhetoricians don't like the term "Rogerian *argument*," preferring instead "Rogerian *rhetoric*" or "Rogerian *communication*." These theorists say that Rogerian listening isn't a form of argument or persuasion at all. Rather, its goal is increased mutual understanding and enlarged perspectives on reality for both writer and audience. According to rhetorician Nathaniel Teich, Rogerian rhetoric seeks to foster discovery of others' perspectives and revision of both parties' worldviews.*

In contrast to this perspective, other scholars view Rogerian argument as a means of manipulating resistant audiences. According to this view, the best way to persuade a hostile audience is to adopt a nonthreatening tone and approach, treat the opponent's views sympathetically, and then lure the opponent into accepting your views. The problem with this perspective is that it is purely instrumental and reduces Rogerian argument to a technique, a clever means to an end.

Our view of Rogerian communication forges a middle path between these two perspectives. Throughout this text, we emphasize that argument includes inquiry. (See particularly Chapters 1 and 2.) Here we treat Rogerian communication as dialogic inquiry in which the writer negotiates with the audience in a mutual search for provisional solutions.

Rogerian Communication as Growth for the Writer

One of the key features of Rogerian communication is the open relationship it establishes between the writer and the subject; it recasts argument as a process of growth for the writer. Because Rogerian communication asks the writer to listen to the opponent's views—views that the writer may find uncomfortable or threatening—it promotes inquiry and self-reflection, a more tentative and exploratory approach to the subject than the writer takes in classical argument or delayed-thesis argument. Rogerian communication urges writers to play Peter Elbow's "believing game," where the writer must try "to get inside the head of someone" who holds unwelcome ideas.** (See our discussion of the believing and doubting game in Chapter 2, pages 17–18). This "dwelling" in unappealing ideas often compels writers to articulate their own values and to achieve a new understanding of them. Extending Elbow's strategy and emphasizing the connection between values and identity, rhetorician James Baumlin argues that Rogerian rhetoric creates "a realm of plural selves or identities" in the process of taking on "another's beliefs and world-view" through role-playing.† Rogerian communication

---

*For one of the most thorough analyses of Carl Rogers's influence on rhetoric and composition, see Nathaniel Teich's scholarly anthology *Rogerian Perspectives: Collaborative Rhetoric for Oral and Written Communication* (Norwood, NJ: Ablex Publishing Corporation, 1992).

**For more suggestions on how to encourage empathic listening, see Elbow's "Bringing the Rhetoric of Assent and the Believing Game Together—and into the Classroom" *College English* (67.4, March 2005), 389.

†For more discussion of the relationship between role-playing, understanding, and identity, see James S. Baumlin's "Persuasion, Rogerian Rhetoric, and Imaginative Play" *Rhetoric Society Quarterly* (17.1, Winter 1987), 36.

Organization Plan for Rogerian Communication

Introduction	• Address the audience and identify the problem that you and your audience want to solve. • Possibly, show the timeliness (*kairos*) of the problem. • Try to establish a friendly or cordial relationship with the audience. • Possibly include information that shows your familiarity with the audience.
Summary of the Audience's Views	• Summarize the audience's views in a fair and neutral way that the audience would accept. • Show that you understand the audience's position. • Also show an understanding of, and respect for, the audience's values and beliefs; the goal of this "saying back" (Rogers's term) is to summarize these views in a way that will be entirely acceptable to the audience.
Common Ground	• Identify common ground you share with your audience. • Demonstrate your growth through empathic consideration of views that you would otherwise find threatening or unwelcome. • Show understanding of the audience's views by "indwelling" with them and perhaps by extending them to other situations through new examples. • Show how your views have been enlarged by empathic listening to the audience's ideas.
Contribution of New Points to the Negotiation	• Respectfully propose your own way of looking at this issue. • Through a respectful and inquiring tone, encourage the audience to listen and work with you to solve the problem.
Conclusion	• Possibly propose a synthesis of the two positions, discuss how both parties gain from an enlarged vision, or invite the audience to ongoing negotiation.

thus promotes a writer's self-examination and exploration of multiple perspectives on a problem. This double process of exploration and reflection can in turn lead to a change of mind or at least a deeper understanding of a problem.

Rogerian Communication as Collaborative Negotiation

A second key feature of Rogerian communication is its altered argumentative purpose and attitude toward the audience. In the absence of the possibility of persuading a resistant audience to accept the writer's views, the writer seeks different goals through a relationship with the audience. These goals include reducing antagonism toward those with different beliefs, initiating small steps in understanding, cultivating mutual respect, and encouraging further problem solving—in short, nurturing conditions for future exchanges. The focus shifts from persuasion toward collaborative negotiation. Thus Rogerian communication is appropriate whenever writers are seeking to open up communication with a resistant audience and are themselves willing to work toward a synthesis of views.

Writing Rogerian Communication

A major thrust of Rogerian communication is building bridges between writer and audience. Because Rogers's principles originated as a communication strategy between two parties in conversation, Rogerian communication most commonly takes the form of a letter or an open letter directed to a specific person or group. Rogerian communication will most likely include the features shown in the chart on page 114, although not necessarily in any set form.

In the following example of a Rogerian letter, student writer Colleen Fontana responds to an article written by Robert A. Levy, a senior fellow for constitutional studies at the Cato Institute, a libertarian think tank. In this open letter, Colleen conducts a collaborative discussion directed toward solving the problem of gun violence.* Annotations in the margins indicate how Colleen is practicing Rogerian principles.

---

*We are indebted to Doug Brent for his insight that Rogerian arguments can often be addressed to the author of an article that a reader finds disturbing. See "Rogerian Rhetoric: Ethical Growth Through Alternative Forms of Argumentation" in Barbara Emmel, Paula Resch, and Deborah Tenney (eds.), *Argument Revisited; Argument Redefined* (Thousand Oaks, CA: Sage, 1996), 81.

An Open Letter to Robert Levy in Response to His Article "They Never Learn"

COLLEEN FONTANA (STUDENT)

Dear Robert Levy,

Writer addresses the audience.

My recent interest in preventing gun violence led me to find your article "They Never Learn" in *The American Spectator* about the mass shooting at Virginia Tech in 2007. I was struck by the similarities between that incident and the recent shooting in Tucson, Arizona, where a young man gunned down U.S. Representative Gabrielle Giffords and nineteen others in a supermarket parking lot. Although your article came several years before this Arizona incident, we can see that gun violence remains an enduring issue. I have long struggled with the question of how we can reduce gun-related violence without detracting from an individual's right to own a gun. Your article shed new light on this question for me.

Writer identifies the problem, shows its current timeliness (kairos), and establishes a cordial relationship with the audience.

Your article stresses the need for something different from our nation's current gun policies. You assert that the solution lies, not in stricter gun control policies, but rather in "liberalized laws." According to you, Mr. Levy, it was primarily the existence of anti-gun laws on the Virginia Tech. campus that prevented an armed citizen from saving the victims of the 2007 shooting. You comment that "gun control does not work. It just prevents weaker people from defending themselves against stronger predators." Your article gives detailed examples of studies that have substantiated that stricter gun laws have not resulted in lower murder rates. You also cite evidence that fewer crimes are likely to happen if the victim brandishes a gun, even if he or she never fires it. According to your article, stricter gun laws are doing nothing to help society, and your solution lies in relaxed laws, allowing more responsible citizens to carry concealed weapons.

Summary: In neutral, fair terms, the writer summarizes the audience's previous argument, the article to which she is responding.

Living currently on a college campus myself, I identify immediately with your concern for preventing school shootings. I appreciate that you are concerned with the safety of the students and the public, and I agree that there exists a need for greater safety on school campuses. I also agree that current gun laws are not effective as is shown by the number of gun-related deaths that happen annually. Even though such laws exist, they are not likely to stop "crazed fanatics undeterred by laws of murder," as you say, from committing certain crimes. I particularly agree with you when you discuss the right of self-defense. I struggle with laws that forbid carrying a gun because I believe in the right of self-defense. As you mentioned in your article, instances do occur in

Common ground: Writer identifies common values that she shares with her audience; she demonstrates empathic listening; she imagines instances where the audience's values make the most sense.

which civilians carrying guns have the ability to save themselves and others. Although I have not experienced this situation personally, I have read of brave acts of self-defense and intervention. For example, my research turned up an article by John Pierce on MonachusLex.com, "It Takes a Gun to Stop a Gunman." In this article Pierce describes an occurrence in Richmond, Virginia, in July of 2009 where a store owner and several customers were saved from an armed robber by a civilian in the store who happened to be carrying a firearm. Granted that Pierce is a long-time gun rights advocate and an NRA certified instructor, the points he brought up were nevertheless striking. If that civilian hadn't been carrying a gun in that store on that day, then everyone in the store might have been killed by the robber. This realization resonates with me. I imagine myself in that store, and I know I would have been quite grateful that he was carrying a weapon that saved my life. Reading this story has forced me to think of the responsibility many gun-owning citizens must feel—a responsibility to protect not only themselves but those around them as well. A similar event happened recently in New York where a person attempting to rob a jewelry shop was shot by the owner in an act of self-defense. His neighbors regard him as a hero (Kilgannon).

Writer moves respect-fully to presenting her own questions and differing perspectives on the problem. Note her tone of negotiation and her willingness to engage in further discussion.

While I agree with you that self-defense is an important right and that armed citizens can sometimes prevent the death of innocent people, I wonder whether the possibility of allowing more guns in public through liberalized gun laws is the best solution. Is there a chance more guns in the hands of more people would foster a more danger-prone climate both from accidents and from sudden fits of rage? I was surprised to learn in a recent *New York Times* article by Charles M. Blow that for every ten people in America there are nine guns. Among major nations, according to a U.N. study, we have both the highest ratio of guns to people and the highest incidence of violence. If liberalizing gun ownership will lead to even more guns, then my concern is that there is a higher chance of children finding a loaded gun in a parent's bed stand or of deaths caused by gang warfare or from momentary rage in an escalating fight between neighbors. Such danger could also exist on school campuses if guns were allowed. On a campus where drinking nurtures the party scene, I worry that rowdy people waving a gun perhaps as a joke might turn a party into a tragedy. Do you have any ideas, Mr. Levy, for reducing gun accidents or irresponsible use of firearms if they are widely available?

Writer expresses a second concern, one that Levy did not mention: assault weapons.

5   I found your point about owning a firearm for self-defense really thought provoking. But even if Virginia Tech had allowed guns on campus, what are the odds that an armed student or teacher would be at the right place at the right time with an actual chance of shooting the gunman? Only in the movies are good guys and heroes *always* on

the spot and capable of taking the right action to protect potential victims. Although I can really see your point about using handguns for self-defense, I don't think self-defense can be used as a justification for assault weapons or automatic weapons with large clips. If guns were freely allowed on campuses, perhaps massacres such as Virginia Tech. might occur more often. Or is there a way to allow people to carry concealed handguns on campus but still to forbid rifles, shotguns, or other weapons more useful for massacres than for self-defense?

Writer concludes her letter with a reiteration of the mutual concerns she shares with her audience; she acknowledges how her perspectives have been widened by Levy's views; she seeks to keep the channel of communication open and expresses interest in further problem solving.

After reading your article I have more understanding of the arguments in favor of guns, and I continue to ponder the ethical and practical issues of gun control versus the right to self-defense. You have underscored for me the importance of our continuing to seek means of preventing these terrible massacres from happening in our nation's schools. You have also opened my eyes to the fact that no amount of enforcement of gun laws can deter determined people from using guns to harm others. I am not sure, however, that your proposal to eliminate gun control laws is the best solution, and I am hoping that you might be willing to consider some of my reasons for fearing guns, especially assault weapons and automatic weapons that can be fired like machine guns. Perhaps we could both agree that pursuing responsible gun ownership is a step in the right direction so that we reduce the number of accidents, keep guns away from children, and reduce access to guns capable of unleashing mass murder. I am hopeful that with our common concern over the current ineffectiveness of gun laws and the desire for safety in our schools, we can find a reasonable solution while still preserving the human right of self-defense.

Sincerely,

Colleen Fontana

Works Cited

Blow, Charles M. "Obama's Gun Play." *The New York Times,* 21 Jan. 2011, www.nytimes.com/2011/01/22/opinion/22blow.html?_r=0.

Kilgannon, Cory. "After Shooting, Merchant Is Hero of Arthur Avenue." *The New York Times,* 12 Feb. 2011, www.nytimes.com/2011/02/18/nyregion/18arthur.html.

Levy, Robert A. "They Never Learn." *The American Spectator,* 25 Apr. 2007, spectator.org/articles/45477/they-never-learn.

Pierce, John. "It Takes a Gun to Stop a Gunman." *MonachusLex.com,* 15 July 2009, monachuslex.com/?p=262.

WRITING ASSIGNMENT   A Classical Argument or a Rogerian Letter

Option 1: A Classical Argument Write a classical argument following the explanations in Chapter 3, pages 44–46, using the guidelines for developing such an argument throughout Chapters 3–7. Depending on your instructor's preferences, this argument could focus on a new issue, or it could be a final stage of an argument-in-progress throughout Part Two. This assignment expands the supporting-reasons assignment from Chapter 5 by adding sections that summarize opposing views and respond to them through refutation or concession. For an example of a classical argument, see "The Dangers of Digital Distraction" by Lauren Shinozuka (pages 119–122).

Option 2: A Rogerian Letter Write a Rogerian communication in the form of a letter addressed to a specific person, either someone you know, someone you have heard deliver a speech, or the author of an article that has disturbed you. Follow the suggestions in the chart that explains the elements of a Rogerian letter on page 114 for determining a purpose and structure for your argument. For an example of a Rogerian letter, see Colleen Fontana's "Open Letter to Robert Levy" on pages 116–118. Your instructor may ask you to attach a reflective response in which you describe how your experience of writing this Rogerian letter differed from your experience of writing classical arguments. ∎

Reading

The following essay by student writer Lauren Shinozuka illustrates a classical argument. This essay grew out of Lauren's own wrestling with her immersion in social media. She decided to persuade her peers to see the problem her way with the goal that they will join her in new awareness and new habits.

The Dangers of Digital Distractedness

LAUREN SHINOZUKA (STUDENT)

We are the Net Generation, the Facebook Generation—digital natives. Cultural critics praise us for our digital skills, our facility with multimedia, and our ability to interact electronically with others through collaboration and co-creation. But at what cost? If we are honest, the following anti-social scene is familiar. You are sitting at a table with friends, and then you hear various pings and look up to see every one of your friends with squinted eyes, checking social media apps and text messages, scrolling away on their phones and furiously punching a reply. What kind of togetherness is this? We seem to feel some urgency or need to know what the world wants from us in that moment, prompting us to check our smartphones every six and a half minutes a day. Rather than being skillfully technologically interactive, I argue that our behavior represents dependence, even addiction, that has deep, pervasive consequences.

It harms us by promoting an unproductive habit of multitasking, by dehumanizing our relationships, and by encouraging a distorted self-image.

I can hear my peers immediately rejecting these claims as too extreme and too critical, and I acknowledge that a good case can be made for our digital savvy and the benefits that brings. Armed with smartphones and laptops, we believe we are masters of technology because we can access so much information easily and immediately. Thanks to our cell phones, all of our friends are only a mere click or swipe away for starting a conversation or sending an invitation to meet up. I also have to admit that our digital knowledge gives us on-the-job advantages. At my part-time job at a high-end retail store, I constantly use a mobile point-of-sale system to ring up customers for fast and easy "on-the-spot checkout," receiving compliments for my competence. With my comfort with the company's technology, I can troubleshoot easily and help other employees. Because technology facilitates much of what we do and keeps us plugged into the rest of the world, I recognize that it can be difficult to see the negative aspects of our relationship to digital technology, but it is time for serious self-examination.

In college, we tell ourselves that multitasking with technology helps us use our time wisely, but in actuality we become even less productive. I notice that while I study, I feel the need to stop every five or ten minutes to check my phone, or log on to a Web site and allow myself to get distracted before going back to my task. These momentary distractions eat away at my time; when I sit down to write a paper at 9 P.M. I am often startled to find that it is suddenly 12 A.M. and I have less than a page written. We Millennials think we are so cutting edge with our multitasking, yet we get little done with our time. We submerge ourselves into a technological bubble consisting of laptops and music and cell phones, convinced that by arming ourselves with these tools, we can really do it all. In actuality, as writer John Hamilton explains in his report for National Public Radio, our brains cannot "focus on more than one thing at a time." Hamilton cites MIT neuroscientist Earl Miller who says that our minds are "not paying attention to...two things simultaneously, but switching between them very rapidly"; thus, multitasking in itself is a myth. Furthermore, as we continue to overload our brains with multiple tasks, we also begin to reshape our thought processes. Technology—the Internet in particular—helps us avoid the hard work of concentration and contemplation. In the article "Is Google Making Us Stupid?" nonfiction business and technology writer Nicholas Carr describes this way we take in and distribute information as a "swiftly moving stream of particles." We skim rather than read; we rapidly switch tasks rather than truly multitask. I recognize this superficial way of operating in the world in my own behavior. I often turn to Google for an immediate answer to a question I have: Who's the current Speaker of the House? How many ounces are in a cup? Then I click on the first link I see, and more often than not, I see the little subheading that states, "You've visited this page X times." I realize my mental instincts tell me that it's much easier to Google an answer multiple times rather than just *learn* the information. Because I constantly overindulge in my technology, I have engrained the habits of skimming streams of information, constantly bouncing from one task to another, but never stopping to bask in its depths.

Our obsession with technology and social media not only reshapes the way we think, but also fosters a type of false superficial friendship with people we barely know, dehumanizing the kinds of relationships we have. Since coming to college, I've had hundreds of new Facebook friends and dozens of new followers on Twitter. To be fair, a number of these people are truly my good friends, but most of these "friendships" came from a one-time meeting at a party or a class I had with them during my sophomore year. Although some will insist on the vital role social media plays in keeping them connected to distant family and friends, we need to address more directly the extent and pervasive effects of our more common arbitrary cyber friendships. Last summer, while I taught a program at a local elementary school, I would occasionally post a Facebook status of something funny that happened that day, or a picture of my class. Back home later for a short vacation, I ran into a girl from high school whom I hadn't seen in four years and barely knew then. When we stopped to chat, she asked me all about my summer program, and commented that all my students were so cute! After our chat, I left feeling perturbed and uneasy. Immediately, I thought she was so "creepy," but I realized that ultimately I chose to share my life with the rest of the world. Speaking about these digital relationships, Sherry Turkle, MIT professor and author of *Alone Together: Why We Expect More from Technology and Less from Each Other,* labels our behavior "a Goldilocks effect": "we can't get enough of one another if we can use technology to keep one another at distances we can control: not too close, not too far, just right." That moment when my distant "friend" reached out to me about my summer felt so disturbing because she crossed that Goldilocks line through a personal face-to-face conversation. I am embarrassed to say that I was comfortable only when she was one of the masses; I didn't want to engage in a true interpersonal connection.

5   This lack of intimacy through false relationships leads to the creation of a distorted identity. We begin to form a social identity through our conscious decisions of what we choose to share with the rest of the digital world. We want to post pretty pictures that will garner us a number of "likes," and we want to tweet something witty or profound so others will retweet us. When I began to reevaluate my own social media identity, I found that I consciously try to word my Facebook status in order for people to find it funny, and I'm obsessed with editing my pictures with the right filters to achieve that hipster artist effect. I realized that I was interpreting my own life experiences in such a way that I would seem interesting or entertaining to all of my "friends," as if I were performing for an audience I was trying to please. That image of myself is dishonest: It conveys the person I want people to think I am, not the real me.

We see this willful self-distortion in a growing trend called "catfishing": an Internet phenomenon where one person creates a false online identity to engage in a romantic relationship with another person physically far removed. The "catfisher" uses fake pictures of attractive people and an image of talent to create a different person. Coined by a documentary of the same name, *Catfish,* a reality show spin-off, features these long-distance lovers traveling across the country for a chance to meet who really is on the other side of the screen. Often that person's appearance and even gender and motives are strikingly at odds with the self-portrayal. While it is easy for us to judge negatively these extreme cases of catfishing, Molly McHugh, writer for *Digital Trends*, points out what she calls the "slippery slope of catfishdom." These cases may seem extreme, but to an extent, all of us who embrace social media are indeed "catfish" as well. We succumb to what McHugh calls the "aspirational beast" of social media, bending the truth online to some degree in order to portray the self that we want to be. With our growing reliance on social media and technology, the tendency for our romantic relationships to blend into our digital selves becomes even more prevalent. When we continue to mix this intimate, personal self with the demands and desires of social media, we produce tragic, ill-formed identities that no longer resemble our true selves.

Of course, we may draw a sharp distinction between our own digital dependence and the growing number of young users who are actual technological addicts. (According to Carolyn Gregoire's *Huffington Post* article, there is now an inpatient Internet rehabilitation center designed specifically for true addicts.) However, our own participation in the more wide-spread digital craze remains a serious problem too. Yet by taking the first step of making the unconscious conscious, I believe we can combat the digital damage in our lives. I have begun by taking several steps. I purposefully put my phone across the table so I physically need to get up to check it; I only let myself binge-check all my social media apps just before going to bed rather than ten times a day, and I have stopped trying to take pictures of every pretty meal I consume or sunset I see because I know that those are my own special moments, not some glamorous, envious image I want to project. I have begun to avoid friends who find their phones more interesting than the immediate world around them, and this new company has made it easier to break away from my own addiction. I am trying to rehumanize my friendships, and I am finding solace in deep reading once more without the distractions of cell phone vibrations. I invite members of my generation to join me, so we can be together, no longer alone together.

Works Cited

Carr, Nicholas. "Is Google Making Us Stupid?: What the Internet Is Doing to Our Brains." *The Atlantic,* July-Aug. 2008, www.theatlantic.com/magazine/archive/2008/07/is-google-making-us-stupid/306868.

Gregoire, Carolyn. "Welcome to Internet Rehab." *The Huffington Post,* 25 Sept. 2013, updated 25 Oct. 2013, www.huffingtonpost.com/2013/09/25/this-is-where-people-are-_n_3976240.html.

Hamilton, John. "Think You're Multitasking? Think Again." *National Public Radio,* 2 Oct. 2008, www.npr.org/templates/story/story.php?storyId=95256794.

McHugh, Molly. "It's Catfishing Season! How to Tell Lovers from Liars Online, and More." *Digital Trends,* 23 Aug. 2013, www.digitaltrends.com/web/its-catfishing-season-how-to-tell-lovers-from-liars-online-and-more.

Turkle, Sherry. "The Flight from Conversation." *The New York Times,* 21 Apr. 2012, www.nytimes.com/2012/04/22/opinion/sunday/the-flight-from-conversation.html.

Analyzing Arguments

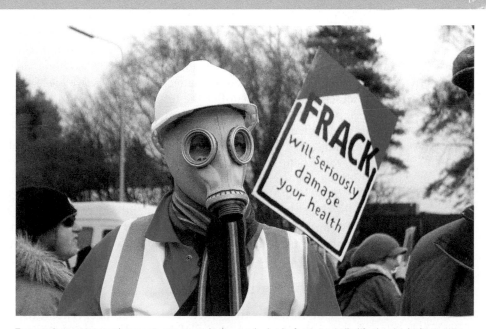

To meet their energy needs, countries are increasingly using hydraulic fracturing (called fracking), which extracts natural gas from deeply buried shale. Burning natural gas is cleaner than burning gasoline, oil, and coal and emits less carbon dioxide. However, each fracking site uses millions of gallons of water, leaves contaminated waste water, and often emits methane. Also, environmentalists fear that fracking may contaminate aquifers. This photo depicts anti-fracking views in a protest near Manchester, England, in January 2014. How does this protestor try to make verbal and visual appeals to *logos* and *pathos* to turn viewers against fracking?

Analyzing Arguments Rhetorically

What you will learn in this chapter:

8.1 To explain what it means to *think rhetorically* about texts
8.2 To conduct a rhetorical analysis of a specific text
8.3 To construct essays that analyze the rhetorical effectiveness of arguments

In Part Two of this book, we explained thinking and writing strategies for composing your own arguments. Now, in Part Three, we show you how to use your new rhetorical knowledge to conduct in-depth analyses of other people's arguments. To analyze an argument rhetorically means to examine closely how it is composed and what makes it an effective or ineffective piece of persuasion. A rhetorical analysis identifies the text under scrutiny, summarizes its main ideas, presents some key points about the text's rhetorical strategies for persuading its audience, and elaborates on these points.

Becoming skilled at analyzing arguments rhetorically will provide multiple payoffs for you. Rhetorical analyses are common assignments in courses in critical thinking and argument. Additionally, thinking rhetorically about texts is crucial for writing the "literature review" section of research assignments across the disciplines and for summarizing and responding to opposing views in your own arguments. This chapter focuses on the rhetorical analysis of written arguments; Chapter 9 equips you to analyze visual arguments.

Thinking Rhetorically about a Text

8.1 To explain what it means to *think rhetorically* about texts

Before we turn directly to rhetorical analysis of specific texts, let's focus on the key word "rhetoric." In popular usage, *rhetoric* often means empty or deceptive language, as in the phrase, "Well, that's just rhetoric." Another related meaning of rhetoric is decorative or artificial language. Most contemporary rhetoricians, however, adopt a larger view of rhetoric articulated by Greek philosopher Aristotle: the art of determining what will be persuasive in every situation. Focusing on this foundational meaning of rhetoric, this chapter will show you how to analyze a writer's motivation, purpose, and rhetorical choices for persuading a targeted audience. This chapter draws primarily on rhetorical concepts with which you are already familiar: audience-based reasons, the STAR criteria for evidence, and the classical appeals of *logos, ethos,* and *pathos.*

Questions for Rhetorical Analysis

Conducting a rhetorical analysis asks you to bring to bear on an argument your knowledge of argument and your repertoire of reading strategies. The questions in the following table can help you examine an argument in depth. Although a rhetorical analysis will not include answers to all these questions, using some of them in your thinking stages can give you a thorough understanding of the argument while helping you generate insights for your own rhetorical analysis essay.

Questions for Rhetorical Analysis

What to Focus On	Questions to Ask	Applying These Questions
The kairotic moment and writer's motivating occasion	■ What motivated the writer to produce this piece? ■ What social, cultural, political, legal, or economic conversations does this argument join?	■ Is the writer responding to a bill pending in Congress, a recent speech by a political leader, or a local event that provoked controversy? ■ Is the writer addressing cultural trends such as the impact of science or technology on values?
Rhetorical context: Writer's purpose and audience	■ What is the writer's purpose? ■ Who is the intended audience? ■ What assumptions, values, or beliefs would readers have to hold to find this argument persuasive? ■ How well does the text suit its particular audience and purpose?	■ Is the writer trying to change readers' views by offering a new interpretation of a phenomenon, calling readers to action, trying to muster votes, or inspiring further investigations? ■ Does the audience share a political or religious orientation with the writer?
Rhetorical context: Writer's identity and angle of vision	■ Who is the writer and what is his or her profession, background, and expertise? ■ How does the writer's personal history, education, gender, ethnicity, age, class, sexual orientation, and political leaning influence the angle of vision? ■ What is emphasized and what is omitted in this text? ■ How much does the writer's angle of vision dominate the text?	■ Is the writer a scholar, researcher, scientist, policymaker, politician, professional journalist, or citizen blogger? ■ Is the writer affiliated with conservative or liberal, religious or lay publications? ■ Is the writer advocating a stance or adopting a more inquiry-based mode? ■ What points of view and pieces of evidence are "not seen" by this writer?

(Continued)

What to Focus On	Questions to Ask	Applying These Questions
Rhetorical context: Genre	▪ What is the argument's original genre? ▪ What is the original medium of publication? How do the genre and its place of publication influence its content, structure, and style?	▪ How popular or scholarly, informal or formal is this genre? ▪ Does the genre allow for in-depth or only sketchy coverage of an issue? (See Chapter 2, pages 19–22, for detailed explanations of genre.)
Logos **of the argument**	▪ What is the argument's claim, either explicitly stated or implied? ▪ What are the main reasons in support of the claim? Are the reasons audience-based? ▪ How effective is the writer's use of evidence? How is the argument supported and developed? ▪ How well has the argument recognized and responded to alternative views?	▪ Is the core of the argument clear and soundly developed? Or do readers have to unearth or reconstruct the argument? ▪ Is the argument one-sided, multisided, or dialogic? ▪ Does the argument depend on assumptions the audience may not share? ▪ What evidence does the writer employ? Does this evidence meet the STAR criteria? (See pages 77–78.)
Ethos **of the argument**	▪ What *ethos* does the writer project? ▪ How does the writer try to seem credible and trustworthy to the intended audience? ▪ How knowledgeable does the writer seem in recognizing opposing or alternative views and how fairly does the writer respond to them?	▪ If you are impressed or won over by this writer, what has earned your respect? ▪ If you are filled with doubts or skepticism, what has caused you to question this writer? ▪ How important is the character of the writer in this argument?
Pathos **of the argument**	▪ How effective is the writer in using audience-based reasons? ▪ How does the writer use concrete language, word choice, narrative, example, and analogies to tap readers' emotions, values, and imaginations?	▪ What examples, connotative language, and uses of narrative or analogy stand out for you in this argument? ▪ Does this argument rely heavily on appeals to *pathos*? Or is this argument more brainy and logical?

What to Focus On	Questions to Ask	Applying These Questions
Writer's style	■ How do the writer's language choices and sentence length and complexity contribute to the impact of the argument? ■ How well does the writer's tone (attitude toward the subject) suit the argument?	■ How readable is this argument? ■ Is the argument formal, scholarly, journalistic, informal, or casual? ■ Is the tone serious, mocking, humorous, exhortational, confessional, urgent, or something else?
Design and visual elements	■ How do design elements—layout, font sizes and styles, and use of color—influence the effect of the argument? (See Chapter 9 for a detailed discussion of these elements.) ■ How do graphics, images, or other visuals contribute to the persuasiveness of the argument?	■ Do design features contribute to the logical or the emotional/imaginative appeals of the argument? ■ How would this argument benefit from visuals and graphics or some different document design?
Overall persuasiveness of the argument	■ What features of this argument contribute most to making it persuasive or not persuasive for its target audience and for you yourself? ■ How would this argument be received by different audiences? ■ What features contribute to the rhetorical complexity of this argument? ■ What is particularly memorable, disturbing, or problematic about this argument? ■ What does this argument contribute to its *kairotic* moment and the argumentative controversy of which it is a part?	■ For example, are appeals to *pathos* legitimate and suitable? Does the quality and quantity of the evidence help to build a strong case or fall short? ■ What specifically would count as a strength for the target audience? ■ If you differ from the target audience, how do you differ and where does the argument derail for you? ■ What gaps, contradictions, or unanswered questions are you left with? ■ How does this argument indicate that it is engaged in a public conversation? How does it "talk" to other arguments you have read on this issue?

Conducting Rhetorical Analysis

8.2 To conduct a rhetorical analysis of a specific text

To illustrate rhetorical analysis in this section and in the student example at the end of the chapter, we will use two articles on reproductive technology—a subject that continues to generate arguments in the public sphere. By *reproductive technology* we mean scientific advances in the treatment of infertility such as egg and sperm donation, artificial insemination, in vitro fertilization, and surrogate motherhood. Our first article, from a decade ago, springs from the early and increasing popularity of these technological options. Our second article—to be used later in our student example—responds to the recent globalization of this technology.

At this point, please read our first article, "Egg Heads" by Kathryn Jean Lopez, and then proceed to the discussion questions that follow. Lopez's article was originally published in the September 1, 1998, issue of the biweekly conservative news commentary magazine *National Review*.

Egg Heads

KATHRYN JEAN LOPEZ

Filling the waiting room to capacity and spilling over into a nearby conference room, a group of young women listen closely and follow the instructions: Complete the forms and return them, with the clipboard, to the receptionist. It's all just as in any medical office. Then they move downstairs, where the doctor briefs them. "Everything will be pretty much normal," she explains. "Women complain of skin irritation in the local area of injection and bloating. You also might be a little emotional. But, basically, it's really bad PMS."

This is not just another medical office. On a steamy night in July, these girls in their twenties are attending an orientation session for potential egg donors at a New Jersey fertility clinic specializing in in-vitro fertilization. Within the walls of IVF New Jersey and at least two hundred other clinics throughout the United States, young women answer the call to give "the gift of life" to infertile couples. Egg donation is a quietly expanding industry, changing the way we look at the family, young women's bodies, and human life itself.

It is not a pleasant way to make money. Unlike sperm donation, which is over in less than an hour, egg donation takes the donor some 56 hours and includes a battery of tests, ultrasound, self-administered injections, and retrieval. Once a donor is accepted into a program, she is given hormones to stimulate the ovaries, changing the number of eggs matured from the usual one per month up to as many as fifty. A doctor then surgically removes the eggs from the donor's ovary and fertilizes them with the designated sperm.

Although most programs require potential donors to undergo a series of medical tests and counseling, there is little indication that most of the young women know what they are getting themselves into. They risk bleeding, infection, and scarring. When too many eggs are matured in one cycle, it can damage the ovaries and leave the donor with weeks of abdominal pain. (At worst, complications may leave her dead.) Longer term, the possibility of early menopause raises the prospect of future regret. There is also some evidence of a connection between the fertility drugs used in the process and ovarian cancer.

5   But it's good money—and getting better. New York's Brooklyn IVF raised its "donor compensation" from $2,500 to $5,000 per cycle earlier this year in order to keep pace with St. Barnabas Medical Center in nearby Livingston, New Jersey. It's a bidding war. "It's obvious why we had to do it," says Susan Lobel, Brooklyn IVF's assistant director. Most New York–area IVF programs have followed suit.

Some infertile couples and independent brokers are offering even more for "reproductive material." The International Fertility Center in Indianapolis, Indiana, for instance, places ads in the *Daily Princetonian* offering Princeton girls as much as $35,000 per cycle. The National Fertility Registry, which, like many egg brokerages, features an on-line catalogue for couples to browse in, advertises $35,000 to $50,000 for Ivy League eggs. While donors are normally paid a flat fee per cycle, there have been reports of higher payments to donors who produce more eggs.

College girls are the perfect donors. Younger eggs are likelier to be healthy, and the girls themselves frequently need money—college girls have long been susceptible to classified ads offering to pay them for acting as guinea pigs in medical research. One 1998 graduate of the University of Colorado set up her own website to market her eggs. She had watched a television show on egg donation and figured it "seemed like a good thing to do"—especially since she had spent her money during the past year to help secure a country-music record deal. "Egg donation would help me with my school and music expenses while helping an infertile couple with a family." Classified ads scattered throughout cyberspace feature similar offers.

The market for "reproductive material" has been developing for a long time. It was twenty years ago this summer that the first test-tube baby, Louise Brown, was born. By 1995, when the latest tally was taken by the Centers for Disease Control, 15 percent of mothers in this country had made use of some form of assisted-reproduction technology in conceiving their children. (More recently, women past menopause have begun to make use of this technology.) In 1991 the American Society for Reproductive Medicine was aware of 63 IVF programs offering egg donation. That number had jumped to 189 by 1995 (the latest year for which numbers are available).

Defenders argue that it's only right that women are "compensated" for the inconvenience of egg donation. Brooklyn IVF's Dr. Lobel argues, "If it is unethical to accept payment for loving your neighbor, then we'll have to stop paying babysitters." As long as donors know the risks, says Glenn McGee of the University of Pennsylvania's Center for Bioethics, this transaction is only "a slightly macabre version of adoption."

10   Not everyone is enthusiastic about the "progress." Egg donation "represents another rather large step into turning procreation into manufacturing," says the University of Chicago's Leon Kass. "It's the dehumanization of procreation." And as in manufacturing, there is quality control. "People don't want to say the word any more, but there is a strong eugenics issue inherent in the notion that you can have the best eggs your money can buy," observes sociology professor Barbara Katz Rothman of the City University of New York.

The demand side of the market comes mostly from career-minded baby-boomers, the frontierswomen of feminism, who thought they could "have it all." Indeed they *can* have it all—with a little help from some younger eggs. (Ironically, feminists are also among its strongest critics; *The Nation*'s Katha Pollitt has pointed out that in egg donation and surrogacy, once you remove the "delusion that they are making babies for other women," all you have left is "reproductive prostitution.")

Unfortunately, the future looks bright for the egg market. Earlier this year, a woman in Atlanta gave birth to twins after she was implanted with frozen donor eggs. The same technology has also been successful in Italy. This is just what the egg market needed, since it avoids the necessity of coordinating donors' cycles with recipients' cycles. Soon, not only will infertile couples be able to choose from a wider variety of donor offerings, but in some cases donors won't even be needed. Young women will be able to freeze their own eggs and have them thawed and fertilized once they are ready for the intrusion of children in their lives.

There are human ovaries sitting in a freezer in Fairfax, Virginia. The Genetics and IVF Institute offers to cut out and remove young women's ovaries and cryopreserve the egg-containing tissue for future implantation. Although the technology was originally designed to give the hope of fertility to young women undergoing treatment for cancer, it is now starting to attract the healthy. "Women can wait to have children until they are well established in their careers and getting a little bored, sometime in their forties or fifties," explains Professor Rothman. "Basically, motherhood is being reduced to a good leisure-time activity."

Early this summer, headlines were made in Britain, where the payment of egg donors is forbidden, when an infertile couple traveled to a California clinic where the woman could be inseminated with an experimental hybrid egg. The egg was a combination of the recipient's and a donor's eggs. The clinic in question gets its eggs from a Beverly Hills brokerage, the Center for Surrogate Parenting and Egg Donation, run by Karen Synesiou and Bill Handel, a radio shock-jock in Los Angeles. Miss Synesiou recently told the London *Sunday Times* that she is "interested in redefining the family. That's why I came to work here."

15   The redefinition is already well under way. Consider the case of Jaycee Buzzanca. After John and Luanne Buzzanca had tried for years to have a child, an embryo was created for them, using sperm and an egg from anonymous donors, and implanted in a surrogate mother. In March 1995, one month before the baby was born, John filed for divorce. Luanne wanted child support from John, but he refused—after all, he's not the father.

Luanne argued that John is Jaycee's father legally. At this point the surrogate mother, who had agreed to carry a baby for a stable two-parent household, decided to sue for custody.

Jaycee was dubbed "Nobody's Child" by the media when a California judge ruled that John was not the legal father nor Luanne the legal mother (neither one was genetically related to Jaycee, and Luanne had not even borne her). Enter Erin Davidson, the egg donor, who claims the egg was used without her permission. Not to be left out, the sperm donor jumped into the ring, saying that his sperm was used without his permission, a claim he later dropped. In March of this year, an appeals court gave Luanne custody and decided that John is the legal father, making him responsible for child support. By contracting for a medical procedure resulting in the birth of a child, the court ruled, a couple incurs "the legal status of parenthood." (John lost an appeal in May.) For Jaycee's first three years on earth, these people have been wrangling over who her parents are.

In another case, William Kane left his girlfriend, Deborah Hect, 15 vials of sperm before he killed himself in a Las Vegas hotel in 1991. His two adult children (represented by their mother, his ex-wife) contested Miss Hect's claim of ownership. A settlement agreement on Kane's will was eventually reached, giving his children 80 percent of his estate and Miss Hect 20 percent. Hence she was allowed three vials of his sperm. When she did not succeed in conceiving on the first two tries, she filed a petition for the other 12 vials. She won, and the judge who ruled in her favor wrote, "Neither this court nor the decedent's adult children possess reason or right to prevent Hect from implementing decedent's pre-eminent interest in realizing his 'fundamental right' to procreate with the woman of his choice." One day, donors may not even have to have lived. Researchers are experimenting with using aborted female fetuses as a source of donor eggs.

And the market continues to zip along. For overseas couples looking for donor eggs, Bill Handel has the scenario worked out. The couple would mail him frozen sperm of their choice (presumably from the recipient husband); his clinic would use it to fertilize donor eggs, chosen from its catalogue of offerings, and reply back within a month with a frozen embryo ready for implantation. (Although the sperm does not yet arrive by mail, Handel has sent out embryos to at least one hundred international customers.) As for the young women at the New Jersey clinic, they are visibly upset by one aspect of the egg-donation process: they can't have sexual intercourse for several weeks after the retrieval. For making babies, of course, it's already obsolete.

■ ■ ■ **FOR CLASS DISCUSSION** Identifying Rhetorical Features

Working in groups, develop responses to the following questions:

1. How does Lopez appeal to *logos*? What is her main claim and what are her reasons? What does she use for evidence? What ideas would you have to include in a short summary?

2. What appeals to *pathos* does Lopez make in this argument? How well are these suited to the conservative readers of the *National Review*?

3. How would you characterize Lopez's *ethos*? Does she seem knowledgeable and credible? Does she seem fair to stakeholders in this controversy?

4. Choose an additional focus from the "Questions for Rhetorical Analysis" on pages 125–127 to apply to "Egg Heads." How does this question expand your understanding of Lopez's argument?

5. What strikes you as problematic, memorable, or disturbing in this argument? ■ ■ ■

Our Own Rhetorical Analysis of "Egg Heads"

Now that you have identified some of the rhetorical features of "Egg Heads," we offer our own notes for a rhetorical analysis of this argument.

Rhetorical Context As we began our analysis, we reconstructed the rhetorical context in which "Egg Heads" was published. In the late 1990s, a furious debate about egg donation rippled through newspapers, popular journalism, Web sites, and scholarly commentary. This debate had been kicked off by several couples placing ads in the newspapers of the country's most prestigious colleges, offering up to $50,000 for the eggs of brilliant, attractive, athletic college women. Coinciding with these consumer demands, advances in reproductive technology provided an increasing number of complex techniques to surmount the problem of infertility, including fertilizing eggs in petri dishes and implanting them into women through surgical procedures. These procedures could use either a couple's own eggs and sperm or donated eggs and sperm. All these social and medical factors created the *kairotic* moment for Lopez's article and motivated her to protest the increasing use of these procedures.

Genre and Writer When we considered the genre and writer of this article and its site of publication, we noted that this article appeared in the *National Review*, which describes itself as "America's most widely read and influential magazine and web site for Republican/conservative news, commentary, and opinion." Currently the editor-at-large of *National Review Online*, she has also been published in the *Wall Street Journal*, *New York Post*, and *Washington Times*. This information told us that in her article "Egg Heads," Lopez is definitely on home territory, aiming her article at a conservative audience.

Logos   Turning to the *logos* of Lopez's argument, we decided that the logical structure of Lopez's argument is clear throughout the article. Her claim is that egg donation and its associated reproductive advances have harmful, long-reaching consequences for society. Basically, she argues that egg donation and reproductive technology represent bad scientific developments for society because they are potentially harmful to the long-range health of egg donors and because they are dehumanizing of human sexuality. She states a version of this last point at the end of the second paragraph: "Egg donation is a quietly expanding industry, changing the way we look at the family, young women's bodies, and human life itself" (126).

The body of her article elaborates on each of these reasons. In developing her reason that egg donation endangers donors, Lopez lists the risks but doesn't supply supporting evidence about the frequency of these problems: damage to the ovaries, persistent pain, early menopause, possible ovarian cancer, and even death. She supports her claim about "the expanding industry" by showing how the procedures have become commercialized. To show the popularity of these procedures as well as their commercial value, she quotes a variety of experts such as directors of *in vitro* clinics, fertility centers, bioethicists, and the American Society for Reproductive Medicine. She also cleverly bolsters her own case by showing where even liberal cultural critics agree with her views about the big ethical questions raised by the reproductive technology business. In addition to quoting experts, Lopez has sprinkled impressive numbers and vivid examples throughout the body of her argument, which give her argument momentum as it progresses from the potential harm to young egg donors to a number of case studies that depict increasingly disturbing ethical problems.

Pathos   Much of the impact of this argument, we noted, comes from Lopez's appeals to *pathos*. By describing in detail the waiting rooms for egg donors at fertility clinics, Lopez relies heavily on pathetic appeals to move her audience to see the physical and social dangers of egg donation. She conveys the growing commercialism of reproductive technology by giving readers an inside look at the egg donation process as these young college women embark on the multi-step process of donating their eggs. These young women, she suggests in her title "Egg Heads," are largely unaware of the potential physical dangers to themselves and of the ethical implications and consequences of their acts. She asserts that they are driven largely by the desire for money. Lopez also appeals to *pathos* in her choice of emotionally loaded and often cynical language that creates an angle of vision opposing reproductive technology: "turning procreation into manufacturing"; "reproductive prostitution"; "the intrusion of children in their lives"; "motherhood . . . reduced to a leisure-time activity"; "aborted female fetuses as a source of donor egg"; and intercourse as an "obsolete" way "to make babies" (pages 128–131).

Audience   Despite Lopez's success at spotlighting serious medical and ethical questions, her lack of attention to alternative views and the alarmism of her language caused us to wonder: who might find this argument persuasive and who would challenge it? What is noticeably missing from her argument is the perspective of infertile couples hoping for a baby. Pursuing our question, we decided that a very provocative feature of this argument—one worthy of deeper analysis—is the disparity between how well this argument is suited to its target audience and yet how unpersuasive it is for readers who do not share the assumptions, values, and beliefs of this primary audience.

To Lopez's credit, she has attuned her reasons to the values and concerns of her conservative readers of the *National Review* who believe in traditional families, gender differences, and gender roles. Lopez's choice and orchestration of evidence are intended to play to her audience's fears that science has fallen into the hands of those who have little regard for the sanctity of the family or traditional motherhood. For example, in playing strongly to the values of her conservative readers, Lopez belabors the physical, social, and ethical dangers of egg donation, mentioning worst-case scenarios; however, these appeals to *pathos* will most likely strike other readers who do some investigation into reproductive technology as overblown. She emphasizes the commercialism of the process as her argument moves from college girls as egg donors to a number of sensationalist case studies that depict intensifying ethical ambiguity. In other words, both the *logos* and *pathos* of her argument skillfully focus on details that tap her target audience's values and beliefs and feed their fears and revulsion.

Use of Evidence   For a broader or skeptical audience, the alarmism of Lopez's appeals to *pathos*, her use of atypical evidence, and her distortion of the facts weaken the *logos* and *ethos* of her argument. First, Lopez's use of evidence fails to measure up to the STAR criteria (that evidence should be sufficient, typical, accurate, and relevant). She characterizes all egg donors as young women seeking money. But she provides little evidence that egg donors are only out to make a buck. She also paints these young women as short-sighted, uninformed, and foolish. Lopez weakens her *ethos* by not considering the young women who have researched the process and who may be motivated, at least in part, by compassion for couples who can't conceive on their own. Lopez also misrepresents the people who are using egg donation, placing them all into two groups: (1) wealthy couples eugenically seeking designer babies with prerecorded special traits and (2) feminist career women. She directs much of her criticism toward this latter group: "The demand side of the market comes mostly from career-minded baby boomers, the frontierswomen of feminism, who thought they could 'have it all'" (page 129). However, readers who do a little research on their own, as we did, will learn that infertility affects one in seven couples; that it is often a male and female problem, sometimes caused by an incompatibility between the husband's and wife's reproductive material; and that most couples who take the big step of investing in these expensive efforts to have a baby have been trying to get pregnant for a number of years. Rather than being casual about having children, they are often deeply desirous of children and depressed about their inability to conceive. In addition, far from being the sure thing and quick fix that Lopez suggests, reproductive technology has a success rate of only 50 percent overall and involves a huge investment of time, money, and physical discomfort for women receiving donor eggs.

Another way that Lopez violates the STAR criteria is her choice of extreme cases. For readers outside her target audience, her argument appears riddled with straw man and slippery slope fallacies. (See Appendix 1 on Informal Fallacies). Here are some specific instances of extreme, atypical cases:

- her focus on career women casually and selfishly using the service of young egg donors
- the notorious case of Jaycee Buzzanca dubbed "Nobody's Child" because her adoptive parents who commissioned her creation divorced before she was born
- the legal contest between a dead man's teen girlfriend and his ex-wife and adult children over his vials of sperm
- the idea of taking eggs from aborted female fetuses

By keeping invisible the vast majority of ordinary couples who come to fertility clinics out of desperation, Lopez uses extreme cases to create a "brave new world" intended to evoke a vehement rejection of these reproductive advances. Skeptical readers would offer the alternative view of the sad, ordinary couples of all ages sitting week after week in fertility clinics, hoping to conceive a child through the "miracle" of these reproductive advances and grateful to the young women who have contributed their eggs.

Concluding points   In short, we concluded that Lopez's angle of vision, although effectively in sync with her conservative readers of the *National Review*, exaggerates and distorts her case against these reproductive advances. Lopez's traditional values and slanting of the evidence undermine her *ethos*, limit the value of this argument for a wider audience, and compel that audience to seek out alternative perspectives for a more complete view of egg donation.

WRITING ASSIGNMENT   A Rhetorical Analysis

8.3 To construct essays that analyze the rhetorical effectiveness of arguments

Write a thesis-driven rhetorical analysis essay in which you examine the rhetorical effectiveness of an argument specified by your instructor. Unless otherwise stated, direct your analysis to an audience of your classmates. In your introduction, establish the argumentative conversation to which this argument is contributing. Briefly summarize the argument and present your thesis highlighting two or more rhetorical features of the argument that you find central to the effectiveness or ineffectiveness of this argument. To develop and support your own points, you will need to include textual evidence in the form of examples or short quotations from the argument. Use attributive tags to distinguish your ideas from those of the writer of the argument. Use MLA documentation to cite points and quotations in your essay and in a Works Cited list at the end. For an example of an essay written to this assignment, see Zachary Stumps's analysis of Ellen Goodman's "Womb for Rent" on pages 138–141.

Generating Ideas for Your Rhetorical Analysis

To develop ideas for your essay, you might follow these steps:

Steps for Writing a Rhetorical Analysis

Step	How to Do It
Familiarize yourself with the article you are analyzing.	Read your article several times. Divide it into sections to understand its structure.
Place the article in its rhetorical context.	Follow the strategies in Chapter 2 and use the "Questions for Rhetorical Analysis" on pages 125–127.
Summarize the article.	Follow the steps in Chapter 2 on pages 27–29. You may want to produce a longer summary of 150–200 words as well as a short one-sentence summary.
Reread the article, identifying "hot spots."	Note hot spots in the article—points that impress you, disturb you, confuse you, or puzzle you.
Use the "Questions for Rhetorical Analysis" on pages 125–127.	Choose several of these questions and freewrite responses to them.
From your notes and freewriting, identify the focus for your analysis.	Choose several features of the article that you find particularly important and that you want to discuss in depth in your essay. Identify points that will bring something new to your readers and that will help them see this article with new understanding. You may want to list your ideas and then look for ways to group them together around main points.
Write a thesis statement for your essay.	Articulate your important points of interest in one or two sentences that will set up these points clearly for your audience.

In finding a meaningful focus for your rhetorical analysis essay, you will need to create a focusing thesis statement that avoids wishy-washy formulas such as, "This argument has some strengths and some weaknesses." To avoid a vapid thesis statement, focus on the complexity of the argument, the writer's strategies for persuading the target audience, and the features that might impede its persuasiveness for skeptics.

These thesis statements articulate how their writers see the inner workings of these arguments as well as the arguments' contributions to their public conversations.

> Lopez's angle of vision, although effectively in sync with her conservative readers of the *National Review,* exaggerates and distorts her case against these reproductive advances, weakening her ethos and the value of her argument for a wider audience. [This is the thesis we would use if we were writing a stand-alone essay on Lopez.]

> In his *New Yorker* article "The Pay is Too Damn Low," Surowiecki adopts an angle of vision empathetic to low-wage workers rather than owners; by linking an increase in minimum wage with other liberal causes such as universal health care, investment in infrastructure, and establishing European style safety nets, Surowiecki appeals to his liberal audience but may alienate the business community by under-representing economic arguments opposing the minimum wage.

To make your rhetorical analysis of your article persuasive, you will need to develop each of the points stated or implied in your thesis statement using textual evidence, including short quotations. Your essay should show how you have listened carefully to the argument you are analyzing, summarized it fairly, and probed it deeply.

Organizing Your Rhetorical Analysis

The organization plan that follows provides a possible structure for your rhetorical analysis. ■

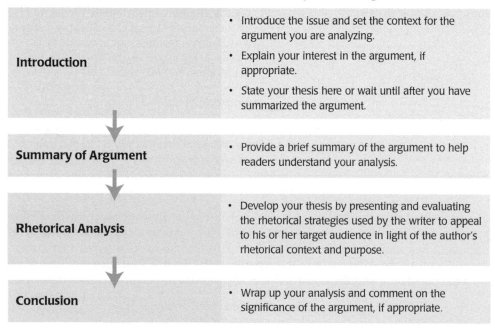

Organization Plan for a Rhetorical Analysis of an Argument

Introduction	• Introduce the issue and set the context for the argument you are analyzing. • Explain your interest in the argument, if appropriate. • State your thesis here or wait until after you have summarized the argument.
Summary of Argument	• Provide a brief summary of the argument to help readers understand your analysis.
Rhetorical Analysis	• Develop your thesis by presenting and evaluating the rhetorical strategies used by the writer to appeal to his or her target audience in light of the author's rhetorical context and purpose.
Conclusion	• Wrap up your analysis and comment on the significance of the argument, if appropriate.

Readings

Our first reading is by Pulitzer Prize–winning columnist, author, and speaker Ellen Goodman. This op-ed piece is analyzed rhetorically by student Zachary Stumps in our second reading.

Womb for Rent

ELLEN GOODMAN

By now we all have a story about a job outsourced beyond our reach in the global economy. My own favorite is about the California publisher who hired two reporters in India to cover the Pasadena city government. Really.

There are times as well when the offshoring of jobs takes on a quite literal meaning. When the labor we are talking about is, well, labor.

In the last few months we've had a full nursery of international stories about surrogate mothers. Hundreds of couples are crossing borders in search of lower-cost ways to fill the family business. In turn, there's a new coterie of international workers who are gestating for a living.

Many of the stories about the globalization of baby production begin in India, where the government seems to regard this as, literally, a growth industry. In the little town of Anand, dubbed

"The Cradle of the World," 45 women were recently on the books of a local clinic. For the production and delivery of a child, they will earn $5,000 to $7,000, a decade's worth of women's wages in rural India.

But even in America, some women, including Army wives, are supplementing their income by contracting out their wombs. They have become surrogate mothers for wealthy couples from European countries that ban the practice.

This globalization of baby-making comes at the peculiar intersection of a high reproductive technology and a low-tech work force. The biotech business was created in the same petri dish as Baby Louise, the first IVF baby. But since then, we've seen conception outsourced to egg donors and sperm donors. We've had motherhood divided into its parts from genetic mother to gestational

mother to birth mother and now contract mother.

We've also seen the growth of an international economy. Frozen sperm is flown from one continent to another. And patients have become medical tourists, searching for cheaper health care whether it's a new hip in Thailand or an IVF treatment in South Africa that comes with a photo safari thrown in for the same price. Why not then rent a foreign womb?

I don't make light of infertility. The primal desire to have a child underlies this multinational Creation, Inc. On one side, couples who choose surrogacy want a baby with at least half their own genes. On the other side, surrogate mothers, who are rarely implanted with their own eggs, can believe that the child they bear and deliver is not really theirs.

As one woman put it, "We give them a baby and they give

---

us much-needed money. It's good for them and for us." A surrogate in Anand used the money to buy a heart operation for her son. Another raised a dowry for her daughter. And before we talk about the "exploitation" of the pregnant woman, consider her alternative in Anand: a job crushing glass in a factory for $25 a month.

10   Nevertheless, there is—and there should be—something uncomfortable about a free market approach to baby-making. It's easier to accept surrogacy when it's a gift from one woman to another. But we rarely see a rich woman become a surrogate for a poor family. Indeed, in Third World countries, some women sign these contracts with a fingerprint because they are illiterate.

For that matter, we have not yet had stories about the contract workers for whom pregnancy was a dangerous occupation, but we will. What obligation does a family that simply contracted for a child have to its birth mother? What control do—should—contractors have over their "employees" lives while incubating "their" children? What will we tell the offspring of this international trade?

"National boundaries are coming down," says bioethicist Lori Andrews, "but we can't stop human emotions. We are expanding families and don't even have terms to deal with it."

It's the commercialism that is troubling. Some things we cannot sell no matter how good "the deal." We cannot, for example, sell ourselves into slavery. We cannot sell our children. But the surrogacy business comes perilously close to both of these deals. And international surrogacy tips the scales.

So, these borders we are crossing are not just geographic ones. They are ethical ones. Today the global economy sends everyone in search of the cheaper deal as if that were the single common good. But in the biological search, humanity is sacrificed to the economy and the person becomes the product. And, step by step, we come to a stunning place in our ancient creation story. It's called the marketplace.

A Rhetorical Analysis of Ellen Goodman's "Womb for Rent"

ZACHARY STUMPS (STUDENT)

Introduction provides context and poses issue to be addressed

Provides background on Goodman

With her op-ed piece "Womb for Rent," published in the *Seattle Times* on April 11, 2008 (and earlier in the *Washington Post*), syndicated columnist Ellen Goodman enters the murky debate about reproductive technology gone global. Since Americans are outsourcing everything else, "Why not then rent a foreign womb?" she asks. Goodman, a Pulitzer Prize–winning columnist for the Washington Post Writers Group, is known for helping readers understand the "tumult of social change and its impact on families" and for shattering "the mold of men writing exclusively about politics" ("Ellen Goodman"). This op-ed piece continues her tradition of examining social change from the perspective of family issues.

Summarizes the op-ed piece

Goodman launches her short piece by asserting that one of the most recent and consequential "jobs" to be outsourced is having babies. She explains how the "globalization of baby production" is thriving because it brings together the reproductive desires of people in developed countries and the bodily resources of women in developing countries such as India. Briefly tracing how both reproductive technology and medical tourism have taken advantage of global possibilities, Goodman acknowledges that the thousands of dollars Indian women earn by carrying the babies of foreign couples represent a much larger income than these women could earn in any other available jobs.

After appearing to legitimize this global exchange, however, Goodman shifts to her ethical concerns by raising some moral questions that she says are not being addressed in this trade. She concludes with a full statement of her claim that this global surrogacy is encroaching on human respect and dignity, exploiting business-based science, and turning babies into products.

Thesis paragraph

In this piece, Goodman's delay of her thesis has several rhetorical benefits: it gives Goodman space to present the perspective of poor women, enhanced by her appeals to *pathos,* and it invites readers to join her journey into the complex contexts of this issue; however, this strategy is also risky because it limits the development of her own argument.

Develops first point in thesis: use of *pathos* in exploring perspective of poor women

5   Instead of presenting her thesis up front, Goodman devotes much of the first part of her argument to looking at this issue from the perspective of foreign surrogate mothers. Using the strategies of pathos to evoke sympathy for these women, she creates a compassionate and progressively minded argument that highlights the benefits to foreign surrogate mothers. She cites factual evidence showing that the average job for a woman in Anand, India, yields a tiny "$25 a month" gotten through the hard work of "crushing glass in a factory," compared to the "$5,000 to $7,000" made carrying a baby to term. To carry a baby to term for a foreign couple represents "a decade's worth of women's wages in rural India." Deepening readers' understanding of these women, Goodman cites one woman who used her earnings to finance her son's heart operation and another who paid for her daughter's dowry. In her fair presentation of these women, Goodman both builds her own positive ethos and adds a dialogic dimension to her argument by helping readers walk in the shoes of otherwise impoverished surrogate mothers.

Develops second point in thesis: the complex contexts of this issue—outsourcing and medical tourism

The second rhetorical benefit of Goodman's delayed thesis is that she invites readers to explore this complex issue of global surrogacy with her before she declares her own view. To help readers understand and think through this issue, she relates it to two other familiar global topics: outsourcing and medical tourism. First, she introduces foreign surrogacy as one of the latest forms of outsourcing: "This globalization of baby-making comes at the peculiar intersection of a high reproductive technology and a low-tech work force." Presenting these women as workers, she explains that women in India are getting paid for "the production and delivery of a child" that is analogous to the production and delivery of sneakers or bicycle parts. Goodman also sets this phenomenon in the context of global medical tourism. If people can pursue lower-cost treatment for illnesses and health conditions in other countries, why shouldn't an infertile couple seeking to start a family not also have such access to these more affordable and newly available means? This reasoning provides a foundation for readers to begin understanding the many layers of the issue.

Shows how the delayed-thesis structure creates two perspectives in conflict

The result of Goodman's delayed-thesis strategy is that the first two-thirds of this piece seem to justify outsourcing surrogate motherhood. Only after reading the whole op-ed piece can readers see clearly that Goodman has been dropping hints about her view all along through her choice of words. Although she clearly sees how outsourcing surrogacy can help poor women economically, her use of market language such as "production," "delivery," and "labor" carry a double meaning. On first reading of this op-ed piece, readers don't know if Goodman's punning is meant to be catchy and entertaining or serves another purpose. This other purpose becomes clear in the last third of the article when Goodman forthrightly asserts her criticism of the commercialism of the global marketplace that promotes worldwide searching for a "cheaper deal": "humanity is sacrificed to the economy and the person becomes the product." This is a bold and big claim, but does the final third of her article support it?

Restates the third point in his thesis: lack of space limits development of Goodman's argument

In the final five paragraphs of this op-ed piece, Goodman begins to develop the rational basis of her argument; however, the brevity of the op-ed genre and her choice not to state her view openly initially have left Goodman with little space to develop her own claim. The result is that she presents some profound ideas very quickly. Some of the ethically complex ideas she introduces but doesn't explore much are these:

- The idea that there are ethical limits on what can be "sold"
- The idea that surrogate motherhood might be "dangerous work"
- The idea that children born from this "international trade" may be confused about their identities

Discusses examples of ideas raised by Goodman but not developed

Goodman simply has not left herself enough space to develop these issues and perhaps leaves readers with questions rather than with changed views. I am particularly struck by several questions. Why have European countries banned surrogacy in developing countries and why has the United States not banned this practice? Does Goodman intend to argue that the United States should follow Europe's lead? She could explore more how this business of finding illiterate women to bear children for the wealthy continues to exploit third-world citizens much as sex tourism exploits women in the very same countries. It seems to perpetuate a tendency for the developed world to regard developing countries as a poor place of lawlessness where practices outlawed in the rest of the world (e.g. child prostitution, slave-like working conditions) are somehow tolerable. Goodman could have developed her argument more to state explicitly that a woman who accepts payment for bearing a baby becomes an indentured servant to the family. Yet another way to think of this issue is to see that the old saying of "a bun in the oven" is more literal than metaphoric when a woman uses her womb as a factory to produce children, a body business not too dissimilar to the commercialism of prostitution. Goodman only teases readers by mentioning these complex problems without producing an argument.

Conclusion

10   Still, although Goodman does not expand her criticism of outsourced surrogate motherhood or explore the issues of human dignity and rights, this argument does introduce the debate on surrogacy in the global marketplace, raise awareness, and begin to direct the conversation toward a productive end of seeking a responsible, healthy, and ethical future. Her op-ed piece lures readers into contemplating deep, perplexing ethical and economic problems and lays a foundation for readers to create an informed view of this issue.

Works Cited

Uses MLA format to list sources cited in the essay

"Ellen Goodman." *Washingtonpost.com,* www.washingtonpost.com/wp-srv/post/writersgroup/biogoodman.htm. Accessed 8 Apr. 2016.

Goodman, Ellen. "Womb for Rent." *The Washington Post,* 11 Apr. 2008, p. B6.

Analyzing Visual Arguments

9

To see how images can make powerful arguments, consider the rhetorical persuasiveness of the "polar bear" marching in a small-town parade (Figure 9.1). Sponsored by local environmentalists advocating action against global warming, the polar bear uses arguments from *logos* (drawing on audience knowledge

FIGURE 9.1 A visual argument about climate change

that climate change threatens polar bears), *pathos* (evoking the bears' vulnerability), and *ethos* (conveying the commitment of the citizens group). Delighting children and adults alike, the bear created a memorable environmental argument.

When an image such as the parade photograph is joined with words, the resulting text is often called a "multimodal argument." The word multimodal combines the concept of "multi" (more than one) and "modality" (a channel, medium, mode of communication). Multimodal arguments published on the Web might take the form of videos, podcasts, blogs, and advocacy Web pages with arguments blending texts and images, all of which make complex rhetorical appeals to viewers. In static print texts, the visual element of a multimodal text might be an image, a drawing, or a graph, but it might also include purposeful uses of fonts, type size, and document design. This chapter focuses on the visual component of such multimodal texts.

Understanding Design Elements in Visual Argument

9.1 To explain the elements of design in visual arguments

To understand how visual images can produce an argument, you need to understand the design elements that work together to create a visual text.

The Components of Visual Design

There are four basic components of visual design: use of type, use of space and layout, use of color, and use of images. The most important considerations in using these design components to achieve readability, visual appeal, and suitability are show in Table 9.1.

TABLE 9.1   Components of Visual Design

Design Component	Key Variables	Key Principles
Use of type	▪ Font style ranging from conservative (Times New Roman, Courier) to playful and decorative (*Zapf Chancery* and other specialty fonts) ▪ Font size ▪ Variables for emphasis (**boldface**, *italics*, underlining, ALL CAPS)	▪ Choose *display type* (sans serif—without the little extensions on letters—like Century Gothic and Ariel) for headings, titles, and slogans. ▪ Choose *body type* (serif—with the little extensions on letters—like Times New Roman and Courier New) for long documents and main text. ▪ Make type functional and appealing by using only two or three typestyles per document. ▪ Use consistent patterns of type to indicate relationships among items. ▪ Choose type to project a specific impression. To create a formal, businesslike impression, as in scholarly publications, use a structured combination of serif and sans serif type. To create an informal look, as in popular magazine publications and highly visual posters and fliers, use sans serif and specialty type.

(continued)

Design Component	Key Variables	Key Principles
Use of headings and other means of breaking text into visual units	• Page size and type of paper • Proportion of text to white space • Arrangement of text on page (space, margins, columns, size of paragraphs, spaces between paragraphs, justification of margins) • Use of highlighting elements such as bulleted lists, tables, sidebars, boxes • Use headings and other means of breaking text into visual units	• Use layout to make documents highly readable and to guide readers with structural clues (headings, paragraph breaks, and bulleted lists). • Focus on creating meaning and coherence with layout. • For academic arguments, use simple, functional layouts. For popular magazine arguments and visual arguments, vary the layout and make the page visually attractive. However, for visual arguments, avoid clutter and confusion by limiting the amount of text and the number of visual items on a page.
Use of color	• Variations in font color for effect • Use of color in images and graphics • Use of background tints and colored shading	• Use color to meet audience and genre expectations (minimal use of color in academic arguments and often lavish color in popular magazines). • For visual arguments, use color functionally (to indicate relationships) or decoratively (to create visual appeal). • For visual arguments, decide whether color will be used to make images look documentary-like (realistic), to create symbolic associations (for example, psychedelic colors and the 1960s), or to create a specific aesthetic effect (for example, pleasing, disturbing, or soothing).
Images and graphics	• Photographs • Drawings • Numeric graphics	• For visual arguments, consider how the image will work in the argument: to convey an idea, illustrate a point, evoke an emotional response. • For all arguments, consider how to establish the relationship between the image or graphic and the verbal text. (Images and graphics are described in detail later in this chapter.)

As Table 9.1 suggests, in arguments that don't use images and graphics the writer's primary visual concern is document design. In planning how the document will look, the writer hopes to make it easy to read (choosing plain, conventional typefaces); to meet the readers' expectations for format (double-spacing manuscripts, following expected genre conventions if the argument is to be desktop published); and to provide appropriate structural cues that highlight points and guide the reader through the argument (using headings, paragraph breaks, bulleted lists). But in moving from verbal-only arguments to arguments that use visual elements for direct persuasive effect—for example in producing a flier, poster, or one-page newspaper advertisement—the writer can make creative use of all the elements of visual design, including images and quantitative graphics, as we explain in the rest of the chapter.

An Analysis of a Visual Argument Using Type and Spatial Elements

To illustrate the persuasive power of type and layout, we ask you to consider Figure 9.2, which shows a public affairs ad sponsored by the Ad Council and an advocacy organization, StopBullying.gov, as part of an ongoing campaign to curtail bullying among young people.

This ad demonstrates how use of type can create powerful visual and verbal rhetorical effects to convey its argument. The ad's creators chose to use lettering—not

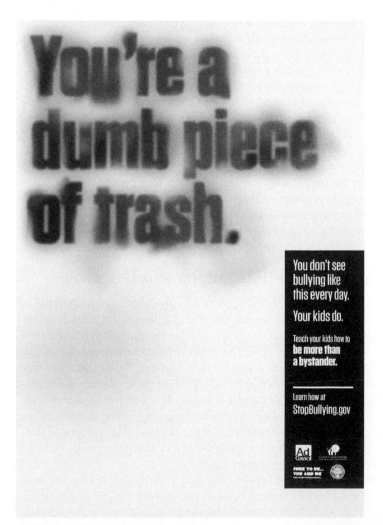

FIGURE 9.2 Anti-bullying public affairs ad

an image—to illustrate bullying. The type style, presentation of the letters, and words themselves create a strange effect—simultaneously personal and impersonal—that draws viewers into the ad more than an image would. The type style and font make strong appeals to *pathos* through the blend of the shocking abusive language and disturbing lettering style. The words "dumb," "piece," and "trash" are all harshly derogatory. The direct address to the viewer in the word "you" conveys that bullying is an attack, sometimes verbal, and often physical.

Note how the blurring of the message in the large bold type makes a visual statement about the act of bullying and about both perception and psychological damage. These large, heavy, blurred letters convey multiple messages. Bullying can be crude and forceful, but it is often carried on covertly where authority figures cannot see or stop it. The lettering itself bullies the viewers while at the same time reinforcing the idea that not everyone is aware of bullying. The blurring of these letters also suggests that bullying damages and erases the personhood of victims. In addition, the ad makes it look as though these dark letters have smudged and stained the yellow background, suggesting that bullying harms the social environment.

The layout of this ad also contributes to the *logos* and *ethos* of the ad. The shock of reading the bold message propels readers to the black sidebar in the lower right side of the ad, where the message in smaller type interprets and explains the message of the blurred letters. The text speaks directly to parents' unawareness of the hostility of their kids' environment and makes an urgent appeal to parental responsibility. While the lettering and layout convey the causal reasons behind the need for action, the message in the smaller letters states the proposal claim: Instruct your kids how to be more than passive observers of bullying. In addition to delivering a strong message, this ad conveys a positive *ethos* by demonstrating knowledge of the problem and directing readers to authoritative sources of information and help in engaging with this serious social issue.

The Compositional Features of Photographs and Drawings

9.2 To analyze the compositional features of photographs and drawings rhetorically

Now that we have introduced you to the four major elements of visual design—type, layout, color, and images—we turn to an in-depth discussion of photographic images and drawings. Used strategically in product advertisements, photos and drawings can be employed with equal shrewdness in posters, fliers, advocacy ads, and Web sites. Although such images often are made to seem spontaneous and "natural," they are almost always composed: designers consciously select the details of staging and composition as well as manipulate camera techniques (filters, camera angle, lighting) and digital or chemical development techniques (airbrushing, merging of images). Even news photography can have a composed feel. For example, public officials often try to control the effect of photographs by creating "photo-ops" (photographing opportunities), wherein news photographers are allowed to photograph an event only during certain times and from certain angles. Political photographs appearing in newspapers often are press releases officially approved by the politician's staff. To analyze a photograph or drawing, or to create visual images for your own arguments, you need to think both about the composition of the image and about the camera's relationship to the subject. Because drawings produce a perspective on a scene analogous to that of a camera, design considerations for photographs can be applied to drawings as well. The following list of questions can guide your analysis of any persuasive image.

- **Type of photograph or drawing:** Is the image documentary-like (representing a real event), fictionlike (intended to tell a story or dramatize a scene), or conceptual (illustrating or symbolizing an idea or theme)? The two photos of the protest for higher wages for fast-food workers on page 1 and of the anti-fracking march on page 123 are documentary photos capturing real events in action.

- **Distance from the subject:** Is the image a close-up, medium shot, or long shot? Close-ups tend to increase the intensity of the image and suggest the importance of the subject; long shots tend to blend the subject into the background. In the baby photograph opposing phthalates in children's toys (Chapter 1, page 4), the effect of the baby's wearing a "poison" bib is intensified by the close-up shot without background. In contrast, the medium shot of the boy holding the toy he has found in the wreckage caused by typhoon Haiyan (Chapter 6, page 95) focuses on both the boy and his surroundings. While the photo captures the magnitude of the disaster, it also shows the child's interests and his attempt to recover some of his past life.

- **Orientation of the image and camera angle:** Is the camera (or artist) positioned in front of or behind the subject? Is it positioned below the subject, looking up (a low-angle shot)? Or is it above the subject, looking down (a high-angle shot)? Front-view shots—for example, the photo of the fracking protestor (page 123)—tend to emphasize the people being photographed. In contrast, rear-view shots often emphasize the scene or setting. A low-angle perspective tends to make the subject look superior and powerful, whereas a high-angle perspective can reduce the size—and by implication, the importance—of the subject. A level angle tends to imply equality. The low-angle perspective of Katniss Everdeen, the main character of *The Hunger Games* (page 153), accentuates her heroic stature.

- **Point of view:** Does the camera or artist stand outside the scene and create an objective effect? Or is the camera or artist inside the scene as if the photographer or artist is an actor in the scene, creating a subjective effect?

- **Use of color:** Is the image in color or in black and white? Is this choice determined by the restrictions of the medium (such as images designed to run in black and white in newspapers) or is it the conscious choice of the photographer or artist? Are the colors realistic or muted? Have special filters been used (a photo made to look old through the use of brown tints)? Are bright colors intended to be catchy and attractive or dominant or disturbing?

- **Compositional special effects:** Is the entire image clear and realistic? Is any portion of it blurred? Is it blended with other realistic or nonrealistic images (a car ad that blends a city and a desert; a body lotion ad that merges a woman and a cactus)? Is the image an imitation of some other famous image such as a classic painting (as in parodies)?

- **Juxtaposition of images:** Are several different images juxtaposed, suggesting relationships between them? Juxtaposition can suggest sequential or causal relationships or can metaphorically transfer the identity of a nearby image or background to the subject (as when a bath soap is associated with a meadow). This technique frequently is used in public relations to shape viewers' perceptions of political figures by photographing them with the American flag or patriotic monuments.

■ **Manipulation of images:** Are staged images made to appear real, natural, or documentary-like? Are images altered with airbrushing? Are images actually composites of a number of images (for instance, using images of different women's bodies to create one perfect model in an ad or film)? Are images cropped for emphasis? What is left out? Are images downsized or enlarged?

■ **Settings, furnishings, props:** Is the photo or drawing an outdoor or indoor scene? What is in the background and foreground? What furnishings and props, such as furniture, objects in a room, pets, and landscape features, help create the scene? What social associations of class, race, and gender are attached to these settings and props?

■ **Characters, roles, actions:** Does the photo or drawing tell a story? Are the people in the scene models? Are the models instrumental (acting out real-life roles) or are they decorative (extra and included for visual or sex appeal)? What are the facial expressions, gestures, and poses of the people? What are the spatial relationships of the figures? (Who is in the foreground, center, and background? Who is large and prominent?) What social relationships are implied by these poses and positions? In the "Save the Children" advocacy ad in Figure 9.3, the pose of the health care worker and baby—the health worker intently treating the baby and the baby happily trusting the health worker—tells the story of successful health care.

■ **Presentation of images:** Are images separated from each other in a larger composition or connected to each other? Are the images large in proportion to verbal text? How are images labeled? How does the text relate to the image(s)? Does the image illustrate the text? Does the text explain or comment on the image?

An Analysis of a Visual Argument Using All the Design Components

We would like to illustrate how all four of the design components—use of type, layout, color, and images—can reinforce and support each other to achieve a rhetorical effect. Consider the "Save the Children" advocacy ad from *Newsweek* (Figure 9.3). This advocacy ad highlights the design features of image, color, and layout, with type used to interpret and reinforce the message delivered by the other features. The layout of the page highlights the connection between the adorable baby on the left side and the female health care worker on the right. The "story" of the ad is told in unobtrusive text (in small white font), which leads the readers' eyes from the baby's face to the heart of the health worker. Interestingly, from a design perspective, a third figure, probably the baby's mother, is just partly visible in the form of hands holding the baby. The text itself celebrates the effectiveness of this local health healer. At the bottom of the page, text conveys the call to action in the form of memorable tag lines "HELP ONE. SAVE MANY"; and "See where the good goes at GoodGoes.org."

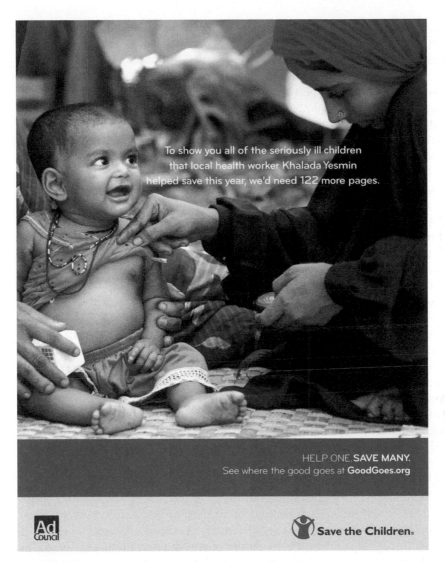

To show you all of the seriously ill children that local health worker Khalada Yesmin helped save this year, we'd need 122 more pages.

HELP ONE. **SAVE MANY.**
See where the good goes at **GoodGoes.org**

Ad Council

Save the Children.

FIGURE 9.3 Save the Children advocacy ad

This advocacy ad works on readers by blending three themes—the universal appeal of babies; the beneficial effects of educating local workers, particularly women; and the symbolic meaning of helping/healing hands—to convey how those of us in the developed world can provide aid that empowers people in developing countries to help themselves. These themes are portrayed through various visual strategies. In this ad, a baby, the health worker, and a third figure outside the frame of the photo (probably the baby's mother) sit on a woven mat, inside a structure. The use of bright colors to create a feeling of warmth and love, the arrangement of the figures, and the close-up shots of the baby and health worker draw viewers into the scene. The close-up, slightly low-angle shot accentuates faces, hands, feet, and traditional clothing. The blurred background suggests palm trees and the doorway to a house. The building is, most likely, the home of the mother and baby, which the health worker is visiting on her rounds. The baby, wearing an orange-beaded blouse or smock, pink shorts or skirt, and a necklace of purple beads, sits and smiles alertly at the health worker, who is engrossed in taking the baby's temperature. She seems to be holding the thermometer under the baby's arm with one hand and holding a watch with the other. Her focus on her task conveys her expertise; she knows what she is doing, an idea reinforced by the caption, which tells us that this health worker, Khalada Yesmin, "has helped 122 sick children this year." This caption and the prominence of hands in this photo—Khalada Yesmin's hands, the baby's hand, and the mother's hands supporting the baby—accentuate the idea of direct, grassroots aid that is improving the lives of mothers and children in a community through compassion and knowledge. The slogans at the bottom of the ad "Help one. Save many" and "See where the good goes" extend this network of help to viewers of the ad. If we contribute money to the training and medical supplies of health workers like Khalada Yesmin, we will help expand the web of aid.

In choosing to make this ad portray a positive, upbeat scene of medical success, instead of portraying scenes of sick and dying children, the designers of this ad gave a memorable embodiment to the ideas in the words "help," "save," and "good." Perhaps most importantly, unlike some global ads, this one empowers people in the developing world. Rather than depict them as victims or helpless people in backward countries, this ad shows them as primary agents in the improvements in their lives. Rather than take control and rush in to solve problems, viewers in developed countries are invited to contribute to this success, figuratively lending a hand through financial support.

■ ■ ■ **FOR CLASS DISCUSSION** *Analyzing Photos and Drawings Rhetorically*

Working individually or in groups, imagine that you have been asked to compose a flier advertising a self-defense workshop for women on your university campus. This workshop will include some basic self-defense moves and some fundamentals of martial arts and blocking. Your task is to choose one of the four photos or images in Figures 9.4–9.7 for the poster. Your goal is to get students to notice your poster, appreciate what is at stake in the workshops, and become motivated to sign up. What image might best encourage women to attend? What image might encourage men to urge their female friends or girlfriends to attend?

1. Study the four photos in Figures 9.4 through 9.7, and then answer the following questions:
   a. What camera techniques and composition features do you see in each photo or image? Consider all the composition features described on pages 147–148 for each image.
   b. What do you think is the dominant impression of each photo? In other words, what is each photo's implicit argument?

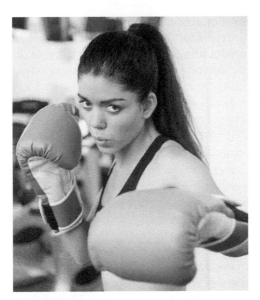

FIGURE 9.4 Photo of girl practicing boxing moves

FIGURE 9.5 Photo of a guy in a hoodie

FIGURE 9.6 Drawing of a girl booting a guy

FIGURE 9.7 Photo of a woman executing a martial arts move

The Genres of Visual Arguments

9.3 To explain the genres of visual argument

We have already mentioned that verbal arguments today frequently are accompanied by photographs or drawings that contribute to the text's persuasive appeal. For example, a verbal argument promoting U.N. action to help AIDS victims in Africa might be accompanied by a photograph of a dying mother and child. However, some genres of argument are dominated by visual elements. In these genres, the visual design carries most of the argumentative weight; verbal text is used primarily for labeling, for focusing the argument's claim, or for commenting on the images. In this section, we describe specifically these highly visual genres of argument.

Posters and Fliers

To persuade audiences, an arguer might create a poster designed for placement on walls or kiosks or a flier to be passed out on street corners. Posters dramatically attract and direct viewers' attention toward a subject or issue. They often seek to rally supporters to promote a strong stance on an issue, and call people to action. For example, during World War II, posters asked Americans to invest in war bonds and urged women to join the workforce to free men for active combat. During the Vietnam War, famous posters used slogans such as "Make Love Not War" or "Girls say yes to boys who say no" to increase national resistance to the war.

The hallmark of an effective poster is the way it focuses and encodes a complex meaning in a verbal-visual text, often with one or more striking images. These images are often symbolic—for example, using children to symbolize family and home, a soaring bird to symbolize freedom, or three firefighters raising the American flag over the World Trade Center rubble in September 2001 to symbolize American heroism, patriotism, and resistance to terrorism. These symbols derive potency from the values they share with their target audience. Posters tend to use words sparingly, either as slogans or as short, memorable directives. This terse verbal text augments the message encoded in an eye-catching, dominant image.

As an example of a contemporary poster, consider the poster on page 153 urging people to see the second *Hunger Games* film, *Catching Fire*. This poster for this popular culture film shows actress Jennifer Lawrence as lead character Katniss Everdeen aiming her weapon of choice, her bow. She is framed by a large version of her mockingjay pin (a symbol of District 12, her home) and a ring of fire. Readers who know Susan Collins's dystopian novels and/or the films know that Katniss appeared in a costume with special effect flames in the first film and that her defiant spirit fuels the rebellion against the Capital and its repressive government. The impact of the poster is intensified by the angry reds and dark colors and by the centrality and size of the image of Katniss (Jennifer Lawrence) that dominates the poster. The tagline at the top of the poster "Remember who the enemy is" intimates the plotline of the film and calls all potential rebels to be discerning and ready for courageous and risky acts of solidarity.

Fliers and brochures often use visual elements similar to those in posters. An image might be the top and center attraction of a flier or the main focus of the front cover of a brochure. However, unlike posters, fliers and brochures offer additional space for verbal arguments, which often present the writer's claim supported with bulleted lists of reasons. Sometimes pertinent data and statistics, along with testimony from supporters, are placed in boxes or sidebars.

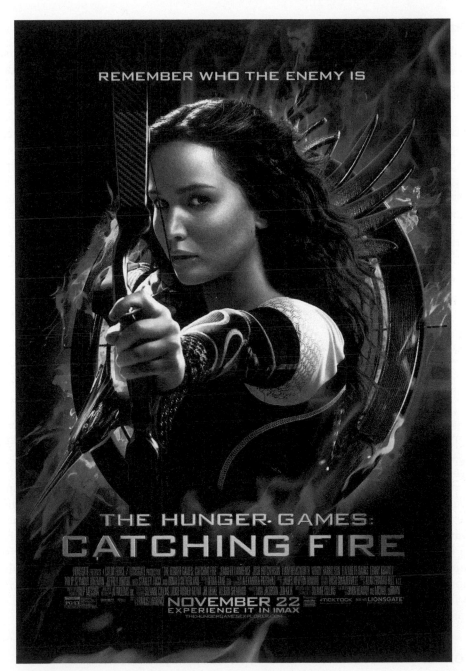

FIGURE 9.8 Poster for *The Hunger Games: Catching Fire*

Public Affairs Advocacy Advertisements

Public affairs advocacy advertisements share with posters an emphasis on visual elements, but they are designed specifically for publication in newspapers and magazines or Web sites and, in their persuasive strategies, are directly analogous to product advertisements. Public affairs advocacy ads are usually sponsored by a corporation or an advocacy organization, often are part of a particular campaign with a theme, and have a more immediate and defined target audience than posters. Designed as condensed arguments aimed at influencing public opinion on civic issues, these ads are characterized by their brevity, audience-based appeals, and succinct, sound bite style. Often, in order to sketch out their claim and reasons clearly and concisely, they employ headings and subheadings, bulleted lists, different sizes and styles of type, and a clever, pleasing layout on the page. They usually have some attention-getting slogan or headline like "MORE KIDS ARE GETTING BRAIN CANCER. WHY?" or "STOP THE TAX REVOLT JUGGERNAUT!" And they usually include a call to action, whether it be a donation, a letter of protest to legislators, or an invitation to join the advocacy group.

The balance between verbal and visual elements in an advocacy advertisement varies. Some advocacy ads are verbal only, with visual concerns focused on document design (for example, an "open letter" from the president of a corporation appearing as a full-page newspaper ad). Other advocacy ads are primarily visual, using images and other design elements with the same shrewdness as product advertisements. We looked closely at advocacy ads when we examined the StopBullying.gov ads (Figure 9.2) and the Save the Children ad (Figure 9.3).

As another example of a public affairs advocacy ad, consider the ad in Chapter 14, page 246, that attempts to counter the influence of the pro-life movement's growing campaign against abortion. As you can see, this ad is dominated by one stark image: a question mark formed by the hook of a coat hanger. The shape of the hook draws the reader's eye to the concentrated type centered below it. The hook carries most of the weight of the argument. Simple, bold, and harsh, the image of the hanger—tapping readers' cultural knowledge—evokes the dangerous experience of illegal abortions performed crudely by nonmedical people in the dark back streets of cities. The ad wants viewers to think of the dangerous last resorts that desperate women would have to turn to if they could not obtain abortions legally. The hanger itself creates a visual pun: as a question mark, it conveys the ad's dilemma about what will happen if abortions are made illegal. As a coat hanger, it provides the ad's frightening answer to the printed question—desperate women will return to back-street abortionists who use coat hangers as tools.

■ ■ ■ **FOR CLASS DISCUSSION**   Analyzing an Advocacy Poster Rhetorically

Working individually or in groups, examine the advocacy poster shown in Figure 9.9 on page 155 that shows a photo of an attractive girl behind the line "HEATHER'S LIFE ENDED TOO SOON." This poster, which appears on the TxtResponsibly.org Web site,

FIGURE 9.9 Poster argument warning against texting while driving

reaches out to young drivers and their parents, using both images and text. Use the following questions to guide your analysis.

   a. What visual features of this poster immediately attract your eyes? What principles for effective use of type, layout, color, and image does this ad exemplify?

   b. What is the core argument of this ad?

   c. Why did Heather's parents choose a large photo of her? How does that photo work with the other photo of a completely mangled car?

   d. How does the frankness of the text and the size and color of the lettering combine to convey the message of the ad?

   e. How would you design a poster warning against texting while driving? Consider use of type, layout, and image; the core argument; and appeals to *ethos, pathos,* and *kairos.*

Cartoons

An especially charged kind of visual argument is the editorial or political cartoon and its extended forms, the comic strip and graphic novel. Here we focus on political cartoons, which are often mini-narratives, portraying an issue dramatically, compactly, and humorously through images and a few well-chosen words that dramatize conflicts and problems. Using caricature, exaggeration, and distortion, a cartoonist distills an issue down to an image that boldly reveals the creator's perspective on an issue. The purpose of political cartoons is usually satire, or, as one famous cartoonist says, "afflicting the comfortable and comforting the afflicted."* Because they are so condensed and are often connected to current affairs, political cartoons are particularly dependent on the audience's background knowledge of cultural and political events. When political cartoons work well, through their perceptive combination of images and words, they flash a brilliant, clarifying light on a perspective or open a new lens on an issue, often giving readers a shock of insight.

As an illustration, note the cartoon by Milt Priggee in Figure 9.10, which was posted on the cartoon Web site www.caglecartoons.com. The setting of the cartoon envisions a humorous blend of prehistoric and contemporary times. This cartoon responds to the recent scientific discussions—with points about dark matter, a kind of energy-mass concept from physics and astronomy—of the creation and development of the universe and the aging of Earth. However, the main story of the cartoon connects the dinosaur characters with the behavior of people today who go about walking and tweeting, oblivious to anything around them, including dangerous environments. Thus, the cartoon links discussions of evolution to discussions of the contemporary obsession with cell phones and forms of social media.

---

*"The Truth Told in Jest: Interview: Martin Rowson." *Morning Star.* Morning Star Online, July 2007 Web. 6 June 2011.

FIGURE 9.10 Tweeting and evolution cartoon

■ ■ ■ **FOR CLASS DISCUSSION** **Analyzing Cartoons**

Cartoons can provide insight into how the public is lining up on issues. Choose a current issue such as health care reform, use of drones, dependence on foreign oil, income inequality, or identity theft. Then, using an online cartoon index such as Daryl Cagle's Professional Cartoonists Index (www.cagle.com) or a Web search of your own, find several cartoons that capture different perspectives on your issue.

1. What is the mini-narrative, the main claim, and the use of caricature, exaggeration, or distortion in each?
2. How is *kairos*, or timeliness, important to each cartoon?   ■ ■ ■

Web Pages

So far we have only hinted at the influence of the World Wide Web in accelerating the use of visual images in argument. Multimodal Web pages, with their hypertext design, exhibit the Web's complex mix of text and image, a mix that has changed the way many writers think of argument. The home page of an advocacy site, for example, often has many features of a poster argument with hypertext links to galleries of images on the one hand, and to verbal arguments on the other. These verbal arguments themselves often contain photographs, drawings, and graphics. The strategies discussed in this chapter for analyzing and interpreting visual texts also apply to Web pages.

Because the Web is such an important tool in research, we have placed our main discussion of Web sites in Appendix 2. There you will find our explanations for reading, analyzing, and evaluating Web sites.

Constructing Your Own Visual Argument

9.4 To construct your own visual argument

The most common visual arguments you are likely to create are posters and fliers, and public affairs advocacy ads. You may also decide that in longer verbal arguments, the use of visuals or graphics could clarify your points while adding visual variety to your paper. The following guidelines will help you apply your understanding of visual elements in the construction of your own visual arguments.

Guidelines for Creating Visual Arguments

1. **Genre:** Determine where this visual argument is going to appear (bulletin board, flier, a one-page magazine or newspaper spread, or as a Web page).
2. **Audience-based appeals:** Determine who your target audience is.
   - What values and background knowledge of your issue can you assume your audience has?
   - What specifically do you want your audience to think or do after reading your visual argument?
   - If you are promoting a specific course of action (sign a petition, send money, vote for or against a bill, attend a meeting), how can you make that request clear and direct?
3. **Core of your argument:** Determine what clear claim and reasons will form the core of your argument; decide if this claim and these reasons will be explicitly stated or implicit in your visuals and slogans.
   - How much verbal text will you use?
   - If the core of your argument will be largely implicit, how can you still make it readily apparent and clear for your audience?
4. **Visual design:** What visual design and layout will grab your audience's attention and be persuasive?
   - How can font sizes and styles, layout, and color be used in this argument to create a strong impression?
   - What balance and harmony can you create between the visual and verbal elements of your argument? Will your verbal element be a slogan, express the core of the argument, or summarize and comment on the image(s)?
5. **Use of images:** If your argument lends itself to images, what photo or drawing would support your claim or have emotional appeal? (If you want to use more than one image, be careful not to clutter your page and confuse your message. Simplicity and clarity are important.)
   - What image would be memorable and meaningful to your audience? Would a photo or a drawing be most effective?
   - Will your image(s) be used to provide evidence for your claim or illustrate a main idea, evoke emotions, or enhance your credibility and authority?

■ ■ ■   **FOR CLASS DISCUSSION**   Developing Ideas for an Advocacy Ad
                                      or Poster Argument

This exercise asks you to do the thinking and planning for an advocacy ad or poster argument to be displayed on your college or university campus. Working individually, in small groups, or as a whole class, choose an issue that is controversial on your campus (or in your town or city), and follow the Guidelines for Creating Visual Arguments on page 158 to envision the view you want to advocate on that issue. What might the core of your argument be? Who is your target audience? Are you representing a group, club, or other organization? What image(s) might be effective in attracting and moving this audience? Possible issues might be commuter parking; poor conditions in the computer lab; student reluctance to use the counseling center; problems with dorm life, financial aid programs, or intramural sports; ways to improve orientation programs for new students, work-study programs, or travel-abroad opportunities; or new initiatives such as study groups for the big lecture courses or new service-learning opportunities.   ■ ■ ■

Using Information Graphics in Arguments

9.5 To use information graphics rhetorically in arguments

Besides images in the form of photographs and drawings, writers often use quantitative graphics to support arguments using numbers. In Chapter 5, we introduced you to the use of quantitative data in arguments. We discussed the persuasiveness of numbers and showed you ways to use them responsibly in your arguments. With the availability of spreadsheet and presentation programs, today's writers often create and import quantitative graphics into their documents. These visuals—such as tables, pie charts, and line or bar graphs—can have great rhetorical power by making numbers tell a story at a glance. In this section, we'll show you how quantitative graphics can make numbers speak. We'll also show you how to incorporate graphics into your text and reference them effectively.

How Tables Contain a Variety of Stories

Data used in arguments usually have their origins in raw numbers collected from surveys, questionnaires, observational studies, scientific experiments, and so forth. Through a series of calculations, the numbers are combined, sorted, and arranged in a meaningful fashion, often in detailed tables. Some of the tables published by the U.S. Census Bureau, for example, contain dozens of pages. The more dense the table, the more their use is restricted to statistical experts who pore over them to analyze their meanings. More useful to the general public are midlevel tables contained on one or two pages that report data at a higher level of abstraction.

Consider, for example, Table 9.2, published by the U.S. Census Bureau and based on the 2010 census. This table shows the marital status of people age 15 and older, broken into gender and age groupings, in March 2010. It also provides comparative data on the "never married" percentage of the population in March 2010 and March 1970.

Take a few moments to peruse the table and be certain you know how to read it. You read tables in two directions: from top to bottom and from left to right. Always begin with the title, which tells you what the table contains and includes elements from

TABLE 9.2 Marital Status of People 15 Years and Over by Age and Sex: March 1970 and March 2010 (Numbers in Thousands, Except for Percentages)

Characteristic	Total	March 2010 Number Married spouse present	Married spouse absent	Separated	Divorced	Widowed	Never married	Percent never married	March 1970 percent never married*
Both Sexes									
Total 15 years old and over	242,047	120,768	3,415	5,539	23,742	14,341	74,243	30.7	24.9
15 to 19 years old	21,079	178	109	151	60	22	20,559	97.5	93.9
20 to 24 years old	21,142	2,655	202	309	195	17	17,765	84.0	44.5
25 to 29 years old	21,445	7,793	406	594	766	60	11,826	55.1	14.7
30 to 34 years old	19,623	10,896	337	632	1,447	72	6,239	31.8	7.8
35 to 44 years old	40,435	25,729	733	1,331	4,697	345	7,599	18.8	5.9
45 to 54 years old	44,373	28,619	703	1,295	6,951	1,080	5,725	12.9	6.1
55 to 64 years old	35,381	23,621	463	763	5,750	1,923	2,861	8.1	7.2
65 years old and over	38,569	21,276	461	465	3,875	10,823	1,668	4.3	7.6
Males									
Total 15 years old and over	117,686	60,384	1,789	2,352	9,981	2,974	40,206	34.2	28.1
15 to 19 years old	10,713	61	55	62	30	8	10,498	98.0	97.4
20 to 24 years old	10,677	946	86	123	49	3	9,469	88.7	54.7
25 to 29 years old	10,926	3,343	220	224	318	21	6,800	62.2	19.1
30 to 34 years old	9,759	5,143	188	246	593	28	3,561	36.5	9.4
35 to 44 years old	20,066	12,614	392	578	1,998	81	4,402	21.9	6.7
45 to 54 years old	21,779	14,280	367	539	3,063	284	3,246	14.9	7.5
55 to 64 years old	16,980	11,958	244	343	2,465	424	1,545	9.1	7.8
65 years old and over	16,786	12,039	237	237	1,464	2,124	685	4.1	7.5
Females									
Total 15 years old and over	124,361	60,384	1,626	3,187	13,760	11,368	34,037	27.4	22.1
15 to 19 years old	10,365	118	55	90	30	13	10,061	97.1	90.3
20 to 24 years old	10,465	1,708	116	185	146	14	8,296	79.3	35.8
25 to 29 years old	10,519	4,451	186	370	448	39	5,026	47.8	10.5
30 to 34 years old	9,864	5,753	150	386	854	44	2,678	27.1	6.2
35 to 44 years old	20,369	13,115	341	753	2,698	264	3,198	15.7	5.2
45 to 54 years old	22,594	14,339	337	756	3,889	794	2,479	11.0	4.9
55 to 64 years old	18,401	11,663	220	420	3,284	1,499	1,315	7.1	6.8
65 years old and over	21,783	9,238	224	227	2,412	8,700	983	4.5	7.7

*The 1970 percentages include 14-year-olds, and thus are for 14+ and 14–19.
Source: U.S. Census Bureau, Current Population Survey, March 2010 and March 1970.

both the vertical and the horizontal dimensions of the table. In this case the vertical dimension presents demographic categories for people "15 years old and over" for both sexes, males and females. Each of these gender categories is subdivided into age categories. The horizontal dimension provides information about "marital status." Seven of the columns give total numbers (reported in thousands) for March 2010. The eighth column gives the "percent never married" for March 2010, while the last column gives the "percent never married" for March 1970. To make sure you know how to read the table, pick a couple of rows at random and say to yourself what each number means. For example, the first row under "Both sexes" gives total figures for the entire population of the United States age 15 and older. In March 2010 there were 242,047,000 people age 15 and older (remember that the numbers are presented in thousands). Of these, 120,768,000 were married and living with their spouses. As you continue across the columns, you'll see that 3,415,000 people were married but not living with their spouses (a spouse may be stationed overseas or in prison; or a married couple may be maintaining a "commuter marriage" with separate households in different cities). Continuing across the columns, you'll see that 5,539,000 people were separated from their spouses, 23,742,000 were divorced, and 14,341,000 were widowed, and an additional 74,243,000 were never married. In the next-to-last column, the number of never-married people is converted to a percentage: 30.7 percent. Finally, the last column shows the percentage of never-married people in 1970: 24.9 percent. These last two columns show us that the number of unmarried people in the United States rose 5.8 percentage points since 1970.

Now that you know how to read the table, examine it carefully to see the kinds of stories it tells. What does the table show you, for example, about the percentage of married people age 25–29 in 1970 versus 2010? What does it show about different age-related patterns of marriage in males and females? By showing you that Americans are waiting much later in life to get married, a table like this initiates many causal questions for analysis and argument. What happened in American culture between 1970 and 2010 to explain the startling difference in the percentage of married people within, say, the 20–24 age bracket? In 2010 only 16 percent of people in this age bracket were married (we converted "unmarried" to "married" by subtracting 84 from 100). However, in 1970, 55.5 percent of people in this age bracket were married.

Using a Graph to Tell a Story

Table 9.2, as we have seen, tells the story of how Americans are postponing marriage. However, one has to tease out the story from the dense columns of numbers. To focus on a key story and make it powerfully immediate, you can create a graph.

Bar Graphs   Suppose you are writing an argument in which you want to show that the percentage of married women in the 20–29 age bracket has dropped significantly since 1970. You could tell this story through a bar graph (Figure 9.11).

Bar graphs use bars of varying length, extending either horizontally or vertically, to contrast two or more quantities. As with any graphic presentation, you must create a comprehensive title. In the case of bar graphs, titles tell readers what is being

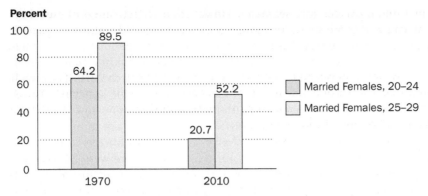

FIGURE 9.11 Percentage of married females, ages 20–29, 1970 and 2010

Source: U.S. Census Bureau, *Current Population Survey*, March 2000.

compared to what. Most bar graphs also have "legends," which explain what the different features on the graph represent. Bars are typically distinguished from each other by use of different colors, shades, or patterns of crosshatching. The special power of bar graphs is that they can help readers make quick comparisons.

Pie Charts   Another vivid kind of graph is a pie chart or circle graph, which depicts different percentages of a total (the pie) in the form of slices. Pie charts are a favorite way of depicting the way parts of a whole are divided up. Suppose, for example, that you wanted your readers to notice the high percentage of widows among women age 65 and older. To do so, you could create a pie chart (Figure 9.12) based on the data in the last row of Table 9.2. As you can see, a pie chart shows at a glance how the

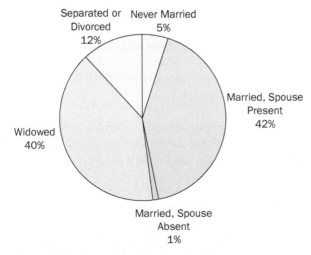

FIGURE 9.12 Marital status of females, age 65 and older, 2010

Source: U.S. Census Bureau, *Current Population Survey*, March 2010.

whole of something is divided into segments. However, the effectiveness of pie charts diminishes as you add more slices. In most cases, you'll begin to confuse readers if you include more than five or six slices.

Line Graphs   Another powerful quantitative graphic is a line graph, which converts numerical data into a series of points on a grid and connects them to create flat, rising, or falling lines. The result gives us a picture of the relationship between the variables represented on the horizontal and vertical axes.

Suppose you wanted to tell the story of the rising number of separated/divorced women in the U.S. population. Using Table 9.2, you can calculate the percentage of separated/divorced females in 2010 by adding the number of separated females (3,187,000) and the number of divorced females (13,760,000) and dividing that sum by the total number of females (124,361,000). The result is 13.6 percent. You can make the same calculations for 2000, 1990, 1980, and 1970 by looking at U.S. census data from those years (available on the Web or in your library). The resulting line graph is shown in Figure 9.14.

To determine what this graph is telling you, you need to clarify what's represented on the two axes. By convention, the horizontal axis of a graph contains the predictable, known variable, which has no surprises—what researchers call the "independent variable." In this case the horizontal axis represents the years 1970–2010 arranged predictably in chronological order. The vertical axis contains the unpredictable variable, which forms the graph's story—what researchers call the "dependent variable"—in this case, the percentage of separated or divorced females. The ascending curve tells the story at a glance.

Note that with line graphs, the steepness of the slope (and hence the rhetorical effect) can be manipulated by the intervals chosen for the vertical axis. Figure 9.13 shows vertical intervals of 2 percent. The slope could be made less dramatic by choosing intervals of, say, 10 percent and more dramatic by choosing intervals of 1 percent.

Incorporating Graphics into Your Argument

Today, writers working with quantitative data usually use graphing software that automatically creates tables, graphs, or charts from data entered into the cells of a spreadsheet. For college papers, some instructors may allow you to make your graphs with pencil and ruler and paste them into your document.

Designing the Graphic   When you design your graphic, your goal is to have a specific rhetorical effect on your readers, not to demonstrate all the bells and whistles available on your software. Adding extraneous data to the graph or chart or using such features as a three-dimensional effect can often distract from the story you are trying to tell. Keep the graphic as uncluttered and simple as possible and design it so that it reinforces the point you are making.

Numbering, Labeling, and Titling the Graphic   In newspapers and popular magazines, writers often include graphics in boxes or sidebars without specifically referring to them in the text itself. However, in academic and professional workplace writing, graphics are always labeled, numbered, titled, and referred to directly in the

Percent

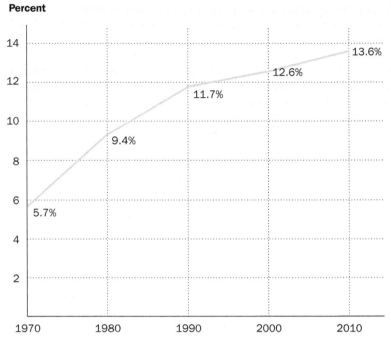

FIGURE 9.13 Percentage of females age 15 and older who are separated or divorced, 1970–2010

Source: U.S. Census Bureau, *Current Population Survey*, March 2010.

text. By convention, tables are listed as "Tables," whereas line graphs, bar graphs, pie charts, or any other kinds of drawings or photographs are labeled as "Figures." Suppose you create a document that includes four graphics—a table, a bar graph, a pie chart, and a photograph. The table would be labeled as Table 1. The rest would be labeled as Figure 1, Figure 2, and Figure 3.

In addition to numbering and labeling, every graphic needs a comprehensive title that explains fully what information is being displayed. Look back over the tables and figures in this chapter and compare their titles to the information in the graphics. In a line graph showing changes over time, for example, a typical title will identify the information on both the horizontal and vertical axes and the years covered. Bar graphs also have a "legend" explaining how the bars are coded if necessary. When you import the graphic into your own text, be consistent in where you place the title—either above the graphic or below it.

Referencing the Graphic in Your Text   Academic and professional writers follow a referencing convention called *independent redundancy*. The general rule is this: The graphic should be understandable without the text; the text should be understandable without the graphic; the text should repeat the most important information in the graphic. An example is shown in Figure 9.14.

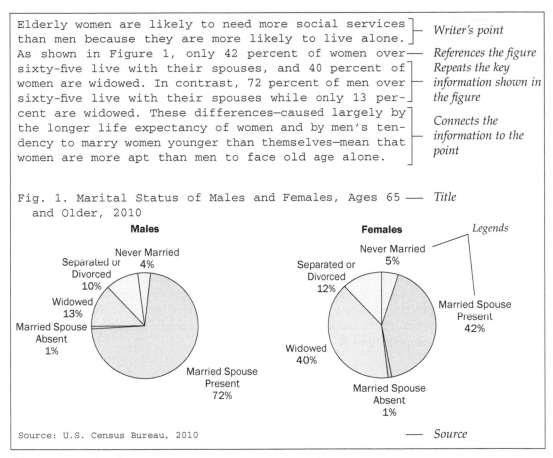

Elderly women are likely to need more social services ⎤ *Writer's point*
than men because they are more likely to live alone. ⎦
As shown in Figure 1, only 42 percent of women over— *References the figure*
sixty-five live with their spouses, and 40 percent of ⎤ *Repeats the key*
women are widowed. In contrast, 72 percent of men over ⎬ *information shown in*
sixty-five live with their spouses while only 13 per- ⎦ *the figure*
cent are widowed. These differences—caused largely by ⎤
the longer life expectancy of women and by men's ten- ⎬ *Connects the*
dency to marry women younger than themselves—mean that ⎥ *information to the*
women are more apt than men to face old age alone. ⎦ *point*

Fig. 1. Marital Status of Males and Females, Ages 65 —— *Title*
and Older, 2010

Males

Never Married
Separated or 4%
Divorced
10%
Widowed
13%
Married Spouse
Absent
1%

Married Spouse
Present
72%

Females

Legends

Never Married
Separated or 5%
Divorced
12%

Married Spouse
Present
42%

Widowed
40%

Married Spouse
Absent
1%

Source: U.S. Census Bureau, 2010 —— *Source*

FIGURE 9.14 Example of a student text with a referenced graph

WRITING ASSIGNMENT **A Visual Argument Rhetorical Analysis, a Visual Argument, or a Microtheme Using Quantitative Data**

Option 1: **Writing a Rhetorical Analysis of a Visual Argument** Write a thesis-driven rhetorical analysis essay in which you examine the rhetorical effectiveness of a visual argument, either one of the visual arguments in this text or one specified by your instructor. Unless otherwise stated, direct your analysis to an audience of your class-mates. In your introduction, establish the argumentative conversation to which this argument is contributing. Briefly summarize the argument and describe the visual text. Present your thesis, highlighting two or more rhetorical features of the argument that you find central to the effectiveness or ineffectiveness of this argument. To develop and support your own points, you will need to include visual features and details (such as color, design, camera angle, framing, and special effects) as well as short quotations from any verbal parts of the argument.

Option 2: Multimodal Assignment: A Poster Argument Working with the idea of an advocacy ad or poster argument that you explored in the For Class Discussion feature on page 159, use the visual design concepts and principles presented on page 158, your understanding of visual argument and the genre of poster arguments, and your own creativity to produce a poster argument that can be displayed on your campus or in your town or city. Try out the draft of your poster argument on people who are part of your target audience. Based on these individuals' suggestions for improving the clarity and impact of this visual argument, prepare a final version of your poster argument.

Option 3: Multimodal Assignment: Cartoon Choose a controversial issue important to you and create a single-frame political cartoon that presents your perspective on the issue in a memorable way. Use the cartoon strategies of mini-narrative, caricature, exaggeration, distortion, and the interaction between image and text.

Option 4: A Microtheme Using a Quantitative Graphic Write a microtheme that tells a story based on data you select from Table 9.2 or from some other table provided by your instructor or located by you. Include in your microtheme at least one quantitative graphic (table, line graph, bar graph, pie chart), which should be labeled and referenced according to standard conventions. Use as a model the short piece shown in Figure 9.14 on page 165. ■

PART FOUR
Arguments in Depth
Types of Claims

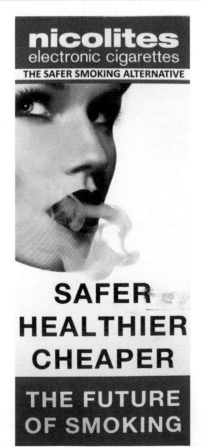

The advertisement for Nicolites is one voice in the public controversy over e-cigarettes. The ad claims that e-cigarettes are safer than regular cigarettes but chooses to use the word "smoking" rather than the more sanitized word "vaping." The vapor from e-cigarettes usually includes nicotine (and may have added flavors) but not the tar from cigarettes. However, as the discussion in Chapter 10 on pages 170–173 shows, the safety, healthfulness, and advisability of e-cigarettes are hotly debated issues. Using strategies from Chapter 9 on analyzing visual texts, how do the words and images in this ad work together to make positive claims about e-cigarettes?

167

An Introduction to the Types of Claims

10

What you will learn in this chapter:

10.1 To identify different claim types and show how each type has characteristic patterns of development

10.2 To use strategies based on claim types to help focus an argument, generate ideas for it, and structure it persuasively

10.3 To be mindful of how different claim types work together in hybrid arguments

In Parts One, Two, and Three of this text, we showed how argument entails both inquiry and persuasion. We explained strategies for creating a compelling structure of reasons and evidence for your arguments (*logos*), for linking your arguments to the beliefs and values of your audience (*pathos*), and for establishing your credibility and trustfulness (*ethos*). We also explained how to do a rhetorical analysis of both verbal and visual texts.

Now in Part Four, we examine arguments in depth by explaining five types of claims, each of which has its own characteristic patterns of development and support. Because almost all arguments use one or more of these types of claims as basic argumentative "moves" or building blocks, knowing how to develop each claim type will advance your skills in argument. The claims we examine in Part Four are related to an ancient rhetorical concept called *stasis,* from a Greek term meaning "stand," as in "to take a *stand* on something." There are many competing theories of stasis, so no two rhetoricians discuss stasis in exactly the same way.

The Types of Claims and Their Typical Patterns of Development

10.1 To identify different claim types and show how each type has characteristic patterns of development

To appreciate what a study of claim types can do, imagine one of those heated but frustrating arguments in which the question at issue keeps shifting. Everyone talks at cross-purposes, each speaker's point unconnected to the previous speaker's. Suppose your heated discussion is about the use of steroids. You might get such a discussion back on track if one person says: "Hold it for a moment. What are we actually arguing about here? Are we arguing about whether steroids are a health risk or whether steroids should be banned from sports? These are two different issues. We can't debate both at once." Whether she recognizes it or not, this person is applying the concept of claim types to get the argument focused.

To understand how claim types work, let's return to the concept of stasis. A stasis is an issue or question that focuses a point of disagreement. You and your audience might agree on the answer to questions A and B, but on question C, you disagree. For example, you and your audience might agree that steroids, if used carefully under a physician's supervision, pose few long-term health risks but still disagree on whether steroids should be banned from sports. This last issue constitutes a stasis, the point where you and your audience part company.

Rhetoricians have discovered that the kinds of questions that divide people have classifiable patterns. In this text, we identify several broad types of claims—each type originating in a different kind of question. The following chart gives you a quick overview of these types of claims, each of which is developed in more detail in subsequent chapters. It also shows you a typical structure for each type of argument. Note that the first three claim types concern questions of truth or reality, whereas the last two concern questions of value. You'll appreciate the significance of this distinction as this chapter progresses.

Claims about Reality, Truth, or the Way Things Are

Claim Type and Generic Question	Examples of Issue Questions	Typical Methods for Structuring an Argument
Definition arguments: *In which category does this thing belong?* Chapter 11	▪ Is solitary confinement cruel and unusual punishment? ▪ Is a skilled video game player an athlete?	▪ Create a definition that establishes criteria for the category. ▪ Use examples to show how the contested case meets the criteria.
Resemblance arguments: *To what is this thing similar?* Chapter 11	▪ Is opposition to gay marriage like opposition to interracial marriage? ▪ Is investing in the stock market like gambling?	▪ Let the analogy or precedent itself create the desired rhetorical effect. [or] ▪ Elaborate on the relevant similarities between the given case and the analogy or precedent.
Causal arguments: *What are the causes or consequences of this event or phenomenon?* Chapter 12	▪ What are the causes of bee colony collapse disorder? ▪ What might be the consequences of raising the minimum wage?	▪ Explain the links in a causal chain going from cause to effect, or summarize experimental studies showing cause or consequence [or] ▪ Speculate about causes (consequences) or propose a surprising cause (consequence)

Claims about Values

Claim Type and Generic Question	Examples of Issue Questions	Typical Methods for Structuring an Argument
Evaluation arguments: *What is the worth or value of this thing?* Chapter 13	▪ Is talk therapy a good approach for treating anxiety? ▪ Is it ethical to use reproductive technology to make "designer babies"?	▪ Establish the criteria for a "good" or "ethical" member of this class or category. ▪ Use examples to show how the contested case meets the criteria.
Proposal arguments: *Should we take this proposed action?* Chapter 14	▪ Should colleges abolish the SAT and ACT for admissions? ▪ Should the federal government enact a carbon tax?	▪ Make the problem vivid for the audience. ▪ Explain your proposed action to solve the problem. ▪ Justify your solution by showing how it is motivated by principle, by good consequences, or by resemblance to a previous action the audience approves.

▪ ▪ ▪   **FOR CLASS DISCUSSION** Identifying Types of Claims

Working as a whole class or in small groups, decide which claim type is represented by each of the following questions. Sometimes there might be several different ways to classify, so if you think the question fits two different categories, explain your reasoning.

[handwritten margin note: Evaluation or Causal / Causal / Causal]

1. Should the president be authorized to employ weaponized drones to kill terrorists?
2. Is taking Adderall to increase concentration for an exam a form of cheating?
3. What would be the economic consequences of a carbon tax aimed at reducing carbon emissions?
4. Were the terrorist attacks of September 11, 2001, more like Pearl Harbor (an act of war) or more like an earthquake (a natural disaster)?
5. How effective is acupuncture in reducing morning sickness?
6. Is acupuncture quackery or real medicine?

▪ ▪ ▪

Using Claim Types to Focus an Argument and Generate Ideas: An Example

10.2 To use strategies based on claim types to help focus an argument, generate ideas for it, and structure it persuasively

Having provided an overview of the types of claims, we now show you some of the benefits of this knowledge. First of all, understanding claim types will help you focus an argument by asking you to determine what's at stake between you and your audience. Where do you and your audience agree and disagree?

Second, it will help you generate ideas for your argument by suggesting the kinds of reasons, examples, and evidence you'll need.

To illustrate, let's take the recent public controversy about e-cigarettes, which use a battery powered heating element to vaporize the liquid in a small cartridge. The user inhales the vapor (an act often called "vaping"). Cartridges can be purchased containing various amounts of nicotine or no nicotine at all; flavored liquids (such as apple cinnamon or peach cobbler) are also available. Although there is debate about whether the vapors from e-cigarettes are harmful, everyone agrees that the nicotine-laced liquid itself is poisonous if ingested in its liquid form.

In the absence of federal regulations, many states and cities have enacted their own laws about e-cigarettes, often treating them exactly as if they were real cigarettes—banning them from bars, restaurants, and other public places, forbidding their sale to minors, and restricting the ways they can be advertised.

Let's now take the hypothetical case of a city debating a policy on e-cigarettes. Imagine three different writers. Writer 1 wants to ban e-cigarettes, while Writer 2 wants to promote them as a preferred alternative to real cigarettes. Writer 3, a libertarian, advocates minimal restrictions. Let's consider how familiarity with claim types can help each writer generate ideas for his or her argument.

Writer 1: Ban E-Cigarettes

Writer 1 believes that e-cigarettes are harmful. Her goal is to portray e-cigarettes negatively in order to persuade her audience that e-cigarettes should be banned.

- **Definition argument:** Because regular cigarettes are already banned in public places, Writer 1 wants to place e-cigarettes in the same category as real cigarettes. For part of her argument she can use a definitional strategy showing that e-cigarettes and regular cigarettes belong in the same category, in that they both deliver nicotine extracted from tobacco leaves. She can argue that the differences between e-cigarettes and regular cigarettes, such as one producing smoke and the other vapor, are superficial. What makes them the same is the delivery of nicotine.
- **Resemblance argument:** Using a resemblance strategy, Writer 1 can also show how e-cigarettes are designed to look like regular cigarettes and make smoking look cool again. You can blow "smoke" rings with the exhaled vapor, just as you can with real tobacco smoke.
- **Causal argument:** To increase her negative portrayal of e-cigarettes, Writer 1 can also use a causal strategy. She can argue that e-cigarettes will hook children and teenagers on real cigarettes. She can show how the creation of flavored vapors such as "bubble gum" or "pancake" seem marketed to children and how the availability of cartridges that combine flavored vapors with nicotine give Big Tobacco a new way to create the next generation of nicotine addicts.
- **Evaluation argument:** Here Writer 1 will have to summarize and rebut counterviews that e-cigarettes are a good replacement for regular cigarettes. Supporters

will say the e-cigarettes are better than regular cigarettes because they produce fewer carcinogens and are thus safer. Writer 1 will need to argue that the negative aspects of e-cigarettes—nicotine addiction and the enticement of children toward smoking—outweigh the increased safety. She can also argue that the propellant ingredients in the cartridges haven't yet been proven safe and can refer to research showing the liquid itself is extremely poisonous if ingested directly.

- **Proposal argument:** The city council should ban e-cigarettes.

Writer 2: Promote E-Cigarettes as a Preferred Alternative to Real Cigarettes

Writer 2 shares with his audience a belief that cigarettes are harmful and that smoking should be banned. However, he wants to emphasize the benefits of e-cigarettes to people who already smoke. Like Writer 1, he can use the five claim types to generate strategies for his argument.

- **Definition argument:** To portray e-cigarettes more positively, Writer 2 can make the definitional claim that e-cigarettes are *not* the same as real cigarettes and thus belong in a different category. He can argue that the essential trait of real cigarettes is cancer-causing tar derived from the combustion of tobacco leaves. It is the danger of the tar, not the nicotine, that caused the anti-smoking movement in the first place, especially the danger of secondhand smoke to others. By arguing that the delivery of nicotine is a superficial rather than essential criterion for defining cigarettes, he can show that the absence of tar and secondhand smoke makes e-cigarettes essentially different from real cigarettes.
- **Resemblance argument:** Using this strategy, Writer 2 can show that although e-cigarettes are essentially different from real cigarettes, the two have pleasing similarities. Vaping provides the same physical and social pleasures as does smoking, but without the harm to self and others.
- **Causal argument:** Writer 2 can also portray e-cigarettes positively through the causal argument that they can save the lives of current smokers by converting them from the dangerous to less dangerous way of getting nicotine. Without condoning nicotine addiction, Writer 2 can point to the positive health consequences of getting a nicotine hit without the carcinogens. Writer 2 can also argue that e-cigarettes can help people stop smoking because they can gradually reduce the nicotine content in the cartridges they purchase.
- **Evaluation argument:** Here Writer 2 can claim that e-cigarettes are better than real cigarettes by arguing that the health benefits of no smoke and tar outweigh the addiction to nicotine, which in itself causes little health risk.
- **Proposal argument:** E-cigarettes should be promoted as a safe alternative to real cigarettes.

Writer 3: Place No Restrictions on E-Cigarettes

Writer 3 is a libertarian who dislikes nanny-state restrictions on our individual freedoms. She wants to argue that the only restrictions on e-cigarettes should be federally mandated childproofing of the cartridges, truth-in-labeling about what is contained in the cartridges, and prevention of sales of nicotine-containing cartridges to minors.

- **Definition argument:** Writer 3, like Writer 2, can argue that e-cigarettes are in a different category from regular cigarettes. They present no proven dangers either to self or to others through secondhand smoke.
- **Resemblance argument:** To celebrate the libertarian endorsement of individual freedom, Writer 3 can show the resemblance between taking a pleasurable hit on an e-cigarette with other pleasures frowned on by the nanny state—drinking sugary sodas, buying a big Mac, or owning a muscle car.
- **Causal argument:** Whereas Writer 2 argues that e-cigarettes are safer than regular cigarettes, Writer 3 can argue that no one has demonstrated any firsthand or secondhand health hazards for e-cigarettes. She can make the additional causal argument that government wants to treat e-cigarettes like regular cigarettes so that they can tax them heavily to produce sin-tax revenue. She can also argue that nanny-state regulations lead to increased loss of personal freedoms and the shutting down of markets for free enterprise.
- **Evaluation argument:** Writer 3 can argue that people should be free to make their own evaluations of e-cigarettes.
- **Proposal argument:** For consenting adults, the city should place no restrictions on e-cigarettes.

Hybrid Arguments: How Claim Types Work Together in Arguments

10.3 To be mindful of how different claim types work together in hybrid arguments

As the e-cigarette example shows, hybrid arguments can be built from different claim types. A writer might develop a proposal argument with a causal subargument in one section, a resemblance subargument in another section, and an evaluation subargument in still another section. Although the overarching proposal argument follows the typical structure of a proposal, each of the subsections follows a typical structure for its own claim type.

Some Examples of Hybrid Arguments

The following examples show how these combinations of claim types can play out in actual arguments.

Evaluation Argument Addressed to Parents

Shooter video games are bad for kids	Evaluation claim —— Values claim
because they are socially toxic.	Definition claim
because they have been shown to promote violence in some males.	Causal claim ⎫ Truth/reality claims
because they desensitize users to violence in the same way that army training games do.	Resemblance claim ⎭

Proposal Argument Addressed to Local Newspaper Readers

Our region should build a light-rail transportation system	Proposal claim —— Values claim
because light rail would get a substantial number of commuters out of cars.	Causal claim ⎫
because light rail has been successful in other regions.	Resemblance claim ⎬ Truth/reality claims
because light rail is cost effective and environmentally sound.	Evaluation claim ⎭

■ ■ ■ **FOR CLASS DISCUSSION** **Exploring Different Claim Types and Audiences**

Working in small groups or as a whole class, try to develop hybrid arguments for each of the authorial purposes below. How might supporting reasons for each argument be based on different claim types (definition, resemblance, cause, evaluation, proposal)? Use as your models our example arguments about e-cigarettes. Imagine an audience skeptical of your chosen position.

1. Carbon footprint: You want (do not want) the Environmental Protection Agency to regulate the amount of carbon dioxide that can be emitted from power plants.
2. Gun restrictions: You want (do not want) the federal government to ban assault rifles and high-volume ammunition cartridges.
3. Diet: You want your classmates to adopt (or not adopt) the paleo diet.   ■ ■ ■

An Extended Example of a Hybrid Argument

As the previous examples illustrate, different claim types often serve as building blocks for larger arguments. We ask you now to consider the following argument from *Outside Magazine* aimed at enthusiasts of outdoor sports such as hiking, mountain climbing, skiing, biking, and distance running. The magazine's readers are often health-conscious consumers of multivitamins and other diet supplements ranging from fish oil capsules to energy drinks. In this startling article the writer uses recent scientific studies to make the evaluation claim that these supplements are either "useless" or "worse than useless." Notice how this overall evaluation claim is supported by claims from definition, resemblance, and cause.

Your Daily Multivitamin May Be Hurting You

ALEX HUTCHINSON

Introduces the **evaluation** *issue "Are supplements good/bad?"*

In JUNE, at this year's European College of Sport Science conference in Barcelona, Mari Carmen Gomez-Cabrera, a physiologist at the University of Valencia and one of the world's leading experts on antioxidants, was debating the merits of supplements with two top researchers. For more than 90 minutes they went back and forth, parsing the accumulated evidence in front of a packed auditorium. Finally, Gomez-Cabrera landed on a provocative question that summarized her position.

Restates **evaluation** *issue with implied claim: Supplements are either useless or worse than useless.*

The debate, she explained, isn't whether supplements are good or bad for athletes. Rather, it's "are they useless, or are they worse than useless?"

The question may come as a shock to the more than half of Americans who take some sort of dietary supplement—a vast catch-all term that includes everything from vitamins and minerals to herbal remedies to exotic performance boosters like deer-antler spray and glutamine.

Further develops **evaluation claim**: *Supplements are bad because they make unproven claims and because they may come with hazardous side effects.*

It's no surprise that the purported muscle-building supplements make unproven claims and may come with hazardous side effects. But in the past few years, Gomez-Cabrera and a growing number of researchers have come to believe that even respectable mainstream supplements like vitamins C and E suffer from the same basic flaw: few apparent benefits and increasing evidence of negative effects.

Uses **causal arguments** *to illustrate bad side effects.*

For example, in July's issue of the *Journal of Physiology,* researchers discovered that resveratrol, an antioxidant in red wine, actually limited the positive effects of cardiovascular exercise—like an increased VO2 max—when taken daily in high concentrations. In July, scientists at the Fred Hutchinson Cancer Research Center found that men with high levels of the omega-3 fatty acid DHA in their blood, often from fish-oil supplements, had a significantly greater risk of prostate cancer.

Definition claim: *Supplements belong to one of two categories: (1) safe but don't work or (2) work but have bad side effects.*

According to Pieter Cohen, a professor at Harvard Medical School, there are really only two types of sports supplements: those that are safe but don't work, and those that might work but have side effects, especially at higher than normal levels. "If any supplement, no matter how beneficial, has a pharmaceutical effect, it's also got a downside," he says. "There's no way to get around that basic principle."

Develops definition argument by showing how supplements meet criteria of being safe but useless or having bad side effects.

5   Most supplements stay firmly in the first category. Taking a daily multivitamin, Cohen emphasizes, won't harm you, but it usually won't help either, which is why major health organizations like the American Heart Association and the American College of Sports Medicine don't recommend supplements to healthy people.

It's not that vitamins and minerals aren't important. If you don't get enough vitamin C, you can get scurvy; without enough iron, you can become anemic; and if you live far enough north to see Russia from your backyard, you may need some extra vitamin D. But all three of these substances have also been linked to negative effects at high doses. Same goes for prolonged use of other common supplements like vitamin E and calcium. In short, unless tests have shown that you're low in a particular vitamin or mineral, there's no evidence to suggest that you should take a daily supplement.

Causal argument showing bad side effects

That rule also applies if you're an athlete who takes supplements because, say, you assume your training requires an anti-oxidant boost to speed recovery. Gomez-Cabrera and her colleagues at the University of Valencia have shown that antioxidant supplements suppress the oxidative stress that signals your body to adapt and get stronger. The result: regular use of something seemingly innocuous like vitamin C can actually block gains in endurance-boosting mitochondria.

Causal argument showing still more bad side effects

The balance between risk and return also works in subtler ways, as Wen-Bin Chiou, a psychologist at National Sun Yatsen University in Taiwan, has shown in a series of experiments on a phenomenon called the licensing effect. As part of a battery of tests, subjects were asked to take a pill; half were told the pill was a multivitamin, while the other half were told it was a placebo. In truth, they were all placebos.

Causal argument from psychology showing different bad effect: People who take supplements feel they are healthier and thus actually act in less healthy ways.

In subsequent tests, the subjects who thought they'd taken a vitamin consistently behaved in less healthy ways. When asked to try out a pedometer, they were more likely to choose a shorter walking route; at lunch, they chose less healthy food. In follow-up studies, Chiou has also discovered that smokers who think they've been given a vitamin smoke more, and people who are given a weight-loss supplement are less likely to stick to their diet. The same thing happens when you go to the gym or eat a plate of spinach. The difference is that exercise and vegetables have real benefits, so you've still got a chance to come out ahead. If you take a pill with no benefits, the best you can do is break even.

Brief resemblance argument: Taking a vitamin is NOT like eating spinach or going to the gym.

Conclusion

> Which brings us back to Gomez-Cabrera in Barcelona. She, of all people, has enormous respect for the powers of micronutrients like antioxidants—she has devoted her life to studying them. "But if you eat enough fruits and vegetables, five servings a day," she says, "I don't think you need anything else." And if you're not eating like that, then taking a pill isn't a solution. In fact, it may be part of the problem.

As this editorial demonstrates, awareness of different kinds of claims can help you increase your flexibility and effectiveness as an arguer. In the following chapters in Part Four, we discuss each of the claim types in more detail, showing how they work and how you can develop skills and strategies for supporting each type of claim.

Definition and Resemblance Arguments

11

What you will learn in this chapter:

11.1 To explain what is at stake in categorical arguments

11.2 To explain four types of categorical arguments

11.3 To explain the criteria match structure of categorical arguments based on definition

11.4 To use criteria-match reasoning to generate ideas for your own definition argument

11.5 To write your own definitional argument

Arguments about definition or resemblance concern disputes about what category something belongs to, either directly by definition or indirectly or metaphorically through comparison or resemblance. They are among the most common argument types you will encounter.

Case 1   Are Global Warming Skeptics Like The Outlier Frog In This Cartoon?

This cartoon by award-wining political cartoonist (as well as children's book author) Pat Bagley makes two overlapping resemblance arguments. First, it argues that global warming happens slowly, like a heating pot of water. Second, it argues that the Republican Science Committee, comprised of global warming skeptics, selects its evidence from outlier sources, analogous to the outlier frog in this cartoon. This striking visual analogy makes a resemblance argument against the objectivity of the GOP Science Committee.

Case 2   Is a Frozen Embryo a Person or Property?

An infertile couple conceived several embryos in a test tube and then froze the fertilized embryos for future use. During the couple's divorce, they disagreed about the disposition of the embryos. The woman wanted to use the frozen embryos to try to get pregnant, and the man wanted to destroy them. When the courts were asked to decide what should be done with the embryos, several questions of definition arose: Should the frozen embryos be categorized as "persons," thus becoming analogous to children in custody disputes? Or should they be divided up as "property," with the man getting half and the woman getting the other half? Or should a new legal category be created for them that regards them as more than property but less than actual persons? The judge decided that frozen embryos "are not, strictly speaking, either 'persons' or 'property,' but occupy an interim category that entitles them to special respect because of their potential for human life."*

What is at Stake in a Categorical Argument?

11.1 To explain what is at stake in categorical arguments

Definition and resemblance arguments occur whenever a community disagrees about the category a particular person, thing, act, or phenomenon should be placed in or identified with. Here are some examples:

Issues Involving Categories

Question	Does this specific phenomenon...	...belong to (or is it similar to) this category?
Is atmospheric carbon dioxide a pollutant?	Atmospheric carbon dioxide	Pollutant
Is LASIK surgery for nearsightedness "medically necessary" surgery or "cosmetic" surgery?	LASIK surgery for nearsightedness	Medically necessary surgery (or cosmetic surgery)
Is women's obsession with thinness today similar in effect to women's foot binding in ancient China?	Women's obsession with thinness	Foot binding in ancient China

Much is at stake when we place things into categories because the category that something belongs to can have real consequences. Naming the category that something belongs to makes an implicit mini-argument.

---

*See Vincent F. Stempel, "Procreative Rights in Assisted Reproductive Technology: Why the Angst?" *Albany Law Review* 62 (1999), 1187.

Consequences Resulting from Categorical Claims

To appreciate the consequences of categorical claims, consider the competing categories proposed for whales in the international controversy over commercial whaling. What category does a whale belong to? Some arguers might say that "whales are sacred animals," implying that their intelligence, beauty, grace, and power mean they should never be killed. Others might argue that "whales are a renewable food resource" like tuna, crabs, cattle, and chickens. This category implies that we can harvest whales for food the same way we harvest tuna for tuna fish sandwiches or cows for beef. Still others might argue that "whales are an endangered species"—a category that argues for the preservation of whale stocks but not necessarily for a ban on controlled hunting of individual whales. Each of these whaling arguments places whales in a separate, different category that implicitly urges the reader to adopt that category's perspective on whaling.

Significant consequences can also result from resemblance claims. Consider the way that media analysts tried to make sense of the September 11, 2001, terrorist attacks on the World Trade Center and the Pentagon by comparing them to different kinds of previous events. Some commentators said, "The September 11 attacks are like Timothy McVeigh's bombing of the Alfred P. Murrah Federal Building in Oklahoma City in 1995"—an argument that framed the terrorists as criminals who must be brought to justice. Others said, "The September 11 attacks are like the 1941 Japanese attack on Pearl Harbor"—an argument suggesting that the United States should declare war on some as-yet-to-be-defined enemy. Still others said, "The September 11 attacks are like an occasionally disastrous earthquake or an epidemic," arguing that terrorists will exist as long as the right conditions breed them and that it is useless to fight them using the strategies of conventional war. Under this analogy, the "war on terror" is a metaphorical war like the "war on poverty" or the "war against cancer." Clearly, each of these resemblance claims had high-stakes consequences. In 2001, the Pearl Harbor claim prevailed, and the United States went to war, first in Afghanistan and then in Iraq. Many critics of these wars continue to say that war is an inappropriate strategy for fighting the "disease of terrorism."

The Rule of Justice: Things in the Same Category Should Be Treated the Same Way

As you can see, the category we place something into—either directly through definition or indirectly through comparison—can have significant implications for people's actions or beliefs. To ensure fairness, philosophers refer to the rule of justice, which states that "beings in the same essential category should be treated in the same way." For example, the problem of how the courts should treat the users or sellers of marijuana depends on the category marijuana belongs to. Marijuana might be placed in the same category as tobacco and alcohol, in which case the possession and sale of marijuana would be legal but subject to regulation and taxes. Or marijuana could be placed in the same category as meth, cocaine, and heroin; in this case, it would be an illegal drug subject to criminal prosecution. Some states have placed marijuana in the same category as penicillin and insulin, making it a legal drug so long as it is obtained from a licensed dispensary with a doctor's prescription. Many states are not happy with any of these categories and are trying to define marijuana in some fourth way. Or to take a more homely example, suppose your professor says that absence from an exam can be excused for emergencies only. How would you define "emergency"? Clearly if you broke your leg on the morning of an exam, you would be excused. But is attending your grandmother's funeral or your best friend's wedding an "emergency"? How about missing an exam because your car wouldn't start? Although your interests might be best served by a broad definition of emergency, your professor might prefer a narrow definition, which would permit fewer exemptions.

The rule of justice becomes especially hard to apply when we consider contested cases marked by growth or slow change through time. At what point does a child become an adult? When does a binge drinker become an alcoholic, an Internet poker player a compulsive gambler, or a fetus a human person? In most category debates, an argument, not a quick trip to the dictionary, is required to settle the matter.

■ ■ ■   **FOR CLASS DISCUSSION** **Applying the Rule of Justice**

Suppose your landlord decides to institute a "no pets" rule. The rule of justice requires that all pets have to go—not just your neighbor's barking dog, but also Mrs. Brown's cat, the kids' hamster downstairs, and your own pet tarantula. That is, all these animals have to go, unless you can argue that some of them are not "pets" for purposes of the landlord's "no pets" rule.

1. Working in small groups or as a whole class, define pets by establishing the criteria an animal would have to meet to be included in the category "pets." Consider your landlord's "no pets" rule as the cultural context for your definition.
2. Based on your criteria, which of the following animals is definitely a pet that would have to be removed from the apartment? Based on your criteria, which animals could you exclude from the "no pets" rule? How would you make your argument to your landlord?
   - a German shepherd
   - a small housecat
   - a tiny, well-trained lapdog
   - a gerbil in a cage
   - a canary
   - a tank of tropical fish
   - a tarantula

■ ■ ■

Types of categorical Arguments

11.2 To explain four types of categorical arguments

Categorical arguments assert that a disputed phenomenon is (or is not) either a member of a certain category or is like a certain category. Such arguments can be divided into four kinds:

1. **Simple categorical arguments,** in which there is no dispute about the definition of the category.
2. **Definition arguments,** in which there is a dispute about the boundaries of the category and hence of its definition.

3. **Resemblance arguments by analogy,** in which the writer uses metaphor or other figurative language to link the phenomenon to a certain category.
4. **Resemblance arguments by precedent,** in which the arguer claims that one phenomenon or situation is similar to another phenomenon or situation.

Let's look at each in turn.

Simple Categorical Arguments

A categorical argument can be said to be "simple" if there is no disagreement about the definition of the category into which a person, event, or phenomenon is placed. For example, if you make the claim that "Joe is bossy," you are placing him in the category of "bossy people." In this case, you assume that you and the audience agree on what "bossy" means. Your dispute is simply whether Joe meets the criteria for "bossy." To support your claim, you would provide examples of his bossiness (his poor listening skills, his shouting at people, his making decisions without asking the committee). To support or rebut a simple categorical claim, you would provide evidence to show that the person, event, or phenomenon does or does not meet the criteria for the category.

■ ■ ■   **FOR CLASS DISCUSSION**   **Supporting and Rebutting Simple Categorical Claims**

Working individually or in small groups, consider how you would support the following simple categorical claims. What examples or other data would convince readers that the specified case fits within the named category? Then discuss ways you might rebut each claim.

1. Bottled water is environmentally unfriendly. (That is, bottled water belongs in the category of "environmentally unfriendly substances.")
2. Macklemore is a pure rapper.
3. Americans today are obsessed with their appearance. (That is, Americans belong in the category of "people obsessed with their appearance.")
4. Competitive cheerleading is physically risky.   ■ ■ ■

Definition Arguments

Simple categorical arguments morph into definition arguments whenever stakeholders disagree about the boundaries of a category. Suppose in the previous exercise that you had said about Macklemore, "Well, that depends on how you define 'pure rapper.'" The need to define the term "pure rapper" adds a new layer of complexity to your arguments about Macklemore. You are disputing not only specifics about Macklemore but also the definition of "pure rapper" itself.

Full-blown definition arguments occur, then, when the disputants don't agree on the definition of the category into which a person, event, or phenomenon is placed. Consider, for example, the environmental controversy over the definition of *wetland*. Section 404 of the federal Clean Water Act provides for federal protection of wetlands, but it leaves the task of defining *wetland* to administrative agencies and the courts. Currently, about

5 percent of the land surface of the contiguous forty-eight states is potentially affected by the wetlands provision, and 75 percent of this land is privately owned. Efforts to define *wetland* have created a battleground between pro-environment and pro-development or property rights groups. Farmers, homeowners, and developers often want a narrow definition of wetlands so that more property is available for commercial or private use. Environmentalists favor a broad definition in order to protect different habitat types and maintain the environmental safeguards that wetlands provide (control of water pollution, spawning grounds for aquatic species, floodwater containment, and so forth).

The problem is that defining *wetland* is tricky. For example, one federal regulation defines a wetland as any area that has a saturated ground surface for twenty-one consecutive days during the year. But how would you apply this law to a pine flatwood ecosystem that was wet for ten days this year but thirty days last year? And how should the courts react to lawsuits claiming that the regulation itself is either too broad or too narrow? One can see why the wetlands controversy provides hefty incomes for lawyers and congressional lobbyists.

As we will explain later, definition arguments require a "criteria-match" structure in which the arguer must first define the category term by specifying the criteria that must be met for something to be placed in that category. The writer then shows that the disputed person, event, or phenomenon matches those criteria.

Resemblance Argument Using Analogy

Whereas definition arguments claim that a particular phenomenon belongs to a certain category, resemblance arguments simply compare one thing to another. A common kind of resemblance argument uses analogies—imaginative kinds of comparisons often with subtle persuasive effects. If you don't like your new boss, you can say that she's like a Marine drill sergeant or the cowardly captain of a sinking ship. Each of these analogies suggests a different category in which to place your boss, clarifying the nature of your dislike while conveying an emotional charge. The arguer's intention is to transfer the audience's understanding of (or feelings about) the second thing back to the first. The risk of resemblance arguments is that the differences between the two things being compared are often so significant that the argument collapses under close examination.

Sometimes, as in the "My boss is like a Marine drill sergeant" example, arguers use short, undeveloped analogies for quick rhetorical effect. At other times, arguers develop extended analogies that carry a substantial portion of the argument. As an example of an extended analogy, consider the following excerpt from a professor's argument opposing a proposal to require a writing proficiency exam for graduation. In the following portion of his argument, the professor compares development of writing skills to the development of physical fitness.

> A writing proficiency exam gives the wrong symbolic messages about writing. It suggests that writing is simply a skill, rather than an active way of thinking and learning. It suggests that once a student demonstrates proficiency then he or she doesn't need to do any more writing.
>
> Imagine two universities concerned with the physical fitness of their students. One university requires a junior-level physical fitness exam in which students must run a mile in less than 10 minutes, a fitness level it considers minimally competent. Students at this university see the physical fitness exam as a one-time hurdle. As many as 70 percent of them can pass the

exam with no practice; another 10–20 percent need a few months' training; and a few hopeless couch potatoes must go through exhaustive remediation. After passing the exam, any student can settle back into a routine of TV and potato chips having been certified as "physically fit."

The second university, however, believing in true physical fitness for its students, is not interested in minimal competency. Consequently, it creates programs in which its students must take one credit physical fitness course each term for the entire four years of the undergraduate curriculum. There is little doubt which university will have the most physically fit students. At the second university, fitness becomes a way of life with everyone developing his or her full potential. Similarly, if we want to improve our students' writing abilities, we should require writing in every course throughout the curriculum.

Thus analogies have the power to get an audience's attention like virtually no other persuasive strategy. But seldom are they sufficient in themselves to provide full understanding. At some point, with every analogy, you need to ask yourself, "How far can I legitimately go with this? At what point are the similarities between the two things I am comparing going to be overwhelmed by their dissimilarities?" Analogies are useful attention-getting devices, but they can conceal and distort as well as clarify.

■ ■ ■ **FOR CLASS DISCUSSION** Developing Analogies

The following exercise will help you clarify how analogies function in the context of arguments. Working individually or in small groups, think of two analogies for each of the following topics. One analogy should urge readers toward a positive view of the topic; the other should urge a negative view. Write each of your analogies in the following one-sentence format:

_____ is like _____: A, B, C…(in which the first term is the contested topic being discussed; the second term is the analogy; and A, B, and C are the points of comparison).

Example

Topic: Cramming for an exam

Negative analogy: Cramming for an exam is like pumping iron for ten hours straight to prepare for a weight-lifting contest: exhausting and counterproductive.

Positive analogy: Cramming for an exam is like carbohydrate loading before a big race: it gives your brain a full supply of facts and concepts, all fresh in your mind.

1. Checking social media constantly
2. Using racial profiling for airport security
3. Using steroids to increase athletic performance
4. Paying college athletes
5. Eating at fast-food restaurants

■ ■ ■

Resemblance Arguments Using Precedent

Another kind of resemblance argument uses precedent for its persuasive force. An argument by precedent tries to show that a current situation is like a past situation and that therefore a similar action or decision should be taken or reached. You can refute a precedence argument by showing that the present situation differs substantially from the past situation.

EXAMINING VISUAL ARGUMENTS

Claim about Category (Definition)

This cartoon, by political cartoonist Randy Bish of the *Pittsburgh Tribune Review*, creates a visual pun that makes a categorical argument against heroin. How does Bish's rendering of the letter "r" make a categorical claim? What is that claim? How effective do you find this cartoon in highlighting the seductive danger of heroin addiction?

Precedence arguments are very common. For example, during the debate about health care reform in the first year of Barack Obama's presidency, supporters of a single-payer, "Medicare-for-all" system pointed to Canada as a successful precedent. Supporters said that since a single-payer system was successful in Canada, it would also be successful in the United States. But opponents also used the Canadian precedent to attack a single-payer system. They pointed to problems in the Canadian system as a reason to reject a Medicare-for-all system in the United States.

■ ■ ■ **FOR CLASS DISCUSSION** Using Claims of Precedent

Consider the following claims of precedent, and evaluate how effective you think each precedent might be in establishing the claim. How would you develop the argument? How would you cast doubt on it?

1. To increase alumni giving to our university, we should put more funding into our football program. When University X went to postseason bowls for three years in a row, alumni donations to building programs and academics increased by 30 percent. We can expect the same increases here.

2. Postwar democracy can be created successfully in Afghanistan because it was created successfully in Germany and Japan following World War II.
3. Euthanasia laws work successfully in the Netherlands. Therefore they will work successfully in the United States.

The Criteria-Match Structure of Definition Arguments

11.3 To explain the criteria-match structure of categorical arguments based on definition

Of the four types of categorical arguments explained in the previous section, definition arguments require the fullest range of argumentative skills. For the rest of this chapter, we'll explain more fully the argumentative moves required to write your own definition argument.

Overview of Criteria-Match Structure

Definition arguments usually have a two-part structure: (1) a definition part that tries to establish the boundaries of the category, and (2) a match part that argues whether a given case meets that definition. To describe this structure, we use the term *criteria-match.* Here are two examples:

> **Definition issue:** In a divorce proceeding, is a frozen embryo a "person" rather than "property"?
> **Criteria part:** What criteria must be met for something to be a "person"?
> **Match part:** Does a frozen embryo meet these criteria?

> **Definition issue:** Is this thirty-acre parcel of land near Swan Lake a "wetland"?
> **Criteria part:** What criteria must be met for something to be a wetland?
> **Match part:** Does this parcel of land meet these criteria?

To show how a definition issue can be developed into a claim with supporting reasons, let's look more closely at a third example:

> **Definition issue:** For purposes of my feeling good about buying my next pair of running shoes, is the Hercules Shoe Company a socially responsible company?
> **Criteria part:** What criteria must be met for a company to be deemed "socially responsible"?
> **Match part:** Does the Hercules Shoe Company meet these criteria?

Let's suppose you work for a consumer information group that wishes to encourage patronage of socially responsible companies while boycotting irresponsible ones. Your group's first task is to define *socially responsible company*. After much discussion and research, your group establishes three criteria that a company must meet to be considered socially responsible:

> *Your definition:* A company is socially responsible if it (1) avoids polluting the environment, (2) sells goods or services that contribute to the well-being of the community, and (3) treats its workers justly.

The criteria section of your argument would explain and illustrate these criteria.

The match part of the argument would then try to persuade readers that a specific company does or does not meet the criteria. A typical thesis statement might be as follows:

> *Your thesis statement:* Although the Hercules Shoe Company is nonpolluting and provides a socially useful product, it is not a socially responsible company because it treats workers unjustly.

Toulmin Framework for a Definition Argument

Here is how the core of the preceding Hercules definition argument could be displayed in Toulmin terms. Note how the reason and grounds constitute the match argument while the warrant and backing constitute the criterion argument.

Toulmin Analysis of the Hercules Shoe Company Argument

ENTHYMEME

CLAIM The Hercules Shoe Company is not a socially responsible company

REASON because it treats workers unjustly.

GROUNDS

Evidence of unjust treatment:

- Evidence that the company manufactures its shoes in East Asian sweatshops

- Evidence of the inhumane conditions in these shops

- Evidence of hardships imposed on displaced American workers

CONDITIONS OF REBUTTAL

Attacking reasons and grounds

- Possible counter evidence that the shops maintain humane working conditions

- Possible questioning of statistical data about hardships on displaced workers

WARRANT

Socially responsible companies treat workers justly.

BACKING

- Arguments showing that just treatment of workers is right in principle and also benefits society

- Arguments that capitalism helps society as a whole only if workers achieve a reasonable standard of living, have time for leisure, and are not exploited

CONDITIONS OF REBUTTAL

Attacking warrant and backing

Justice needs to be considered from an emerging nation's standpoint:

- The wages paid workers are low by American standards but are above average by East Asian standards.

- Displacement of American workers is part of the necessary adjustment of adapting to a global economy and does not mean that a company is unjust.

As this Toulmin schema illustrates, the warrant and backing constitute the criteria section of the argument by stating and defending "just treatment of workers" as a criterion for a socially responsible company. The reason and grounds constitute the match section of the argument by arguing that the Hercules Shoe Company does not treat its workers justly. How much emphasis you need to place on justifying each criterion and supporting each match depends on your audience's initial beliefs. The conditions of rebuttal help you imagine alternative views and see places where opposing views need to be acknowledged and rebutted.

■ ■ ■   **FOR CLASS DISCUSSION** Identifying Criteria and Match Issues

Consider the following definition claims. Working individually or in small groups, identify the criteria issue and the match issue for each of the following claims.

> **Definition issue:** A Honda assembled in Ohio is (is not) an American-made car.
>
> **Criteria part:** What criteria have to be met before a car can be called "American made"?
>
> **Match part:** Does a Honda assembled in Ohio meet these criteria?

1. American Sign Language is (is not) a "foreign language" for purposes of a college graduation requirement.
2. The violence in *Grand Theft Auto* is (is not) constitutionally protected free speech.
3. Bungee jumping from a crane is (is not) a "carnival amusement ride" subject to state safety inspections.
4. For purposes of a state sales tax on "candy," a Twinkie is (is not) candy.
5. A skilled video game player is (is not) a true athlete.   ■ ■ ■

Creating Criteria Using Aristotelian Definition

When creating criteria for a category, you can often follow the pattern of *Aristotelian definition.* The Aristotelian definitional strategy, regularly used in dictionaries, defines a term by placing it within the next larger class or category and then showing the specific attributes that distinguish the term from other terms within the same category. For example, according to a legal dictionary, *robbery* is "the felonious taking of property" (next larger category) that differs from other acts of theft because it seizes property "through violence or intimidation." Legal dictionaries often provide specific examples to show the boundaries of the term. Here is one example:

> There is no robbery unless force or fear is used to overcome resistance. Thus, surreptitiously picking a man's pocket or snatching something from him without resistance on his part is *larceny,* but not robbery.

Many states specify degrees of robbery with increasingly heavy penalties. For example, *armed robbery* involves the use of a weapon to threaten the victim. In all cases, *robbery* is distinguished from the lesser crime of *larceny,* in which no force or intimidation is involved.

As you can see, an Aristotelian definition of a term identifies specific attributes or criteria that enable you to distinguish it from other members of the next larger class. We created an Aristotelian definition in our example about socially responsible companies. A socially responsible company, we said, is any company (next larger class) that meets three criteria: (1) it doesn't pollute the environment; (2) it creates goods or services that promote the well-being of the community; and (3) it treats its workers justly.

Creating Criteria Using an Operational Definition

In some rhetorical situations, particularly those arising in the physical and social sciences, writers need precise, *operational definitions* that can be measured empirically and are not subject to problems of context and conflicting values and beliefs. A social scientist studying the effects of television on aggression in children needs a precise, measurable definition of *aggression*. Typically, the scientist might measure "aggression" by counting the number of blows a child gives to an inflatable bobo doll over a fifteen-minute period when other play options are available. In our wetlands example, a federal authority created an operational definition of *wetland*: a wetland is a parcel of land that has a saturated ground surface for twenty-one consecutive days during the year.

Such operational definitions are useful because they are precisely measurable, but they are also limited because they omit criteria that may be unmeasurable but important. Thus, we might ask whether it is adequate to define an *honors student* as someone with a 3.8 GPA or higher or a *successful sex-education program* as one that results in a 25 percent reduction in teenage pregnancies. What important aspects of an honors student or a successful sex-education program are not considered in these operational definitions?

Conducting the Match Part of a Definition Argument

In conducting a match argument, you need to supply examples and other evidence showing that your contested case does (does not) meet the criteria you established in your definition. In essence, you support the match part of your argument in much the same way you would support a simple categorical claim.

For example, if you were developing the argument that the Hercules Shoe Company is not socially responsible because it treats its workers unjustly, your match section would provide evidence of this injustice. You might supply data about the percentage of shoes produced in East Asia, about the low wages paid these workers, and about the working conditions in these factories. You might also describe the suffering of displaced American workers when Hercules closed its American factories and moved operations to Asia, where the labor is nonunion and cheap. The match section should also summarize and respond to opposing views.

Idea-Generating Strategies for Creating Your Own Criteria-Match Argument

11.4 To use criteria-match reasoning to generate ideas for your own definition argument

In constructing criteria to define your contested term, you can either research how others have defined your term or make your own definitions. If you use the first strategy, you turn to standard or specialized dictionaries, judicial opinions, or expert testimony to establish a definition based on the authority of others. The second strategy is to use your own critical thinking to make your own definition, thereby defining the contested term yourself. This section explains these approaches in more detail.

Strategy 1: Research How Others Have Defined the Term

When you take this approach, you search for authoritative definitions acceptable to your audience yet favorable to your case. When the state of Washington tried to initiate a new sales tax on candy, lawyers and legislators wrestled with a definition. They finally created the following statute available to the public on a government Web site:

What Is the Definition of Candy?

"Candy" is a preparation of sugar, honey, or other natural or artificial sweeteners combined with chocolate, fruits, nuts, or other ingredients or flavorings in the form of bars, drops, or pieces. Candy does not require refrigeration, and does not include flour as an ingredient.

"Natural or artificial sweeteners" include, but are not limited to, high fructose corn syrup, dextrose, invert sugar, sucrose, fructose, sucralose, saccharin, aspartame, stevia, fruit juice concentrates, molasses, evaporated cane juice, and rice syrup.

"Flour" includes any flour made from a grain, such as wheat flour, rice flour, and corn flour.

Items that require "refrigeration," either before or after opening, are not candy. For example, popsicles, ice cream bars, and fruits in sweetened syrups are not candy.

This definition made it easy for state officials to exclude from the "candy tax" any snack food that contained flour. Thus Twinkies, Fruit Loops cereal, and chocolate-covered pretzels were exempt from the tax. But considerable debate occurred over cough drops. The state decided to exclude cough drops if the package contained a "drug facts" panel and a list of active ingredients. (Such cough drops were then classified as "over the counter drugs.")

Turning to established definitions is thus a first step for many definition arguments. Common sources of these definitions are specialized dictionaries such as *Black's Law Dictionary*, which form a standard part of the reference holdings of any library. Other sources of specialized definitions are state and federal appellate court decisions, legislative and administrative statutes, and scholarly articles examining a given definition conflict. Lawyers use this research strategy exhaustively in preparing court briefs. They begin by looking at the actual text of laws as passed by legislatures or written by administrative authorities. Then they look at all the court cases in which the laws have been tested and examine the ways courts have refined legal definitions and applied them to specific cases. Using these refined definitions, lawyers then apply them to their own case at hand.

If your research uncovers definitions that seem ambiguous or otherwise unfavorable to your case, you can sometimes appeal to the "original intentions" of those who defined the term. For example, if a scientist is dissatisfied with definitions of *wetlands* based on consecutive days of saturated ground surface, she might proceed as follows: "The original intention of Congress in passing the Clean Water Act was to preserve the environment." What Congress intended, she could then claim, was to prevent development of those wetland areas that provide crucial habitat for wildlife or that inhibit water pollution. She could then propose an alternative definition based on criteria other than consecutive days of ground saturation.

Strategy 2: Create Your Own Extended Definition*

Often, however, you need to create your own definition of the contested term. An effective strategy is to establish initial criteria for your contested term by thinking of hypothetical cases that obviously fit the category you are trying to define and then by altering one or more variables until the hypothetical case obviously doesn't fit the category. You can then test and refine your criteria by applying them to borderline cases. For example, suppose you work at a homeless agency where you overhear street people discuss an incident that strikes you as potential "police brutality." You wonder whether you should write to your local paper to bring attention to the incident.

A Possible Case of Police Brutality

Two police officers confront an inebriated homeless man who is shouting obscenities on a street corner. The officers tell the man to quiet down and move on, but he keeps shouting obscenities. When the officers attempt to put the man into the police car, he resists and takes a wild swing at one of the officers. As eyewitnesses later testified, this officer shouted obscenities back at the drunk man, pinned his arms behind his back in order to handcuff him, and lifted him forcefully by the arms. The man screamed in pain and was later discovered to have a dislocated shoulder. Is this officer guilty of police brutality?

To your way of thinking, this officer seems guilty: An inebriated man is too uncoordinated to be a threat in a fight, and two police officers ought to be able to arrest him without dislocating his shoulder. But a friend argues that because the man took a swing at the officer, the police were justified in using force. The dislocated shoulder was simply an accidental result of using justified force.

---

*The defining strategies and collaborative exercises in this section are based on the work of George Hillocks and his research associates at the University of Chicago. See George Hillocks Jr., Elizabeth A. Kahn, and Larry R. Johannessen, "Teaching Defining Strategies as a Mode of Inquiry: Some Effects on Student Writing," *Research in the Teaching of English* 17 (October 1983), 275–84. See also Larry R. Johannessen, Elizabeth A. Kahn, and Carolyn Calhoun Walter, *Designing and Sequencing Prewriting Activities* (Urbana, IL: NCTE, 1982).

To make your case, you need to develop a definition of "police brutality." You can begin by creating a hypothetical case that is obviously an instance of "police brutality":

A Clear Case of Police Brutality

A police officer confronts a drunk man shouting obscenities and begins hitting him in the face with his police baton. *[This is an obvious incidence of police brutality because the officer intentionally tries to hurt the drunk man without justification; hitting him with the baton is not necessary for making an arrest or getting the man into the police car.]*

You could then vary the hypothetical case until it is clearly *not* an instance of police brutality.

Cases That Are Clearly Not Police Brutality

Case 1: The police officer handcuffs the drunk man, who, in being helped into the police car, accidentally slips on the curb and dislocates his arm while falling. *[Here the injury occurs accidentally; the police officer does not act intentionally and is not negligent.]*

Case 2: The police officer confronts an armed robber fleeing from a scene and tackles him from behind, wrestling the gun away from him. In this struggle, the officer pins the robber's arm behind his back with such force that the robber's shoulder is dislocated. *[Here aggressive use of force is justified because the robber was armed, dangerous, and resisting arrest.]*

Using these hypothetical cases, you decide that the defining criteria for police brutality are (1) *intention* and (2) use of *excessive force*—that is, force beyond what was required by the immediate situation. After more contemplation, you are convinced that the officer was guilty of police brutality and have a clearer idea of how to make your argument. Here is how you might write the "match" part of your argument:

Match Argument Using Your Definition

If we define police brutality as the *intentional* use of *excessive* force, then the police officer is guilty. His action was intentional because he was purposefully responding to the homeless man's drunken swing and was angry enough to be shouting obscenities back at the drunk (according to eyewitnesses). Second, he used excessive force in applying the handcuffs. A drunk man taking a wild swing hardly poses a serious danger to two police officers. Putting handcuffs on the drunk may have been justified, but lifting the man's arm violently enough to dislocate a shoulder indicates excessive force. The officer lifted the man's arms violently not because he needed to but because he was angry, and acting out of anger is no justification for that violence. In fact, we can charge police officers with "police brutality" precisely to protect us from being victims of police anger. It is the job of the court system to punish us, not the police's job. Because this officer acted intentionally and applied excessive force out of anger, he should be charged with police brutality.

The strategy we have demonstrated—developing criteria by imagining hypothetical cases that clearly do and do not belong to the contested category—gives you a systematic procedure for developing your own definition for your argument.

■ ■ ■   **FOR WRITING AND CLASS DISCUSSION** **Developing a Definition**

Individual task:

1. Suppose you want to define the concept of courage. In each of the following cases, decide whether the person in question is acting courageously or not. In each instance explain your reasoning.

   a. A neighbor rushes into a burning house to rescue a child from certain death and emerges, coughing and choking, with the child in his arms. Is the neighbor courageous?

   b. A firefighter rushes into a burning house to rescue a child from certain death and emerges with the child in her arms. The firefighter is wearing protective clothing and a gas mask. When a newspaper reporter calls her courageous, she says, "Hey, this is my job." Is the firefighter courageous?

   c. A teenager rushes into a burning house to recover a memento given to him by his girlfriend, the first love of his life. Is the teenager courageous?

   d. A parent rushes into a burning house to save a trapped child. The fire marshal tells the parent to wait because there is no chance that the child can be reached from the first floor. The fire marshal wants to try cutting a hole in the roof to reach the child. The parent rushes into the house anyway and is burned to death. Was the parent courageous?

2. Now formulate your own definition of a "courageous act." "An act would be considered courageous if it meets the following criteria: [you specify]."

3. Finally, apply your definition to the following case: An extreme sport enthusiast sets a record for a hang gliding descent from a certain state's highest cliff. Is this record-setting descent a courageous act? Write a paragraph in which you argue that the descent is or is not courageous.

Group task: Share the results from the individual task on courage. Then make up your own series of controversial cases, like those given previously for "courage," for one or more of the following concepts:

   a. cruelty to animals
   b. child abuse
   c. true athlete
   d. sexual harassment
   e. free speech protected by the First Amendment

Finally, using the strategy of making up hypothetical cases that do and do not belong to each category, construct a definition of your chosen concept.   ■ ■ ■

WRITING ASSIGNMENT   A Definition Argument

11.5 To write your own definitional argument

The assignment for this chapter focuses on definition disputes about categories. Write an essay in which you argue that a borderline or contested case fits (or does not fit) within a given category. In the opening of your essay, introduce the borderline case you will examine and pose your definition question. In the first part of your argument, define the boundaries of your category (criteria) by reporting a definition used by others or by developing your own extended definition. In the second part of your argument (the match), show how your borderline case meets (or doesn't meet) your definition criteria.

Exploring Ideas

Ideally, in writing this argument you will join an ongoing conversation about a definition issue that interests you. What cultural and social issues that concern you involve disputed definitions? In the public arena, you are likely to find numerous examples simply by looking through news stories—for example, the disputes about the definition of "torture" in interrogating terrorist suspects or about "freedom of religion" in debates about religious organizations having to pay for contraception in employees' health insurance. Often you can frame your own definition issues even if they aren't currently in the news. Is using TiVo to avoid TV commercials a form of theft? Is flag burning protected free speech? Is solitary confinement "cruel and unusual punishment"? Is Wal-Mart a socially responsible company? Are voter ID laws racist?

If you have trouble discovering a local or national issue that interests you, you can create fascinating definition controversies among your classmates by asking whether certain borderline cases are "true" or "real" examples of some category: Are highly skilled video game players (race car drivers, synchronized swimmers, marbles players) true athletes? Is a gourmet chef (skilled furniture maker, tagger) a true artist? Is a chiropractor (acupuncturist, naturopathic physician) a "real doctor"? Working as a whole class or in small groups inside or outside class, create an argumentative discussion on one or more of these issues. Listen to the various voices in the controversy, and then write out your own argument.

You can also stimulate definition controversies by brainstorming borderline cases for such terms as *courage* (Is mountain climbing an act of courage?), *cruelty to animals* (Are rodeos [zoos, catch-and-release trout fishing, use of animals for medical research] guilty of cruelty to animals?), or *war crimes* (Was the American firebombing of Tokyo in World War II a war crime?).

As you explore your definition issue, try to determine how others have defined your category. If no stable definition emerges from your search, create your own definition by deciding what criteria must be met for a contested case to fit within your category. Try using the strategy for creating criteria that we discussed on pages 191–192 with reference to police brutality. Once you have determined your criteria, freewrite for five or ten minutes, exploring whether your contested case meets each of the criteria.

Identifying Your Audience and Determining What's at Stake

Before drafting your argument, identify your targeted audience and determine what's at stake. Consider your responses to the following questions:

- What audience are you targeting? What background do they need to understand your issue? How much do they already care about it?

- Before they read your argument, what stance on your issue do you imagine them holding? What change do you want to bring about in their views?
- What will they find new or surprising about your argument?
- What objections might they raise? What counterarguments or alternative points of view will you need to address?
- Why does your argument matter? Who might be threatened or made uncomfortable by your views? What is at stake?

Organization Plan 1: Definition Argument with Criteria and Match in Separate Sections

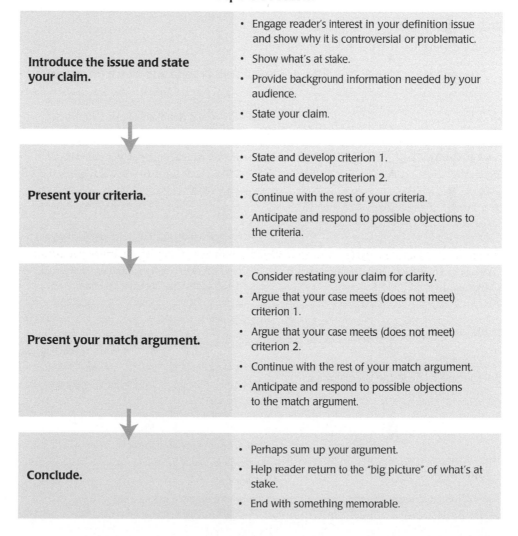

Introduce the issue and state your claim.	• Engage reader's interest in your definition issue and show why it is controversial or problematic. • Show what's at stake. • Provide background information needed by your audience. • State your claim.
Present your criteria.	• State and develop criterion 1. • State and develop criterion 2. • Continue with the rest of your criteria. • Anticipate and respond to possible objections to the criteria.
Present your match argument.	• Consider restating your claim for clarity. • Argue that your case meets (does not meet) criterion 1. • Argue that your case meets (does not meet) criterion 2. • Continue with the rest of your match argument. • Anticipate and respond to possible objections to the match argument.
Conclude.	• Perhaps sum up your argument. • Help reader return to the "big picture" of what's at stake. • End with something memorable.

Organizing a Definition Argument

As you compose a first draft of your essay, you may find it helpful to know typical structures for definition arguments. There are two basic approaches, as shown in Organization Plans 1 and 2. You can either discuss the criteria and the match separately or interweave the discussion.

Questioning and Critiquing a Definition Argument

A powerful way to stimulate global revision of a draft is to role-play a skeptical audience. The following questions will help you strengthen your own argument or rebut the definition arguments of others. In critiquing a definition argument, you need to appreciate its criteria-match structure because you can question your criteria argument, your match argument, or both.

Organization Plan 2: Definition Argument with Criteria and Match Interwoven

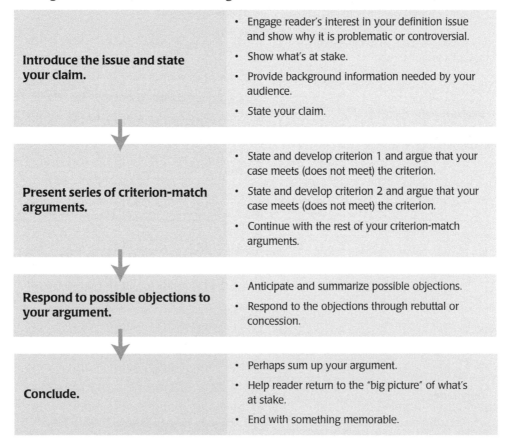

Introduce the issue and state your claim.	• Engage reader's interest in your definition issue and show why it is problematic or controversial. • Show what's at stake. • Provide background information needed by your audience. • State your claim.
Present series of criterion-match arguments.	• State and develop criterion 1 and argue that your case meets (does not meet) the criterion. • State and develop criterion 2 and argue that your case meets (does not meet) the criterion. • Continue with the rest of your criterion-match arguments.
Respond to possible objections to your argument.	• Anticipate and summarize possible objections. • Respond to the objections through rebuttal or concession.
Conclude.	• Perhaps sum up your argument. • Help reader return to the "big picture" of what's at stake. • End with something memorable.

Questioning Your Criteria

- Could a skeptic claim that your criteria are not the right ones? Could he or she offer different criteria or point out missing criteria?
- Could a skeptic point out possible bad consequences of accepting your criteria?
- Could a skeptic cite unusual circumstances that weaken your criteria?
- Could a skeptic point out bias or slant in your definition?

Questioning Your Match

- Could a skeptic argue that your examples or data don't meet the STAR criteria (see Chapter 5, pages 77–78) for evidence?
- Could a skeptic point out counterexamples or alternative data that cast doubt on your argument?
- Could a skeptic reframe the way you have viewed your borderline case? ■

READING

This reading, by student Alex Mullen, was written for the definition assignment on pages 193–194. Alex's argument was stimulated by class discussions of property ownership in digital environments.

A Pirate But Not a Thief: What Does "Stealing" Mean in a Digital Environment?

ALEX MULLEN (STUDENT)

I am a pirate. In the eyes of the law, I could face serious punishment in fines, up to thousands of dollars, or jail time for my crime. Legally, it matters very little that my crime is one perpetrated by millions of people every year (you yourself may be guilty of it) or that there are far worse offenders out there. But before we get out the noose and head for the yardarm, I think I ought to describe my crime. In my History of Film class we were asked to watch Jean Renoir's *La Grande Illusion*. Now, if you've spent any time searching for 1930s foreign films you will undoubtedly know what a pain it is to find them, and of the twenty or so films we watched for my class a grand total of three were available on streaming sites such as Netflix, Hulu, and YouTube. While there were several copies of this particular film at my University Library, all had been checked out. I planned to make a journey to the fabled Scarecrow Video (one of the largest rental libraries in the United States), but time was running low at this point. Finally, I broke down and used a person-to-person torrent site to download the film illegally. In the end all the trouble was worthwhile, as *La Grande Illusion* remains one of the greatest films I have ever seen. After watching it several times and writing a brief paper, I deleted the film from my computer. Although I feel that my action was justifiable, many people think what I did was no better than shoplifting and that I am guilty of theft. As a film lover and aspiring filmmaker I am conflicted on the issue of online piracy. Nevertheless, I contend that what I did wasn't stealing because I deprived no one of either property or profit.

Let's take a step back from online piracy and focus simply on what stealing is in its most basic form. In my mind, stealing is the unlawful taking of another's property or profits without permission. The underlying assumption that makes stealing wrong needs to be considered. In the case of property, stealing is wrong not because the thief has the property but because the original owner has been deprived of it. The owner's loss causes the wrong, not the thief's gain. To give an example in very simple terms, if you have a phone case and I make a copy of that case (as is quite possible with a 3D printer), you still possess the original case, so no harm has been done to you the owner. However, suppose that you made your living by selling these phone cases. If I made exact duplicates with my 3-D printer and then sold these cases to others, then you could be deprived of profits that might otherwise have been received. Again, the wrong comes from the creator's loss and not the thief's gain.

Now let's focus on my particular example of online piracy. While I concede that piracy has the distinct potential to be stealing, I reject the accusation that all piracy is stealing. Based on the first part of my definition of stealing, my downloading *La Grande Illusion* deprived no consumer or creator of his or her copy of the film. This is why accusations that compare online piracy to shoplifting are false. In the case of shoplifting the owner/creator has one fewer piece of merchandise to make a profit on; with online piracy such loss does not occur because the original copy still exists.

However, the second part of my definition, which focuses on profits, still remains to be examined. Perhaps by downloading the film I have deprived the creators/owners of profits they would normally receive. Let me begin by saying that I never intended to purchase *La Grande Illusion*. While intention does not often register in legal matters, it does have a bearing on the type and degree of wrongdoing. Film industry lawyers often argue that every time a film is pirated the rightful owner is deprived of money because the pirate would have otherwise purchased the film. This claim, however, is fallacious because there is no way to show that these potential consumers would have purchased the film (I certainly wouldn't have). So while we may agree that some of these people would have purchased the film, it would be inaccurate to claim that in all cases piracy directly deprives creators of profit. I argue that what I did in the case of *La Grande Illusion* was more like borrowing than theft. Borrowing a film from a library (or renting it from a video store) has the same basic effect on the owner/creator as online piracy. That is, a library or video store purchases a copy and then loans it or rents to others. Thus, many persons may not purchase a copy from the owner/creator because they can use this single public or commercial copy. Yet we do not consider borrowing or renting stealing even though it can have the same economic ramification as piracy. To go a step further, any time I borrow a film from a friend I cause the same outcome found so reprehensible in online piracy. In my case, instead of borrowing *La Grande Illusion* from an institution or business, I borrowed it from another individual via the Internet.

5   There is, of course, the counterargument that I could have rented the film from Scarecrow and thus stole profit from this film rental store much loved by film buffs. While it is true that I did not benefit Scarecrow with my patronage (a fact that I partially regret because I do try to support Scarecrow as often as possible), it would be inaccurate to say that I stole from Scarecrow. I am under no obligation to supply them with profits. When I pay money to a rental organization I am not paying for the film; I am paying for the service of being able to use their copy of the film for 24 hours. Had I purchased the film directly from the filmmaker, I would do the same harm to Scarecrow. Thus my not utilizing Scarecrow to obtain *La Grande Illusion* is not theft.

While I understand why the film industry (and also the music industry) views downloading from file-sharing torrent sites as piracy, their motives focus on preserving profits and blur the distinctions among "buying," "renting," and "borrowing." If I owned a DVD version of a movie and loaned it to a friend, no one would object. But if I make the same movie available to a friend via a torrent or file-sharing site, I become a pirate subject to huge fines. The intention is the same, only the format changes. The problem stems from the hazy concept of "ownership" in a digital environment where physical copies are replaced by digital copies. Certainly, we pay to possess digital copies of films, music, and video games, but is this really the same as physical ownership? After all I can lend, rent, or even sell a physical DVD, but such actions are impossible with digital copies without committing piracy. Our consumption of media is evolving rapidly, and while undoubtedly there will always be those who exploit these changes for personal gain, I feel we need to realize that our understanding of ownership, stealing, and illegal use must evolve along with these changes.

Critiquing "A Pirate But Not a Thief: What Does 'Stealing' Mean in a Digital Environment?"

1. Identify the following features of Alex's essay: (1) his definition of "stealing"; (2) his examples to illustrate the definition; (3) his "match" argument showing whether his downloading of the film fits each of the criteria; and (4) his summary of and responses to objections and opposing views.
2. Do you agree with Alex's contention that his downloading the film was an act of "borrowing" rather than "stealing"?
3. What do you see as the major strengths of Alex's argument? How about weaknesses?
4. Do you think that the laws about online piracy should be changed? At what point does online piracy clearly become "stealing"?

Causal Arguments

12

What you will learn in this chapter:

12.1 To explain and illustrate kinds of causal arguments

12.2 To explain how different causal mechanisms function in cause/consequence arguments

12.3 To understand key causal terms and the need to avoid inductive fallacies in causal arguments

12.4 To write your own cause or consequence argument

We encounter causal issues all the time. What has caused the declining birth rate among teens in the United States? Why has the dance exercise called Zumba become popular globally? Why are white teenage girls seven times more likely to smoke than African American teenage girls? In addition to asking questions about case, we pose consequence questions as well: What might be the consequences of installing stricter proof-of-citizenship requirements for voting? What might be the consequences—expected or unexpected—of expanding commercial use of drones? Often, arguments about causes and consequences have important stakes because they shape our view of reality and influence government policies and individual decisions. This chapter explains how to wrestle responsibly with cause/consequence issues to produce effective causal arguments.

Case 1 What Causes Global Warming?

One of the early clues linking global warming to atmospheric carbon dioxide (CO_2) came from side-by-side comparisons of graphs plotting atmospheric carbon dioxide and global temperatures over time. These graphs show that increases in global temperature parallel increases in the percentage of carbon dioxide in the atmosphere. However, the graphs show only a correlation, or link, between increased carbon dioxide and higher average temperature. To argue that an increase in CO_2 could cause global warming, scientists needed to explain the links in a causal chain. They could do so by comparing the earth to a greenhouse. Carbon dioxide, like glass in a greenhouse, lets some of the earth's heat radiate into space but also reflects some of it back to the earth. The higher the concentration of carbon dioxide, the more heat is reflected back to the earth.

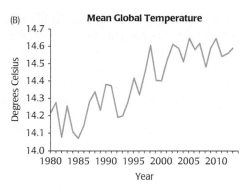

Source: Data from Dr. Pieter Tans, NOAA/ESRL

Source: Data from NASA Goddard Institute for Space Studies Surface Temperature Analysis

---

Case 2   What Has Caused the Change in the Rate of Teen Pregnancies in the United States in the Last Five Years?

Although the United States still has the highest rate of teen pregnancies among developed countries, studies show a decline in teen pregnancies since the early 1990s. What has caused this decline? Some economists point to the recession, claiming that teens are afraid of not being able to get jobs if encumbered with babies. Other sources credit the role of parents in cautioning teens about irresponsible sexual choices. A quite different explanation comes from a recent study analyzing the impact of media images on viewers. This study has found a correlation between the decline in teen pregnancies and the popularity of the MTV docudrama *16 and Pregnant* (premiered in 2009) and its spinoff *Teen Moms*. While some critics argue that these shows sensationalize and glamorize the lives of the teen moms, researchers, using Nielsen ratings and geographic data on viewership and data from Google Trends and Twitter, found that watching these shows "led to more searches and tweets regarding birth control and abortion, and ultimately led to a 5.7 percent reduction in teen births in the eighteen months" after *16 and Pregnant* first aired.*

An Overview of Causal Arguments

12.1 To explain and illustrate kinds of causal arguments

Typically, causal arguments try to show how one event brings about another. When causal investigation focuses on material objects—for example, one billiard ball striking another—the notion of causality appears fairly straightforward. But when humans become the focus of a causal argument, the nature of causality becomes more vexing. If we say that something happened that "caused" a person to act in a certain way, what do we mean? Do we mean that she was "forced" to act in a certain way, thereby negating her free will (as in, an

---

*Melissa S. Kearney and Phillip B. Levine. "Media Influences on Social Outcomes: The Impact of MTV's *16 and Pregnant* on Teen Childbearing," NBER Working Paper No. 19795, National Bureau of Economic Research, January 2014.

undiagnosed brain tumor caused her to act erratically), or do we mean more simply that she was "motivated" to act in a certain way (as in, her anger at her parents caused her to act erratically)? When we argue about causality in human beings, we must guard against confusing these two senses of "cause" or assuming that human behavior can be predicted or controlled in the same way that nonhuman behavior can. A rock dropped from a roof will always fall at thirty-two feet per second squared, and a rat zapped for turning left in a maze will always quit turning left. But if we raise interest rates, will consumers save more money? If so, how much? This is the sort of question we debate endlessly.

Kinds of Causal Arguments

Arguments about causality can take a variety of forms. Here are three typical kinds:

- **Speculations about possible causes.** Sometimes arguers speculate about possible causes of a phenomenon. For example, whenever a shooter opens fire on innocent bystanders (as in the 2012 Sandy Hook Elementary School massacre), investigators begin analyzing the causes. One of the most heavily debated shooting incidents occurred in 1999 at Columbine High School in Littleton, Colorado, when two male students opened fire on their classmates, killing thirteen people, wounding twenty-three others, and then shooting themselves. Figure 12.1 illustrates some of the proposed theories for the Columbine shootings. What was at stake was not only our desire to understand the sociocultural sources of school violence but also our desire to institute policies to prevent future school shootings. If a primary cause is the availability of guns, then we might push for more stringent gun control laws. But if the primary cause is the disintegration of the traditional family, the shooters'

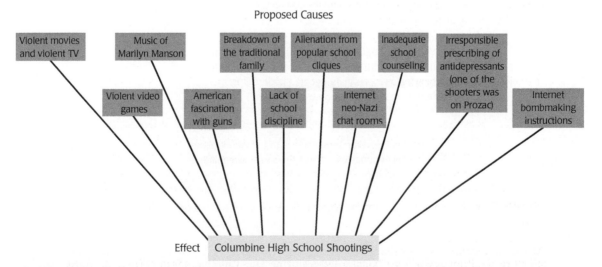

FIGURE 12.1 Speculation about possible causes: Columbine High School Massacre

alienation from high school cliques, or the dangerous side effects of Prozac, then we might seek different solutions.

■ **Arguments for an unexpected or surprising cause.** Besides sorting out possible causes of a phenomenon, sometimes arguers try to persuade readers to see the plausibility of an unexpected or surprising cause. This was the strategy used by syndicated columnist John Leo, who wanted readers to consider the role of violent video games as a contributing cause to the Columbine massacre.* After suggesting that the Littleton killings were partly choreographed on video game models, Leo suggested the causal chain shown in Figure 12.2.

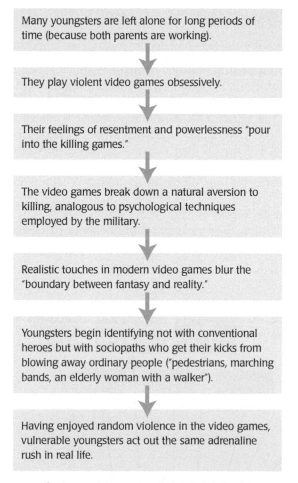

FIGURE 12.2 Argument for a surprising cause: Role of violent video games in the Columbine massacre

---

*John Leo, "Kill-for-Kicks Video Games Desensitizing Our Children," *Seattle Times* 27 April 1999, B4.

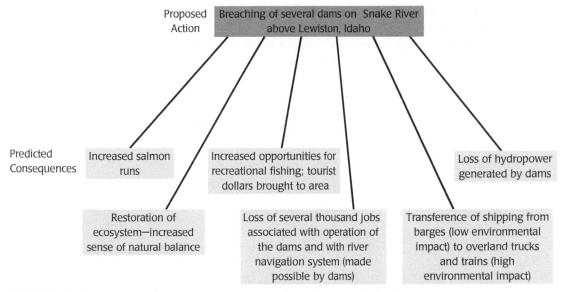

FIGURE 12.3 Predictions about consequences: Breaching dams on the Snake River

■ **Predictions of consequences.** Still another frequently encountered kind of causal argument predicts the consequences of current, planned, or proposed actions or events. Consequence arguments have high stakes because we often judge actions on whether their benefits outweigh their costs. As we will see in Chapter 14, proposal arguments usually require writers to predict the consequences of a proposed action, do a cost/benefit analysis, and persuade readers that no unforeseen negative consequences will result. Just as a phenomenon can have multiple causes, it can also have multiple consequences. Figure 12.3 shows the consequence arguments considered by environmentalists who propose eliminating several dams on Idaho's Snake River in order to save salmon runs.

Toulmin Framework for a Causal Argument

Because causal arguments can involve lengthy or complex causal chains, they are often harder to summarize in *because* clauses than are other kinds of arguments. Likewise, they are not as likely to yield quick analysis through the Toulmin schema. Nevertheless, a causal argument can usually be stated as a claim with *because* clauses. Typically, a *because* clause pinpoints one or two key elements in the causal chain rather than summarizes every link. John Leo's argument linking the Columbine massacre to violent video games could be summarized in the following claim with a *because* clause:

> Violent video games may have been a contributing cause to the Littleton massacre because playing these games can make random, sociopathic violence seem pleasurable.

Once stated as an enthymeme, the argument can be analyzed using Toulmin's schema. It is easiest to apply Toulmin's schema to causal arguments if you think of the grounds as the observable phenomena at any point in the causal chain and the warrants as the shareable assumptions about causality that join links together.

Toulmin Analysis of the Violent Video Games Argument

ENTHYMEME

CLAIM Violent video games may have been a contributing cause to the Columbine school shooting

REASON because playing these games can make random, sociopathic violence seem pleasurable.

→ Qualifiers

GROUNDS

- Evidence that the killers, like many young people, played violent video games
- Evidence that the games are violent
- Evidence that the games involve random, sociopathic violence (not good guys versus bad guys) such as killing ordinary people—marching bands, little old ladies, etc.
- Evidence that young people derive pleasure from these games

CONDITIONS OF REBUTTAL
Attacking the reason and grounds

- Perhaps the killers didn't play violent video games.
- Perhaps the video games are no more violent than traditional kids' games such as cops and robbers.
- Perhaps the video games do not feature sociopathic killing.

WARRANT

If young people derive pleasure from random, sociopathic killing in video games, they can transfer this pleasure to real life, thus leading to the Columbine shooting.

BACKING

- Testimony from psychologists
- Evidence that violent video games desensitize people to violence
- Analogy to military training in which video games are used to "make killing a reflex action"
- Evidence that the distinction between fantasy and reality becomes especially blurred for unstable young people

CONDITIONS OF REBUTTAL
Attacking the warrant and backing

- Perhaps kids are fully capable of distinguishing fantasy from reality.
- Perhaps the games are just fun with no transference to real life.
- Perhaps the games are substantially different from military training games.

■ ■ ■   **FOR CLASS DISCUSSION** Developing Causal Chains

1. Working individually or in small groups, create a causal chain to show how the item on the left could help lead to the item on the right.

   a. Invention of the automobile   Changes in sexual mores

   b. Popularity of cell phones   Reduction in size and importance of phone directories

   c. Millennials' desire for an urban lifestyle   Redesign of cities

   d. Development of way to prevent rejections in transplant operations   Liberalization of euthanasia laws

2. For each of your causal chains, compose a claim with an attached because clause summarizing one or two key links in the causal chain—for example, "Millennials' desire for an urban lifestyle is spurring the redesign of cities because Millennials' car free habits are prompting developers to build new high-density urban communities that are close to work and play."

■ ■ ■

Two Methods for Arguing that One Event Causes Another

12.2 To explain how different causal mechanisms function in cause/consequence arguments

One of the first things you need to do when preparing a causal argument is to note exactly what sort of causal relationship you are dealing with—a onetime phenomenon, a recurring phenomenon, or a puzzling trend. Here are some examples.

Kind of Phenomenon	Examples
Onetime phenomenon	■ Mysterious disappearance of Malaysia Airlines Flight 370 in March 2014 ■ Firing of a popular teacher at your university
Recurring phenomenon	■ Eating disorders ■ Road rage
Puzzling trend	■ Declining audience for TV news ■ Declining populations of both bats and honeybees

With recurring phenomena or with trends, one has the luxury of being able to study multiple cases, often over time. You can interview people, make repeated observations, or study the conditions in which the puzzling phenomenon occurs. But with a onetime occurrence, one's approach is more like that of a detective than a scientist. Because one can't repeat the event with different variables, one must rely only on the immediate evidence at hand, which can quickly disappear.

Having briefly stated these words of caution, let's turn now to two main ways that you can argue that one event causes another.

First Method: Explain the Causal Mechanism Directly

The most convincing kind of causal argument identifies every link in the causal chain, showing how an initiating cause leads step by step to an observed effect. A causes B, which causes C, which causes D. In some cases, all you have to do is fill in the missing links. In other cases—when your assumptions about how one step leads to the next may seem questionable to your audience—you have to argue for the causal connection with more vigor.

A careful spelling out of each step in the causal chain is the technique used by science writer Robert S. Devine in explaining a negative consequence of dams. In the following passage, he explains how dams reduce salmon flows by slowing the migration of smolts (newly hatched, young salmon) to the sea.

Causal Argument Describing a Causal Chain

Such transformations lie at the heart of the ongoing environmental harm done by dams. Rivers are rivers because they flow, and the nature of their flows defines much of their character. When dams alter flows, they alter the essence of rivers.

Consider the erstwhile river behind Lower Granite (a dam on Idaho's Snake River). Although I was there in the springtime, when I looked at the water it was moving too slowly to merit the word "flow"—and Lower Granite Lake isn't even one of the region's enormous storage reservoirs, which bring currents to a virtual halt. In the past, spring snowmelt sent powerful currents down the Snake during April and May. Nowadays hydropower operators of the Columbia and Snake systems store the runoff behind the dams and release it during the winter, when demand—and the price—for electricity rises. Over the ages, however, many populations of salmon have adapted to the spring surge. The smolts used the strong flows to migrate, drifting downstream with the current. During the journey smolts' bodies undergo physiological changes that require them to reach salt water quickly. Before dams backed up the Snake, smolts coming down from Idaho got to the sea in six to twenty days; now it takes from sixty to ninety days, and few of the young salmon reach salt water in time. The emasculated current is the single largest reason that the number of wild adult salmon migrating up the Snake each year has crashed from predevelopment runs of 100,000–200,000 to what was projected to be 150–750 this year.[*]

This tightly constructed passage connects various causal chains to explain the decline of salmon runs:

Smolts use river flow to reach the sea → dams restrict flow of river → a trip that before development took 6–20 days now takes 60–90 days → migrating smolts undergo physiological changes that demand quick access to salt water → delayed migration time kills the smolts.

Second Method: Infer Causal Links Using Inductive Reasoning

If we can't explain a causal link directly, we often employ a reasoning strategy called *induction*. Through induction we infer a general conclusion based on a limited number of specific cases. For example, if on several occasions you got a headache after drinking red wine but not after drinking white wine, you would be likely to conclude

---

[*]Robert S. Devine, "The Trouble with Dams," *Atlantic* (August 1995), 64–75. The example quotation is from page 70.

inductively that red wine causes you to get headaches, although you can't explain directly how it does so. However, because there are almost always numerous variables involved, inductive reasoning gives only probable truths, not certain ones.

Three Ways of Thinking Inductively   When your brain thinks inductively, it sorts through data looking for patterns of similarity and difference. In this section we explain three ways of thinking inductively: looking for a common element, looking for a single difference, and looking for correlations.

1. **Look for a common element.** One kind of inductive thinking places you on a search for a common element that can explain recurrences of the same phenomenon. For example, psychologists attempting to understand the causes of anorexia have discovered that many anorexics (but not all) come from perfectionist, highly work-oriented homes that emphasize duty and responsibility. This common element is thus a suspected causal factor leading to anorexia.

2. **Look for a single difference.** Another approach is to look for a single difference that may explain the appearance of a new phenomenon. When infant death rates in the state of Washington shot up in July and August 1986, one event making these two months different stood out: increased radioactive fallout over Washington from the April Chernobyl nuclear meltdown in Ukraine. This single difference led some researchers to suspect radiation as a possible cause of the increase in infant deaths.

3. **Look for correlations.** Still another method of induction is correlation, which means that two events or phenomena tend to occur together but this doesn't imply that one causes the other. For example, there is a correlation between nearsightedness and intelligence. (That is, in a given sample of nearsighted people and people with normal eyesight, the nearsighted group will have a somewhat higher mean IQ score.) But the direction of causality isn't clear. It could be that high intelligence causes people to read more, thus ruining their eyes (high intelligence causes nearsightedness). Or it could be that nearsightedness causes people to read more, thus raising their intelligence (nearsightedness causes high intelligence). Or it could be that some unknown phenomenon, perhaps a gene, is related to both nearsightedness and intelligence. So keep in mind that correlation is not causation—it simply suggests possible causation.

■ ■ ■ **FOR CLASS DISCUSSION** **Developing Plausible Causal Chains Based on Correlations**

Working individually or in small groups, develop plausible causal chains that may explain the relationship between the following pairs of phenomena:

a. A person who registers a low stress level on an electrochemical stress meter — does daily meditation

b. A binge drinker at college parties — has increased risk of becoming a perpetrator or victim of sexual violence

c. A person who grew up in a house with two bathrooms — is likely to have higher SAT scores than a person who grew up in a one-bathroom home

■ ■ ■

EXAMINING VISUAL ARGUMENTS

A Causal Claim

This billboard is part of a Texas campaign to fight sex trafficking. How do both the text and image in this billboard suggest links in a causal chain? Although this ad oversimplifies the complex issue of human trafficking, and some would say it represents only one view of sex workers, how do both the words and the choice of images make powerful appeals to both *logos* and *pathos*?

Key Terms and Inductive Fallacies in Causal Arguments

12.3 To understand key causal terms and the need to avoid inductive fallacies in causal arguments

Because causal arguments are often easier to conduct if writer and reader share a few specialized terms and concepts, this section explains key terms in causal reasoning and offers ways to avoid inductive fallacies.

A Glossary of Key Terms

- **The problem of oversimplified cause.** One of the great temptations is to look for *the* cause of something, as if a phenomenon had only one cause rather than multiple causes. For example, in recent years the number of persons in the United States sending out Christmas cards has declined substantially. Many commentators attribute the decline to the increasing use of Facebook, which keeps old friends in touch year-round, eliminating the need for holiday "family letters." But there may be other causes also, such as a decline in the number of nuclear families, fewer networks of long-term friends, or generational shifts away from older traditions. When you make a causal argument, be especially careful how you use words such as *all, most, some, the,* or *in part.* For example, *some* (but not *all*) of the decline in Christmas cards may be caused by Facebook. Arguers sometimes deliberately mix up these quantifiers to misrepresent and dismiss opposing views.
- **Immediate and remote causes.** Every causal chain extends backward indefinitely into the past. An immediate cause is the closest in time to the event being examined.

Consider the causes for the release of nuclear contaminants around the Fukushima nuclear power plant following the 2011 earthquake off the coast of Japan. The immediate cause was loss of power to the water pumps that cooled the reactor's fuel rods, causing the rods to overheat and partially melt. A slightly less immediate cause (several days earlier) was the earthquake-produced tsunami that had swept away the diesel fuel tanks needed to run the backup generators. These immediate causes can be contrasted with a remote cause—in this case, a late-1960s design decision that used backup diesel generators to power the water pumps in case of an electrical power loss to the reactor facility. Still more remote causes were the economic and regulatory systems in the late 1960s that led to this particular design.

- **Precipitating and contributing causes.** These terms are similar to *immediate* and *remote* causes but don't designate a temporal link going into the past. Rather, they refer to a main cause emerging out of a background of subsidiary causes. If, for example, a husband and wife decide to separate, the *precipitating cause* may be a stormy fight over money, after which one of the partners (or both) says, "I've had enough." In contrast, *contributing causes* would be all the background factors that are dooming the marriage. Note that contributing causes and the precipitating cause all coexist at the same time.

- **Constraints.** Sometimes an effect occurs because some stabilizing factor—a *constraint*—is removed. In other words, the presence of a constraint may keep a certain effect from occurring. For example, in the marriage we have been discussing, the presence of children in the home may be a constraint against divorce; as soon as the children graduate from high school and leave home, the marriage may well dissolve.

- **Necessary and sufficient causes.** A *necessary cause* is one that has to be present for a given effect to occur. For example, fertility drugs are necessary to cause the conception of septuplets. Every couple who has septuplets must have used fertility drugs. In contrast, a *sufficient cause* is one that always produces a given effect. Smoking more than a pack of cigarettes per day is sufficient to raise the cost of one's life insurance policy. If you are a smoker, no matter how healthy you appear to be, life insurance companies will always place you in a higher, more expensive risk bracket. In some cases, a single cause can be both necessary and sufficient. For example, lack of ascorbic acid is both a necessary and a sufficient cause of scurvy. It is a necessary cause because you can't get scurvy any other way except through absence of ascorbic acid; it is a sufficient cause because the absence of ascorbic acid always causes scurvy.

Avoiding Common Inductive Fallacies that Can Lead to Wrong Conclusions

Largely because of its power, informal induction can often lead to wrong conclusions. You should be aware of two common fallacies of inductive reasoning that can tempt you into erroneous assumptions about causality. (Both fallacies are treated more fully in the Appendix.)

- ***Post hoc* fallacy:** The *post hoc, ergo propter hoc* fallacy ("after this, therefore because of this") mistakes sequence for cause. Just because event A regularly precedes event B doesn't mean that event A causes event B. The same reasoning that tells us that flipping a switch causes the light to go on can make us believe that low levels of radioactive fallout from the Chernobyl nuclear disaster caused a sudden rise in infant death rates in the state of Washington. The nuclear disaster clearly preceded the rise in death rates. But did it clearly *cause* it?

■ **Hasty generalization:** The *hasty generalization* fallacy occurs when you make a generalization based on too few cases or too little consideration of alternative explanations: You flip the switch, but the lightbulb doesn't go on. You conclude—too hastily—that the lightbulb has burned out. (Perhaps the power has gone off or the switch is broken.) How many trials does it take before you can make a justified generalization rather than a hasty generalization? It is difficult to say for sure.

Both the *post hoc* fallacy and the hasty generalization fallacy remind us that induction requires a leap from individual cases to a general principle and that it is always possible to leap too soon.

■ ■ ■ **FOR CLASS DISCUSSION** **Brainstorming Causes and Constraints**

The terms in the preceding glossary can be effective brainstorming tools for thinking of possible causes of an event. For the following events, try to think of as many causes as possible by brainstorming possible *immediate causes, remote causes, precipitating causes, contributing causes,* and *constraints:*

1. Why did you decide to attend your present college?
2. Why are women's fashion and beauty magazines the most frequently purchased magazines in college bookstores?
3. Why do American students consistently score below Asian and European students in academic achievement?   ■ ■ ■

WRITING ASSIGNMENT **A Causal Argument**

12.4 To write your own cause or consequence argument

Choose an issue about the causes or consequences of a trend, event, or other phenomenon. Write an argument that persuades an audience to accept your explanation of the causes or consequences of your chosen phenomenon. Within your essay you should examine alternative hypotheses or opposing views and explain your reasons for rejecting them. You can imagine your issue either as a puzzle or as a disagreement. If a puzzle, your task will be to create a convincing case for an audience that doesn't have an answer to your causal question already in mind. If a disagreement, your task will be more overtly persuasive because your goal will be to change your audience's views.

Exploring Ideas

Arguments about causes and consequences abound in public, professional, or personal life, so you shouldn't have difficulty finding a causal issue worth investigating and arguing. If you have trouble finding a causal issue to write about, you can often create provocative controversies among your classmates through the following strategies:

■ **Make a list of unusual likes and dislikes.** Think about unusual things that people like or dislike. You could summarize the conventional explanations that people give for an unusual pleasure or aversion and then argue for a surprising or unexpected cause. What attracts people to extreme sports? How do you explain the popularity of the paleo diet or of *The Hunger Games*?

■ **Make a list of puzzling events or trends.** Another strategy is to make a list of puzzling phenomena and then try to explain their causes. Start with onetime events (a curriculum change at your school, the sudden popularity of a new app). Then list puzzling recurring events (failure of knowledgeable teenagers to practice safe sex). Finally, list some recent trends (growth of naturopathic medicine, increased interest in tattoos). Engage classmates in discussions of one or more of the items on your list. Look for places of disagreement as entry points into the conversation.

■ **Brainstorm consequences of a recent or proposed action.** Arguments about consequences are among the most interesting and important of causal disputes. If you can argue for an unanticipated consequence of a real or proposed action, whether good or bad, you can contribute importantly to the conversation. What might be the consequences, for example, of placing "green taxes" on coal-produced electricity; of legalizing marijuana; of overturning Roe v. Wade; or of requiring national public service for all young adults?

Identifying Your Audience and Determining What's at Stake

Before drafting your argument, identify your targeted audience and determine what's at stake. Consider your responses to the following questions:

■ What audience are you targeting? What background do they need to understand your issue? How much do they already care about it?

■ Before they read your argument, what stance on your issue do you imagine them holding? What change do you want to bring about in their views?

■ What will they find new or surprising about your argument?

■ What objections might they raise? What counterarguments or alternative points of view will you need to address?

■ Why does your argument matter? Who might be threatened or made uncomfortable by your views? What is at stake?

Organizing a Causal Argument

At the outset, it is useful to know some of the standard ways that a causal argument can be organized. Later, you may decide on a different organizational pattern, but the standard ways shown in Organization Plans 1, 2, and 3 on pages 215–216 will help you get started.

Plans 2 and 3 are similar in that they examine numerous possible causes or consequences. Plan 2, however, tries to establish the relative importance of each cause or consequence, whereas Plan 3 aims at rejecting the causes or consequences normally assumed by the audience and argues for an unexpected, surprising cause or consequence. Plan 3 can also be used when your purpose is to change your audience's mind about a cause or consequence.

Questioning and Critiquing a Causal Argument

Knowing how to question and critique a causal argument will help you anticipate opposing views in order to strengthen your own. It will also help you rebut another person's causal argument. Here are some useful questions to ask:

- When you explain the links in a causal chain, can a skeptic point out weaknesses in any of the links?
- If you speculate about the causes of a phenomenon, could a skeptic argue for different causes or arrange your causes in a different order of importance?
- If you argue for a surprising cause or a surprising consequence of a phenomenon, could a skeptic point out alternative explanations that would undercut your argument?
- If your argument depends on inferences from data, could a skeptic question the way the data were gathered or interpreted? Could a skeptic claim that the data weren't relevant (for example, research done with lab animals might not apply to humans)?
- If your causal argument depends on a correlation between one phenomenon and another, could a skeptic argue that the direction of causality should be reversed or that an unidentified, third phenomenon is the real cause? ■

Organization Plan 1: Argument Explaining Links in a Causal Chain

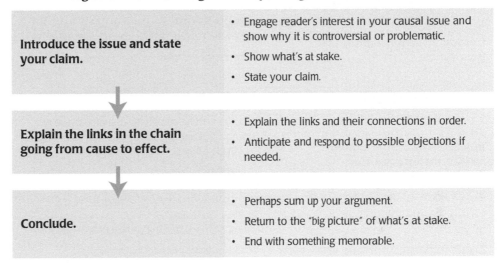

Introduce the issue and state your claim.	• Engage reader's interest in your causal issue and show why it is controversial or problematic. • Show what's at stake. • State your claim.
Explain the links in the chain going from cause to effect.	• Explain the links and their connections in order. • Anticipate and respond to possible objections if needed.
Conclude.	• Perhaps sum up your argument. • Return to the "big picture" of what's at stake. • End with something memorable.

Organization Plan 2: Argument Proposing Multiple Causes or Consequences of a Phenomenon

Introduce the issue and state your claim.	• Engage reader's interest in your causal issue and show why it is problematic or controversial. • Show what's at stake. • State your claim.
Propose relative contributions of different causes of a phenomenon or relative importance of different consequences.	• Describe the first possible cause or consequence and explain your reasoning. • Continue with the rest of your causes or consequences. • Arrange causes or consequences in increasing order of importance, significance, or surprise.
Respond to possible objections to your argument (if needed).	• Anticipate and summarize possible objections. • Respond through rebuttal or concession.
Conclude.	• Perhaps sum up your argument. • Return to the "big picture" of what's at stake. • End with something memorable.

Organization Plan 3: Argument Proposing a Surprising Cause or Consequence

Introduce the issue and state your claim.	• Engage reader's interest in your causal issue and show why it is problematic or controversial. • Show what's at stake. • State your claim.
Reject commonly assumed causes or consequences.	• Describe the first commonly assumed cause or consequence and show why you don't think the explanation is adequate. • Continue with the rest of your commonly assumed causes or consequences.
Argue for your surprising cause or consequence.	• Describe your surprising cause or consequence. • Explain your causal reasoning. • Anticipate and respond to possible objections if needed.
Conclude.	• Perhaps sum up your argument. • Return to the "big picture" of what's at stake. • End with something memorable.

READING

Student Julee Christianson wrote this causal argument in response to the assignment in this chapter. Julee was entering an intense public debate about the underrepresentation of women in science, a controversy initiated by Lawrence Summers, then president of Harvard, who suggested there might be fewer women than men on prestigious science faculties because women have less innate talent for science and math. A furious reaction ensued. The Web site of the Women in Science and Engineering Leadership Institute has extensive coverage of the controversy, including Summers's original speech.

Julee's paper is documented and formatted in the style of the American Psychological Association. For more on APA style, see Appendix 2.

Why Lawrence Summers Was Wrong: Culture Rather Than Biology
Explains the Underrepresentation of Women in Science and Mathematics
Julee Christianson
December 8, 2008

APA

WHY LAWRENCE SUMMERS WAS WRONG   2

Why Lawrence Summers Was Wrong: Culture Rather
Than Biology Explains the Underrepresentation of
Women in Science and Mathematics

In 2005, Harvard University's president, Lawrence H. Summers, gave a controversial speech that suggested that the underrepresentation of women in tenured
positions in math and science departments is partly caused by biological differences.
In his address, Summers proposed three hypotheses explaining why women shy away
from math and science careers. First, he gave a "high-powered job hypothesis" that
stated that women naturally want to start a family and therefore will not have the
time or desire to commit to the high-stress workload required for research in math
and science. His second hypothesis was that genetic differences between the sexes
cause more males than females to have high aptitude for math and science. Lastly, he
mentioned the hypothesis that women are underrepresented because of discrimination, but he dismissed discrimination as an insignificant factor. It was Summers's
second hypothesis about biological differences that started a heated national debate.
The academic world seems split over this nature/nurture issue. Although there is
some evidence that biology plays a role in determining math ability, I argue that culture plays a much larger role, both in the way that women are socialized and in the
continued existence of male discrimination against women in male-dominated fields.

Evidence supporting the role of biology in determining math ability is effectively presented by Steven Pinker (2005), a Harvard psychologist who agrees with
Summers. In his article "The Science of Difference: Sex Ed," Pinker focuses extensively on Summers's argument. According to Pinker, "in many traits, men show
greater variance than women, and are disproportionately found at both the low and
high ends of the distribution" (p. 16). He explains that males and females have similar average scores on math tests but that there are more males than females in the top
and the bottom percentiles. This greater variance means that there are disproportionately more male than female math geniuses (and math dunces) and thus more male
than female candidates for top math and science positions at major research universities. Pinker explains this greater variance through evolutionary biology: men can pass
on their genes to dozens of offspring, whereas women can pass on their genes to only
a few. Pinker also argues that men and women have different brain structures that
result in different kinds of thinking. For example, Pinker cites research that shows
that on average men are better at mental rotation of figures and mathematical word

problems, while women are better at remembering locations, doing mathematical calculations, reading faces, spelling, and using language. Not only do males and females think differently, but they release different hormones. These hormones help shape gender because males release more testosterone and females more estrogen, meaning that men are more aggressive and apt to take risks, while women "are more solicitous to their children" (p. 16). One example Pinker uses to support his biological hypothesis is the case of males born with abnormal genitals and raised as females. These children have more testosterone than normal female children, and many times they show characteristically male interests and behavior. Pinker uses these cases as evidence that no matter how a child is raised, the child's biology determines the child's interests.

Although Pinker demonstrates that biology plays some role in determining math aptitude, he almost completely ignores the much larger role of discrimination and socialization in shaping the career paths of women. According to an editorial from Nature Neuroscience (2005), "[t]he evidence to support [Summers's] hypothesis of 'innate difference' turns out to be quite slim" ("Separating," p. 253). The editorial reports that intercultural studies of the variance between boys' and girls' scores on math tests show significant differences between countries. For example, in Iceland girls outscore boys on math tests. The editorial also says that aptitude tests are not very good at predicting the future success of students and that the "SATs tend to underpredict female and over-predict male academic performance" (p. 253). The editorial doesn't deny that men and women's brains work differently, but states that the differences are too small to be blamed for the underrepresentation of women in math and science careers.

If biology doesn't explain the low number of women choosing math and science careers, then what is the cause? Many believe the cause is culture, especially the gender roles children are taught at a very young age. One such believer is Deborah L. Rhode (1997), an attorney and social scientist who specializes in ethics and gender, law, and public policy. Rhode describes the different gender roles females and males are expected to follow from a very young age. Gender roles are portrayed in children's books and television shows. These gender roles are represented by male characters as heroes and problem solvers, while the female characters are distressed damsels. Another example of gender roles is that only a very small number of these shows and books portray working mothers or stay-at-home fathers. Rhodes also discusses how movies and popular music, especially rap and heavy metal, encourage violence and objectify women. As girls grow up, they face more and more gender stereotypes,

APA

WHY LAWRENCE SUMMERS WAS WRONG   4

from toys to magazines. Parents give their boys interactive, problem-solving toys such as chemistry sets and telescopes, while girls are left with dolls. Although more organizations such as the Girl Scouts of America, who sponsor the Web site Girls Go Tech.org, are trying to interest girls in science and math and advertise careers in those fields to girls, the societal forces working against this encouragement are also still pervasive. For example, magazines for teenage girls encourage attracting male attention and the importance of looks, while being smart and successful is considered unattractive. Because adolescents face so many gender stereotypes, it is no wonder that these stereotypes shape the career paths they choose later in life. The gender roles engraved in our adolescents' minds cause discrimination against women later in life. Once women are socialized to see themselves as dependent and not as smart as males, it becomes very difficult to break away from these gender stereotypes. With gender bias so apparent in our society, it is hard for females to have high enough self-confidence to continue to compete with males in many fields.

The effect of socialization begins at a very early age. One study (Clearfield & Nelson, 2006) shows how parents unconsciously send gendered messages to their infants and toddlers. This study examined differences in mothers' speech patterns and play behaviors based on the gender of infants ranging from six months to fourteen months. Although there was no difference in the actual play behavior of male and female infants, the researchers discovered interesting differences in the way mothers interacted with daughters versus sons. Mothers of daughters tended to ask their daughters more questions, encouraging social interaction, whereas mothers of sons were less verbal, encouraging their sons to be more independent. The researchers concluded that "the mothers in our study may have been teaching their infants about gender roles through modeling and reinforcement....Thus girls may acquire the knowledge that they are 'supposed' to engage in higher levels of interaction with other people and display more verbal behavior than boys....In contrast, the boys were reinforced for exploring on their own" (p. 136).

One of the strongest arguments against the biological hypothesis comes from a transgendered Stanford neurobiologist, Ben A. Barres (2006), who has been a scientist first as a woman and then as a man. In his article "Does Gender Matter?" Barres states that "there is little evidence that gender differences in [mathematical] abilities exist, are innate or are even relevant to the lack of advancement of women in science" (p. 134). Barres provides much anecdotal evidence of the way women are discriminated against in this male-dominated field. Barres notes that simply putting a male name rather than a female name on an article or résumé increases its perceived value. He also describes research showing that men and women do equally well in gender-blind academic competitions but that men win disproportionately in contests where gender is revealed.

As Barres says, "The bar is unconsciously raised so high for women and minority candidates that few emerge as winners" (p. 134). In one study reported by Barres, women applying for a research grant needed more than twice the productivity of men in order to be considered equally competent. As a female-to-male transgendered person, Barres has personally experienced discrimination when trying to succeed in the science and math fields. When in college, Barres was told that her boyfriend must have done her homework, and she later lost a prestigious fellowship competition to a male even though she was told her application was stronger and she had published "six high-impact papers," while the man that won published only one. Barres even notices subtle differences, such as the fact that he can now finish a sentence without being interrupted by a male.

Barres urges women to stand up publicly against discrimination. One woman he particularly admires as a strong female role model is MIT biologist Nancy Hopkins, who sued the MIT administration for discrimination based on the lesser amount of lab space allocated to female scientists. The evidence from this study was so strong that even the president of MIT publicly admitted that discrimination was a problem (p. 134). Barres wants more women to follow Hopkins's lead. He believes that women often don't realize they are being discriminated against because they have faith that the world is equal. Barres explains this tendency as a "denial of personal disadvantage" (p. 134). Very few women will admit to seeing or experiencing discrimination. Until discrimination and sexism are addressed, women will continue to be oppressed.

As a society, we should not accept Lawrence Summers's hypothesis that biological differences are the reason women are not found in high-prestige tenured jobs in math and science. In fact, in another generation the gap between men and women in math and science might completely disappear. In 2003–2004, women received close to one-third of all doctorates in mathematics, up from 15 percent of doctorates in the early 1980s (American Mathematical Society, 2005). Although more recent data are not yet available, the signs point to a steadily increasing number of women entering the fields of math, science, and engineering. Blaming biology for the lack of women in these fields and refusing to fault our culture is taking the easy way out. Our culture can change.

WHY LAWRENCE SUMMERS WAS WRONG   6
References

American Mathematical Society. (2005, July 6). *Women in mathematics: Study shows gains.* Retrieved from http://www/ams.org/news?news_id=489

Barres, B. A. (2006). Does gender matter? *Nature, 44*(7), 133–136. doi:10.1038/442133a

Clearfield, M. W., & Nelson, N. M. (2006). Sex differences in mothers' speech and play behavior with 6-, 9-, and 14-month-old infants. *Sex Role, 54*(1–2), 127–137. doi:.10.1007/s11199-005-8874-1

Pinker, S. (2005, February 14). The science of difference: Sex ed. *New Republic. 232,* 15–17.

Rhode, D. L. (1997). *Speaking of sex: The denial of gender inequality.* Cambridge, MA: Harvard University Press.

Separating science from stereotype [Editorial]. (2005). *Nature Neuroscience, 8*(3) 253. doi:10.1038/nn0305-253

Summers, L. H. (2005, January 14). Remarks at NBER conference on diversifying the science and engineering workforce. Retrieved from http://designintelligences .wordprcss.com/lawrence-h-summers-remarks-at-nber-conference/

APA

Evaluation and Ethical Arguments

13

What you will learn in this chapter:

13.1 To explain and illustrate the difference between categorical and ethical evaluation arguments

13.2 To conduct a categorical evaluation argument using a criteria-match strategy

13.3 To conduct an ethical evaluation argument using principles or consequences

13.4 To be mindful of common problems encountered in evaluation arguments

13.5 To write your own categorical or ethical evaluation argument

---

In our roles as citizens and professionals, we are continually expected to make evaluations and to persuade others to accept them. In this chapter, you will learn to conduct two kinds of evaluation arguments: categorical and ethical. Both have clarifying power to help us make difficult choices about good or bad, right or wrong.

Case 1 How Should We Evaluate The Film *District 9*?

In the film *District 9* (2009), directed by South African Neill Blomkamp and produced by Peter Jackson, a spaceship has stalled out over Johannesburg, South Africa, where it has hovered for several decades. Its starving alien passengers, derogatorily called "The Prawns" for their appearance, have been placed in what has become a crowded, militarized prison ghetto called District 9. As the film begins, South Africans have grown disgusted with and intolerantly fearful of the growing alien population, while corporate powers seek these aliens' technologically advanced bio-weapons. As this poster suggests—based on its "No Humans Allowed" sign, its ominous "You are not welcome here" slogan, and its barbed wire perimeter—the film includes graphic echoes of the racism of apartheid and disturbing depiction of xenophobia, abusive corporate powers, and mistreatment of refugees (the aliens). Nominated for numerous awards, *District 9* has sparked heated evaluation arguments about whether it is a good or a flawed film. Part of the debate focuses on what evaluative criteria to use—a decision that depends on the category into which the film should be placed. Should it be evaluated as a science fiction film, as a corporate espionage thriller, or as a commentary on global social justice? Some critics, for example, have argued that *District 9* is not a great science fiction film, but it is a deeply provocative and moving commentary on social justice.

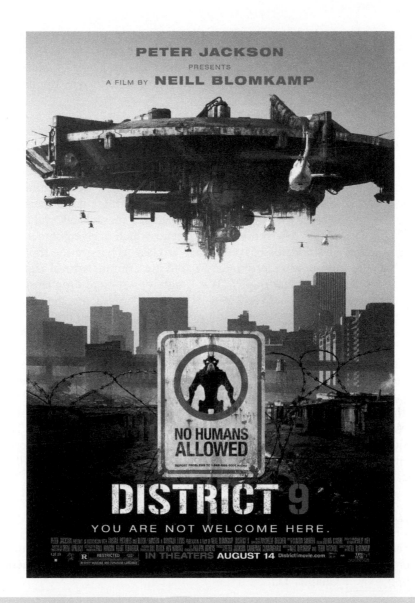

Case 2   What Is a "Good Organ" for a Transplant? How Can an Ill Person Ethically Find an Organ Donor?

In the United States some 87,000 sick people have been waiting as long as six years for an organ transplant, with a portion of these dying before they can find a donor. The problem of organ shortages raises two kinds of evaluation issues. First, doctors are reevaluating the criteria by which they judge a "good" organ—that is, a good lung, kidney, or liver suitable for transplanting. Formerly, people who were elderly or obese or who had engaged in risky behaviors or experienced heart failure or other medical conditions were not considered sources of good organs. Now doctors are reconsidering these sources as well as exploring the use of organs from pigs. Second, the shortage of organs for donation has raised numerous ethical issues: Is it ethical for people to bypass the national waiting list for organs by advertising on billboards and Web sites in search of a volunteer donor? Is it morally right for people to sell their organs? Is it right for patients and families to buy organs or in any way remunerate living organ donors? Some states are passing laws that allow some financial compensation to living organ donors.

An Overview of Categorical and Ethical Evaluation Arguments

13.1 To explain and illustrate the difference between categorical and ethical evaluation arguments

In this chapter we explain strategies for conducting two different kinds of evaluation arguments. First, we examine categorical evaluations of the kind "Is this thing a good member of its class?"* (Is Ramon a good leader?) In such an evaluation, the writer determines the extent to which a given something possesses the qualities or standards of its category or class. What are the traits of good leaders? Does Ramon possess these traits? Second, we examine ethical arguments of the kind "Is this action right (wrong)?" (Was it right or wrong to drop atomic bombs on Hiroshima and Nagasaki in World War II?) In these arguments, the writer evaluates a given act from the perspective of some system of morality or ethics.

To see the difference between the two kinds of evaluations, consider the case of terrorists. From a nonethical standpoint, you could make a categorical evaluation by saying that certain people are "good terrorists" in that they fully realize the purpose of the class "terrorist": they cause great anguish and damage with a minimum of resources, and they bring much attention to their cause. In other words, they are good at what they do—terrorism. However, if we want to condemn terrorism on ethical grounds, we have to construct an ethical argument that terrorism is wrong. The ethical question is not whether a person fulfills the purposes of the class "terrorist," but whether it is wrong for such a class to exist. In the rest of this chapter we will explain categorical evaluations and ethical evaluations in more detail.

Constructing a Categorical Evaluation Argument

13.2 To conduct a categorical evaluation argument using a criteria-match strategy

A categorical evaluation uses a criteria-match structure similar to the structure we examined in definition arguments (see Chapter 11).

Criteria-Match Structure of Categorical Evaluations

A typical claim-with-reasons frame for an evaluation argument has the following structure:

> This thing/phenomenon is/is not a good member of its class because it meets (fails to meet) criteria A, B, and C.

---

*In addition to the term *good*, a number of other evaluative terms involve the same kind of thinking—*effective, successful, workable, excellent, valuable,* and so forth.

The main conceptual difference between an evaluation argument and a definition argument is the nature of the contested category. In a definition argument, one argues whether a particular thing belongs within a certain category. (Is this swampy area a *wetland*?) In an evaluation argument, we know what category something belongs to. For example, we know that this 2008 Chevy Cobalt is a *used car*. For an evaluation argument, the question is whether this Chevy Cobalt is a *good used car*. Or, to place the question within a rhetorical context, is this Chevy Cobalt a *good used car for me to buy for college*?

To illustrate the criteria-match structure of an evaluation argument, let's ask whether hydraulic fracturing (commonly called fracking) is a good means for extracting natural gas from shale formations. Supporters of fracking might say, "yes," because it meets three major criteria:

- It is technologically efficient at extracting huge supplies of otherwise untappable natural gas.
- It is cost effective.
- It is environmentally safe.

Opponents might make two counterarguments: First, they might claim that fracking is not environmentally safe. (Safety is still a crucial criterion. Opponents argue that fracking doesn't meet this criterion.) Second, they might argue that fracking, by producing lots of relatively cheap natural gas, removes the urgency from efforts to convert to renewable energy such as solar and wind. Thus it might be cost effective (criterion 2) in the short run, but disastrous in the long run. Page 228 provides a Toulmin analysis of how proponents of fracking might develop their third reason: "Fracking is environmentally safe."

Developing Your Criteria

To help you develop your criteria, we suggest a three-step thinking process:

1. Place the thing you are evaluating in the smallest relevant category so that you don't compare apples to oranges.
2. Develop criteria for your evaluation based on the purpose or function of this category.
3. Determine the relative weight of your criteria.

Let's look at each of these steps in turn.

Step 1: Place the Thing You Are Evaluating in the Smallest Relevant Category

Placing your contested thing in the smallest category is a crucial first step. Suppose, for example, that you want a professor to write you a letter of recommendation for a summer job. The professor will need to know what kind of summer job. Are you applying to become a camp counselor, a law office intern, a retail sales clerk, or a tour guide at a wild animal park? Each of these jobs has different criteria for excellence. Or to take a different example, suppose that you want to evaluate e-mail as a medium of correspondence. To create a stable context for your evaluation, you need to place e-mail in

TOULMIN ANALYSIS OF THE FRACKING ARGUMENT SUPPORTING ENVIRONMENTAL SAFETY

ENTHYMEME

CLAIM Fracking is a good method for extracting natural gas from shale formations

REASON because it is environmentally safe.

GROUNDS

- Descriptions of safety measures employed by industry
- Descriptions of local, state, and federal regulations aimed at insuring safety
- Summaries of peer-reviewed studies and government studies showing the safety of fracking
- Refutation of anecdotal scare stories told by environmentalists

WARRANT

Environmental safety is an important criterion for evaluating a method of drilling for natural gas

BACKING

Arguments that safety must be a prime consideration of any business plan. One major accident could undermine public support of fracking. [Backing tries to counter the arguments of environmentalists that business interests put profit ahead of safety.]

CONDITIONS OF REBUTTAL

Attacking the reason and grounds

Arguments that fracking is not environmentally safe

- Studies pointing to possible dangers such as contamination of aquifers, earthquakes, flaring of methane, and so forth
- Arguments that local, state, and federal regulations are too loose and unenforced
- Statistics about environmental costs in doing the fracking (huge amounts of required water, recovering contaminated water, use of carbon fuels to run the machinery, and so forth)

CONDITIONS OF REBUTTAL

Attacking the warrant and backing

- Environmentalists will endorse the warrant, but may say that even if fracking is safe, it undermines the urgency of finding alternative energy sources.
- Business interests might want to loosen an insistence on absolute safety by acknowledging that some accidents are inevitable.

its smallest relevant category. You may choose to evaluate e-mail as a medium for business communication (by contrasting e-mail with direct personal contact, phone conversations, or postal mail), as a medium for staying in touch with high school friends (in contrast, say, to text messaging or Facebook), or as a medium for carrying on a long-distance romance (in contrast, say, to old-fashioned "love letters"). Again, criteria will vary across these different categories.

By placing your contested thing in the smallest relevant class, you avoid the apples-and-oranges problem. That is, to give a fair evaluation of a perfectly good apple, you need to judge it under the class "apple" and not under the next larger class, "fruit," or a neighboring class such as "orange." And to be even more precise, you may wish to evaluate your apple in the class "eating apple" as opposed to "pie apple" because the latter class is supposed to be tarter and the former class juicier and sweeter.

Step 2: Develop Criteria for Your Evaluation Based on the Purpose or Functions of This Category   Suppose that the summer job you are applying for is tour guide at a wild animal park. The functions of a tour guide are to drive the tour buses, make people feel welcome, give them interesting information about the wild animals in the park, make their visit pleasant, and so forth. Criteria for a good tour guide would thus include reliability and responsibility, a friendly demeanor, good speaking skills, and knowledge of the kinds of animals in the wild animal park. In our e-mail example, suppose that you want to evaluate e-mail as a medium for business communication. The purpose of this class is to provide a quick and reliable means of communication that increases efficiency, minimizes misunderstandings, protects the confidentiality of internal communications, and so forth. Based on these purposes, you might establish the following criteria:

> A good medium for business communication:
>
> ■ Is easy to use, quick, and reliable
> ■ Increases employee efficiency
> ■ Prevents misunderstandings
> ■ Maintains confidentiality where needed

Step 3: Determine the relative weight of your criteria   In some evaluations all the criteria are equally important. However, sometimes a phenomenon to be evaluated is strong in one criterion but weak in another—a situation that forces the evaluator to decide which criterion takes precedence. For example, the supervisor interviewing candidates for tour guide at the wild animal park may find one candidate who is very knowledgeable about the wildlife but doesn't have good speaking skills. The supervisor would need to decide which of these two criteria gets more weight.

Making Your Match Argument

Once you've established and weighed your criteria, you'll need to use examples and other evidence to show that the thing being evaluated meets or does not meet the criteria. For example, your professor could argue that you would be a good wildlife park tour guide because you have strong interpersonal skills (based on your work on a college orientation committee), that you have good speaking skills (based on a speech you gave in the professor's class), and that you have quite a bit of knowledge about animals and ecology (based on your major in environmental science).

In our e-mail example, you might establish the following working thesis:

> Despite its being easy to learn, quick, and reliable, e-mail is often not an effective medium for business communication because it reduces worker efficiency, leads to frequent misunderstandings, and often lacks confidentiality.

EXAMINING VISUAL ARGUMENTS

An Evaluation Claim

This photograph of Stephen Colbert and Jon Stewart of *The Colbert Report* and *The Daily Show* was taken at the October 30, 2010 "Rally to Restore Sanity 'or Fear,'" on the Washington, DC, National Mall, an event that drew thousands of people. The event followed by two months the "Restoring Honor Rally" led by conservative Fox News talk show celebrity Glenn Beck on August 28, 2010. Political commentators debated whether the Colbert and Stewart rally was simply satirical entertainment mocking the Beck rally or whether it was serious political activism supporting the liberal left. If your goal was to portray this event as serious political activism, would this photograph be a good image to accompany your argument? What criteria would you establish for selecting a photograph to support your argument that Colbert and Stewart are effective political activists and not simply entertainers?

You could develop your last three points as follows:

- **E-mail reduces worker efficiency.** You can use personal anecdotes and research data to show how checking e-mail is addictive and how it eats into worker time (one research article says that the average worker devotes ten minutes of every working hour to reading and responding to e-mail).
- **E-mail leads to misunderstandings.** Because an e-mail message is often composed rapidly without revision, e-mail can cause people to state ideas imprecisely, to write something they would never say face-to-face, or to convey an unintended tone. You could give a personal example of a high-consequence misunderstanding caused by e-mail.
- **E-mail often lacks confidentiality.** You could provide anecdotal or research evidence of cases in which a person clicked on the "reply to all" button rather than the "reply" button, sending a message intended for one person to a whole group of people. Also, people sometimes forward e-mails without the sender's permission. Finally, e-mail messages are archived forever, so messages that you thought were deleted may show up years later in a lawsuit.

As these examples illustrate, the key to a successful match argument is to use sufficient examples and other evidence to show how your contested phenomenon meets or does not meet each of your criteria.

■ ■ ■ **FOR CLASS DISCUSSION** Developing Criteria/Match Arguments

The following small-group exercise can be accomplished in one or two class hours. It gives you a good model of the process you can go through in order to write your own categorical evaluation.

1. Choose a specific controversial person, thing, or event to evaluate. To help you think of ideas, try brainstorming controversial members of various categories such as *people* (athletes, political leaders, musicians); *technology* (new car features, phone apps); *media* (a social network, a TV program); *government and world affairs* (an economic policy, a Supreme Court decision); *your college or university* (food service, an administrative policy); *the world of work* (a job, a company operation, a dress policy); or any other categories of your choice.
2. Place your controversial person or thing within the smallest relevant class, thus providing a rhetorical context for your argument and showing what is at stake. Do you want to evaluate Harvey's Hamburger Haven in the broad category of *restaurants,* in the narrow category of *hamburger joints,* or in a different narrow category such as *late-night study places*?
3. Make a list of the purpose or function of that class, and then list the criteria that a good member of that class would need to have in order to accomplish the purpose or function. (What is the purpose or function of a hamburger joint versus a late-night study place? What criteria for excellence can you derive from these purposes or functions?)

4. If necessary, rank your criteria from most to least important. (For a late-night study place, what is more important: good ambience, Wi-Fi availability, good coffee, or convenient location?)

5. Provide examples and other evidence to show how your contested something matches or does not match each of your criteria. (As a late-night study place, Carol's Coffee Closet beats out Harvey's Hamburger Haven. Although Harvey's Hamburger Haven has the most convenient location, Carol's Coffee Closet has Wi-Fi, an ambience conducive to studying, and excellent coffee.)

Constructing an Ethical Evaluation Argument

13.3 To conduct an ethical evaluation argument using principles or consequences

A second kind of evaluation argument focuses on moral or ethical issues, which can often merge or overlap with categorical evaluations. For example, many apparently straightforward categorical evaluations can turn out to have an ethical dimension. Consider again the criteria for buying a car. Most people would base their evaluations on cost, safety, comfort, and so forth. But some people may feel morally obligated to buy the most fuel-efficient car, to buy an American car, or not to buy a car from a manufacturer whose labor policies they find morally repugnant. Depending on how large a role ethical considerations play in the evaluation, we may choose to call this an ethical argument based on moral considerations rather than a categorical evaluation based on the purposes of a class or category.

When we are faced with an ethical issue, we must move from arguments of good or bad to arguments of right or wrong. The terms *right* and *wrong* are clearly different from the terms *good* and *bad* when the latter terms mean, simply, "effective" (meets purposes of class, as in "This is a good laptop") or "ineffective" (fails to meet purposes of class, as in "This is a bad cookbook"). But *right* and *wrong* often also differ from what seems to be a moral use of the terms *good* and *bad*. We may say, for example, that sunshine is good because it brings pleasure and that cancer is bad because it brings pain and death, but that is not quite the same thing as saying that sunshine is "right" and cancer is "wrong." It is the problem of "right" and "wrong" that ethical arguments confront.

There are many schools of ethical thought—too many to cover in this brief overview—so we'll limit ourselves to two major systems: arguments from consequences and arguments from principles.

Consequences as the Base of Ethics

Perhaps the best-known example of evaluating acts according to their ethical consequences is utilitarianism, a down-to-earth philosophy that grew out of nineteenth-century British philosophers' concern to demystify ethics and make it work in the practical world. Jeremy Bentham, the originator of utilitarianism, developed the goal of the greatest good for the greatest number, or "greatest happiness," by which he meant the most pleasure for the least pain. John Stuart Mill, another British philosopher, built on Bentham's utilitarianism by using predicted consequences to determine the morality of a proposed action.

Mill's consequentialist approach allows you readily to assess a wide range of acts. You can apply the principle of utility—which says that an action is morally right if it produces a greater net value (benefits minus costs) than any available alternative action—in virtually any situation, and it will help you reach a decision. Obviously, however, it's not always easy to make the calculations called for by this approach because, like any prediction of the future, an estimate of consequences is conjectural. In particular, it's often very hard to assess the long-term consequences of any action. Too often, utilitarianism seduces us into a short-term analysis of a moral problem simply because long-term consequences are difficult to predict.

Principles as the Base of Ethics

Any ethical system based on principles will ultimately rest on moral tenets that we are duty bound to uphold, no matter what the consequences. Sometimes the moral tenets come from religious faith—for example, the Ten Commandments. At other times, however, the principles are derived from philosophical reasoning, as in the case of German philosopher Immanuel Kant. Kant held that no one should ever use another person as a means to his own ends and that everyone should always act as if his acts are the basis of universal law. In other words, Kant held that we are duty bound to respect other people's sanctity and to act in the same way that we would want all other people to act. The great advantage of such a system is its clarity and precision. We are never overwhelmed by a multiplicity of contradictory and difficult-to-quantify consequences; we simply make sure we are following (or not violating) the principles of our ethical system and proceed accordingly.

Example Ethical Arguments Examining Capital Punishment

To show you how to conduct an ethical argument, let's now apply these two strategies to the example of capital punishment. In general, you can conduct an ethical evaluation by using the frame for either a principles-based argument or a consequences-based argument, or a combination of both.

> **Principles-Based Frame:** An act is right (wrong) because it follows (violates) principles A, B, and C.
>
> **Consequences-Based Frame:** An act is right (wrong) because it will lead to consequences A, B, and C, which are good (bad).

A principles-based argument looks at capital punishment through the lens of one or more guiding principles. Kant's principle that we are duty bound not to violate the sanctity of other human lives could lead to arguments opposing capital punishment. One might argue as follows:

> *Principles-based argument opposing capital punishment:* The death penalty is wrong because it violates the principle of the sanctity of human life.

You could support this principle either by summarizing Kant's argument that one should not violate the selfhood of another person or by pointing to certain religious systems such as Judeo-Christian ethics, where one is told, "Vengeance is mine, saith the Lord" or "Thou shalt not kill." To develop this argument further, you might examine two exceptions in which principles-based ethicists may allow killing—self-defense and war—and show how capital punishment does not fall into either category.

Principles-based arguments can also be developed to support capital punishment. You may be surprised to learn that Kant himself—despite his arguments for the sanctity of life—supported capital punishment. To make such an argument, Kant evoked a different principle about the suitability of the punishment to the crime:

> There is no sameness of kind between death and remaining alive even under the most miserable conditions, and consequently there is no equality between the crime and the retribution unless the criminal is judicially condemned and put to death.

Stated as an enthymeme, Kant's argument is as follows:

> *Principles-based argument supporting capital punishment:* Capital punishment is right because it follows the principle that punishments should be proportionate to the crime.

In developing this argument, Kant's burden would be to show why the principle of proportionate retribution outweighs the principle of the supreme worth of the individual. Our point is that a principles-based argument can be made both for and against capital punishment. The arguer's duty is to make clear what principle is being evoked and then to show why this principle is more important than opposing principles.

Unlike a principles-based argument, which appeals to certain guiding maxims or rules, a consequences-based argument looks at the consequences of a decision and measures the positive benefits against the negative costs. Here is the frame that an arguer might use to oppose capital punishment on the basis of negative consequences:

> *Consequences-based argument opposing capital punishment:* Capital punishment is wrong because it leads to the following negative consequences:
>
> - The possibility of executing an innocent person
> - The possibility that a murderer who may repent and be redeemed is denied that chance
> - The excessive legal and political costs of trials and appeals
> - The unfair distribution of executions so that one's chances of being put to death are much greater if one is a minority or is poor

To develop this argument, the reader would need to provide facts, statistics, and other evidence to support each of the stated reasons.

A different arguer might use a consequences-based approach to support capital punishment:

> *Consequences-based argument supporting capital punishment:* Capital punishment is right because it leads to the following positive consequences:
>
> - It may deter violent crime and slow down the rate of murder.
> - It saves the cost of lifelong imprisonment.

- It stops criminals who are menaces to society from committing more murders.
- It helps grieving families reach closure and sends a message to victims' families that society recognizes their pain.

It should be evident, then, that adopting an ethical system doesn't lead to automatic answers to one's ethical dilemmas. A system offers a way of proceeding—a way of conducting an argument—but it doesn't relieve you of personal responsibility for thinking through your values and taking a stand. When you face an ethical dilemma, we encourage you to consider both the relevant principles and the possible consequences the dilemma entails. In many arguments, you can use both principles-based and consequences-based reasoning as long as irreconcilable contradictions don't present themselves.

■ ■ ■ FOR WRITING AND DISCUSSION Developing an Ethical Argument

Individual task: Develop a frame for an ethical argument (based on principles, consequences, or both) for or against any two of the following actions. Use the previous examples on capital punishment as a model.

1. Eating meat
2. Using public transportation instead of owning a car
3. Legalizing assisted suicide for the terminally ill
4. Selling organs
5. Allowing concealed weapons on college campuses

Group task: Share your arguments with classmates   ■ ■ ■

Common Problems in Making Evaluation Arguments

13.4 To be mindful of common problems encountered in evaluation arguments

When conducting evaluation arguments (whether categorical or ethical), writers can bump up against recurring problems that are unique to evaluation. In some cases these problems complicate the establishment of criteria; in other cases they complicate the match argument. Let's look briefly at some of these common problems.

- **The problem of standards—what is commonplace versus what is ideal:** In various forms, we experience the dilemma of the commonplace versus the ideal all the time. Is it fair to get a ticket for going seventy miles per hour on a sixty-five-mile-per-hour freeway when most of the drivers go seventy miles per hour or faster? (Does what is *commonplace*—going seventy—override what is *ideal*—obeying the law?) Is it better for high schools to pass out free contraceptives to students because students are having sex anyway (what's *commonplace*), or is it better not to pass them out in order to support abstinence (what's *ideal*)?
- **The problem of mitigating circumstances:** This problem occurs when an arguer claims that unusual circumstances should alter our usual standards of judgment. Ordinarily, it is fair for a teacher to reduce a grade if you turn in a paper late. But what if you were up all night taking care of a crying baby? Does that count as

a *mitigating circumstance* to waive the ordinary criterion? When you argue for mitigating circumstances, you will likely assume an especially heavy burden of proof. People assume the rightness of usual standards of judgment unless there are compelling arguments for abnormal circumstances.

■ **The problem of choosing between two goods or two bads:** Often an evaluation issue forces us between a rock and a hard place. Should we cut pay or cut people? Should we put our parents in a nursing home or let them stay at home, where they have become a danger to themselves? In such cases one has to weigh conflicting criteria, knowing that the choices are too much alike—either both bad or both good.

■ **The problem of seductive empirical measures:** The need to make high-stakes evaluations has led many people to seek quantifiable criteria that can be weighed mathematically. Thus we use grade point averages to select scholarship winners, student evaluation scores to decide merit pay for teachers, and combined scores of judges to evaluate figure skaters. In some cases, empirical measures can be quite acceptable, but they are often dangerous because they discount important non-quantifiable traits. The problem with empirical measures is that they seduce us into believing that complex judgments can be made mathematically, thus rescuing us from the messiness of alternative points of view and conflicting criteria.

■ **The problem of cost:** A final problem in evaluation arguments is cost. Something may be the best possible member of its class, but if it costs too much, we have to go for second or third best. We can avoid this problem somewhat by placing items into different classes on the basis of cost. For example, a Mercedes will exceed a Kia on almost any criterion, but if we can't afford more than a Kia, the comparison is pointless. It is better to compare a Mercedes to a Lexus and a Kia to an equivalent Ford. Whether costs are expressed in dollars, personal discomfort, moral repugnance, or some other terms, our final evaluation of an item must take cost into account.

WRITING ASSIGNMENT An Evaluation or Ethical Argument

13.5 To write your own categorical or ethical evaluation argument

Write an argument in which you try to change your readers' minds about the value, worth, or ethics of something. Choose a phenomenon to be evaluated that is controversial so that your readers are likely at first to disagree with your evaluation or at least to be surprised by it. Somewhere in your essay you should summarize alternative views and either refute them or concede to them (see Chapter 7).

Exploring Ideas

Evaluation issues are all around us. Think of disagreements about the value of a person, thing, action, or phenomenon within the various communities to which you belong—your dorm, home, or apartment community; your school community, including clubs or organizations; your academic community, including classes you are currently taking; your work community; and your city, state, national, and world communities. Once you have settled on a controversial thing to be evaluated, place it in its smallest relevant category, determine the purposes of that category, and develop your criteria. If you are making an ethical evaluation, consider your argument from the perspective of both principles and consequences.

Identifying Your Audience and Determining What's at Stake

Before drafting your argument, identify your targeted audience and determine what's at stake. Consider your responses to the following questions:

- What audience are you targeting? What background do they need to understand your issue? How much do they already care about it?
- Before they read your evaluation argument, what stance on your issue do you imagine them holding? What change do you want to bring about in their view?
- What will they find new or surprising about your argument?
- What objections might they raise? What counterarguments or alternative points of view will you need to address?
- Why does your evaluation matter? Who might be threatened or made uncomfortable by your views? What is at stake?

Organizing an Evaluation Argument

As you write a draft, you may find useful the following prototypical structures for evaluation arguments shown in Organization Plans 1 and 2 on pages 238 and 239. Of course, you can always alter these plans if another structure better fits your material.

Critiquing a Categorical Evaluation Argument

Here is a list of questions you can use to critique a categorical evaluation argument:

Will a skeptic accept my criteria? Many evaluative arguments are weak because the writers have simply assumed that readers will accept their criteria. Whenever your audience's acceptance of your criteria is in doubt, you will need to argue for your criteria explicitly.

Will a skeptic accept my general weighting of criteria? Another vulnerable spot in an evaluation argument is the relative weight of the criteria. How much anyone weights a given criterion is usually a function of his or her own interests relative to your contested something. You should always ask whether some particular group might have good reasons for weighting the criteria differently.

Organization Plan 1: Criteria and Match in Separate Sections

Introduce the issue and state your claim.	• Engage reader's interest in your evaluation issue and show why it is controversial or problematic. • Show what's at stake. • Provide background information needed by your audience. • State your claim.
Present your criteria.	• State and develop criterion 1. • State and develop criterion 2. • Continue with the rest of your criteria. • Anticipate and respond to possible objections to the criteria.
Present your match argument.	• Consider restating your claim for clarity. • Argue that your case meets (does not meet) criterion 1. • Argue that your case meets (does not meet) criterion 2. • Continue with the rest of your match argument. • Anticipate and respond to possible objections to the match argument.
Conclude.	• Perhaps sum up your argument. • Help reader return to the "big picture" of what's at stake. • End with something memorable.

Will a skeptic accept my criteria but reject my match argument? The other major way of testing an evaluation argument is to anticipate how readers may object to your stated reasons and grounds. Will readers challenge you by showing that you have cherry-picked your examples and evidence? Will they provide counterexamples and counterevidence?

Organization Plan 2: Criteria and Match Interwoven

Introduce the issue and state your claim.	• Engage reader's interest in your evaluation issue and show why it is controversial or problematic. • Show what's at stake. • Provide background information needed by your audience. • State your claim.
Present series of criterion-match arguments.	• State and develop criterion 1 and argue that your case meets (does not meet) the criterion. • State and develop criterion 2 and argue that your case meets (does not meet) the criterion. • Continue with the rest of your criterion-match arguments.
Respond to possible objections to your argument.	• Anticipate and summarize possible objections. • Respond to the objections through rebuttal or concession.
Conclude.	• Perhaps sum up your argument. • Help reader return to the "big picture" of what's at stake. • End with something memorable.

Critiquing an Ethical Argument

Ethical arguments can be critiqued through appeals to consequences or principles. If an argument appeals primarily to principles, it can be vulnerable to a simple cost analysis. What are the costs of adhering to this principle? There will undoubtedly be some, or else there would be no real argument. If the argument is based strictly on consequences, we should ask whether it violates any rules or principles, particularly such commandments as the Golden Rule—"Do unto others as you would have others do unto you"—which most members of our audience adhere to. By failing to mention these alternative ways of thinking about ethical issues, we undercut not only our argument but our credibility as well. ■

READINGS

Our first reading, by student writer Lorena Mendoza-Flores, critiques her former high school for the way it marginalizes Hispanic students. Lorena, a physics major in college, has changed the name of her high school and chosen not to reveal her home state.

Silenced and Invisible: Problems of Hispanic Students at Valley High School

LORENA MENDOZA-FLORES (STUDENT)

Every year, thousands of Mexican families come to the United States in order to escape economic hardships in Mexico and hope for better schools for their children. While many American schools try to accommodate immigrant non-native speakers, many immigrant families, according to case study interviews, have increasingly negative perceptions of these attempts (Roessingh). There are action plans to bridge the gap between disadvantaged and advantaged students, yet Hispanic ESL (English as a Second Language) youth continue to perform considerably below that of other students (Good et al.). These problems pose the question: what is wrong with the way our schools treat Hispanic immigrants? Perhaps we could gain some understanding if we looked at a specific school—my own Valley High School in an agricultural region of [name of state]. Valley High School is a perfect example of a school with a growing Hispanic population, well-intentioned teachers, and hopes for their success that simply fall through. The failures at my school include inadequate ESL training for teachers, inadequate counseling for immigrant students, poor multicultural training for all teachers, and failure to value Hispanic identity and provide support for transitioning families.

Despite the fact that the Valley School District has 52 percent Hispanic students, a large percentage of whom have Spanish as their first language and parents who only speak Spanish, the staff at Valley High School is overwhelmingly white with only one Hispanic teacher and only three or four teachers who speak Spanish. Even with a large number of ESL students, Valley High School has not hired teachers who are adequately trained in ESL. There is only one ESL teacher, who is responsible for all the ESL students. They are assigned to regular classes and then go to the ESL classrooms for what is supposed to be extra support. When I've gone into the ESL classroom, I've found students surfing random sites online and the teacher, also the yearbook advisor, working on pages for the annual. Because I was senior editor of the yearbook, he was very open to talking to me about his students, always complaining that they didn't work hard enough even though I could see they weren't being given meaningful work. I was frustrated because it was obvious that the ESL classroom did not engage either the students or the teacher. The students' language progress remained stagnant, while the expectations of standardized testing became increasingly more demanding, dooming ESL students to failure.

Another problem is inadequate counseling for Hispanic students and inadequate methods of assessing their progress so they can be placed in the right classes. When immigrant students need help, teachers often recruit other students to address their needs. As a student mentor, I was called upon a few times to speak with students about their performance in class. In one particular situation, the math teacher called me in to talk to a student who had decided to drop out. The teacher was visibly concerned for the student's welfare but didn't have any means for understanding or addressing the student's issues. The student told me that he did not feel like he belonged at school. The lack of adequate counseling sent the message that immigrant students were not worth fighting for to stay in our school.

Additionally, when students enter the school, their skills in other coursework are not taken into consideration. All ESL students are placed in the basic Math and English courses and while they might move down, sometimes as far as being placed in special education classes, they're never moved up. A student's aptitude in math or science may never get recognized in the four years that he or she is in high school because the ESL students move as a single group and take just about all coursework together. Their status as ESL students becomes the sole determinant of their identity as a student within the school system, and they are not given the same considerations and levels of attention required to grow and develop academically. Personally, I have fallen victim to our school's overlooking of student progress. When I entered the Valley School District in 8th grade, I had already taken several years of algebra and tested far above other students in my grade. At my previous school in another district, I had surpassed the school's highest level of math. In fact, my 5th–7th grade math instructor had to find advanced online material for me so that I could keep progressing. Entering the Valley School District, however, I regressed two years. Even though I communicated to both my math teacher and the counselor that I was being placed too low and that the nearby high school had several higher-level courses, I was kept in the same class. The next year, I was shocked to see that two 8th grade white students were in my 9th grade geometry class; the system had catered to them while it had denied to me an acknowledgement of the same earned achievement. I felt dismissed because I was Hispanic.

5   A third problem is that outside of the ESL classroom, in the regular classroom settings, teachers are often untrained in how to create safe multicultural dialogue. One time in sociology my teacher asked the class why the Hispanic students were performing so much worse than white students. I tried to explain that our support was inadequate. I stated that since most Hispanic students came from immigrant backgrounds, our parents weren't able to help us maneuver through the school system. In doing our homework, we had no one to turn to, and if the instructions were unclear, we did not have access to a resource such as an English speaking parent, something that many white students and faculty never even thought about

when considering this gap in performance. When I started talking about these things, white students around the room started becoming upset. They argued that they were hard workers and didn't have their parents do their homework for them. Obviously, my point was not to dismiss their efforts but to emphasize that these are two different worlds we're living in. Coming from an immigrant background, I and my fellow Hispanic students undoubtedly had more obstacles to overcome every step of the way. What was most troubling about this situation was that at no point did my sociology teacher step up and defend the validity of my arguments. Teachers need to know how to facilitate these multicultural clashes by helping make injustices more visible rather than marginalizing someone for bringing up uncomfortable issues.

Finally, Valley High School does little to honor cultural identity or reach out to immigrant families. My senior year I was president of the International Club (the only club at our school that had lots of immigrant student participation). Without my consent, or that of the members, my advisor began a transition to convert the International Club into the InterAct club affiliated with the community's Rotaract Club (part of Rotary). While this new connection with the Rotary would provide more funding, the only club that was primarily made up of Hispanic members was now being taken over by one sponsored by an all-white organization. In this transition, our advisor had pre-elected leaders to move it forward (also all white). By the time I graduated, the transition was well under way. In fact, on Cinco de Mayo, International Club's major event every year, our club members realized that our advisor didn't think this event was worth our time. As the only Mexican teacher, this advisor did not even advocate for the desires of our community. Ultimately, she turned her back on the members, and the following year InterAct became a primarily white club just like every other club at school.

The loss of a club supporting Hispanic students is matched by failure to create a welcoming environment for Hispanic parents and families. When immigrant parents come to the school, they have to wait around until they can find a translator if they want to speak to a teacher or administrator. Usually this interpreter is another student, creating awkward moments for parents who don't want to discuss their children's problems in front of another student. The school occasionally does try to reach out to Hispanic parents by holding Hispanic Nights where all the events are held in Spanish. However, all the other school events are held only in English. Considering that the school population is more than half Hispanic, the absence of any interpreters makes it clear the school thinks of itself as white. In addition, there are no translators at larger school events such as academic award nights or sporting banquets. As a result, immigrant parents and families feel isolated from the school and unwelcomed.

Debate remains over the exact or best procedures for helping immigrant ESL students successfully integrate into schools, but what is not debated is that these students deserve equal opportunities to learn and grow. Just as any other student, immigrant students should meet the demanding academic standards needed for higher education, but first they must have adequate support. It is essential that schools support educational reforms that address the problem areas apparent at Valley High School. Particularly, schools need to hire qualified ESL instructors, provide adequate counseling for immigrant students, enable teachers to develop multicultural sensitivity and skills at handling ethnic conflict, and provide outreach to immigrant families while valuing their culture.

Works Cited

Good, Mary Ellen, et al. "Latino English Language Learners: Bridging Achievement and Cultural Gaps between Schools and Families." *Journal of Latinos & Education,* vol. 9, no. 4, 2010, pp. 321-39.

Roessingh, Hetty. "The Teacher Is the Key: Building Trust in ESL High School Programs." *Canadian Modern Language Review,* vol. 62, no. 4, 2006, pp. 563-90.

Our final reading, by Judith Daar and Erez Aloni, addresses ethical issues emerging from recent research on therapeutic cloning at the Oregon Health and Sciences University. It appeared as an op-ed piece in the *Los Angeles Times* on March 21, 2014. Judith Daar, a professor of both law and medicine, is a member of the Ethics Committee of the American Society for Reproductive Medicine. Her coauthor, Erez Aloni, is a professor at Whittier Law School.

Three Genetic Parents—For One Healthy Baby

JUDITH DAAR AND EREZ ALONI

Since January, a new California law allows for a child to have more than two legal parents. But children are still limited to two genetic parents. That could change soon, if the Food and Drug Administration approves human clinical trials for a technique known as mitochondrial replacement, which would enable a child to inherit DNA from three parents.

News of the pending application has caused a kind of panic not seen since Dolly the sheep was cloned, raising the possibility of a single genetic parent. But far from being the end of the human race as we know it, the technique might be a way to prevent hundreds of mitochondrial-linked diseases, which affect about one in 5,000 people.

The idea of multi-person reproductive collaborations is not new. Over the last several decades we have acclimated to various forms of assisted reproductive technologies. Indeed, in the U.S. about 75,000 infants are born each year to parents who enlist the aid of egg donors, sperm donors or gestational carriers. These methods, however, still involve the "traditional" merger of DNA from one male and one female.

Mitochondrial replacement would alter this two-genetic-parent model by introducing a third set of DNA into the procreative process. The technique would enable women who carry harmful mutations in their mitochondria to have a child without those harmful mutations. As with all human reproduction, the child would carry a combination of genes from one male and one female. However, in this technique, the nucleus of the mother's egg would be injected into a "third parent's" nucleus-free egg containing healthy mitochondrial DNA. As a result, the child would inherit the characteristics of the original male and female but have healthy mitochondria from a third person.

5   Experiments employing the technique conducted on monkeys resulted in healthy offspring that did not carry the harmful mutation. Now, a team at Oregon Health and Sciences University is seeking approval from the FDA to begin human clinical trials.

It seems likely that, if it is proved safe and effective, mitochondrial replacement will eventually join the panoply of techniques facilitating the birth of healthy children through assisted conception. But it should be no surprise that the new technology is causing a furor.

The introduction of assisted reproductive technologies has followed a predictable pattern: initial panic followed by widespread condemnation, followed by gradual acceptance as a technique becomes more widespread. In the 1950s, when reports of pregnancies using donor sperm first appeared in medical journals, lawmakers declared the process "mechanical adultery" and sought its criminalization. Early reports of success with in vitro fertilization in the 1970s provoked editorials that decried the process as totally immoral. In the 1990s, the introduction of pre-implantation diagnosis of genetic diseases provoked allegations of a war on disabled individuals.

Today, detractors remain, but the methods have been embraced as the standard of care in reproductive medicine. Once a technique proves safe and effective, its ability to assist in the birth of healthy children generally paves the way for public approval.

For some, the introduction of a third genetic parent is alarming because the novel genetic configuration could be embedded in the child's DNA in perpetuity, with unknown implications for future generations. But the panic also rests in part on simple discomfort with upending the notion of genetic parenthood involving just two people.

10   A similar anxiety seized the public this year after California authorized judges to recognize more than two people as a child's lawful parents. The law grew out of a horrendous situation in which the court's inability to recognize a third parent diverted a young child into foster care. Though it's hardly on par with the scientific breakthrough represented by mitochondrial replacement, the so-called three-parent law stirred deep fears about the durability of traditional family life in the modern era.

But the fears about three-parent possibilities—both genetic and legal—are likely to subside as people realize that they are aimed at one goal: the well-being of children. The California law orders judges to recognize three parents when not doing so "would otherwise be detrimental to the child." And mitochondrial replacement will be employed to avoid transmission of a heritable disease. If the "power of three" has the ability to improve a child's well-being, isn't that something worth embracing?

Proposal Arguments

14

What you will learn in this chapter:

14.1 To explain the special features and concerns of proposal arguments

14.2 To use a problem-solution-justification structure to develop proposal arguments

14.3 To use heuristic strategies to develop supporting reasons for your proposal argument

14.4 To use words and images to create an advocacy poster or advertisement

14.5 To write your own proposal argument

Proposal arguments—which identify problems and propose solutions—are essential for the workings of a free and open society. Whether you are writing a grant proposal to seek funding for a research project, a practical proposal for remedying a problem at your workplace, or a policy proposal to address a national issue, proposal arguments are among the most important kinds of writing you will ever be called upon to produce.

Case 1   Should the Supreme Court Overturn *Roe v. Wade*?

Among the most heated debates in the United States is whether the due process and privacy protections of the Fourteenth Amendment can be extended to a woman's right to an abortion. The right-to-life movement has intensified its efforts to restrict access to abortions at the state level and to overturn *Roe v. Wade* in the U.S. Supreme Court. Meanwhile, pro-choice advocates such as Planned Parenthood have vigorously defended a woman's right to an abortion. Both sides make effective use of visual arguments. Right-to-life groups frequently use posters showing ultrasound images of unborn babies (often not using the word "fetus"). The poster on the next page, sponsored by Planned Parenthood, features a starkly black question mark that on second look is made from a coat hanger. It makes an implied proposal claim ("Abortion should remain legal") and supports it with a consequence argument: If abortions are outlawed, women will have abortions anyway—using coat hangers instead of medically safe procedures. The image of the coat hanger (reminiscent of horror stories about abortions prior to *Roe v. Wade*) appeals simultaneously to *logos* and *pathos*.

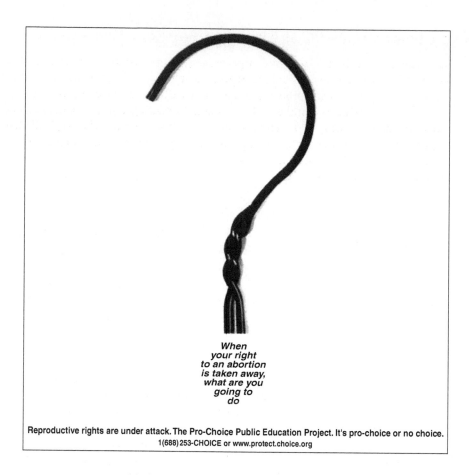

*When
your right
to an abortion
is taken away,
what are you
going to
do*

Reproductive rights are under attack. The Pro-Choice Public Education Project. It's pro-choice or no choice.
1(688)253-CHOICE or www.protect.choice.org

Case 2   How Should the United States Reduce the Carbon Footprint of Automobiles?

The concern for climate change—combined with the high price of gasoline—has increased the popularity of small, energy-efficient cars. Much debated among policy makers is the role that federal or state governments should play in further promoting a green transportation system. Some argue that the government should stay out of free markets, letting buyers decide for themselves what kinds of cars they want to buy. Others argue that free markets do not currently make gasoline consumers pay for the "externalities" of gasoline consumption—particularly the cost to the environment of loading more carbon into the atmosphere. Concerned citizens have proposed dozens of ideas for reducing the carbon footprint of cars and trucks. Among the proposals are the following: placing a "green tax" on gasoline; requiring auto manufacturers to increase the fuel efficiency of their fleets; giving tax credits for buying a fuel-efficient car; increasing incentives for carpooling or taking public transportation; increasing the cost of parking; charging different gas prices at the pump (with higher prices for less fuel-efficient cars); retrofitting cars to burn natural gas; and rebuilding cities so that housing is closer to work sites.

The Special Features and Concerns of Proposal Arguments

14.1 To explain the special features and concerns of proposal arguments

Although proposal arguments are the last type of argument we examine, they are among the most common arguments that you will encounter or be called upon to write. The essence of proposal arguments is that they call for action. In reading a proposal, the audience is enjoined to make a decision and then to act on it—to *do* something. They typically have a three-part structure: (1) description of a problem, (2) proposed solution, and (3) justification for the proposed solution. In the justification section of your proposal argument, you develop *because* clauses of the kinds you have practiced throughout this text.

Practical Proposals versus Policy Proposals

For instructional purposes, we distinguish between two kinds of proposal arguments—*practical proposals,* which propose an action to solve some kind of local or immediate problem, and *policy proposals,* which propose a broad plan of action to solve major social, economic, or political problems affecting the common good. A student's proposal to build bike paths on campus would be an example of a practical proposal. In contrast, an argument that the United States should abolish the income tax would be a policy proposal.

Toulmin Framework for a Proposal Argument

The Toulmin schema is particularly useful for proposal arguments because it helps you find good reasons and link them to your audience's beliefs, assumptions, and values. Suppose that your university is debating whether to banish fraternities and sororities. Suppose further that you are in favor of banishing the Greek system. One of your arguments is that eliminating the Greek system will improve your university's academic reputation. The chart on page 248 shows how you might use the Toulmin schema to make this line of reasoning as persuasive as possible.

Special Concerns for Proposal Arguments

In their call for action, proposal arguments entail certain emphases and audience concerns that you don't generally face with other kinds of arguments. Let's look briefly at some of these special concerns.

- **The need for presence.** To persuade people to *act* on your proposal, particularly if the personal or financial cost of acting is high, you must give your argument presence as well as intellectual force. By *presence,* we mean an argument's ability to grip your readers' hearts and imaginations as well as their intellects. You can give presence to an argument through appeals to *pathos,* such as effective use of details, provocative statistics, dialogue, illustrative narratives, and compelling examples that show the reader the seriousness of the problem you are addressing or the consequences of not acting on your proposal.
- **The need to overcome people's natural conservatism.** Another difficulty with proposals is the innate conservatism of all human beings, whatever their political persuasion, as suggested by the popular adage "If it ain't broke, don't fix it." The

Toulmin Analysis of the Greek System Argument

ENTHYMEME

CLAIM Our university should eliminate the Greek system

REASON because doing so will improve our university's academic reputation.

GROUNDS

Evidence that eliminating the Greek system will improve our academic reputation:

- Excessive party atmosphere of some Greek houses emphasizes social life rather than studying—we are known as a party school.

- Last year the average GPA of students in fraternities and sororities was lower than the GPA of non-Greek students.

- New pledges have so many house duties and initiation rites that their studies suffer.

- Many new students think about rush more than about the academic life.

CONDITIONS OF REBUTTAL
Attacking the reason and grounds

- Many of the best students are Greeks. Last year's highest-GPA award went to a sorority woman, and several other Greeks won prestigious graduate school scholarships.

- Statistics on grades are misleading. Many houses had a much higher average GPA than the university average. Total GPA was brought down by a few rowdy houses.

- Many other high-prestige universities have Greek systems.

- There are ways to tone down the party atmosphere on campus without abolishing the Greek system.

- Greeks contribute significantly to the community through service projects.

WARRANT

It is good for our university to achieve a better academic reputation.

BACKING

- The school would attract more serious students, leading to increased prestige.

- Campus would be more academically focused and attract better faculty.

- Losing the "party-school" reputation would put us in better light for taxpayers and legislators.

- Students would graduate with more skills and knowledge.

CONDITIONS OF REBUTTAL
Attacking the warrant and backing

- No one will argue that it is not good to have a strong academic reputation.

- However, skeptics may say that eliminating sororities and fraternities won't improve the university's academic reputation but will hurt its social life and its wide range of living options.

difficulty of proving that something needs fixing is compounded by the fact that frequently the status quo appears to be working. So sometimes when writing a proposal, you can't argue that what we have is bad, but only that what we could have would be better. Often, then, a proposal argument will be based not on present evils but on the evils of lost potential. And getting an audience to accept lost potential may be difficult indeed, given the inherently abstract nature of potentiality.

■ **The difficulty of predicting future consequences.** Further, most proposal makers will be forced to predict consequences of their proposed action. As the "law of unintended consequences" suggests, few major decisions lead neatly to their antic-ipated results without surprises along the way. So when we claim that our proposal will lead to good consequences, we can expect our audience to be skeptical.

■ **The problem of evaluating consequences.** A final problem for proposal writers is the difficulty of evaluating consequences. In government and industry, manag-ers often use a *cost-benefit analysis* to reduce all consequences to a single-scale comparison, usually money. Although this scale may work well in some circum-stances, it can lead to grotesquely inappropriate conclusions in other situations. Just how does one balance the environmental benefits of high gasoline prices against the suffering of drivers who can't afford to get to work? Also, a benefit of one group often entails a cost for others. For example, a higher minimum wage will benefit low-wage workers, but at a cost to consumers who must pay higher prices or to other low-wage workers who get laid off.

EXAMINING VISUAL ARGUMENTS

A Proposal Claim

This advocacy poster, sponsored by the Endangered Wildlife Trust, presents a photograph of a dead baby albatross on a beach on Midway Island, a main nesting ground for albatrosses. The photo is part of environmental photographer Chris Jordan's exhibit "Midway: Message from the Gyre." In this exhibit, Jordan exposes the effects of increasing volumes of ocean garbage on albatrosses, who mistake the garbage for food. What policy proposal is the Endangered Wildlife Trust making in this poster? What action is it asking people to take? The colorful, plastic-filled carcass of the baby albatross creates a complex appeal to *pathos* in its effort to give presence to the problem. How does the verbal text help to interpret this appeal while driving home the *logos* of the argument?

These, then, are some of the general difficulties facing someone who sets out to write a proposal argument. Although these difficulties may seem daunting, the rest of this chapter offers strategies to help you overcome them and produce a successful proposal.

Developing a Proposal Argument

14.2 To use a problem-solution-justification structure to develop proposal arguments

Writers of proposal arguments must focus in turn on three main phases or stages of the argument: showing that a problem exists, explaining the proposed solution, and offering a justification.

Convincing Your Readers that a Problem Exists

There is one argumentative strategy generic to all proposal arguments: calling your reader's attention to a problem. In some situations, your intended audience may already be aware of the problem and may have even asked for solutions. In such cases, you do not need to develop the problem extensively or motivate your audience to solve it. But in most situations, awakening your readers to the existence of a problem—a problem they may well not have recognized before—is your first important challenge. You must give your problem presence through anecdotes, telling statistics, or other means that show readers how the problem affects people or otherwise has important stakes. Your goal is to gain your readers' intellectual assent to the depth, range, and potential seriousness of the problem and thereby motivate them to want to solve it.

Typically, the arguer develops the problem in one of two places in a proposal argument—either in the introduction prior to the presentation of the arguer's proposal claim or in the body of the paper as the first main reason justifying the proposal claim. In the second instance the writer's first *because* clause has the following structure: "We should do this action *because* it addresses a serious problem."

Here is how one student writer gave presence to a proposal, addressed to the chair of the mathematics department at her school, calling for redesign of the first-year calculus curriculum in order to slow its pace. She wants the chair to see the problem from her perspective.

Example Passage Giving Presence to a Problem

For me, who wants to become a high school math teacher, the problem with introductory calculus is not its difficulty but its pace. My own experience in the Calculus 134 and 135 sequence last year showed me that it was not the learning of calculus that was difficult for me. I was able to catch on to the new concepts. My problem was that it went too fast. Just as I was assimilating new concepts and feeling the need to reinforce them, the class was on to a new topic before I had full mastery of the old concept.... Part of the reason for the fast pace is that calculus is a feeder course for computer science and engineering. If prospective engineering students can't learn the calculus rapidly, they drop out of the program. The high dropout rate benefits the Engineering School because they use the math course to weed out an overabundance of engineering applicants. Thus the pace of the calculus course is geared to the needs of the engineering curriculum, not to the needs of someone like me, who wants to be a high school mathematics teacher and who believes that my own difficulties with math—combined with my love for it—might make me an excellent math teacher.

By describing the fast pace of the math curriculum from the perspective of a future math teacher rather than an engineering student, this writer brings visibility to a problem. What before didn't look like a problem (it is good to weed out weak engineering majors) suddenly became a problem (it is bad to weed out future math teachers). Establishing herself as a serious student genuinely interested in learning calculus, she gave presence to the problem by calling attention to it in a new way.

Showing the Specifics of Your Proposal

Having decided that there is a problem to be solved, you should lay out your thesis, which is a proposal for solving the problem. Your goal now is to stress the feasibility of your solution, including costs. The art of proposal making is the art of the possible. To be sure, not all proposals require elaborate descriptions of the implementation process. If you are proposing, for example, that a local PTA chapter buy new tumbling mats for the junior high gym classes, the procedures for buying the mats will probably be irrelevant. But in many arguments the specifics of your proposal—the actual step-by-step methods of implementing it—may be instrumental in winning your audience's support.

You will also need to show how your proposal will solve the problem either partially or wholly. Sometimes you may first need to convince your reader that the problem is solvable, not something intractably rooted in "the way things are," such as earthquakes or jealousy. In other words, expect that some members of your audience will be skeptical about the ability of any proposal to solve the problem you are addressing. You may well need, therefore, to "listen" to this point of view in your refutation section and to argue that your problem is at least partially solvable.

In order to persuade your audience that your proposal can work, you can follow any one of several approaches. A typical approach is to lay out a causal argument showing how one consequence will lead to another until your solution is effected. Another approach is to turn to resemblance arguments, either analogy or precedent. You try to show how similar proposals have been successful elsewhere. Or, if similar things have failed in the past, you try to show how the present situation is different.

Convincing Your Readers that the Benefits of Your Proposal Outweigh the Costs

The justification phase of a proposal argument will need extensive development in some arguments and minimal development in others, again depending on your particular problem and the rhetorical context of your proposal. If your audience already acknowledges the seriousness of the problem you are addressing and has simply been waiting for the right solution to come along, then your argument will be successful so long as you can convince your audience that your solution will work and that it won't cost too much. Such arguments depend on the clarity of your proposal and the feasibility of its being implemented.

But what if the costs are high? What if your readers don't think the problem is serious? What if they don't appreciate the benefits of solving the problem or the bad consequences of not solving it? In such cases you have to develop persuasive reasons for enacting your proposal. You may also have to determine who has the power to act on your proposal and apply arguments directly to that person's or agency's immediate interests. You need to know to whom or to what your power source is beholden or responsive and what values your power source holds that can be appealed to. You're looking, in short, for the best pressure points.

Using Heuristic Strategies to Develop Supporting Reasons for Your Proposal

14.3 To use heuristic strategies to develop supporting reasons for your proposal argument

To help you find supporting reasons for your proposal—the pressure points that will move your audience—we offer two heuristic strategies. (A *heuristic* is an exploratory problem-solving technique or invention aid that helps you generate ideas.) We call these heuristics the "claim types" strategy and the "stock issue" strategy.

The "Claim Types" Strategy

In Chapter 10 we explained how evaluation and proposal claims often depend for their supporting reasons on claims about category, cause, or resemblance. This fact leads to a powerful idea-generating strategy based on arguments from category (particularly from a category of actions that adhere to a certain principle), on arguments from consequences, or on arguments from resemblance. This "claim types" strategy is illustrated in the following chart:

Claim Type	Generic Template	Example from Biotechnology Issue
Argument from principle or category	We should do this action ■ because doing so adheres to this good principle [or] ■ because this action belongs to this good category	We should support genetically modified foods ■ because doing so values scientific reason over emotion [or] ■ because genetically modified foods are safe [belong to the category of safe things]

(continued)

Claim Type	Generic Template	Example from Biotechnology Issue
Argument from consequences	■ because this action will lead to these good consequences	■ because biotech crops can reduce world hunger ■ because biotech crops can improve the environment by reducing use of pesticides
Argument from resemblance	■ because this action has been done successfully elsewhere [or] ■ because this action is like this other good action	■ because genetic modification is like natural crossbreeding that has been accelerated [or] ■ because genetic modification of food is like scientific advancements in medicine

Before we give you some simple strategies for using this approach, let's illustrate it with another example.

The United States should levy a "carbon tax" on carbon-based fuels.

- Because such a tax accords with the free-market principle that the price of a good should reflect the full cost of production (category/principle)
- Because such a tax will accelerate the transition to cleaner fuels and thus help reduce global warming (cause/consequence)
- Because this approach is similar to the market-based tax on sulfur emissions that helped solve the problem of acid rain (resemblance)

Note how each of these supporting reasons appeals to the value system of different kinds of voters. The writer argues that a carbon tax belongs to the category of things that use free market principles (particularly valued by conservative, pro-business voters); that it will lead to the good consequence of reducing global warming (valued particularly by environmentalists and others worried about climate change); and is similar to something that has already proved successful (the market-based approach to fighting acid rain, which has been hailed by both liberals and conservatives). The claim types strategy for generating ideas is easy to apply in practice. The following chart shows you how.

Suggestions for Applying the Claim Types Strategy to Your Proposal

Claim Type	Your Goal	Thinking Strategy
Argument from principle or category	Show how your proposed action follows a principle valued by your audience or belongs to a category valued by your audience.	Think of how your proposed action adheres to an audience-valued rule or principle or belongs to an audience-valued category (for example, "doing this action is kind, just, constitutional, appropriately restrained, safe, efficient," and so forth.

(*continued*)

Claim Type	Your Goal	Thinking Strategy
Argument from consequences	Show how your proposed action will lead to consequences valued by your audience.	Brainstorm consequences of your proposal and identify those that the audience will agree are good.
Argument from resemblance	Show how your proposed action has been done successfully elsewhere or is like another action valued by your audience.	Find analogies that compare your proposed action to something the audience already values or find previous places or times that your proposed action (or something similar to it) has been done successfully.

■ ■ ■ **FOR CLASS DISCUSSION** Generating Ideas Using the
                                   Claim Types Strategy

Working in small groups or as a whole class, use the strategies of principle/category, consequence, and resemblance to create *because* clauses that support each of the following claims. Try to have at least one *because* clause from each of the claim types, but generate as many reasons as possible. Don't worry about whether any individual reason exactly fits the category. The purpose is to stimulate thinking, not fill in the slots. When you have shared ideas, then repeat the exercise taking the opposite position on each issue.

Example

Congress should not pass gun control laws (proposal claim)

- because the Second Amendment guarantees the right to own guns (principle or category)
- because owning a gun allows citizens to protect themselves, their homes, and their loved ones from intruders (consequence)
- because laws to ban guns will be as ineffective as laws to ban alcohol during Prohibition (resemblance)

   1. Colleges should require a service learning course for graduation.
   2. Restaurants should be required to post calorie counts and other ingredient information for all menu items.
   3. Division I college athletes should receive salaries.   ■ ■ ■

The "Stock Issues" Strategy

Another effective heuristic for a proposal argument is to ask yourself a series of questions based on the "stock issues" strategy. Suppose, for example, you wanted to develop the following argument: "In order to solve the problem of students who won't take risks with their writing, the faculty should adopt a pass/fail method of grading in all writing courses." The stock issues strategy invites the writer to consider "stock" ways (that is, common, usual, frequently repeated ways) that such arguments can be conducted.

Stock issue 1: ***Is there really a problem here that needs to be solved?*** Is it really true that a large number of student writers won't take risks in their writing? Is this problem more serious than other writing problems such as undeveloped ideas, lack of organization, and poor sentence structure? This stock issue invites the writer to convince her audience that a true problem exists. Conversely, an opponent to the proposal may argue that a true problem does not exist.

Stock issue 2: ***Will the proposed solution really solve this problem?*** Is it true that a pass/fail grading system will cause students to take more risks with their writing? Will more interesting, surprising, and creative essays result from pass/fail grading? Or will students simply put less effort into their writing? This stock issue prompts a supporter to demonstrate that the proposal will solve the problem; in contrast, it prompts the opponent to show that the proposal won't work.

Stock issue 3: ***Can the problem be solved more simply without disturbing the status quo?*** An opponent of the proposal may agree that a problem exists and that the proposed solution might solve it. However, the opponent may say, "Are there not less radical ways to solve this problem? If we want more creative and risk-taking student essays, can't we just change our grading criteria so that we reward risky papers and penalize conventional ones?" This stock issue prompts supporters to show that *only* the proposed solution will solve the problem and that no minor tinkering with the status quo will be adequate. Conversely, opponents will argue that the problem can be solved without acting on the proposal.

Stock issue 4: ***Is the proposed solution really practical? Does it stand a chance of actually being enacted?*** Here an opponent to the proposal may agree that the proposal would work but contends that it involves pie-in-the-sky idealism. Nobody will vote to change the existing system so radically; therefore, it is a waste of our time to debate it. Following this prompt, supporters would have to argue that pass/fail grading is workable and that enough faculty members are disposed to it that the proposal is worth debating. Opponents may argue that the faculty is so traditional that pass/fail has utterly no chance of being accepted, despite its merits.

Stock issue 5: ***What will be the unforeseen positive and negative consequences of the proposal?*** Suppose we do adopt a pass/fail system. What positive or negative consequences may occur that are different from what we at first predicted? Using this prompt, an opponent may argue that pass/fail grading will reduce the effort put forth by students and that the long-range effect will be writing of even lower quality than we have now. Supporters would try to find positive consequences—perhaps a new love of writing for its own sake rather than for the sake of a grade.

■ ■ ■   **FOR CLASS DISCUSSION** **Brainstorming Ideas for a Proposal**

The following collaborative task takes approximately two class days to complete. The exercise takes you through the process of creating a proposal argument.

1. In small groups, identify and list several major problems facing students in your college or university.
2. Decide among yourselves which are the most important of these problems and rank them in order of importance.
3. Take your group's number one problem and explore answers to the following questions. Group recorders should be prepared to present their group's answers to the class as a whole:
   a. Why is the problem a problem?
   b. For whom is the problem a problem?
   c. How will these people suffer if the problem is not solved? (Give specific examples.)
   d. Who has the power to solve the problem?
   e. Why hasn't the problem been solved up to this point?
   f. How can the problem be solved? (That is, create a proposal.)
   g. What are the probable benefits of acting on your proposal?
   h. What costs are associated with your proposal?
   i. Who will bear those costs?
   j. Why should this proposal be enacted?
   k. Why is it better than alternative proposals?
4. As a group, draft an outline for a proposal argument in which you
   a. describe the problem and its significance.
   b. propose your solution to the problem.
   c. justify your proposal by showing how the benefits of adopting that proposal outweigh the costs.
5. Recorders for each group should write their group's outline on the board and be prepared to explain it to the class.   ■ ■ ■

Proposal Arguments as Advocacy Posters or Advertisements

14.4 To use words and images to create an advocacy poster or advertisement

A frequently encountered kind of proposal argument is the one-page newspaper or magazine advertisement often purchased by advocacy groups to promote a cause. Such arguments also appear as Web pages or as posters or fliers. These condensed advocacy arguments are marked by their bold, abbreviated, tightly planned format. The creators of these arguments know they must work fast to capture our attention, give presence to a problem, advocate a solution, and enlist our support. Advocacy advertisements frequently use photographs, images, or icons that appeal to a reader's emotions and imagination. In addition to images, they often use different type sizes and styles. Large-type text in these documents frequently takes the form of slogans or condensed thesis statements written in an arresting style. To outline and justify their solutions, creators of advocacy ads often put main supporting reasons in bulleted lists and sometimes enclose care-fully selected facts and quotations in boxed sidebars. To add an authoritative *ethos,* the arguments often include fine-print footnotes and bibliographies. (For more detailed discussion of how advocacy posters and advertisements use images and arrange text for rhetorical effect, see Chapter 9 on visual argument.)

Another prominent feature of these condensed, highly visual arguments is their appeal to the audience through a direct call for a course of action: go to an advocacy Web site to find more information on how to support the cause; cut out a postcardlike form to send to a decision maker; vote for or against the proposition or the candidate; write a letter to a political representative; or donate money to a cause.

An example of a student-produced advocacy advertisement is shown in Figure 14.1. Here, environmental studies student Janie Bube urges residents of her city to build rain

Is Stormwater Turning Your Street Into a Lake?

Installing green stormwater infrastructure technologies like rain gardens will address this problem.

Install a rain garden to:

- Slow, retain, and absorb runoff
- Replicate the functioning of a forest in cleaning pollutants from the water
- Add natural beauty

For further information contact RainWise through Seattle Public Utilities at rainwise@seattle.gov

FIGURE 14.1 Student advocacy poster

gardens to help solve the problem of excess storm water. At the top of this poster, Janie uses a photo of a flood she took during her internship fieldwork to give the problem presence. She then offers her proposed solution, made visually appealing by another of her own photos—a neighborhood rain garden. She offers three reasons to justify the choice of rain gardens, asserting why and how rain gardens work. The final lines of the poster give readers a Web site for more information. The rhetorical effect of the text, image, and layout is to attract readers' attention, remind them of the problem, and push them toward adopting her proposed solution.

WRITING ASSIGNMENT A Proposal Argument

14.5 To write your own proposal argument

Option 1: A Practical Proposal Addressing a Local Problem   Write a practical proposal offering a solution to a local problem. Your proposal should have three main sections: (1) description of the problem, (2) proposed solution, and (3) justification. Proposals are usually accompanied by a *letter of transmittal*—a one-page business letter that introduces the proposal to its intended audience and provides some needed background about the writer.

Option 2: A Policy Proposal as a Guest Editorial   Write a two- to three-page policy proposal suitable for publication as a feature editorial in a college or city newspaper, on an appropriate Web site, or in a publication associated with a particular group, such as a church newsletter or employee bulletin. The voice and style of your argument should be aimed at readers of your chosen publication or Web site. Your editorial should have the following features:

1. The identification of a problem (Persuade your audience that this is a genuine problem that needs solving; give it presence.)
2. A proposal for action that will help alleviate the problem
3. A justification of your solution (the reasons why your audience should accept your proposal and act on it)

Option 3: A Researched Argument Proposing Public Policy   Write an eight- to twelve-page proposal argument as a formal research paper, using researched data for development and support. In business and professional life, this kind of research proposal is often called a *white paper*, which recommends a course of action internally within an organization or externally to a client or stakeholder. An example of a researched policy proposal is student writer Ivan Snook's "Flirting with Disaster: An Argument against Integrating Women into the Combat Arms" on pages 264–268.

Option 4: Multimedia Project: A One-Page Advocacy Poster or Advertisement   Using the strategies of visual argument discussed in Chapter 9 and on pages 256–258 of this chapter, create a one-page advocacy advertisement urging action on a public issue. Your advertisement should be designed for publication in a newspaper or on a Web site, or for distribution as a poster or flier. An example of a student-produced advocacy advertisement is shown in Figure 14.1 on page 257.

Option 5: Multimedia Project: A Proposal Speech with Visual Aids Deliver a proposal argument as a prepared but extemporaneous speech of approximately five to eight minutes, supported with visual aids created on presentation software such as PowerPoint or Prezi. Your speech should present a problem, propose a solution, and justify the solution with reasons and evidence. Use visual aids to give "presence" to the problem and to enhance appeals to *logos*, *ethos*, and *pathos*. Good aids use visual strategies to create encapsulated visual arguments; they are not simply bullet point outlines of your speech. Sandy Wainscott's speech outline and selected PowerPoint slides (pages 269–270) illustrate this genre.

Exploring Ideas

Because *should* or *ought* issues are among the most common sources of arguments, you may already have ideas for proposal issues. To think of ideas for practical proposals, try making an idea map of local problems you would like to see solved. For initial spokes, try trigger words such as the following:

- Problems at my university (dorms, parking, registration system, financial aid, campus appearance, clubs, curriculum, intramural program, athletic teams)
- Problems in my city or town (dangerous intersections, ugly areas, inadequate lighting, parks, police policy, public transportation, schools)
- Problems at my place of work (office design, flow of customer traffic, merchandise display, company policies)
- Problems related to my future career, hobbies, recreational time, life as a consumer, life as a homeowner

If you can offer a solution to the problem you identify, you may make a valuable contribution to some phase of public life.

To find a topic for policy proposals, stay in touch with the news, which will keep you aware of current debates on regional and national issues. Also, visit the Web sites of your congressional representatives to see what issues they are currently investigating and debating. You might think of your policy proposal as a white paper for one of your legislators.

Once you have decided on a proposal issue, we recommend you explore it by trying one or more of the following activities:

- Explore ideas by using the claim types strategy (see pages 252–254).
- Explore ideas by using the "stock issues" strategy (see pages 254–255).
- Explore ideas using the eleven questions (3a–3k) on pages 256.

Identifying Your Audience and Determining What's at Stake

Before drafting your argument, identify your targeted audience and determine what's at stake. Consider your responses to the following questions:

- What audience are you targeting? What background do they need to understand your problem? How much do they already care about it? How could you motivate them to care?

- After they read your argument, what stance do you imagine them holding? What change do you want to bring about in their view or their behavior?
- What will they find uncomfortable or threatening about your proposal? Particularly, what costs will they incur by acting on your proposal?
- What objections might they raise? What counterarguments or alternative solutions will you need to address?
- Why does your proposal matter? What is at stake?

Organizing a Proposal Argument

When you write your draft, you may find it helpful to have at hand an organization plan for a proposal argument. The plan on page 261 shows a typical structure for a proposal argument. In some cases, you may want to summarize and rebut opposing views before you present the justification for your own proposal.

Designing a One-Page Advocacy Advertisement

As an alternative to a traditional written argument, your instructor may ask you to create a one-page advocacy advertisement. The first stage of your invention process should be the same as that for a longer proposal argument. Choose a controversial public issue that needs immediate attention or a neglected issue about which you want to arouse public passion. As with a longer proposal argument, consider your audience in order to identify the values and beliefs on which you will base your appeal.

When you construct your argument, the limited space available demands efficiency in your choice of words and in your use of document design. Your goal is to have a memorable impact on your reader in order to promote the action you advocate. The following questions may help you design and revise your advocacy ad.

1. How could photos or other graphic elements establish and give presence to the problem?
2. How can type size, type style, and layout be used to present the core of your proposal, including the justifying reasons, in the most powerful way for the intended audience?
3. Can any part of this argument be presented as a memorable slogan or catchphrase? What key phrases could highlight the parts or the main points of this argument?
4. How can document design clarify the course of action and the direct demand on the audience this argument is proposing?
5. How can use of color enhance the overall impact of your advocacy argument? (Note: One-page advertisements are expensive to reproduce in color, but you might make effective use of color if your advocacy ad were to appear as a poster or Web page.)

Designing PowerPoint Slides or Other Visual Aids for a Speech

In designing visual aids, your goal is to increase the persuasive effect of your speech rather than to demonstrate your technical wizardry. If you find yourself thinking about special effects (animations, fade-outs, flashing letters) rather than about "at a glance" visual appeals to *logos* or *pathos*, you may be on the wrong track. Another common mistake is to use slides simply to project a bullet point outline of your speech. Our best advice in designing slides is to "think visual argument."

Organization Plan for a Proposal Argument

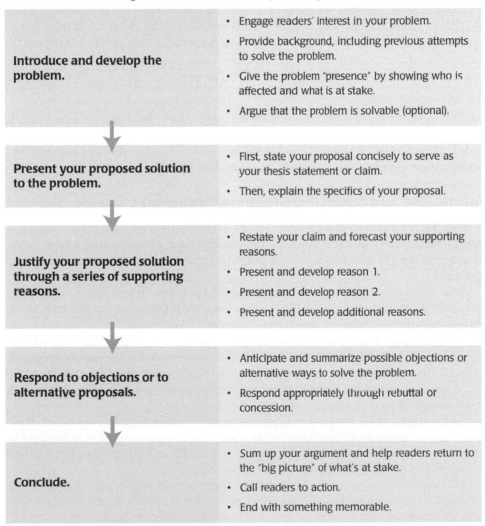

Introduce and develop the problem.	• Engage readers' interest in your problem. • Provide background, including previous attempts to solve the problem. • Give the problem "presence" by showing who is affected and what is at stake. • Argue that the problem is solvable (optional).
Present your proposed solution to the problem.	• First, state your proposal concisely to serve as your thesis statement or claim. • Then, explain the specifics of your proposal.
Justify your proposed solution through a series of supporting reasons.	• Restate your claim and forecast your supporting reasons. • Present and develop reason 1. • Present and develop reason 2. • Present and develop additional reasons.
Respond to objections or to alternative proposals.	• Anticipate and summarize possible objections or alternative ways to solve the problem. • Respond appropriately through rebuttal or concession.
Conclude.	• Sum up your argument and help readers return to the "big picture" of what's at stake. • Call readers to action. • End with something memorable.

In terms of visual argument, effective presentation slides can usually be placed into three design categories:

- Slides using images (photographs, drawings) to enhance *pathos* or to create snapshot visual clarity of a concept (*logos*)
- Slides using graphs or other visual displays of numbers to make numeric arguments
- Slides using bulleted (all text) subpoints for evidence

All the strategies for visual arguments discussed in Chapter 9 and in this chapter under "Proposal Arguments as Advocacy Posters or Advertisements" (pages 256–258) apply equally to presentation slides.

In most cases, the "title" of the slide should put into words the "take-away point" of the slide—a verbal summary of the slide's visual argument. Most rhetoricians suggest that the title of a slide be a short sentence that makes a point rather than just a topic phrase.

Topic as Title (Weak)	Point as Title (Strong)
Coal and the Environment	Burning Coal Produces Dangerous Greenhouse Gases
The Effect of Money on Happiness	More Money Doesn't Mean More Happiness

Student writer Sandy Wainscott tried to follow these principles in her speech and accompanying PowerPoint slides shown on pages 269–270. ■

Questioning and Critiquing a Proposal Argument

As we've suggested, proposal arguments need to overcome the innate conservatism of people, the difficulty of anticipating all the consequences of a proposal, and so forth. What questions, then, can we ask about proposal arguments to help us anticipate these problems?

Will a skeptic deny that my problem is really a problem? Be prepared for skeptics who aren't bothered by your problem, who see your problem as limited to a small group of people, or who think you are exaggerating.

Will a skeptic doubt the effectiveness of my solution? A skeptic might agree that your problem is indeed important, but will not be convinced that your solution will work. For these skeptics, you'll need to provide evidence that your solution is workable. Also be prepared for skeptics who focus on the potential negative or unintended consequences of your proposed solution.

Will a skeptic think my proposal costs too much? The most commonly asked question of any proposal is simply, "Do the benefits of enacting the proposal outweigh the costs?" Be wary of the understandable tendency to underestimate costs and exaggerate the benefits of a proposal. Honesty will enhance your *ethos*.

Will a skeptic suggest counterproposals? Once you've convinced readers that a problem exists, they are likely to suggest solutions different from yours. It only makes sense to anticipate alternative solutions and to work out ways to argue why your solution is better. And who knows, you may end up liking the counterproposal better and changing your mind about what to propose!

READING

Our first reading, by student writer Ivan Snook, is a researched public policy proposal written in response to the option 3 assignment on page 258. Snook's argument is based both on library and Internet research, and on personal experience (he is a returning veteran who served as a Marine infantry soldier in Iraq). It is formatted as a formal research paper using the documentation style of the Modern Language Association (MLA). An explanation of this format is given in Appendix 2.

Snook 1

Ivan Snook

Dr. Johnson

Argumentative Writing

March 31, 2014

Flirting with Disaster: An Argument Against Integrating
Women into the Combat Arms

In 2005 I was a rifleman for the elite 1st Reconnaissance Battalion in Iraq. My deployment was not all bad. When we returned to Camp Fallujah to repair our humvee we ate great chow, enjoyed good entertainment, and drank contraband vodka. I never had a girlfriend, though. I was too busy working in my all-male infantry unit. At the time I wished we had a few girls in the unit. What can I say? I wanted female companionship like the guys in non-combat jobs had. But I realized that women could never serve in the infantry because of the negative impact of boyfriend/girlfriend dramatics on unit morale, cohesiveness, and ultimately combat effectiveness.

However, America's civilian leadership recently moved towards integrating women into frontline combat arms units such as infantry, tanks, and artillery. In January, 2014, Secretary of Defense Leon Panetta lifted the Pentagon's policy on all-male combat arms occupations. "The department's goal...is to ensure that the mission is met with the best qualified and most capable people, regardless of gender," he said. "I'm not talking about reducing the qualifications for the job—if they can meet the qualifications for the job, then they should have a right to serve" (qtd. in Michaels and Vanden Brook). President Obama expanded upon Panetta's sentiment by saying, "Every American can be proud *that our military will grow even stronger*, with our mothers, wives, sisters, and daughters playing a greater role in protecting this country we love" (qtd. in Michaels and Vanden Brook, emphasis mine).

If this policy change will indeed strengthen our military, every American should support it. However, no one has specified how integrating women into the combat arms will strengthen our military. I wholeheartedly agree with integrationists who claim that women can meet the rigorous physical and mental requirements for frontline combat. Any CrossFit has at least half a dozen women more physically and mentally fit than some of my Marine brothers in arms. If those were the sole criteria by which we evaluate infantrymen, I would endorse integration. But, how an individual soldier affects the combat unit as a whole must be considered. The great military theorist Carl von Clausewitz coined the term "friction" to represent the "[c]ountless minor incidents ...[that] combine to lower the general level of performance [of the military machine]." He continues, "We should bear in mind that none of its components is of one piece: each part is composed of individuals, every one of whom retains his potential of friction." Therefore, we must not judge individual soldiers only by their individual physical capabilities, but also by their impact on the unit as a whole.

Introducing women to previously all-male combat units means introducing the friction of romantic relationships. Petty jealousies and other dramatic relational issues combine to lower the general level of performance. In 1997, the non-profit global policy think tank RAND Corporation studied how romantic relationships affect coed military units. The study reported that such relationships "sexualize" the work environment, making it "difficult for colleagues to regard one another as just coworkers. Thus, the cohesion of the unit is negatively affected" (Harrell and Miller 81). One respondent complained, "The [cafeteria]...at night looks more like a singles club or promenade deck than a cafeteria [for a military unit]." Another said, "I get tired of seeing a junior enlisted female and her boyfriend [at the cafeteria].... This place is like high school all over again. Everyone is dating others. To me this is not the military. We are here to do a job not meet our spouse. Guys seem more worried about getting a girl than doing their job" (Harrell and Miller 81-82).

Integrationists claim the military's high level of discipline coupled with strict rules against fraternization will prevent romantic relationships. However, those strict rules have always been in place and have never worked. During the Gulf War, 5 percent of deployed women were sent home early due to pregnancy. The Navy sends home on average 10 percent of deployed female sailors for the same reason. The USS *Theodore Roosevelt,* one of America's largest aircraft carriers, lost 45 of its 300 female sailors to pregnancy leave and became one of the many U.S. Navy ships to earn the nickname "The Love Boat" (Browne 246). My point is not about morality. These statistics demonstrate that despite strict rules against fraternization, 18-25 year olds succumb to their natural urges. What else should one expect when young adults are locked away on ship or deployed to Afghanistan for months at a time? It is analogous to locking the doors on a coed college dormitory for a year and making rules against sex. It is preposterous to expect 18-25 year olds to work, live, and relax together in such close proximity and expect no romantic relationships to sprout.

MLA

These problems are more than just trifling lovers' quarrels. They affect a serious decline in performance and can lead to a total breakdown of command structure. In 2005, Brian Kates of the *New York Daily News* visited Camp Bucca, a military prison in Southern Iraq, which he described as a drunken "out-of-control frat party." "In front of a cheering male audience, two young women wearing only bras and panties threw themselves into a mud-filled plastic kiddie pool and rolled around in a wild wrestling match." Sergeant Emil Ganim, who refereed the match, said other non-commissioned officers "had been lending out their rooms for soldiers to have sex." These were not just young privates, either. A witness told investigators that a drunken first sergeant and master sergeant, two high-ranking non-commissioned officers, were in attendance (Kates). Although Camp Bucca was far away from any actual fighting, it is safe to assume similar sexual antics and command structure breakdowns will occur in coed frontline combat units whose members confront their own mortality on a daily basis.

Still, Camp Bucca is not the worst case scenario. The military is currently battling an epidemic of rape and sexual assault. A study conducted by the Department of Veterans' Affairs reported that one-third of female veterans say they were victims of rape or attempted rape. A third of those claim they were raped multiple times, and 14 percent claim they were gang raped (Browne). Introducing females to frontline combat units will only exacerbate the problem. Dr. David Grossman, one of the world's foremost experts on human aggression and the psychology of combat, has explained how combat stress affects human sex drive. He analogizes the human body's ability to cope with stress to a bathtub: it can hold only so much water before overflowing. When our body overflows with stress the midbrain releases hormones causing a fight or flight response, often followed by a dramatic change in hunger and sex drive. Grossman writes, "Some people lose their appetite for food in response to stress, but many have an enhanced craving to eat. In the same way, some individuals can lose their sex drive in response to great stress, but other people experience a tremendous sex drive, especially after a combat situation in which they were triumphant" (275). Frontline combat is fueled by stress hormones, and the potential for a woman to be sexually assaulted is very high. An inter-unit sexual assault costs the unit two soldiers: the victim is typically transferred to a new unit, the assaulter is sent to prison. Replacing two comrades integrated in a tight-knit unit with two new recruits is a difficult blow to a unit's esprit de corps and trust members have in one another. Thus, to put at risk a female soldier's sexual well-being is to also put at risk her unit's combat ability.

Rather than respond to the physiological realities of preparing for and engaging in combat, integrationists such as CNN's Maren Leed deflect to a false analogy connecting integration of women to past arguments against integrating minorities and homosexuals. Regarding minorities, race is a social construct not a biological difference. Whereas the military somewhat successfully trained its men to not act on racial prejudices, it is improbable that 18-25 year old men can be trained to be not sexually attracted to women. Regarding homosexuals, one homosexual has little effect on a group of heterosexuals, but one female can have a significant impact on a large group of stress hormone driven heterosexual men.

Another integrationist argument is that changes in modern warfare already put women in combat. They say modern warfare is "asymmetric" and attacks can come from anywhere. It is true that women have served in combat in Afghanistan and Iraq, but integrationists erroneously believe the nature of warfare has evolved beyond traditional frontlines. Every American military engagement since World War II has been a limited war, but that does not mean all future wars will be. The wars our military must prepare to fight are global conflicts where combat troops face well-armed and well-trained enemies on traditional frontlines.

Perhaps the most important argument made by integrationists, and one to which I am sympathetic, concerns fairness and equity. It is extremely difficult to be promoted to General without infantry training. Some may say the Army should change its promotion policy, but this would harm overall morale. Frontline troops more enthusiastically follow leaders who are sharing, or have at one time shared, the toils and dangers of war. Thus, high-ranking female officers hit a glass ceiling because no such experience is available to them. However, there is an alternative to break through this glass ceiling without making all combat units coed. The U.S. Army National Guard consists of every imaginable combat arms occupation. If they were opened to aspirant female soldiers, they would have access to the necessary experience for advancement to the military's upper echelon and have the option of transferring from the National Guard to active duty. General John Vessey began his illustrious career in the National Guard infantry and was later selected as Chairman of the Joint Chiefs of Staff. This compromise would give women the opportunity to get infantry training while still protecting our active duty frontline infantry units from the unnecessary friction caused by romantic relationships.

Snook 5

Although some outsiders call terms like friction, morale, and unit cohesion mere buzzwords, to the Marines they mean life or death. Coed infantry is a parlous experiment with too much at stake. The restriction against women joining the infantry must be reinstated before the policy becomes entrenched and the negative side effects of romantic relationships deteriorate our fighting ability. I fully support gender equality, and I am proud of the brave women in the Marines, Army, Navy, and Air Force who have sacrificed so much defending this country I love. But when one considers the ultimate mission of the military, which is to win wars, we must not risk losing the cohesion of combat units when there is no exigent reason to do so except for the sake of expanding military career opportunities for women.

Snook 6

Works Cited

Browne, Kingsley. *Co-Ed Combat: The New Evidence That Women Shouldn't Fight the Nation's Wars.* Sentinel, 2007.

Clausewitz, Carl von. *On War.* Translated by Michael Howard and Peter Paret, Princeton UP, 1984.

Grossman, David. *On Combat: The Psychology and Physiology of Deadly Conflict in War and in Peace.* 3rd ed., Warrior Science, 2008.

Harrell, Margaret C., and Laura L. Miller. "New Opportunities for Military Women: Effects Upon Readiness, Cohesion, and Morale." *RAND Corporation,* 1 Jan. 1997, www.rand.org/pubs/monograph_reports/MR896.html.

Kates, Brian. "Out of Control at Camp Crazy! Female Soldiers Dress Down & Get Dirty for Mud Romps." *New York Daily News,* 6 Feb. 2005, www.nydailynews.com/archives/news/control-camp-crazy-female-soldiers-dress-dirty-mud-romps-g-s-wild-article-1.590262.

Leed, Maren. "Will Infantry Men Accept Women as Peers?" *CNN,* 26 Jan. 2013, www.cnn.com/2013/01/25/opinion/leed-women-in-infantry.

Michaels, Jim, and Tom Vanden Brook. "Women, Men Must Meet Same Combat Standards in Military." *USA Today,* 25 Jan. 2013, www.usatoday.com/story/news/world/2013/01/24/women-in-combat-briefing/1861887.

Our second reading, by student Sandy Wainscott, illustrates option 5, a proposal speech supported by visual aids. We have reproduced Sandy's outline for her speech, along with her scripts for the introduction and conclusion. (Although she delivered the body of the speech extemporaneously from her outline, she scripted the introduction and conclusion to reduce nervousness.) We have also reproduced four of her ten PowerPoint slides. She used these four slides to introduce each of the four main points shown on the outline. Note how she has constructed her slides as visual arguments supporting a main point (stated in the slide title).

Why McDonald's Should Sell Meat and Veggie Pies: A Proposal to End Subsidies for Cheap Meat

SANDY WAINSCOTT (STUDENT)

Script for Introduction: McDonald's hamburgers are popular because they're satisfying and pretty darn cheap. But I will argue that the hamburger is cheap because the American taxpayer subsidizes the cost of meat. Uncle Sam pays agribusiness to grow feed corn while not requiring agribusiness to pay the full cost for water or for cleaning up the environmental damage caused by cattle production. If meat producers had to recover the true cost of their product, the cost of meat would be substantially higher, but there would be offsetting benefits: a healthier environment, happier lives for cows and chickens, and healthier diets for all of us.

1. Meat is relatively cheap partly because taxpayers help feed the cows.
    a. U.S. taxpayers give farmers money to grow feed corn, which is fed to cows.
    b. U.S. taxpayers provide farmers with cheap water.
2. Cheap meat threatens health.
    a. Factory-style farms significantly reduce the effectiveness of antibiotics.
    b. Antibiotic-resistant pathogens are potentially huge killers.
    c. Factory farms are likely sources of new swine and bird flus.
    d. Meat-related food poisoning harms millions of people per year with thousands of deaths.
3. Cheap meat hurts the environment.
    a. Factory farms create 130 times more sewage than humans.
    b. Animal farming contributes more to global warming than all forms of human transportation combined.
    c Farming uses much of the world's land and water.
4. Cheap meat requires cruelty to animals.
    a. Ninety-eight percent of egg-laying hens in the United States spend their entire lives in stacked cubicle cages with 9-inch sides.
    b. Cruel conditions also exist for pigs and cows.

Script for Conclusion: If we quit giving farmers taxpayer subsidies and required them to pay for the pollution they cause, the cost of meat would be much higher—but with great benefits to our health and to our environment. A restaurant like McDonald's would likely adjust its menus. McDonald's would move the burger off its 99 cent menu and replace it with something like a meat pie, a similarly warm, quick, and satisfying choice, but with a lower proportion of meat than a burger. In a fair market, we should have to pay more for a hamburger than for a meat pie or a stir fry. But we would have the benefit of a healthier Earth.

FIGURE 14.2 Sandy's PowerPoint slides used to introduce main points

Informal Fallacies

In this appendix, we look at ways of assessing the legitimacy of an argument within a real-world context of probabilities rather than within a mathematical world of certainty. Whereas formal logic is a kind of mathematics, the *informal fallacies* addressed in this appendix get embedded in everyday arguments, sometimes making fallacious reasoning seem deceptively persuasive, especially to unwary audiences. Fallacies of *pathos* rest on flaws in the way an argument appeals to the audience's emotions and values. Fallacies of *ethos* rest on flaws in the way the argument appeals to the character of opponents or of sources and witnesses within an argument. Fallacies of *logos* rest on flaws in the relationship among statements in an argument.

Fallacies of *Pathos*

Argument to the People (Appealing to Stirring Symbols)   Arguments to the people appeal to the fundamental beliefs, biases, and prejudices of the audience in order to sway opinion through a feeling of solidarity among those of the group. Thus a "Support Our Troops" bumper sticker, often including the American flag, creates an initial feeling of solidarity among almost all citizens of good will. But the car owner may have the deeper intention of actually meaning "support our president" or "support the war in _____." The stirring symbol of the flag and the desire shared by most people to support our troops is used fallaciously to urge support of a particular political act. Arguments to the people often use visual rhetoric, as in the soaring eagle used in Wal-Mart corporate ads or images of happy families in marketing advertisements.

Appeal to Ignorance   This fallacy persuades an audience to accept as true a claim that hasn't been proved false or vice versa. "Jones must have used steroids to get those bulging biceps because he can't prove that he hasn't used steroids." Appeals to ignorance are particularly common in the murky field of pseudo-science. "UFOs (or ghosts, or abominable snowmen) do exist because science hasn't proven that they don't exist." Sometimes, however, it is hard to draw a line between a fallacious appeal to ignorance and a legitimate appeal to precaution: "Genetically modified organisms must be dangerous to our health because science hasn't proven that they are safe."

Appeal to Popularity—Bandwagon   To board the bandwagon means (to use a more contemporary metaphor) to board the bus or train of what's popular. Appeals to popularity are fallacious because the popularity of something is irrelevant to its actual merits. "Living together before marriage is the right thing to do because most couples are now doing it." Bandwagon appeals are common in advertising where the claim that a product is popular substitutes for evidence of the product's excellence. There are times, however, where popularity may indeed be relevant: "Global warming is probably caused by human activity because a preponderance of scientists now hold this position." (Here we assume scientists haven't simply climbed on a bandwagon themselves, but have formed their opinions based on research data and well vetted, peer-reviewed papers.) *College*

Appeal to Pity   Here the arguer appeals to the audience's sympathetic feelings in order to support a claim that should be decided on more relevant or objective grounds. "Honorable judge, I should not be fined $200 for speeding because I was distraught from hearing news of my brother's illness and was rushing to see him in the hospital." Here the argument is fallacious because the arguer's reason, while evoking sympathy, is not a relevant justification for speeding (as it might have been, for instance, if the arguer had been rushing an injured person to the emergency room).

Red Herring   This fallacy's funny name derives from the practice of using a red herring (a highly odiferous fish) to throw dogs off a scent that they are supposed to be tracking. It refers to the practice of throwing an audience off track by raising an unrelated or irrelevant point. "Debating a gas tax increase is valuable, but I really think there should be an extra tax on SUVs." Here the arguer, apparently uncomfortable with the gas tax issue, diverts the conversation to the emotional issue of SUVs.

Fallacies of *Ethos*

Appeal to False Authority   Arguers appeal to false authority when they use famous persons (often movie stars or celebrities) to testify on issues about which these persons have no special competence. "Joe Quarterback says Gooey Oil keeps his old tractor running sharp; therefore, Gooey Oil is a good oil." Real evidence about the quality of Gooey Oil would include technical data about the product rather than testimony from a hired celebrity.

Ad Hominem   Literally, *ad hominem* means "to the person." An *ad hominem* argument is directed at the character of an opponent rather than at the quality of the reasoning. Ideally, arguments are supposed to be *ad rem* ("to the thing"), that is, addressed to the specifics of the case itself. Thus an *ad rem* critique of a politician would focus on her voting record, the consistency and cogency of her public statements, her responsiveness to constituents, and so forth. An *ad hominem* argument would shift attention from her record to irrelevant features of her personality, life circumstances, or the company she keeps. "Senator Sweetwater's views on the gas tax should be discounted because her campaign was supported by the huge oil companies" or "Senator Sweetwater supports tax cuts for the wealthy because she is very wealthy herself and stands to gain." But not all *ad hominem* arguments are *ad hominem* fallacies. Lawyers, for example, when questioning expert witnesses who give damaging testimony, will often make an issue of their honesty, credibility, or personal investment in an outcome.

Poisoning the Well   This fallacy is closely related to *ad hominem*. Arguers poison the well when they discredit an opponent or an opposing view in advance. "Before I yield the floor to the next speaker, I must remind you that persons who oppose my plan do not have the best interests of working people in their hearts."

Straw Man   The straw man fallacy occurs when you oversimplify an opponent's argument to make it easier to refute or ridicule. Rather than summarizing an opposing view fairly and completely, you basically make up the argument you wish your opponent had made because it is so much easier to knock over, like knocking over a straw man or scarecrow in a corn field.

Fallacies of *Logos*

Hasty Generalization   This fallacy occurs when someone makes a broad generalization on the basis of too little evidence. Generally, the evidence needed to support a generalization persuasively must meet the STAR criteria (sufficiency, typicality, accuracy, and relevance) discussed in Chapter 5 (pages 77–78). But what constitutes a sufficient amount of evidence? The generally accepted standards of sufficiency in any given field are difficult to determine. The Food and Drug Administration (FDA), for example, generally proceeds cautiously before certifying a drug as "safe." However, if people are harmed by the side effects of an FDA-approved drug, critics often accuse the FDA of having made a hasty generalization. At the same time, patients eager to have access to a new drug and manufacturers eager to sell a new product may lobby the FDA to quit "dragging its feet" and get the drug to market. Hence, the point at which a hasty generalization passes over into the realm of a prudent generalization is nearly always uncertain and contested.

Part for the Whole   Sometimes called by its Latin name *pars pro toto*, this fallacy is closely related to hasty generalization. In this fallacy, arguers pick out a part of the whole or a sample of the whole (often not a typical or representative part or sample) and then claim what is true of the part is true for the whole. If, say, individuals wanted to get rid of the National Endowment for the Arts (NEA), they might focus on several controversial programs funded by the NEA and use them as justification for wiping out all NEA programs. The flip side of this fallacy occurs when an arguer picks only the best examples to make a case and omits other examples that might weaken the case.

Post Hoc, Ergo Propter Hoc   The Latin name of this fallacy means "after this, therefore because of this." The fallacy occurs when a sequential relationship is mistaken for a causal relationship. (See Chapter 12, pages 211–212, where we discuss this fallacy in more depth.) For example, you may be guilty of this fallacy if you say "Cramming for a test really helps because last week I crammed for my psychology test and I got an A." When two events occur frequently in conjunction with each other, we've got a good case for a causal relationship. But until we can show how one causes the other and until we have ruled out other causes, we cannot be certain that a causal relationship is occurring. For example, the A on your psych test may have been the result of an easy exam. It is often difficult to tell when a *post hoc* fallacy occurs. When the New York police department changed its policing tactics in the early 1990s, the crime rate plummeted. But did the new policing tactics cause the drop in the crime rate? Many experts suggested other causes, including economist Steven Levitt, who attributes the declining crime rate to the legalization of abortion in the 1970s (and hence to a decline in unwanted children who might grow up to be criminals).

Begging the Question—Circular Reasoning   Arguers beg the question when they provide a reason that simply restates the claim in different words. Here is an example: "Abortion is murder because it is the intentional taking of the life of a human being." Because "murder" is defined as "the intentional taking of the life of a human being," the argument is circular. It is tantamount to saying "Abortion is murder because it is murder."

False Dilemma—Either/Or   This fallacy occurs when an arguer oversimplifies a complex issue so that only two choices appear possible. Often one of the choices is made to seem unacceptable, so the only remaining option is the other choice. "It's my way or the highway" is a typical example of a false dilemma. Here is a more subtle one: "Either we allow embryonic stem cell research, or we condemn persons with diabetes, Parkinson's disease, or spinal injuries to a life without a cure." Clearly there may be other options here including other approaches to curing these diseases.

Slippery Slope   The slippery slope fallacy is based on the fear that once we put a foot on a slippery slope heading in the wrong direction we're doomed to slide right out of sight. The controlling metaphor is of a slick mountainside without places to hold on rather than of a staircase with numerous stopping places. Here is an example of a slippery slope: "Once we allow medical use of marijuana, we'll eventually legalize it for everyone, after which we're on a slippery slope toward social acceptance of cocaine and heroin."

False Analogy   In Chapter 11 on resemblance arguments, we explained that no analogy is perfect. Any two things being compared are similar in some ways and different in other ways. Whether an analogy is persuasive or false often depends on the audience's initial degree of skepticism. For example, persons opposed to gun control may find the following argument persuasive: "Banning guns on the basis that guns accidentally kill people is like banning cars on the basis that cars accidentally kill people." In contrast, supporters of gun control are likely to call this argument a false analogy on the basis of dissimilarities between cars and guns. (For example, they might say that banning cars would be far more disruptive on our society than would be banning guns.) Just when a persuasive analogy turns into a false analogy is difficult to say.

Non Sequitur   The name of this fallacy means "it does not follow." *Non sequitur* is a catchall term for any claim that doesn't follow from its premises or that is supported by irrelevant premises. Sometimes the arguer seems to make an inexplicably illogical leap: "Genetically modified foods should be outlawed because they are not natural." (Should anything that is not natural be outlawed? In what way are they not natural?) At other times, there may be a gap in the chain of reasons: "Violent video games have some social value because the Army uses them for recruiting." (There may be an important idea emerging here, but too many logical steps are missing.) At still other times an arguer might support a claim with irrelevant reasons. "I should not receive a C in this course because I currently have a 3.8 GPA."

Loaded Label or Definition   Sometimes arguers will try to influence their audience's view of something by creating a loaded label or definition. For example, people who oppose the "estate tax" (which calls to mind rich people with estates) have relabeled it the "death tax" in order to give it a negative connotation without any markers of class or wealth. Or to take another example, proponents of organic foods could create definitions like the following: "Organic foods are safe and healthy foods grown without any pesticides, herbicides, or other unhealthy additives." "Safe" and "healthy" are evaluative terms used fallaciously in what purports to be a definition. The intended implication is that non-organic foods are not safe and healthy.

A Concise Guide to Evaluating, Using, and Documenting Sources

When you research material for your arguments, you will probably use sources from licensed databases and the World Wide Web as well as from a library's print collection. You must be able to evaluate these sources, use them effectively in your own arguments (avoiding plagiarism), and cite and document them accurately so that readers can retrace your steps. This appendix provides brief instruction for evaluating and using sources and for citing and documenting them using both the MLA (Modern Language Association) and APA (American Psychological Association) systems.

Evaluating Your Sources by Reading Rhetorically

To be an effective researcher, you need to read your sources rhetorically. In this section we show you how to read your sources with your own goals in mind, take purposeful notes, and evaluate sources for reliability, credibility, angle of vision, and degree of advocacy. We also provide some additional advice for evaluating Web sources.

Reading with Your Own Goals in Mind

How you read a source depends to a certain extent on where you are in the research process. Early in the process, when you are in the thesis-seeking, exploratory stage, your goal is to achieve a basic understanding about your research problem. You need to become aware of different points of view, learn what is unknown or controversial about your research question, see what values or assumptions are in conflict, and build up your store of background knowledge.

Given these goals, at the early stages of research you should select overview kinds of sources to get you into the conversation. In some cases, even an encyclopedia or specialized reference work can be a good start for getting general background.

As you get deeper into your research, your questions become more focused, and the sources you read become more specialized. Once you formulate a thesis and plan a structure for your paper, you can determine more clearly the sources you need and read them with purpose and direction.

Reading with Rhetorical Awareness

To read your sources rhetorically, you should keep two basic questions in mind:

1. What was the source author's purpose in writing this piece?
2. What might be my purpose in using this piece?

Table A2.1 sums up the kinds of questions a rhetorical reader typically considers.

Table A2.1 reinforces a point we've made throughout this text: all writing is produced from an angle of vision that privileges some ways of seeing and filters out other ways. You should guard against reading your sources as if they present hard, undisputed facts or universal truths. For example, if one of your sources says that "Saint-John's-wort [an herb] has been shown to be an effective treatment for depression," some of your readers might accept that statement as fact—but many wouldn't. Skeptical readers would want to know who the author is, where his views have been published, and what he uses for evidence. Let's say the author is someone named Samuel Jones. Skeptical readers would ask whether Jones is relying on published research, and if so, whether the studies have been peer reviewed in reputable, scholarly journals and whether the research has been replicated by other scientists. They would also want to know whether a trade association for herbal supplements sponsored the research and whether Jones has financial connections to companies that

TABLE A2.1   Questions Asked by Rhetorical Readers

What was the source author's purpose in writing this piece?	What might be my purpose in using this piece in my own argument?
• Who is this author? What are his or her credentials and affiliations? • What audience is this person addressing? • What is the genre of this piece? (if you downloaded the piece from the World Wide Web, did it originally appear in print?) • If this piece appeared in print, what is the reputation and bias of the journal, magazine, or press? Was the piece peer reviewed? • If this piece appeared only on the Web, who or what organization sponsors the Web site (check the home page)? What is the reputation and bias of the sponsor? • What is the author's thesis or purpose? • How does this author try to change his or her audience's view? • What is this writer's angle of vision or bias? • What is omitted or censored from this text? • How reliable and credible is this author? • What facts, data, and other evidence does this author use and what are the sources of these data? • What are this author's underlying values, assumptions, and beliefs?	• How has this piece influenced or complicated my own thinking? • How does this piece relate to my research question? • How will my own intended audience react to this author? • How might I use this piece in my own argument? • Is it an opposing view that I might summarize? • Is it an alternative point of view that I might compare to other points of view? • Does it have facts and data that I might use? • Would a summary of all or part of this argument support or oppose one or more of my own points? • Could I use this author for testimony? (If so, how should I indicate this author's credentials?) • If I use this source, will I need to acknowledge the author's bias and angle of vision?

produce herbal remedies and supplements. Rather than settling the question about Saint-John's-wort as a treatment for depression, a quotation from Jones may open up a heated controversy about medical research.

Reading rhetorically is thus a way of thinking critically about your sources. It influences the way you take notes, evaluate sources, and shape your argument.

Taking Purposeful Notes

Many beginning researchers opt not to take notes—a serious mistake, in our view. Instead, they simply photocopy or print articles, perhaps using a highlighter to mark passages. This practice, which experienced researchers almost never use, reduces your ability to engage the ideas in a source and to find your own voice in a conversation. When you begin drafting your paper, you'll have no notes to refer to, no record of your thinking-in-progress. Your only recourse is to revisit all your sources, thumbing through them one at a time—a practice that leads to passive cutting and pasting (and possible plagiarism).

Good note taking includes recording bibliographic information for each source, recording information and ideas from each source, and responding to each source with your own ideas and exploratory writing.

Recording Bibliographic Information   To take good research notes, begin by making a bibliographic entry for each source, following the documentation format assigned by your instructor. Although you will be tempted to put off doing this mechanical task, there are two reasons to do it immediately:

- Doing it now, while the source is in front of you, will save you time in the long run. Otherwise you'll have to try to retrieve the source, in a late-night panic, just before the paper is due.
- Doing it now will make you look at the source rhetorically. Is this a peer-reviewed journal article? A magazine article? An op-ed piece? A blog? Making the bibliographic entry forces you to identify the source's genre.

Recording Ideas and Information and Responding to Each Source   To take good research notes, follow the reading habits of summary and exploration discussed in Chapter 2, weaving back and forth between walking in the shoes of the source author and then standing back to believe and doubt what the source says.

- **Your informational notes on each source:** Using the skills of summary writing explained in Chapter 2, summarize each source's argument and record useful information. To avoid the risk of plagiarism later, make sure that you put quotation marks around any passages that you copy word for word (be sure to copy *exactly*). When you summarize or paraphrase passages, be sure to put the ideas entirely into your own words. (For more on quoting, summarizing, and paraphrasing sources, see pages 284–287.)
- **Your own exploratory notes as you think of ideas:** Write down your own ideas as they occur to you. Record your thinking-in-progress as you mull over and speak back to your sources.

An approach that encourages both modes of writing is to keep a dialectic or double-entry journal. Divide a page in half; enter your informational notes on one side and your exploratory writing on the other. If you use a computer, you can put your informational notes in one font and your own exploratory writing in another.

Taking effective notes is different from the mechanical process of copying out passages or simply listing facts and information. Rather, make your notes purposeful by imagining how you might use a given source in your research paper. Table A2.2 shows the different functions that research sources might play in your argument and highlights appropriate note-taking strategies for each function.

TABLE A2.2   Strategies for Taking Notes According to Purpose

Function that Source Might Play in Your Argument	Strategies for Informational Notes	Strategies for Exploratory Notes
Provides background about your problem or issue	• Summarize the information. • Record specific facts and figures useful for background.	• Speculate on how much background your readers will need.
Gives an alternative view that you will mention briefly	• Summarize the source's argument in a couple of sentences; note its bias and perspective. • Identify brief quotations that sum up the source's perspective.	• Jot down ideas on how and why different sources disagree. • Begin making an idea map of alternative views.
Provides an alternative or opposing view that you might summarize fully and respond to	• Summarize the article fully and fairly (see Chapter 2 on summary writing). • Note the kinds of evidence used.	• Speculate about why you disagree with the source and whether you can refute the argument, concede to it, or compromise with it. • Explore what research you'll need to support your own argument.
Provides information or testimony that you might use as evidence	• Record the data or information. • If using authorities for testimony, quote short passages. • Note the credentials of the writer or person quoted.	• Record new ideas as they occur to you. • Continue to think purposefully about additional research you'll need.
Mentions information or testimony that counters your position or raises doubts about your argument	• Note counterevidence. • Note authorities who disagree with you.	• Speculate how you might respond to counterevidence.
Provides a theory or method that influences your approach to the issue	• Note credentials of the author. • Note passages that sparked ideas.	• Freewrite about how the source influences your method or approach.

Evaluating Sources

When you read sources for your research project, you need to evaluate them as you go along. As you read each potential source, ask yourself questions about the author's reliability, credibility, angle of vision, and degree of advocacy.

Reliability   "Reliability" refers to the accuracy of factual data in a source. If you check a writer's "facts" against other sources, do you find that the facts are correct? Does the writer distort facts, take them out of context, or otherwise use them unreasonably? In some controversies, key data are highly disputed—for example, the frequency of date rape or the risk factors for many diseases. A reliable writer acknowledges these controversies and doesn't treat disputed data as fact. Furthermore, if you check out the sources used by a reliable writer, they'll reveal accurate and careful research—respected primary sources rather than hearsay or secondhand reports. Journalists of reputable newspapers (not tabloids) pride themselves on meticulously checking out their facts, as do editors of serious popular magazines. Editing is often minimal for Web sources, however, and they can be notoriously unreliable. As you gain knowledge of your research question, you'll develop a good ear for writers who play fast and loose with data.

Credibility   "Credibility" is similar to "reliability" but is based on internal rather than external factors. It refers to the reader's trust in the writer's honesty, goodwill, and trustworthiness and is apparent in the writer's tone, reasonableness, fairness in summarizing opposing views, and respect for different perspectives. Audiences differ in how much credibility they will grant to certain authors. Nevertheless, a writer can achieve a reputation for credibility, even among bitter political opponents, by applying to issues a sense of moral courage, integrity, and consistency of principle.

Angle of Vision and Political Stance   By "angle of vision," we mean the way that a piece of writing is shaped by the underlying values, assumptions, and beliefs of its author, resulting in a text that reflects a certain perspective, worldview, or belief system. Of paramount importance are the underlying values or beliefs that the writer assumes his or her readers will share. You can get useful clues about a writer's angle of vision and intended audience by doing some quick research into the politics and reputation of the author on the Internet or by analyzing the genre, market niche, and political reputation of the publication in which the material appears.

Degree of Advocacy   By "degree of advocacy" we mean the extent to which an author unabashedly takes a persuasive stance on a contested position as opposed to adopting a more neutral, objective, or exploratory stance. For example, publications affiliated with advocacy organizations (the Sierra Club, the National Rifle Association) will have a clear editorial bias. When a writer has an ax to grind, you need to weigh carefully the writer's selection of evidence, interpretation of data, and fairness to opposing views. Although no one can be completely neutral, it is always useful to seek out authors who offer a balanced assessment of the evidence. Evidence from a more detached and neutral writer may be more trusted by your readers than the arguments of a committed advocate. For example, if you want to persuade corporate executives of the dangers of global warming, evidence from scholarly journals may be more persuasive than evidence from an environmentalist Web site or from a freelance writer for a leftist popular magazine such as *Mother Jones.*

Criteria for Evaluating a Web Source   When you evaluate a Web source, we suggest that you ask five different kinds of questions about the site in which the source appeared, as shown in Table A2.3. These questions, developed by scholars and librarians as points to consider when you are evaluating Web sites, will help you determine the usefulness of a site or source for your own purposes.

As a researcher, the first question you should ask about a potentially useful Web source should be, "Who placed this piece on the Web and why?" You can begin answering this question by analyzing the site's home page, where you will often find navigational buttons linking to "Mission," "About Us," or other identifying information about the site's sponsors. You can also get hints about the site's purpose by asking, "What kind of Web site is it?" Different kinds of Web sites have different purposes,

TABLE A2.3   Criteria for Evaluating Web Sites

Criteria	Questions to Ask
1. Authority	• Is the document author or site sponsor clearly identified? • Does the site identify the occupation, position, education, experience, or other credentials of the author? • Does the home page or a clear link from the home page reveal the author's or sponsor's motivation for establishing the site? • Does the site provide contact information for the author or sponsor such as an e-mail or organization address?
2. Objectivity or Clear Disclosure of Advocacy	• Is the site's purpose clear (for example, to inform, entertain, or persuade)? • Is the site explicit about declaring its point of view? • Does the site indicate whether the author is affiliated with a specific organization, institution, or association? • Does the site indicate whether it is directed toward a specific audience?
3. Coverage	• Are the topics covered by the site clear? • Does the site exhibit a suitable depth and comprehensiveness for its purpose? • Is sufficient evidence provided to support the ideas and opinions presented?
4. Accuracy	• Are the sources of information stated? • Do the facts appear to be accurate? • Can you verify this information by comparing this source with other sources in the field?
5. Currency	• Are dates included in the Web site? • Do the dates apply to the material itself, to its placement on the Web, or to the time the site was last revised and updated? • Is the information current, or at least still relevant, for the site's purpose? For your purpose?

often revealed by the domain identifier following the site name: .com (commercial); .org (nonprofits and advocacy groups); .edu (college or university); .gov (government agency); and .mil (military site).

Using Sources for Your Own Purposes

To illustrate the purposeful use of sources, we will use the following short argument from the Web site of the American Council on Science and Health (ACSH)—an organization of doctors and scientists devoted to providing scientific information on health issues and to exposing health fads and myths. Please read the argument carefully in preparation for the discussions that follow.

Is Vegetarianism Healthier Than Nonvegetarianism?

Many people become vegetarians because they believe, in error, that vegetarianism is uniquely conducive to good health. The findings of several large epidemiologic studies indeed suggest that the death and chronic-disease rates of vegetarians—primarily vegetarians who consume dairy products or both dairy products and eggs—are lower than those of meat eaters....

The health of vegetarians may be better than that of nonvegetarians partly because of nondietary factors: Many vegetarians are health-conscious. They exercise regularly, maintain a desirable body weight, and abstain from smoking. Although most epidemiologists have attempted to take such factors into account in their analyses, it is possible that they did not adequately control their studies for nondietary effects.

People who are vegetarians by choice may differ from the general population in other ways relevant to health. For example, in Western countries most vegetarians are more affluent than nonvegetarians and thus have better living conditions and more access to medical care.

An authoritative review of vegetarianism and chronic diseases classified the evidence for various alleged health benefits of vegetarianism:

■ The evidence is "strong" that vegetarians have (a) a lower risk of becoming alcoholic, constipated, or obese and (b) a lower risk of developing lung cancer.

■ The evidence is "good" that vegetarians have a lower risk of developing adult-onset diabetes mellitus, coronary artery disease, hypertension, and gallstones.

■ The evidence is "fair to poor" that vegetarianism decreases risk of breast cancer, colon cancer, diverticular disease, kidney-stone formation, osteoporosis, and tooth decay.

For some of the diseases mentioned above, the practice of vegetarianism itself probably is the main protective factor. For example, the low incidence of constipation among vegetarians is almost certainly due to their high intakes of fiber-rich foods. For other conditions, nondietary factors may be more important than diet. For example, the low incidence of lung cancer among vegetarians is attributable primarily to their extremely low rate of cigarette smoking. Diet is but one of many risk factors for most chronic diseases.

How you might use this article in your own writing would depend on your research question and purpose. To illustrate, we'll show you three different hypothetical examples of writers who have reason to cite this article.

- **Writer 1: A Causal Argument Showing Alternative Approaches to Reducing Risk of Alcoholism.** Writer 1 argues that vegetarianism may be an effective way to resist alcoholism. She uses just one statement from the ACSH article for her own purpose and then moves on to other sources.

Another approach to fighting alcoholism is through naturopathy, holistic medicine, and vegetarianism. Vegetarians generally have better health than the rest of the population and particularly have, according to the American Council on Science and Health, "a lower risk of becoming alcoholic." This lower risk has been borne out by other studies showing that the benefits of the holistic health movement are particularly strong for persons with addictive tendencies.... [goes on to other arguments and sources]

Writer's claim

Identification of source

Quotation from ACSH

- **Writer 2: A Proposal Argument Advocating Vegetarianism.** Writer 2 proposes that people become vegetarians. Parts of his argument focus on the environmental costs and ethics of eating meat, but he also devotes one paragraph to the health benefits of vegetarianism. As support for this point he summarizes the ACSH article's material on health benefits.

Not only will a vegetarian diet help stop cruelty to animals, but it is also good for your health. According to the American Council on Science and Health, vegetarians have longer life expectancy than nonvegetarians and suffer from fewer chronic diseases. The Council cites "strong" evidence from the scientific literature showing that vegetarians have reduced risk of lung cancer, obesity, constipation, and alcoholism. The Council also cites "good" evidence that they have a reduced risk of adult-onset diabetes, high blood pressure, gallstones, and hardening of the arteries. Although the evidence isn't nearly as strong, vegetarianism may also lower the risk of certain cancers, kidney stones, loss of bone density, and tooth decay.

Writer's claim

Identification of source

Summary of ACSH material

- **Writer 3: An Evaluation Argument Looking Skeptically at Vegetarianism.** Here, Writer 3 uses portions of the same article to make an opposite case from that of Writer 2. She focuses on those parts of the article that Writer 2 consciously excluded.

The link between vegetarianism and death rates is a classic instance of correlation rather than causation. While it is true that vegetarians have a longer life expectancy than nonvegetarians and suffer from fewer chronic diseases, the American Council on Science and Health has shown that the causes can mostly be explained by factors other than diet. As the Council suggests, vegetarians are apt to be more health conscious than nonvegetarians and thus get more exercise, stay slender, and avoid smoking. The Council points out that vegetarians also tend to be wealthier than nonvegetarians and see their doctors more regularly. In short, they live longer because they take better care of themselves, not because they avoid meat.

Writer's claim

Identification of source

Paraphrased points from ACSH

Using Summary, Paraphrase, and Quotation

As a research writer, you need to incorporate sources gracefully into your own prose. Depending on your purpose, you might (1) summarize all or part of a source author's argument, (2) paraphrase a relevant portion of a source, or (3) quote small passages from the source directly. To avoid plagiarism, you'll need to reference the source with an in-text citation, put quotation marks around quoted passages, and convert paraphrases and summaries entirely into your own words. Table A2.4 gives you an overview of summary, paraphrase, and quotation as ways of incorporating sources into your own prose.

Summarizing

Detailed instructions on how to write a summary of an article and incorporate it into your own prose are provided in Chapter 2 (pages 27–29). Summaries can be as short as a single sentence or as long as a paragraph. Make the summary as concise as

TABLE A2.4   Incorporating Sources into Your Own Prose

Strategy	What to Do	When to Use This Strategy
Summarize the source.	Condense a source writer's argument by keeping main ideas and omitting details (see Chapter 2, pages 27–29).	• When the source writer's whole argument is relevant to your purpose • When the source writer presents an alternative or opposing view that you want to push against • When the source writer's argument can be used in support of your own
Paraphrase the source.	Reproduce an idea from a source writer but translate the idea entirely into your own words; a paraphrase should be approximately the same length as the original.	• When you want to incorporate factual information from a source or to use one specific idea from a source • When the source passage is overly complex or technical for your targeted audience • When you want to incorporate a source's point in your own voice without interrupting the flow of your argument
Quote short passages from the source using quotation marks.	Work brief quotations from the source smoothly into the grammar of your own sentences (see pages 286–287).	• When you need testimony from an authority (state the authority's credentials in an attributive tag—see pages 287–288) • In summaries, when you want to reproduce a source's voice, particularly if the language is striking or memorable • In lieu of paraphrase when the source language is memorable
Quote long passages from the source using the block method.	Results in a page with noticeably lengthy block quotations	• When you intend to analyze or critique the quotation—the quotation is followed by your detailed analysis of its ideas or rhetorical features • When the flavor and language of testimonial evidence is important

possible so that you don't distract the reader from your own argument. In many cases, writers summarize only parts of a source, depending on what is relevant to their own argument. Writer 3's summary of the article by the American Council on Science and Health is a good example of a partial summary.

Paraphrasing

Unlike a summary, which is a condensation of a source's whole argument, a **para-phrase** translates a short passage from a source's words into the writer's own words. Writers often choose to paraphrase when the details of a source passage are particularly important or when the source is overly technical and needs to be simplified for the intended audience. When you paraphrase, be careful to avoid reproducing the original writer's grammatical structure and syntax. If you mirror the original sentence structure while replacing occasional words with synonyms or small structural changes, you will be doing what composition specialists call "**patchwriting**"—that is, patching some of your language onto someone else's writing.* Patchwriting is a form of academic dishonesty because you aren't fully composing your own sentences and are thus misrepresenting both your own work and that of the source writer. An acceptable paraphrase needs to be entirely in your own words. To understand patchwriting more fully, track the differences between unacceptable patchwriting and acceptable paraphrase in the following examples.

Original

- The evidence is "strong" that vegetarians have (a) a lower risk of becoming alcoholic, constipated, or obese and (b) a lower risk of developing lung cancer.
- The evidence is "good" that vegetarians have a lower risk of developing adult-onset diabetes mellitus, coronary artery disease, hypertension, and gallstones.

Unacceptable Patchwriting

According to the American Council on Science and Health , there is strong evidence that vegetarians have a lower risk of becoming alcoholic, constipated, or obese . The evidence is also strong that they have a lower risk of lung cancer. The evidence is good that vegetarians are less apt to develop adult-onset diabetes, coronary artery disease, hypertension, or gallstones.

Identification of source

Note phrases taken word for word from original.

---

*We are indebted to the work of Rebecca Moore Howard and others who have led composition researchers to reexamine the use of sources and plagiarism from a cultural and rhetorical perspective. See especially Rebecca Moore Howard, *Standing in the Shadow of Giants: Plagiarists, Authors, Collaborators* (Stamford, CT: Ablex Pub., 1999).

Acceptable Paraphrase

The Council summarizes "strong" evidence from the scientific literature showing that vegetarians have reduced risk of lung cancer, obesity, constipation, and alcoholism. The council also cites "good" evidence that they have a reduced risk of adult-onset diabetes, high blood pressure, gallstones, or hardening of the arteries.	Identification of source
	Doesn't follow original sentence structure
	Quotes "strong" and "good" to indicate distinction made in original

Both the patchwriting example and the acceptable paraphrase reproduce the same ideas as the original in approximately the same number of words. But the writer of the acceptable paraphrase has been more careful to change the sentence structure substantially and not copy exact phrases. In contrast, the patchwritten version contains longer strings of borrowed language without quotation marks.

We'll return to the problem of patchwriting in our discussion of plagiarism (pages 289–291).

Quoting

Besides summary and paraphrase, writers often choose to quote directly in order to give the reader the flavor and style of the source author's prose or to make a memorable point in the source author's own voice. Always quote the source author's words exactly (unless you indicate changes with ellipses or brackets) and don't misrepresent the author's meaning by taking quotations out of context.

In the following sections, we show you the two main ways to use quotations: quoting a complete sentence from your source versus inserting brief words and phrases from your source into your own sentence. For special cases using quotations (brackets, ellipses, quotations within a quotation, or block quotations), consult a good handbook.

Quoting a Complete Sentence   In some cases, you will want to quote a complete sentence from your source.

Original Passage

Many people become vegetarians because they believe, in error, that vegetarianism is uniquely conducive to good health. [found on page 282 of source]*

---

*The cited page is from this text. When quoting from print sources or other sources with stable page numbers, you indicate the page number as part of your citation. To illustrate how to punctuate page citations, we'll assume throughout this section that you found the American Council on Science and Health article in this textbook rather than on the Web, in which case it would not be possible to cite page numbers.

Writer's Quotation of This Passage

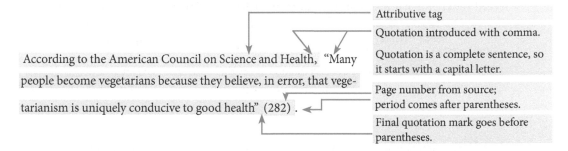

According to the American Council on Science and Health, "Many people become vegetarians because they believe, in error, that vegetarianism is uniquely conducive to good health" (282) .

Attributive tag

Quotation introduced with comma.

Quotation is a complete sentence, so it starts with a capital letter.

Page number from source; period comes after parentheses.

Final quotation mark goes before parentheses.

Quoting Words and Phrases   Instead of quoting a complete sentence, you often want to quote only a few words or phrases from your source and insert them into your own sentence. In these cases, make sure that the grammatical structure of the quotation fits smoothly into the grammar of your own sentence.

Original Passage

The health of vegetarians may be better than that of nonvegetarians partly because of non-dietary factors: Many vegetarians are health-conscious. They exercise regularly, maintain a desirable body weight, and abstain from smoking. [found on page 282]

Quoted Phrase Inserted into Writer's Own Sentence

The American Council on Science and Health argues that the cause of vegetarians' longer life may be "nondietary factors." The Council claims that vegetarians are more "health-conscious" than meat eaters and that they "exercise regularly, maintain a desirable body weight, and abstain from smoking" (282) .

Attributive tag

Quotation marks show where quotation starts and ends.

No comma or capital letter: Punctuation and capitalization determined by grammar of your own sentence.

Period comes after parentheses containing page number.

Creating Attributive Tags to Indicate Use of a Source

Our previous examples use attributive tags to indicate words or ideas taken from a source. *Attributive tags* are phrases such as "according to Hahn ..." or "Smith and Perosi claim that...." Such phrases indicate that the material immediately following the tag is from the cited source. You can also add to the tag a phrase indicating the source author's credentials, biases, or angle of vision: "Climate scientist James Hansen states that …" Although some disciplines (particularly the social sciences) indicate a source only by citing it in parentheses at the end of the borrowed material, the preferred practice for non-specialized audiences is to use attributive tags.

Less Preferred: Indicating Source through Parenthetical Citation

Vegetarians are apt to be more health-conscious than nonvegetarians (American Council on Science and Health).

More Preferred: Indicating Source through Attributive Tag

According to the American Council on Science and Health, vegetarians are apt to be more health-conscious than nonvegetarians.

Avoiding Plagiarism

Unethical use of sources—called **plagiarism**—is a major concern not only for writing teachers but for teachers in all disciplines. To combat plagiarism, many instructors across the curriculum use plagiarism-detection software like turnitin.com. Their purpose, of course, is to discourage students from cheating. But sometimes students who have no intention of cheating can fall into producing papers that look like cheating. That is, they produce papers that might be accused of plagiarism even though the students had no intention of deceiving their readers. Our goal in this section is to explain the concept of plagiarism more fully and to sum up the strategies needed to avoid it.

Why Some Plagiarism May Occur Unwittingly

To understand how unwitting plagiarism might occur, consider Table A2.5, where the middle column—"Misuse of Sources"—shows common mistakes of novice writers. Everyone agrees that the behaviors in the "Fraud" column constitute deliberate cheating and deserve appropriate punishment. Everyone also agrees that good scholarly work meets the criteria in the "Ethical Use of Sources" column. Novice researchers, however, may find themselves unwittingly in the middle column until they learn the academic community's conventions for using research sources.

You might appreciate these conventions more fully if you recognize how they have evolved from Western notions of intellectual property and patent law associated with the rise of modern science in the seventeenth and eighteenth centuries. A person not only could own a house or a horse, but also could own an idea and the words used to express that idea. Laws and professional codes of ethics protect an author's words in the same way they protect song lyrics, drawings, or patents. In the academic world, the conventions protecting a source author's words and ideas are essential if research findings are to win the community's confidence. Effective

TABLE A2.5   Plagiarism and the Ethical Use of Sources

Plagiarism		Ethical Use of Sources
Fraud	Misuse of Sources (*Common Mistakes Made by New Researchers*)	
The writer	The writer	The writer
• buys a paper online • submits someone else's work as his own • copies chunks of text from sources with obvious intention of not being detected • fabricates data or makes up evidence • intends to deceive	• copies passages directly from a source, references the source with an in-text citation, but fails to use quotation marks or block indentation • in attempting to paraphrase a source, makes some changes, but follows too closely the wording of the original ("patchwriting") • fails to indicate the sources of some ideas or data (often is unsure what needs to be cited or has lost track of sources through poor note taking) • in general, misunderstands the conventions for using sources in academic writing	• writes paper entirely in her own words or uses exact quotations from sources • indicates all quotations with quotation marks or block indentation • indicates her use of all sources through attribution, in-text citation, and an end-of-paper list of works cited

research can occur only within ethical and responsible research communities, where people respect the words and ideas of those who have gone before them.

Strategies for Avoiding Plagiarism

Table A2.6 will help you review the strategies presented throughout this appendix for using source material ethically and avoiding plagiarism.

TABLE A2.6   Avoiding Plagiarism or the Appearance of Plagiarism

What to Do	Why to Do It
At the beginning	
Read your college's policy on plagiarism as well as statements from your teachers in class or on course syllabi.	Understanding policies on plagiarism and academic integrity will help you research and write ethically.
Pose a research question rather than a topic area.	Arguing your own thesis gives you a voice, establishes your *ethos,* and urges you to write ethically.

(continued)

TABLE A2.6 **continued**

What to Do	Why to Do It
At the note-taking stage	
Create a bibliographic entry for each source.	This action makes it easy to create an end-of-paper bibliography and encourages rhetorical reading.
When you copy a passage into your notes, copy word for word and enclose it within quotation marks.	It is important to distinguish a source's words from your own words.
When you enter summaries or paraphrases into your notes, avoid patchwriting.	If your notes contain any strings of a source's original wording, you might later assume that these words are your own.
Distinguish your informational notes from your personal exploratory notes.	Keeping these kinds of notes separate will help you identify borrowed ideas when it's time to incorporate the source material into your paper.
When writing your draft	
Except for exact quotations, write the paper entirely in your own words.	This strategy keeps you from patchwriting when you summarize or paraphrase.
Indicate all quotations with quotation marks or block indentation. Use ellipses or brackets to make changes to fit your own grammar.	Be careful to represent the author fairly; don't change meaning by taking quotations out of context.
When you summarize or paraphrase, avoid patchwriting.	Word-for-word strings from a source must either be avoided or placed in quotation marks. Also avoid mirroring the source's grammatical structure.
Never cut and paste a Web passage directly into your draft. Paste it into a separate note file and put quotation marks around it.	Pasted passages are direct invitations to patchwrite.
Inside your text, use attributive tags or parenthetical citations to identify all sources. List all sources alphabetically in a concluding Works Cited or References list.	This strategy makes it easy for readers to know when you are using a source and where to find it.
Cite with attributive tags or parenthetical citations all quotations, paraphrases, summaries, and any other references to specific sources.	These are the most common in-text citations in a research paper.
Use in-text citations to indicate sources for all visuals and media such as graphs, maps, photographs, films, videos, broadcasts, and recordings.	The rules for citing words and ideas apply equally to visuals and media cited in your paper.
Use in-text citations for all ideas and facts that are not common knowledge.	Although you don't need to cite widely accepted and noncontroversial facts and information, it is better to cite them if you are unsure.

■ ■ ■   **FOR CLASS AND DISCUSSION** Avoiding Plagiarism

Reread the original article from the American Council on Science and Health (page 282) and Writer 3's use of this source in her paragraph about how nondietary habits may explain why vegetarians are healthier than nonvegetarians (page 283). Then read the paragraph below by Writer 4, who makes the same argument as Writer 3 but crosses the line from ethical to nonethical use of sources. Why might Writer 4 be accused of plagiarism?

Writer 4's Argument (Example of Plagiarism)

According to the American Council on Science and Health, the health of vegetarians may be better than that of nonvegetarians partly because of nondietary factors. People who eat only vegetables tend to be very conscious of their health. They exercise regularly, avoid getting fat, and don't smoke. Scientists who examined the data may not have adequately controlled for these nondietary effects. Also in Western countries most vegetarians are more affluent than nonvegetarians and thus have better living conditions and more access to medical care.

Working in small groups or as a whole class, respond to the following questions.

1. How does this passage cross the line into plagiarism?
2. The writer of this passage might say, "How can this be plagiarism? I cited my source." How would you explain the problem to this writer?
3. Psychologically or cognitively, what may have caused Writer 4 to misuse the source? How might this writer's note-taking process or composing process have differed from that of Writer 3 on page 283? In other words, what happened to get this writer into trouble?

■ ■ ■

Citing Sources in Your Text in MLA Style

When academic writers cite sources, they use the conventions appropriate to their discipline. In this section, we will explain briefly the MLA style used in the humanities. (We explain the APA system used in the social sciences later in this appendix.) Our discussion of MLA style and our citation examples are based on the eighth edition of the *MLA Handbook* (2016).

In the MLA system of in-text citation, you place the author's last name and the page number of the cited source in parentheses, usually at the end of the material you wish to cite. (If the author's name is mentioned in a preceding attributive tag, such as "according to Karnow" or "Karnow says," only the page number is placed in parentheses.) In the following examples, note that the citation precedes the period. If you are citing a quotation, the parenthetical citation follows the quotation mark but precedes the final period.

The Spanish tried to reduce the status of Filipina women who had been able to do business, get divorced, and sometimes become village chiefs (Karnow 41).

According to Karnow , the Spanish tried to reduce the status of Filipina women who had been able to do business, get divorced, and sometimes become village chiefs (41).

"And, to this day," Karnow continues, "women play a decisive role in Filipino families" (41).

A reader who wishes to look up the source will find the bibliographic information in the Works Cited section by looking for the entry under "Karnow." If more than one work by Karnow was used in the paper, the writer would also include an abbreviated title of the book or article following Karnow's name in the in-text citation.

(Karnow , *In Our Image* 41)

When citing sources and page numbers, you should know about two special cases:

Citing from an Indirect Source   Occasionally you may wish to use a quotation that you have seen cited in one of your sources. You read Jones, who has a nice quotation from Smith, and you want to use Smith's quotation. To do so, quote Smith, but then cite Jones in your text preceded by the terms "qtd. in." List only Jones in your "Works Cited."

> According to the ex-mayor of Gotham City, Rupert Smith, "the rate of crime was at an all-time low" during his term of office (qtd. in Jones 25).

Citing a Work without Page Numbers   If the work you are citing in your paper has no page numbers but does have numbered paragraphs, use *par.* or *pars.* and give the number of the paragraph(s): (Helvarg, par. 10). If the source has neither page nor paragraph numbers, as is typical of many Web sources in HTML format, do not give any numbers in the in-text citation but cite the source in its entirety. (Do not use the page numbers from an HTML printout because they will not be consistent from printer to printer.)

Documenting Sources in a "Works Cited" List (MLA)

In the MLA system, you place a complete bibliography, titled "Works Cited," at the end of the paper. The list includes all the sources that you mention in your paper. However, it does not include works you read but did not use. Entries in the Works Cited follow these general guidelines:

- Entries are arranged alphabetically by author, or by title if there is no author.
- If there is more than one entry by the same author, the second and subsequent entries begin with three hyphens followed by a period and the title.

> Smith, Roberta. *Body Image in Non-Western Cultures.* Bonanza, 1999.
> —. *Body Image in Western Cultures, 1750-Present.* Bonanza, 1995.
> —. "Eating Disorders Reconsidered." *Journal of Appetite Studies*, vol. 45, no. 3, 1999,
>   pp. 295–300.

For an example of how to format a "Works Cited" page in MLA style, see the last page of Ivan Snook's researched argument (p. 268).

Table A2.7 provides MLA models for the most common kinds of citations. This table will help you distinguish the forest from the trees when you try to cite sources. All the major categories of sources are displayed in this table.

TABLE A2.7   **Quick Reference Guide for MLA Citations**

Kind of Source	Basic Citation Model
Print Sources	
Article in scholarly journal	Pollay, Richard W., et al.* "Separate, but Not Equal: Racial Segmentation in Cigarette Advertising." *Journal of Advertising,* vol. 21, no. 1, 1992, pp. 45-57.
Article in print magazine or newspaper	Beam, Alex. "The Mad Poets Society." *The Atlantic,* July–Aug. 2001, pp. 96–103. Lemonick, Michael D. "Teens Before Their Time." *Time,* 30 Oct. 2000, pp. 66–74. Liptak, Adam. "In Abortion Rulings, Idea of Marriage Is Pivotal." *The New York Times,* 2 Nov. 2005, p. A1.
Book	Tannen, Deborah. *The Argument Culture: Moving From Debate to Dialogue.* Random House, 1998.
Article in anthology with an editor	Shamoon, Linda. "International E-mail Debate." *Electronic Communication Across the Curriculum,* edited by Donna Reiss, Dickie Self, and Art Young, NCTE, 1998, pp. 151-61.
Sources That You Have Downloaded from an Academic Database	
Article downloaded from database	Matsuba, M. Kyle. "Searching for Self and Relationships Online." *CyberPsychology and Behavior,* vol. 9, no. 3, 2006, pp. 275 84. *Academic Search Complete,* doi:10.1089/cpb.2006.9.275.**
Other Internet and Web Sources	
Home page (use for citing an entire Web site)	*NRA Programs.* National Rifle Association, home.nra.org/nra-programs. Accessed 15 Apr. 2016.
Document within a Web site	Rosenman, Mark. "A Call for National Service." *The Chronicle of Philanthropy,* vol. 20, no. 1, 18 Oct. 2007, philanthropy.com/article/A-Call-for-National-Service/165721.
Article from scholarly Web journal (retrieved from a database)	Welch, John R., and Ramon Riley. "Reclaiming Land and Spirit in the Western Apache Homeland." *American Indian Quarterly,* vol. 25, no. 4, 2001, pp. 5-14. *JSTOR,* www.jstor.org/stable/1185999?seq=1#.
News article found on the Web	Brennan, Charlie. "Boulder Scientists over the Moon at Chance to Work on Lunar Dust." *Daily Camera Boulder News,* 3 Oct. 2015, www.dailycamera.com/news/boulder/ci_28913824/boulder-scientists-over-moon-at-chance-work-lunar.
Blog posting	Wright, Jeremy. "*MySpace* Is the New Blogosphere." *Ensight.org,* 21 Feb. 2006, www.ensight.org/archives/2006/02/21/myspaceis-the-new-blogosphere.
Miscellaneous Sources	
Interview	Van der Peet, Rob. Personal interview, 24 June 2009.
Lecture, address, or speech	Sharples, Mike. "Authors of the Future." Conference of European Teachers of Academic Writing, 20 June 2001, University of Groningen, Groningen, Netherlands.

*For two authors, give both authors' names in this format: "Smith, John, and Frank Peters." For three or more authors, give only the first author's name, followed by *et al.*

**If a DOI (digital object identifier) is not available, give the URL. If no publication date is provided for the source, end your entry with the date on which you accessed the source.

Student Example of an MLA-Style Research Paper

For an illustration of a student research paper written and formatted in MLA style, see Ivan Snook's researched policy proposal on pages 264–268.

Citing Sources in Your Text in APA Style

Our discussion of APA style is based on the *Publication Manual of the American Psychological Association*, 6th ed. (2010).

To cite sources in the body of your paper in the APA system, you include the year of the source and you place a "p." or "pp." before the page number. The author's last name, date, and page numbers are separated by commas. When the author is mentioned in an attributive tag, place only the date and page number in parentheses, usually directly after the author's name.

> The Spanish tried to reduce the status of Filipina women who had been able to do business, get divorced, and sometimes become village chiefs (Karnow, 1989, p. 41).

> According to Karnow (1989, p. 41), the Spanish tried to reduce the status of Filipina women who had been able to do business, get divorced, and sometimes become village chiefs.

If your readers wish to follow up on this source, they will look for "Karnow" in the References section at the end of the essay. If Karnow had more than one entry in the References section, they would look for the 1989 source. If Karnow had published more than one work in 1989, you would add a lowercase "a" to the date of the first one and a lowercase "b" to the date of the second one. Your in-text parenthetical citation would then be either (Karnow, 1989a) or (Karnow, 1989b).

When you quote or use data from an indirect source, in your parenthetical citation use "as cited in" rather than the MLA's "qtd in."

> According to the ex-mayor of Gotham City, Rupert Smith, "the rate of crime was at an all-time low" during his term of office (as cited in Jones, 1995, p. 25).

Documenting Sources in a "References" List (APA)

The APA system includes a complete bibliography, called "References," at the end of the paper. Entries are listed alphabetically, with a hanging indentation. If you list more than one item for an author, repeat the author's name each time and arrange the items in chronological order beginning with the earliest. If two works appeared in the same year, arrange them alphabetically, adding an "a" and a "b" after the year for purposes of in-text citation. Here is a hypothetical illustration:

> Smith, R. (1995). *Body image in Western cultures, 1750–present*. London, England: Bonanza Press.
>
> Smith, R. (1999a). *Body image in non-Western cultures*. London, England: Bonanza Press.
>
> Smith, R. (1999b). Eating disorders reconsidered. *Journal of Appetite Studies, 45,* 295–300.

Table A2.8 provides examples in APA style for the most common kinds of citations to be placed in a "References" list at the end of the paper.

Student Example of an APA-Style Research Paper

An example of a paper in APA style is Julee Christianson's researched argument on pages 218–223.

TABLE A2.8   Quick Reference Guide for APA Citations

Kind of Source	Basic Citation Model
Print Sources	
Article in scholarly journal	Pollay, R. W., Lee, J.S., & Carter-Whitney, D. (1992). Separate, but not equal: Racial segmentation in cigarette advertising. *Journal of Advertising, 21*(1), 45-57.
Article in magazine or newspaper	Beam, A. (2001, July–August). The mad poets society. *Atlantic Monthly, 288,* 96-103.
	Lemonick, M. D. (2000, October 30). Teens before their time. *Time, 156,* 66-74.
	Cauvin, H. E. (2001, July 18). Political climate complicates food shortage in Zimbabwe. *The New York Times,* p. A13.
Book	Tannen, D. (1998). *The argument culture: Moving from debate to dialogue.* New York, NY: Random House.
Article in anthology with an editor	Shamoon, L. (1998). International e-mail debate. In D. Reiss, D. Self, & A. Young (Eds.), *Electronic communication across the curriculum* (pp. 151-161). Urbana, IL: National Council of Teachers of English.
Sources That You Have Downloaded from a Database	
Article with DOI	Adelt, U. (2008). Trying to find an identity: Eric Clapton's changing conception of "blackness." *Popular Music & Society, 31,* 433–452. doi: 10.1080/03007760802052809
Article without DOI—use periodical's home page	Beckham II, J. M. (2008). Placing *Touch of evil, The border,* and *Traffic* in the American imagination. *Journal of Popular Film & Television 33*(3), 130-141. Retrieved from http://www.heldref.org/pubs/jpft/about.html
Other Internet and Web Sources	
Document within a Web site	Marks, J. Overview: Letter from the president. Retrieved 2004, June 25 from the Search for Common Ground Web site: http://www.sfcg.org/sfcg/sfcg_overview.html
Article from scholarly Web journal	Welch, J. R., & Riley, R. (2001). Reclaiming land and spirit in the western Apache homeland. *American Indian Quarterly, 25,* 5–14. Retrieved from http://muse.jhu.edu/journals/american_indian_quarterly
News article downloaded from Web	Thevenot, B. (2004, July 31). Once in a blue moon. *Times Picayune* [New Orleans]. Retrieved from http://www.nola.com/t-p
Blog posting	Wright, J. (2006, Feb. 21). *MySpace* is the new blogosphere. [Web log post]. Retrieved from http://www.ensight.org/archives
Miscellaneous Sources	
Interview, personal communication	R. Van der Peet (personal communication, June 24, 2009) stated that…[In-text citation only; not included in References]
Lecture, address, or speech	According to Mike Sharples (lecture given at the Conference of European Teachers of Academic Writing, Groningen, June 20, 2001), authors …[in-text citation only; not included in references]

Credits

Text

Pages 15, 17, 28, 29, 30, 36. Trudie Makens

Page 25. James Surowiecki, "The Pay Is Too Damn Low," *The New Yorker*. Reprinted with permission of the Chris Calhoun Agency.

Page 32. Michael Saltsman, "To Help the Poor, Move Beyond 'Minimum Gestures'," Huffington Post. Reprinted by permission of the author.

Page 46. Pearson Education

Pages 54, 68. Carmen Tieu

Page 106. Trudie Makens, "Bringing Dignity to Workers: Make the Minimum Wage a Living Wage"

Page 116. Colleen Fontana, "An Open Letter to Robert Levy in Response to His Article 'They Never Learn'." Used by permission.

Page 119. Lauren Shinozuka, "The Dangers of Digital Distractedness"

Page 128. Kathryn Jean Lopez, "Egg Heads," *National Review*. (c) 1998 National Review, Inc. Reprinted by permission.

Page 138. Zachary Stumps, "A Rhetorical Analysis of Ellen Goodman's 'Womb for Rent'." Reprinted with permission of the author.

Page 175. Alex Hutchinson, "Your Daily Multivitamin May Be Hurting You—The Debate Is On: Just Useless, or Truly Dangerous?" *Outside Magazine*, Oct. 8, 2013. Used with permission.

Page 198. Alex Mullens, "A Pirate but Not a Thief: What Does 'Stealing' Mean in a Digital Environment?" Reprinted by permission of the author.

Page 210. "Buying Sex Causes Sex Trafficking" from Free the Captives. Used by permission.

Page 218. Julee Christianson, "Why Lawrence Summers Was Wrong." Used by permission.

Page 240. Lorena Mendoza-Flores, "Silenced and Invisible: Problems of Hispanic Students at Valley High School"

Page 243. Judith Daar, "Three Genetic Parents for One Healthy Baby," *Los Angeles Times,* March 21, 2014. Reprinted with permission of the author.

Page 264. Ivan Snook, "Flirting with Disaster: An Argument Against Integrating Women into the Combat Arms." Reprinted by permission of the author.

Page 269. Sandy Wainscott, "Why McDonald's Should Sell Meat and Veggie Pies: A Proposal to End Subsidies for Cheap Meat." Used by permission.

Images

Page 1. AP Photo/StephanSavoia

Page 4. United Steelworkers Union

Page 15. www.cartoonstock.com

Page 16. Shmitt, John and Janelle Jones. 2012. "Low-Wage Workers are Older and Better Educated Than Ever." Washington, DC: Center for Economic and Policy Research. Used with permission.

Page 43. Andreas Rentz/Getty Images

Page 83. Top, AP Photo/Toby Talbot. Bottom, AP Photo/Branimir Kvartuc.

Page 95. AP Photo/Bullit Marquez

Page 96. Men Can Stop Rape. Reprinted with permission.

Page 123. Peter Byrne/PA Wire URN:187 98732 (Press Association via AP Images)

Page 142. John Bean

Page 145. Ad Council

Page 149. Save the Children

Page 151. Figure 9.12, Blend Images/Alamy. Figure 9.13, Radius Images/Alamy. Figure 9.14, Eric Basir/Alamy. Figure 9.15, DCPhoto/Alamy.

Page 153. Photos 12/Alamy

Page 155. TXTResponsibly.org

Page 157. Milt Prigee/Cagle Cartoons

Page 165. John Ramage

Page 167. © Kathy deWitt/Alamy

Page 178. Bagley/Cagle Cartoons

Page 185. Bish/Cagle Cartoons

Page 225. AF archive/Alamy

Page 230. AP Photo/Carolyn Kaster

Page 246. DeVito Verdi Advertising Agency

Page 249. © FLPA/Alamy

Page 257. Reprinted with permission of Jane E. Bube.

Page 270. Lower left, Aurora Photos/Alamy. Lower right, Simon Belcher/Alamy.

Index

Academics, 23
Ad hominem, 272–273
Advertisements. *See* Advocacy advertisements/posters
Advocacy, degree of, 24, 280–281
Advocacy advertisements/posters. *See also* Visual arguments
  design elements of, 148–150, 260
  examples of, 155, 210, 246
  function of, 21
  as proposal arguments, 256–260
  public affairs, 21, 154, 155
Advocacy groups, 22–23
Aloni, Erez and Judith Daar, "Three Genetic Parents—For One Healthy Baby," 243–244
Analogy
  to appeal to *pathos*, 93
  resemblance argument by, 183–184
Angle of vision
  of evidence, 80–82
  explanation of, 80
  in photographs, 83
  of source material, 280
Antithesis, 30
Appealing to stirring symbols, 271
Appeal to false authority, 272
Appeal to ignorance, 271
Appeal to pity, 272
Appeal to popularity, 272
Arguments. *See also* Visual arguments; *specific types of arguments*
  categorical, 179, 181–185
  causal, 171–173, 202–221
  classical structure of, 44–47
  consequences-based, 233–235
  creating your own criteria-match, 190–196
  defining features of, 4–9
  definition, 171–173, 178, 181–183, 186–197
  dialogic, 100, 101, 108–111
  evaluation, 171–173
  explicit, 3–4
  frame of, 51–53
  function of, 2–4

  genres of, 19–22
  hybrid, 173–177
  implicit, 3–4
  as inquiry, 12–13
  issue questions for, 47–49
  justification of claims in, 4–6
  logical structure of, 55–71
  match, 229, 231
  multisided, 100, 101
  one-sided, 100, 101
  as persuasion, 7–9
  principles-based, 233–234
  as process and product, 6–7
  proposal, 172, 245–262
  pseudo-, 49–51
  reading to believe, 25–29
  reading to doubt, 29–30
  resemblance, 171–173, 178, 183–185
  role-playing, 11
  Toulmin framework to plan and test, 63–71 (*See also* Toulmin framework)
  truth issues and, 9–10
  as truth seeking combined with persuasion, 7–9
Argument to the people, 271
Aristotelian definition, 188–189
Aristotle, 57–59
Assignments. *See* Writing assignments
Assumptions
  enthymeme and, 56–57
  role of, 56
  shared, 50–51
Attributive tags, 287–288
Audience
  analysis of, 97–98, 133
  appeal to, 257
  authorial purpose and, 23–24
  for causal arguments, 213
  for definition arguments, 194–195
  neutral, 102–103
  for proposal arguments, 259–260
  resistant, 101–102, 108–111
  supportive, 102
  undecided, 102–103
  for visual arguments, 158

Audience-based reasons
  to enhance *logos, ethos,* and *pathos,* 58, 95, 97–98
  power of, 58
Authority, questioning credibility of, 105
Authors. *See* Writers

Backing, 60–63. *See also* Toulmin framework
Bandwagon appeal, 272
Bankers, 23
Bar graphs, 161–162
Base point, for statistical comparisons, 86
Baumlin, James, 113
because clauses, 52–53, 205
Begging the question, 274
Believe, reading to, 25–29
Believing and doubting game, 17–18, 113
Bibliographic information, 278
Blogs, 20
Brainstorming
  consequences of actions, 213
  to identify issues to explore, 13–14
  sources of evidence, 86
"Bringing Dignity to Workers: Make the Minimum Wage a Living Wage" (Makens), 106–108
Brochures, 152
Business professionals, 23

Cartoons
  examples of, 157, 178, 185
  as visual arguments, 156
Cases, as evidence, 76
Categorical arguments
  criteria development for, 227–229
  criteria-match structure of, 226–227
  definition arguments as, 182–183
  explanation of, 226
  function of, 179
  making match argument for, 229, 231
  resemblance argument using analogy as, 183–184

298